BEHOLD THE DARK GRAY MAN

TRIUMPHS AND TRAUMA
THE CONTROVERSIAL LIFE OF
SHOLTO DOUGLAS

BEHOLD THE DARK
GRAY MAN

KATHARINE CAMPBELL

Biteback Publishing

First published in Great Britain in 2021 by
Biteback Publishing Ltd, London
Copyright © Katharine Campbell 2021

Extract from Oswald Boelcke's diaries quoted in Professor Johannes Werner's *Boelcke: Der Mensch, der
Flieger, der Führer der deutschen Jagdfliegerei* reproduced with the kind permission of Casemate UK.

Extracts from Air Chief Marshal Sir John Grandy's letters reproduced
with the kind permission of Sir John Grandy's son, John Grandy.

Extracts from Helen Nimmo's account of the London Blitz reproduced
with the kind permission of Mrs Nimmo's grandchildren.

Extracts from Siegfried Sassoon's letters and Poem 17, *Vigils* © Siegfried Sassoon,
reproduced with the kind permission of the estate of George Sassoon.

Every reasonable effort has been made to trace copyright holders of material reproduced in this book,
but if any have been inadvertently overlooked the publisher would be glad to hear from them.

ISBN 978-1-78590-597-1

10 9 8 7 6 5 4 3 2 1

A CIP catalogue record for this book is available from the British Library.

Set in Adobe Garamond Pro and Futura

Printed and bound in Great Britain by
CPI Group (UK) Ltd, Croydon CR0 4YY

CONTENTS

*Marshal of the Royal Air Force Lord Douglas of Kirtleside
in full dress uniform for the Queen's coronation in 1953.*

FOREWORD

The years of the First World War provided us with an experience that was so extraordinary that it was impossible to understand immediately what it all meant, and so profound that it was to alter the whole course of our lives. We had scarcely more than begun to know what living meant, but we knew all about dying, and for many the experience was so disturbing that it was to leave upon some minds the deepest of scars ... We were young in years, and we had learnt to present a front that was high-spirited and apparently carefree; but in other respects we were indeed old before our time.

THE WORDS OF LORD DOUGLAS CONCERNING THE IMMEDIATE POST-WORLD WAR I YEARS.[1]

Going to war often has a great cost for a person. It is always an individual story. The nature of the trauma of war means that there is often a silence about what has been endured. However, the observations of the lingering effects by the children and spouses of veterans can provide raw and sensitive insights. One example was the deep impression left on Katharine Campbell as a child by her father's nocturnal wanderings during his nightmares. This is a book about the intimacy of these reflections as well as the broad sweep of our shared history, capturing many critical moments of the twentieth century in which Lord Douglas played a substantial part. Survival moulds a strength of character that is defined by knowledge of reality and conviction about right and wrong. This struggle can be the source of motivations that drive great achievement. Such was the life of Lord

Douglas of Kirtleside, who cast a large footprint in the history of the RAF and civil aviation in the UK.

But there is another kind of history, similar to the ones that doctors take from patients. This is an exploration of the life of a man who endured considerable deprivation and challenges prior to his ascendency to senior leadership roles. The past sets the template for a person's values and vulnerabilities. This book considers the world of Lord Douglas and his epic journey from growing up as a child in poverty after his mother was deserted by his father, through his extraordinary survival as a World War I fighter pilot, to taking a number of senior roles in command in World War II and the aftermath. He was a man of extraordinary vision and energy who left a powerful legacy in the world of modern aviation. But this did not happen by accident. This account of Lord Douglas's life grapples with these accumulated realities and the nature of the experiences that were the anvil on which his character was shaped.

Traumatic events such as vivid moments of confrontation with the struggle between life and death in combat are captured by memory in unusual ways. These memories are often left undigested and revisited with an intensity driven by the nonverbal world of imagery, sound, smell and physiological domains. Their undigested nature means that they remain active and are easily brought to awareness by subtle reminders that are unrecognised. These are memories that intrude between the person and the world with which he is trying to engage. As a consequence, the contemporary circumstance is seen through the foreground presence of the past rather than the reality of the current moment. These events can be key drivers of the unconscious decisions that underpin everyday life. The frequent revisitation of these memories also repeatedly activates the stress systems which progressively disrupt an individual's internal physiological homeostasis, as inhibitory systems struggle to maintain some adaptation and equilibrium.

These perturbations come at an increasing cost to a range of biological systems due to the wear and tear of repeated attempts to down-regulate these activations. What is achieved is a state of allostasis where there is an unstable state of internal physiological adaptation.² Eventually the brakes wear out. You cannot drive your car with one foot on the accelerator and the other on the brakes without the vehicle wearing out more quickly. This is what underpins the post-traumatic stress disorder that used to be known as shell-shock or traumatic neurosis in Lord Douglas's era. There are also costs in terms of a range of physical illnesses such as obesity, diabetes, cardiac disease, dementia and autoimmune disease. In Australia, it was recognised that the strains of war brought about premature ageing, leading to the term the 'burnt-out soldier'.³ This was the lingering cost of war for Lord Douglas.

What were the traumatic events that Lord Douglas survived? This is important to keep in mind to understand his motivations. Let us not forget that the mortality of WWI airmen was approximately 50 per cent. He had some extraordinary escapes in bullet-ridden aircraft and had to deal with the death of his younger brother, who had followed him into the Royal Flying Corps. He survived four serious aircraft crashes. Towards the end of the war, he took extreme risks on a particular reconnaissance mission, and such moments can have a haunting legacy when reflection allows the reality of the risk to bubble to the surface. While many veterans live damaged lives because of the scars from such experiences, others manage to use them as a source of wisdom and energy to engage in the present.⁴ Lord Douglas was one of these latter men. However, he wrote of the struggle that this involved in the years after the war when 'we were run down to a state that approached a standstill'.⁵ When he regained his motivation and immersed himself in his career in the RAF, he would still reflect, 'Not being emotional or easily stirred, I miss the heights of life.'⁶ He lived in a somewhat numbed state and at times struggled with his inner withdrawal, which was criticised as aloofness by others. A world without feeling can be one of emotional emptiness. In this emotional state, intimate relationships are challenging and attachments fragile.

The internal meaning and motivations of people's lives come from the cauldron of memories that accumulate in the journey through life and their synthesis by the individual's temperament and intellect. These memories are a mosaic of the journey through different events that are a combination of chance and choice and determine the trajectory of a person's life. The undertone of this book is for the reader to unravel how Lord Douglas's personal confrontations with death and the many losses he suffered drove his motivations. His support for the use of Big Wing formations by Fighter Command during WWII is one example. This strategy was hotly debated and evoked considerable controversy. Lord Douglas's own experience in WWI taught him that formation flying provided protection and maximal capability in combat, in contrast to the vulnerability of a lone aircraft becoming the prey of the enemy. His brother Archie's death and his own lucky escape from his German pursuers are likely to have underpinned a personal intensity in his thinking about these tactical questions.

Lord Douglas, towards the end of his life, bore the scars of his more challenging roles. This cost is often disguised by fame. Not all memories are tolerable, and some become haunting relics. He seems to have lived with the reality of aerial combat and respecting the skills of an adversary: he could act and fight with a knowledge that this was a fair match of intent and a test of skill. However, this was not the case in the aftermath of the war, when Lord Douglas was the Military Governor of the British sector of occupied Germany. He was the final point of appeal in the death sentences for war criminals from the Nuremberg trials, a duty he found deeply troubling. He was a man who abhorred corporal punishment as an adolescent and despised violence. The memories of signing execution warrants were the subject of his nightmares in his old age. He suffered considerably for his acts of leadership.

Lord Douglas's life highlights how any person's journey through the world is inherently unpredictable. The ability to integrate and grow from adversity reveals the character of a person in managing the many throws of the dice that combine to direct the passage from youth to old age. Lord Douglas's life shows that it is not hollow ambition which drives real achievement. Rather, his is the story of how, if a person uses his skills to their best and has an internal sense of commitment to the synthesis of life experience, he will lead a life that leaves an extraordinary legacy. However, this was not without suffering and personal pain but, in part, because of his managing this inner turmoil.

If this biography were written by a scholar or an associate, Lord Douglas's world would not be so personally or sensitively captured. Katharine Campbell's voice as the author is partly moulded by the emotional capacity and life skills learned from her father and his impact on her nurturance and the family's culture. A child carries this legacy, and this creates a lens that brings a unique reflection on the life of the parent. The richness of the historical scholarship of this book is surrounded by this unspoken scaffolding. As a consequence, the book is almost an amalgam of autobiography and biography. This account is a hybrid of these two very different styles of reflection and dissection of a famous life. This matrix adds to a depiction of the humanity of the many dimensions of Lord Douglas's life that sets this biography apart. There is an empathy and reconciliation of the very public and external world of achievement that Lord Douglas's life embodies with the private hardships and suffering.

Eric Maria Remarque wrote of a soldier in the trenches of World War I anticipating life after the war: 'One thing I do know: everything that is sinking into us like a stone now, while we are in the war, will rise up again when the war is over, and that's when the real life-and-death struggle will start.'[7] This turmoil was the world that haunted Lord Douglas in his nightmares in his final years.

Professor Alexander C. McFarlane
AO, MB BS (Hons), MD, FRANZCP, Dip Psychother.
Director, Centre for Traumatic Stress Studies, Adelaide Medical School, University of Adelaide

LIST OF ILLUSTRATIONS

MAPS

1. Map of Sholto's airfields on the Western Front in World War I. Image created by Andy Thomsen and Alan Waters. Courtesy of Katharine Campbell.
2. Fighter Command map of group areas, 1940. Reproduced from Vincent Orange, *Dowding of Fighter Command: Victor of the Battle of Britain*, courtesy of Grub Street Publishing.
3. The British Zone of occupied Germany, 1946/47. Image created by Peter Campbell. Courtesy of Katharine Campbell.

PHOTOGRAPHS

Frontispiece: Marshal of the Royal Air Force Lord Douglas of Kirtleside in full dress uniform, 1953. Courtesy of Katharine Campbell.
1. Winston Churchill and Sholto in a car at Heathrow Airport, with Katharine, January 1960. © *Daily Express*.
2. Sholto with Katharine, 1963. Courtesy of Katharine Campbell.
3. Sholto with Errol Barrow, Prime Minister of Barbados, 1966. Courtesy of Katharine Campbell.
4. Sholto with his mother Maggie, 1894. Courtesy of Katharine Campbell.
5. The three Douglas brothers, Sholto (seated on right), Bobby (resting on arm of chair) and Archie, at Tonbridge, 1911. Courtesy of Katharine Campbell.

6. Lincoln College Oxford, Torpid crew, 1914: Sholto seated in the centre. Courtesy of Lincoln College, Oxford.
7. Sholto's father, Robert Langton Douglas, around the start of World War I. Courtesy of Katharine Campbell.
8. Sholto's second brother, Bobby, 1916. Courtesy of Katharine Campbell.
9. Sholto's youngest brother, Archie, 1916. Courtesy of Katharine Campbell.
10. Major Sholto Douglas, c. 1916. Courtesy of Tangmere Military Aviation Museum.
11. The Campbell family in Stirling, 1912 (the youngest daughter watched Sholto flying from the top of the cliffs next to the castle in 1916). Reproduced by kind permission of Campbell Chesterman.
12. Stirling Castle and King's Park, c. 1912. Courtesy of Stirling Council Archives.
13. Major Sholto Douglas, Commanding Officer of 84 Squadron, standing beside an SE5a, 1918. Courtesy of Katharine Campbell.
14. Wing Commander Sholto Douglas (in the centre of the photo with clipboard) and his pilots standing beside the Nile in Khartoum in 1930, with Belinda, his pet lion cub. Reproduced by kind permission of Durham University Library and Collections, from the collection of E. G. Sarsfield-Hall, ref. SAD.8/48/9.
15. Sholto's half-brother Donald with his wife Anita, 1939. Courtesy of Sholto's niece, Erica Filby.
16. Air Marshal Sholto Douglas as C-in-C Fighter Command talking with ground crew, 1940/41. Courtesy of Katharine Campbell.
17. Sholto at his desk in Bentley Priory, 1942. Courtesy of Katharine Campbell.
18. Air Chief Marshal Sir Sholto Douglas taking the salute as C-in-C Middle East Command, 1943. Courtesy of Katharine Campbell.
19. King Farouk with Sholto and General 'Jumbo' Wilson at RAF gala evening in Cairo, 1943. Courtesy of Katharine Campbell.
20. The Cairo conference, November 1943. Sholto with Churchill and Field Marshal Sir Alan Brooke. Courtesy of Katharine Campbell.
21. Sholto with airmen in Cairo, Christmas 1943. Courtesy of Katharine Campbell.

ABBREVIATIONS

2TAF	Second Tactical Air Force
AA	Anti-Aircraft
AASF	Advanced Air Striking Force
AC2	Aircraftsman Second Class
ACAS	Assistant Chief of the Air Staff
ACC	Anterior Cingulate Cortex
ACE	Adverse Childhood Event
ACM	Air Chief Marshal
AEAF	Allied Expeditionary Air Force
AI	Airborne Interception (radar)
AMDP	Air Member for Development and Production
AMP	Air Member for Personnel
AMRD	Air Member for Research and Development
AOA	Air Officer-in-Charge of Administration
AOC	Air Officer Commanding
AOC-in-C	Air Officer Commander-in-Chief
ASV	Air to Surface Vessel
ATA	Air Transport Auxiliary
AVM	Air Vice-Marshal
AWOL	Absent Without Leave
BAFO	British Air Forces of Occupation
BAOR	British Army of the Rhine
BEA	British European Airways
BEF	British Expeditionary Force
BOAC	British Overseas Airways Corporation
BTB	British Troops in Berlin

CAS   Chief of the Air Staff
CCG   Control Commission for Germany
CFS   Central Flying School
CH   Chain Home
CHL   Chain Home Low
CID   Criminal Investigation Department
CIGS   Chief of the Imperial General Staff
C-in-C   Commander in Chief
CO   Commanding Officer
COGA   Control Office for Germany and Austria
CSSAD   Committee for the Scientific Survey of Air Defence
DAF   Desert Air Force
DCAS   Deputy Chief of the Air Staff
DFC   Distinguished Flying Cross
DGMS   Director General Medical Services
DH   De Havilland
DOP   Distance Offensive Patrol
DPs   Displaced Persons
DSD   Director of Staff Duties
DSM-III   Diagnostic and Statistical Manual of Mental Disorders, Third Edition
DSM-V   Diagnostic and Statistical Manual of Mental Disorders, Fifth Edition
DSO   Distinguished Service Order
EIS   Economic Information Section
ENSA   Entertainments National Service Association
FIU   Fighter Interception Unit
FTS   Flying Training School
F-W   Focke-Wulf
GCB   Knight Grand Cross of the Order of the Bath
GCI   Ground Control Interception (radar)
GL   Gun Laying
GOC   General Officer Commanding
HF   High Frequency
HPA   Hypothalamic-Pituitary-Adrenal
IATA   International Air Transport Association

ICS	Indian Civil Service
IDC	Imperial Defence College
IFF	Identification Friend or Foe (radar)
IMT	International Military Tribunal
KCB	Knight Commander of the Order of the Bath
KLM	*Koninklijke Luchtvaart Maatschappij* – Royal Dutch Airlines
LMF	Lack of Moral Fibre
MAAF	Mediterranean Allied Air Forces
MAC	Mediterranean Air Command
MAP	Ministry of Aircraft Production
MC	Military Cross
Me110	Messerschmitt 110
MEP	Military Entry Permit
MFA&A	Monuments, Fine Arts and Archives
MRAF	Marshal of the Royal Air Force
NCO	Non-Commissioned Officer
NSDAP	*Nationalsozialistische Deutsche Arbeiterpartei* – National Socialist German Workers' Party – Nazi Party
OCTU	Officer Corps Training Unit
OTC	Officer Training Corps
OTU	Operational Training Unit
PAF	Polish Air Force
PSO	Personal Staff Officer
P.-W.	[Captain D.V.] Peyton-Ward
RASC	Royal Army Service Corps
RDF	Radio Direction Finding
RFA	Royal Field Artillery
RFC	Royal Flying Corps
RHA	Royal Horse Artillery
RNAS	Royal Naval Air Service
SA	*Sturmabteilung* – Stormtrooper Division
Sabena	*Societé anonyme belge d'Exploitation de la Navigation aérienne* – Belgian National Airline
SAM	Sympathetic-Adrenal-Medullary
SASO	Senior Air Staff Officer
SCW	Spanish Civil War

SDF	Sudanese Defence Force
SE5a	Scout Experimental 5a
SEAC	South East Asia Command
SEPs	Surrendered Enemy Personnel
SLC	Searchlight Control Radar ('Elsie')
SS	*Schutzstaffel* – Protection Squadron
USAAF	United States Army Air Forces
VC	Victoria Cross
VCAS	Vice Chief of the Air Staff
VHF	Very High Frequency
WAAF	Women's Auxiliary Air Force
WSD	William Sholto Douglas
ZAC	Zonal Advisory Council

CHAPTER ONE

MY MEMORIES OF THE DARK GRAY MAN

It's 3 a.m., and I am lying awake in a cold bedroom that is far too big for me. Decorated with sickly-coloured wallpaper on which is printed a childish design, it no longer appeals to my eleven-year-old self. The light in the equally unfriendly corridor outside my room streams in through the open door. A few years ago, my grandmother suggested that I should have a light on at night so that I would not be frightened. Up to that point I had not been afraid of the dark, but from the moment I saw her rather creepy silhouette in the doorway, I have been scared of it. Now the brightness is hurting my eyes, and I am listening to banging and thumping coming from my father's bedroom, which is directly below mine. I jump out of bed, cross to the door, and run barefoot down the back staircase.

There I find my father, wearing only his pyjama top, pushing the tea trolley that we keep outside his bedroom for his medicines down the corridor towards the kitchen. I guess that he has had a nightmare. 'Poppa, what are you doing?' 'I have to go to a meeting about the Sentences.' I am not sure whether he is asleep or awake; he seems to be in some kind of no man's land between the two. In the daytime he is in his wheelchair, but during these night-time wanderings he is able to walk while holding on to something.

I help him back to bed, and he seems so worried and far away from me, from now. But at other times he is still Poppa, and there is left behind something of the hero that I knew. When I was younger, despite his large size, he used to chase me down our long garden as

I

I squealed with excitement, and tell me the most wonderful stories from his extraordinary life, which went farther back than I could imagine, while I sat at the end of his bed on a Saturday morning, his time of rest after a hard week's work.

I fetch my mother from the other end of the house, and as we tuck Poppa up again, she says to me: 'I had hoped you wouldn't have to see this.' But I am puzzled because how could I not see it? My bedroom is above his, and on the nights when we cannot get nurses, I can see that something like this is bound to happen because I am the one who is closest to it.

My mother has explained to me already that the place to which Poppa returns most often in his frequent bad dreams and sleepwalking episodes is where he passed the unhappiest period of his entire working life: post-war Germany. He is remembering the final judgments that he had to review on the Nuremberg war criminals and the numerous death warrants that he had to sign as Military Governor from proceedings in the Military Courts of the British Zone. Although there are other painful memories that trouble him from the two world wars, his guilt over those death warrants has tormented him ever since he put his name to them. As a child I do not understand that he has left part of himself in that apocalyptic place and it is now, when he is at his most vulnerable, that it has surfaced like an accusing spectre to haunt him.

My father Sholto was sixty-three when I was born in 1957. By that time, he had reached the highest positions in two distinct careers; firstly military, in the Royal Flying Corps (RFC) and Royal Air Force (RAF), and secondly civil, as chairman of British European Airways (BEA), a post he had held for eight years prior to my birth, and which he continued to hold for a further seven. When he retired from the RAF, he was the second most decorated British officer after Field Marshal Montgomery.

Despite his elevated position and his late foray into fatherhood, he was always the gentle, nurturing influence when I was a child. Although he was not always that way with others, he was affectionate and warm with me, endlessly concerned with looking after me when we were together, and eager to answer my questions and teach me new things. He had the most wonderful infectious chuckle, which would come out when I did something funny or silly, as though he was completely delighted from deep inside. He could be stern too, but he never lifted a hand towards me in anger, as my mother did.

I witnessed that Sholto was no respecter of persons, treating everyone as equal even though a stellar list of people passed through our lives, two of whom became my godparents, Aristotle Onassis's first wife, Tina, and Prince Bernhard of the Netherlands, but they do not feature most prominently in my memory. Neither can I remember the time I met Winston Churchill when I was two and a half, as he was going through London Airport on his way to Nice in January 1960, but the photographic evidence remains. Sholto told my mother the whole story and she relayed it to me much later. Due to his position as BEA chairman, he used to greet all important people as they passed through Heathrow, including members of the royal family and political leaders past and present. Often, my mother Hazel, my nanny and I would be there too, and on this occasion, as it was raining and Churchill was in his eighties, his car was driven to the aircraft steps. We were all lined up on the tarmac, and Sholto said to my mother: 'I must go and see the old boy and have a chat with him,' so he walked over to Churchill's car and got in. Seeing Poppa disappearing into the car was more than I could bear, so I broke free from my mother and nanny, rushed towards him and into the car, straight on to his lap and stared into Churchill's face. He was wearing a coat with a furry Astrakhan collar, which I stroked and said, 'Nice, nice.' He thought I meant him, saying, 'And you're a very nice little girl too!'

The nannies my father employed to look after me were almost always German, and this was another small way in which he tried to heal the wounds of war. He wanted me to learn the language and to become familiar with the culture of Germany. We lived in a very European atmosphere, as Sholto and Hazel travelled almost ceaselessly all round Europe to further the interests of the airline. Often, at my father's instigation, my nanny and I would accompany my parents. It was the time of the Cold War, but he engineered a rapprochement with the Soviet Union, meeting both Khrushchev and Bulganin, so that air routes were opened up between London and Moscow, which we visited when I was six. We were taken on a tour of the Kremlin, and I disconcerted the Soviet secret police operatives by losing one of my milk teeth under Lenin's desk. The KGB officers searched for it in vain, and even though I am sure the floor will have been cleaned many times since then, I wonder sometimes if the tooth is still there. Sholto considered that fostering good relations with the Soviets was a high priority, no doubt due to his desire to prevent another global conflict at all costs, but he was no lover of totalitarianism. However, unusually for a senior military commander, he had been left-wing from his adolescence and remained so until the end of his life. I remember him reading the *New Statesman* and *The Observer* when I was very young, and I absorbed from him a sense of fairness and social justice.

Sholto had kept in touch with many RAF personnel who had served under him or whom he knew through his support of the Guinea Pig Club from its inception in 1941 until the end of his life, holding them 'in special affection and regard'.[1] This association consisted initially of RAF aircrew who had suffered burn injuries during World War II and who had been treated at the Queen Victoria Hospital, East Grinstead, by the pioneering plastic surgeon Archibald McIndoe. Sholto was almost unique among former RAF leaders in his support, along with Lord Dowding, the former C-in-C of Fighter Command during the Battle of Britain. One of the Guinea Pigs, William ('Bill') Simpson, was a frequent and favourite visitor to our home.

Simpson had been on a bombing mission over Luxembourg in May 1940 when his plane was hit by anti-aircraft fire and burst into flames.[2] He suffered the most terrible burns to his hands and face and the disastrous initial treatment he received robbed him of all his fingers.[3] By the time he made it to East Grinstead a year later, he had, as he said, 'an ugly fingerless paw for a left hand, and only a few misshapen stumps for fingers on my right hand'.[4] He became public relations officer at BEA and was a frequent guest at our parties; I learned quickly about the effects of serious disability when I was told to hand his glass of whisky gently into the outstretched waxy pale stumps where once his fingers had been.

Uncle Bill, as I knew him, made a very astute assessment of Sholto's character in his book. He had heard that Sholto was 'a rather stiff and unforthcoming Air Marshal', but when he visited him in post-war Germany, he discovered why he

> had the reputation for having a rather forbidding manner: he was
> shy. Also, he undoubtedly missed some popularity because he did
> not court it in the way that was fashionable during the war among
> other senior air officers and army generals. And unlike the run of
> leading RAF officers, who have mainly technical and administrative
> attributes, he was a classical scholar and inherited from his father,
> the art critic, a deep appreciation of art and the humanities.[5]

The long, painful process of losing my father began when I was five with the first of his many strokes in the late autumn of 1962. Sholto was sixty-eight and still chairman of BEA. The stress of that job, plus the weight of two world wars, during and after the second of which he was in high command for a total of eight years, were exacting a heavy toll on him. After an initial period in hospital, he came home but was confined to bed for rest. Looking after him seemed to occupy all of everyone's time, day and night, and my German nanny did not leave the house for three weeks, during which time she cared for my father as though her life depended on it.

Sholto's stroke brought him back into contact with another former RAF officer, Errol Barrow, who had been his personal navigator when he was Military Governor of the British Zone in Germany but who was now Premier of Barbados. Sholto and Errol had formed a solid friendship in Germany, which I realised later operated on both political and filial levels. They were both committed socialists, but also seemed like father and son, Errol being twenty-seven years younger than Sholto. 'Uncle Errol' had suggested to my parents that the beautiful climate and scenery of Barbados might provide the ideal environment in which Sholto could recuperate from his stroke. So, on 29 December 1962, we set sail on the cruise ship *Coronia* to Barbados. It was not an easy crossing due to poor weather, and Sholto, who had only just begun to take tentative steps again, found it almost impossible to keep his balance on the rolling ship. One eventful morning, the waves were so high that one of them broke open the porthole in my cabin and sea water poured into my bed. I was sitting on the end of it trying to get dressed. We were all required to put on life jackets, at which point I became really frightened, started screaming and had to be pacified by the ship's First Officer.

On our arrival, however, Uncle Errol made us feel instantly welcome. I could see immediately the affection that he and Sholto had for each other. Uncle Errol spent as much time with him as his duties would allow, and the memory that I have of him on every occasion that we visited Barbados over the next six years is of him sitting beside my father, leaning forward, and the two of them listening intently to each other. Later, when Sholto became increasingly ill, Uncle Errol would sit with his hand on his arm, or he would take hold of my father's hand. Errol continued to lavish attention on my parents and me whenever we went to Barbados, even after he became their first Prime Minister in 1966. Despite Sholto's increasing physical incapacity, he continued to enjoy intellectual conversation and debate, and he and Errol spent many hours engaged in political discussion.

Sholto had another stroke in December 1963, after which he found it more difficult to walk, using a stick that he held in his left hand. I remember him hating this, and once throwing the stick down the steps of an aircraft with a great clatter as we arrived somewhere, saying that he did not need it. He retired, not a moment before time, on 31 March 1964, when he was seventy, having led a nationalised company for longer than anyone had done before him.[6]

In the ensuing years after his retirement, Sholto became much more emotionally labile and used to cry easily, much as Churchill did after suffering strokes in his old age, when he used to 'blub like a child'.[7] Sholto became increasingly sad, and though I wouldn't have known the word 'depression' back then, that's what it was. On 30 January 1965, he and I watched Churchill's state funeral together. I remember the tears pouring down Poppa's face, and even today, the recollection is almost unbearable. Then, I understood only vaguely what is clear to me now: that Churchill had been Sholto's strong supporter all the way through WWII, even when others had doubted him.

His deterioration at the end of his life followed a very similar pattern to Churchill's as one stroke followed another,[8] although he was almost twenty years younger. His physical condition continued to decline, not helped by his large bulk, and he required frequent physiotherapy. He also started to fall more and since neither my mother, who was very slim, nor I could help him up, we began the habit of calling the local police station to ask if they would send a couple of officers round to help us get him up. This they did very willingly and they became quite a fixture over the next four years, coming round every time my father fell if nurses were not there. The fall that I will never forget happened when I was about ten years old. My father and I were sitting, as we mostly did, in our dining room, and my mother said to me: 'Keep an eye on Poppa while I go and get supper.' As I had homework to do, I went to fetch my books from the bench just outside in the hall, but when I came back after only a minute or two, my father had tried to get up from his chair and had fallen over, hitting his head against the radiator. He was lying on the floor with blood pouring from his scalp. I was horrified at the sight of him, knowing that it was all my fault, and terrified at what my mother would say when she came back into the room, which she did on hearing me call out for her. I remember to this day that we were all crying. We had to get the kind policemen to pick him up, and although my father probably went to hospital for an X-ray, I do not remember that. I do recollect, though, that he did not have a fractured skull, to my eternal relief.

Even after Sholto's retirement from BEA, and despite his increasing physical incapacity, my parents still followed a punishing social schedule. Driving back from London one evening in June 1966, they had a car crash and were both quite severely injured, sustaining wounds to the head and needing to go to hospital. They returned home two days later. I was quite used to my father going to hospital by that time, although not for an emergency as in this case. He was admitted about twice a year for more intensive treatment. My mother was drinking a lot (she always did), and although she said that the accident was the result of her high heel catching under the accelerator, causing her to crash heavily into the car in front, even I thought that she had probably had too much to drink. She was never prosecuted.

My parents also continued their travels abroad after Sholto had retired. They went to Europe often, and my mother made frequent trips to Barbados, as she had decided that we should have a house there so that Sholto could benefit from the climate. As a family, we started going to Barbados in the winter and in the summer, although I sensed that, despite his fondness for Uncle Errol, my father found the journey there by air exhausting, and it was more for my mother's benefit that this was being done. Often, and for reasons that I could not understand then and can only guess at now, my mother went to Barbados when my father was in hospital, on one occasion in 1967 when he was very ill and it was unclear whether he would survive when she left. She may have thought that it was safe for her to go, knowing that he was being cared for. We had nursing care for him at home, but it was not always reliable and there were gaps.

It wasn't only Sholto's physical health that continued to go downhill. His memory, which had always been prodigious, was beginning to fail him too. In fact, as his entire self was subordinated more and more to his battle for survival, I noticed that his character changed a little and that he would become forgetful. But this varied widely from day to day: some days he could be entirely lucid, while other days, as with the sleepwalking, he could be in a completely different place at a different time in his life. He was never 'silly' or stupid, even in his wanderings, but always serious and often distressed over things that had happened in the past. He would sit in his chair in the dining room, crying and saying: 'My brain's going soft.' Little did he know that that was exactly what was happening. In his post-mortem report, which I managed to obtain with some difficulty a few years ago, I read: 'The brain showed fairly marked cerebral atheroma [arterial disease] and there was considerable softening in a number of areas.'

He also began to be profoundly apprehensive in a way that we had not seen before, particularly about what would happen to my mother and me when he died, saying to her: 'I worry about you and Katharine when I am not here.' In one way, this kind of response to a recognition of one's own mortality in the face of increasing infirmity is unsurprising. However, what we did not realise at the time, and which a recent study on the effect of early life stress on anxiety symptoms in late adulthood has shown, is that the start in life that Sholto had had, including his father's desertion and parental divorce when he was very young and subsequent severe poverty, rendered him more vulnerable to anxiety in later life. Evidence also indicates that parental separation is a stronger risk factor for anxiety and other psychopathology than parental loss.[9] It was as though all the traumas from the earliest points in Sholto's life onwards were catching up with him.

His own suffering notwithstanding, my father's concern for me never wavered, and when I was coming up to nine years old, he decided that I should have a pony. Since his own childhood had been impoverished, he wanted me to have what he had not had, although he learned to ride when he was at Oxford due to the kind offices of a fellow student and later served in the Royal Horse Artillery (RHA) in WWI. He and I both loved horses and, much to my mother's disapproval, he was adamant that I start riding lessons aged seven. His view of education was always broad, and he felt that I should have as many experiences as possible. Even though he was often in his wheelchair by this time, he insisted on going to look at various ponies for me, and on the morning of my ninth birthday in July 1966, he gave me a lovely card, which I have still, of a little pony who was exactly the same colour, whitish grey, as the one he had bought for me and who was waiting in the field next to our house. I could not have been more thrilled. Cui Silver became my very best friend, and as well as riding him, I often used to go and cuddle him and kiss his furry neck when the chaos of life in our house was too much to bear.

My father's behaviour became ever more disturbed and he began to have violent outbursts, although he was never physically abusive towards either my mother or me. As a means of controlling his eruptions of temper, his doctors attempted to sedate him with a barbiturate, pentobarbital, otherwise known as Nembutal. I shall never forget the name of that drug, which had such an impact on all of our lives. It had been hailed as a 'truth drug' in the United States during the 1930s, and then used by the British psychiatrist J. S. Horsley as a treatment he termed 'narco-analysis', by which he meant the administration of barbiturates or similar agents to lower his subjects' inhibitions, enabling them to share their experiences and feelings. Of all the drugs that Horsley used in this way, he found Nembutal to be the most effective in producing sedation with the minimum of confusion.[10] Its intravenous counterpart, Pentothal, had been used by two US military psychiatrists, Roy Richard Grinker and John Paul Spiegel, in north Africa during WWII to sedate military personnel suffering from war neurosis. Similarly to Horsley's 'narco-analysis', this was to help patients to access and relive their traumatic memories as a step towards recovery.[11] Grinker and Spiegel termed this process 'narcosynthesis', but it has also been called 'abreaction'.

I do not know whether the doctors treating my father intended simply to use Nembutal as a sedative or whether they expected his traumatic memories (almost always of post-war Germany) to resurface even more. But my mother's and my experience was that my father's confusion became worse and, as has been reported before with this drug, he became more anxious,[12] partly because the recollections upset him so much. When Grinker and Spiegel administered Pentothal in WWII, they did so prior to psychotherapy sessions so that when the patient abreacted, they were there to listen to his traumatic experiences, playing the part of a protective figure, perhaps a kindly parent or good friend, and allowing the patient to recall his trauma before returning him to the current reality.[13] None of this happened with my father. He was left to relive his distressing experiences alone, and when they flooded his mind in the middle of the night, usually when nurses weren't around, the only ones who were there to deal with them were me and my mother. She never knew whether to play along with my father in his delusions or to try to bring him back to the present moment. I was all for the latter, but sometimes when we tried to do this it caused him more anguish. We watched the tormented expressions of guilt that played out in his mind and body.

By the beginning of 1969, my father's physical condition had deteriorated so much that he could no longer sleep in his bedroom upstairs, so modifications were made to the ground floor bedroom and bathroom below mine, to give my father his own space downstairs. Although this was the practical thing to do, it isolated him from my mother, who slept in her bedroom upstairs at the other end of our large house. There is no doubt that the strain on her was enormous, but being alcoholic, she was ill-equipped to deal with the situation. My father drank too, and smoked his pipe and cigars almost incessantly, but I seldom saw him drunk, unlike my mother. Our family doctor prescribed her Durophet, an amphetamine, to 'keep her going', and with both my parents taking psychoactive medication, things got more and more strange, although both of them tried to keep up some sort of normality in their demeanour towards me, to their credit.

One example of my mother's increasingly stressed behaviour stands out in my memory. On my father's lucid days, he and I began to have an intellectual connection. We thought similarly and we enjoyed discussing things such as the English Civil War. I was a committed parliamentarian, and I don't know if he was playing devil's advocate to stimulate argument, but he said he was a royalist. My mother's jealousy of our relationship spilled over one day when we were all in the dining room after supper. I was sitting on the floor by my father's chair. Suddenly, she said that she had had enough of the two of us, and started throwing things off the dining room table and against the radiator. Plates, cups, cutlery, salt and pepper cellars, everything crashed against the radiator. Rather cruelly as I look back on it, my father turned to me and said: 'Katharine, it appears that your mother has gone mad.' I said: 'Yes, and I suppose I'll have to clear up the mess.' My mother left the room, still furious.

In moments like this, Sholto was the one who seemed clear-headed and sane, causing my mother to comment that some days, he could have conducted a BEA board meeting. On these days, his interest in current events was reawakened, and something that caused him profound distress was the start of the Northern Ireland Troubles in 1968. He became very upset when reports of sectarian violence appeared on TV. I did not understand at the time that he had a deep love of Ireland and had been a keen supporter of Irish independence, believing that it should have happened much earlier than it did.

The crunch for Sholto came one day in 1969 when he was watching the news from Northern Ireland. He became so agitated that he picked up the glass urinal next to his bed and hurled it at the TV screen, smashing it. Our family doctor, bless him, said to my mother:

'It's either him or you,' pitting my parents against each other in a life-and-death struggle in which my father was always going to be the loser: of course he would be the first to die, as my mother was twenty-four years younger. Even I could see that, aged eleven. In fact, I had realised about a year before my father died that he could not possibly go on much longer, but never having seen death at close quarters, I could not really picture what it would be like or how deeply distressed I would feel.

In July 1969, before I started secondary school in September, and to give us both a break, my mother decided that she and I would go on holiday to Corfu, somewhere that we all loved and had been many times. My father was taken into the RAF Hospital at Uxbridge on my birthday, the 26th, which looking back now seems rather unkind, and on the same day, my mother and I flew to Corfu. My father hoped so much that he would be well enough to join us in a week or so after intense physiotherapy in hospital, but he was heartbroken to have been left behind, and dictated a painful letter to my mother in Corfu:

RAF Hospital Uxbridge
Middlesex
29 July 1969

Darling Hazel

I'm so homesick and want to be with you so very much. It is worse at night and sometimes spend half the night crying for loneliness and you.

I do hope that you are alright and are not missing me too much; although I wish that sometimes you would.

I am told that I am due to stay here until Saturday and with any luck I should be able to join you on Saturday.

Have you got the small suite for me and Katharine, I hope that K is flourishing and is missing me – I had a very nice letter from her yesterday. If only I could be with you, it would make all the difference because I love you very much. It is sad that we are parted at this very moment, which is when we should be together. In spite of that I hope you are alright, you are probably bearing up under the strain better than I am because it makes me heartbroken and I find it difficult to bear, so I hope that I see you on Saturday as promised.

With lots of love and kisses,

Sholto.

Accompanying this distressing letter was one from the medical director of the hospital, Group Captain Campbell, attempting to reassure us by saying that although my father was missing us, he did not think that he was as depressed as the letter made out, and that he had been very much 'with it' for a large part of the time, reading, talking and enjoying the TV. However, he also said that the RAF neuropsychiatrist, Air Commodore O'Connor, would be seeing my father the following afternoon and that both of them had decided already that he would not be well enough to travel. Finally, Dr Campbell wrote that the civilian consultant psychiatrist to the RAF had agreed to admit my father to the psychogeriatric wing of a private psychiatric hospital in Northampton should that be necessary.

My mother and I sent letters back to my father, trying to encourage him, and two days later, another letter from Dr Campbell reached us in Corfu, saying that my father had been told that he was not well enough to join us and, although outwardly distressed, seemed to accept the situation underneath. He added: 'You know so well he likes to "moan", but don't let that worry you too much.' There is no doubt in my mind which of the two accounts, my father's or Dr Campbell's, was real. My father's letter said it all and, considering his health and the situation that he was in, was entirely unsurprising. He had experienced loneliness throughout his life, from his fragile attachments to his parents in childhood, through frequent threats to his life in WWI, when it assumed an existential quality, and in the isolation of high command in WWII. I suspect that nothing had been able to assuage it: not friendships, not affairs, not even my mother or me. Except that now, the cruellest thing of all was that the two people most precious to him seemed to have deserted him just when he needed them most, giving the loneliness a profound emotional as well as an existential element, assailing him as it did near the end of his life.[14] In his letter, Dr Campbell was simply trying to reassure my mother. Nevertheless, the hospital arranged outings for him, and Henry Marking, a BEA board member who had been appointed chief executive on Sholto's retirement, a close and faithful family friend, visited Sholto to keep his spirits up.

My mother had planned that we should stay three weeks in Corfu, but she received another letter from Dr Campbell saying he did not think that my father would accept this, and he himself did not recommend it. Hard on the heels of that there came a telegram from Uncle Henry saying that he had consulted Group Captain Campbell and they both thought that we should return after two weeks. He even said that he had reserved seats on the appropriate flight and arranged a car to collect us from the airport, adding: 'Sholto has been looking forward to your return on Saturday and will be disappointed if you postpone'. Reading between the lines, the situation was becoming critical.

We returned home on 11 August, and the day afterwards, my father came back from hospital, but for little more than two weeks. On 26 August, he was admitted to the psychogeriatric wing of St Andrews Hospital Northampton, as Group Captain O'Connor had suggested. He would stay there until the end of his life, and I could sense his feeling of being abandoned. We all went up together to get him settled in, but he hated it. He had his own small room opposite the kitchen of the long, low building, so it was noisy. There was a day room down the corridor where, as usually happens with day rooms for older people, the patients sat grimly in chairs all around the walls in a large circle. A nurse asked my father: 'Would you like to go to the day room to meet the other gentlemen?' He replied: 'They're not gentlemen and I don't want to meet them!' So he stayed most of the time in his room, and hardly any effort was made to take him outside or give him any stimulation. No wonder he was miserable.

As if things couldn't get any more chaotic, two weeks later, I started at St Paul's Girls' School, Hammersmith. My parents, principally my mother, had decided that since the commute from our home in Denham to Hammersmith was too long for me to manage at first, I would stay during the week with some friends of my parents in their large flat in Kensington. The father of the family was a foreign diplomat and he and his wife had five children, the eldest of whom was in the same class as me at St Paul's. This was supposed to be a good solution and, certainly, my classmate was kind to me, but I discovered quickly that the household was as dysfunctional as mine was: noisy and disorganised, with small children screaming and suffering from diarrhoea.

During the week, I sent Poppa postcards from London, often of horses or donkeys, and also of Spitfires or pilots being scrambled during WWII. Sometimes, I drew pictures for him. I cringe now when I read my messages to him because although I started always with: 'I hope you are well and happy' (it was a wish – I knew that he wasn't), I almost always went on with something like: 'and behaving yourself' or 'and being good'. I had been shocked by his outbursts at home as well as the consequences of his medication with Nembutal, such as incontinence, and since my mother was continually telling me that I should be 'good', a futile exercise in damage limitation, I passed this on to my father. Now, of course, I am deeply ashamed for not understanding more.

Every weekend, I returned home, which felt very empty in the absence of my father. On Saturdays, my good friend Helen and I went riding together, and on Sundays, my mother and I visited Poppa. Each visit, I took him a present, perhaps one of my most precious toys or an ornament that I would leave with him. I requisitioned his tray table and on it arranged all my gifts for him. He appreciated the care that I took, but I am not sure how thrilled he was with a furry purple cow on a red mat that I had made myself, or a psychedelic enamel flower in a pot. He was always so sad, and was grateful for any kindness shown to him by the staff. The kitchen orderly, Margaret, and one of the nurse assistants, whose name I think was Francesco, spent as much time with him as they could, and when we arrived, we often found them in his room. He was always sitting in his chair, from which he was seldom encouraged to move, and that was to be his final undoing.

About two weeks before my father's death, he started complaining of pain in his right leg and in his chest, but no one, neither doctors nor nurses, seemed to take any notice, even though my mother pointed this out to them on more than one occasion. Then, on 29 October at about 5 p.m., we got a dreadful telephone call. It was my half-term and I had just returned home from riding with Helen. We were planning to take my father out for a long weekend to the Lygon Arms in Broadway, Worcestershire, one of our favourite haunts. My mother took the call in the study, and I rushed into the room because she had started crying. One of the doctors from the hospital told her that my father had died. He said that his death had been 'peaceful' and that he had been sitting in his chair with Margaret and Francesco by his side. My mother and I were both distraught.

In her diary entry for that day, she wrote: 'Sholto has died. I don't believe it, nor does Katharine.' But I did believe it, and it changed my life for ever in ways that I am still discovering. The post-mortem report stated that my father had died from a clot that had travelled to his lung, called a pulmonary embolism, and thromboses (clots) in a major vein in his right leg and in his brain. Underneath, the coroner had written: 'From the degree of adhesion of the pulmonary emboli it is possible that they occurred a week or two ago and may be related to the attack of chest pain reported in the clinical notes.' I understand that my father was incredibly unwell, but if only the doctors had done more than just writing in his notes.

This all looks very 'medical' and somewhat inevitable. Certainly, those clinicians in charge of Sholto's care considered him, and treated him, as a demented and rather badly behaved geriatric patient with the multiple physical concomitants of old age from which he died. They encouraged my mother and me to view him in a similar way, which we did. But the memories of my father's terrible physical and mental disintegration, and, most upsetting of all, his psychological distress, have stayed with me throughout my life, and were fundamental in the choice of my initial profession, nursing, although I specialised finally in newborn intensive care. Subsequently I became a neuroscientist, studying the development of pain processing in babies.

Following my career in neuroscience, I started to research Sholto's life in order to fulfil a long-held but half-buried ambition to write about it, beginning with a look at what I could only describe as 'psychological pain', since I knew that he had carried an agonising burden from the war and especially its aftermath. In my research I had always dealt with physical pain in a pre-verbal, very young population – pre-term and full-term newborns and infants under one year. Furthermore, I had studied those most basic of physical responses, reflexes, so psychology was not my area of expertise. However, for some people, psychological pain, especially that associated with depression, is worse than any physical pain they experience.[15] At least with the latter, there is at least some possibility of withdrawing from the pain. But with psychological pain, there is no immediate escape: it is there in the mind as a constant ache with some of the qualities of chronic physical pain. In fact, there is considerable overlap in the brain areas activated by both physical and psychological pain; the two could be thought of as two sides of the same coin, both engendering deep distress.

My search continued with the *Textbook of Pain*, where, by chance, I came upon a section devoted to post-traumatic stress disorder (PTSD). Thinking back to my father's condition, its features seemed to coincide with what I had seen of his angst, so I began a new trawl through the literature.

At the time that my father was so ill in the late 1960s, no one in Britain talked about PTSD. The term was not introduced until 1980, when, as the result of many years' work, a determined group of Vietnam veterans and the psychiatrists who had treated them fought for it to be included in the third edition of the Diagnostic and Statistical Manual of Mental Disorders (DSM-III), and it entered into medical parlance. The terms 'shell-shock' and 'war neurosis' had been around since WWI,[16] but they were associated with front-line soldiers enduring the appalling conditions of the trenches, not with a sick old man reliving the awful experiences of signing people's lives away in post-war Germany. This was despite the appearance in the medical literature in the 1950s and '60s of reports that the distressing symptoms of 'combat fatigue' or 'gross stress reaction', the terms in vogue at that time, persisted long after the end of WWII. These findings were highlighted in a study conducted in 1965, which found chronic and even irreversible instances of combat fatigue among veterans twenty years after the war had ended.[17] I became fascinated with this subject, explaining as it did so much of my father's behaviour – the nightmares, the sleepwalking, the dislocation to an entirely different place, the crying and distress.

Of course! *This* was what I had seen my father suffer when I was a child. He was not a badly behaved demented old man, as his heartbreaking and lucid letter to my mother had shown. He had PTSD! If he had been part of the Vietnam generation, he would have been diagnosed with this condition, but because he was a WWII survivor, he was classed as a 'psycho-geriatric' patient and treated accordingly, much as his US and Australian counterparts were.[18] So I started looking back into his life through the prism of PTSD, and a new and different story emerged. I realised I was looking at a lifetime of trauma, from his early childhood, through not one but two world wars, and on into the devastation of post-war Germany.

At the same time, one of my psychologist friends put me in touch with the Pain and Suffering Interdisciplinary Program, in which she had participated. I contacted its founder, and through her I was able to contact two eminent experts who explained to me different aspects of what I had observed of my father's distress. They have been my constant companions and friends as I became absorbed in the twists and turns of Sholto's extraordinary story. Through their insights, my extensive searching in the literature, Sholto's own writings and seemingly endless historical documents, I began to rediscover the man who despite his infirmities was a loving and kind father, but who had lived almost a whole life, actually many lives, each with their own traumas and triumphs, before I knew him.

CHAPTER TWO

THE BEGINNINGS OF THE DARK GRAY MAN

Outwardly, my father's life began quite unremarkably. He was born William Sholto Douglas on 23 December 1893 in Headington, Oxford, into a branch of the Scottish aristocratic clan of Douglas that had been denuded of its once considerable wealth. From infancy he was known by his second name, Sholto Douglas being the Gaelic name for the mythical founder of the Douglas clan, and meaning 'Behold the Dark Gray Man' due to this reputed ancestor's swarthy complexion.[1] The name Sholto stuck throughout my father's life, as both airman and senior commander and, as he wrote, 'more often than not, I am glad to say, without any reference to my rank or even to my surname'.[2]

Sholto was the second son of Robert Langton Douglas (also known by his middle name), the first having died in infancy. At the time of Sholto's birth, Langton was an Anglican priest with a growing scholarly interest in literature, history and art, and was assistant chaplain of Merton College, Oxford. He had never wanted to be a clergyman, wishing instead to be a professional singer, as he had a very fine tenor voice. Against his will, his father Robert, an Anglican clergyman of the extreme Evangelical Protestant variety and in whose fervently religious household Langton had had a strict upbringing, had compelled him to enter holy orders following his graduation in Modern History from New College, Oxford.

Sholto's mother, Margaret Jane, known as Maggie, was the daughter of Percival Henry Cannon, a printer, whose wife's family was from Glasgow. Maggie had been a member of Langton's congregation during his first curacy in the church of St Paul Walworth in south London, and he said that he was attracted to her because she reminded him of a Verrocchio Madonna. Only seventeen years old when they married in 1891, Maggie was ten years Langton's junior, tall and very thin with dark hair, the colour of which she kept until she died. After Sholto's birth, two more boys followed: Robert (Bobby) in February 1895, and Archibald (Archie) in September 1896, also named in the Scottish tradition of the Douglas clan. Langton and Maggie's last child was a girl, but once more, like their firstborn, she died while still an infant.

In the late autumn of 1895, when Sholto was nearly two and his brother Bobby nine months old, Langton was appointed to the post of Church of England chaplain in Livorno on the Tuscan coast, where he stayed for approximately a year. He was eager to familiarise himself with the writings and art of Italy, especially those of the Renaissance. Maggie, Sholto and Bobby set out on the journey to Italy with him. Sholto could not recall much of his stay there, his mother telling him later that he learned to speak Italian faster than he did English. However, when I was a child, he told me that he did remember an Italian nanny, who, rather than giving him sweets, gave him olives as treats. From Livorno, the family went to Genoa, where they stayed until 1898.

They returned to England later in that year and once again settled in Oxford, where Langton gave lectures on Italian art under the university's Extension Scheme. The family had been back in Oxford for only two years when in 1900 he decided to accept an appointment to the new chair of Modern History and English Language and Literature at the University of Adelaide. He sailed for Australia in March 1900, leaving his wife and children behind – permanently. Up to this point, his only income had been his clergyman's salary, plus the little that he earned from the Extension Scheme lectures, so when he departed for Australia, he left Maggie with almost nothing, and she was forced to take their three children – Sholto then aged six, Bobby five, and Archie three – to live with her parents in a small house in Tooting, south London.

Sholto wrote a letter to his father at this time, which was returned to him on Langton's death in 1951. Reading it again just over fifty years after it was written, Sholto said:

> I could not help feeling a little sad about the slightly pathetic note that it sounded. It could not have been explained to me that my father had left our home for good because I wrote, in a childish hand, that 'we often think of you as sleeping whilst we are having our dinner', which was a reference to his sojourn in Australia.[3]

There was no support of any kind from Langton for at least the first year of separation, near the end of which Maggie submitted a petition to the divorce court for 'restitution of conjugal rights', after first having written a letter to Langton asking him to return to his family. The letter was posted to his solicitors, because at that point she had no idea of his whereabouts and no means of finding out. She received the following reply:

> Paris. Feb. 19. 1901
>
> My Dear Maggie
>   I have received your letter of Feb. 17. I regret to say that it is quite impossible for me to do what you ask of me. I cannot live with you again. I do not believe that any attempt at a reconciliation would be successful or would really conduce to your happiness or mine, or to the happiness & well-being of our children. Things being as they are, it is better for us to remain apart.
>   I am sorry to pain you, but the decision I have arrived at is final. It has not been arrived at without long and anxious thought.
>   I am
>   Your affectionate husband
>   Robert Langton Douglas.[4]

Without telling Maggie and the children, Langton had returned to Europe temporarily in order to pursue historical studies for his forthcoming book on the history of Siena, but while in Australia, he had fallen madly in love with a beautiful, dark-haired young Australian woman, Gwendolen Henchman. He was still a clergyman in the Church of England, and it is hard to overestimate the impact of a scandal of this kind on his wife and children at that time. From Langton and Maggie's divorce court files, it is clear that Maggie found the whole experience humiliating. Of course, Sholto and his brothers were witnesses to their mother's anguish, and there is ample evidence from the medical literature that the experience before age eleven of maternal distress, and loss of a parent, not only through death but also due to divorce and separation, increases an individual's susceptibility to PTSD. Frequent changes of home before this age are also a risk factor for this condition,[5] and Sholto and his brothers had had a few of those, with more to follow. Moreover, two or more adverse childhood experiences have been significant predictors of PTSD symptoms in soldiers both pre- and post-deployment.[6] All of this heightened Sholto's vulnerability in the face of what was to come.

In one of the files dating from 1901, there are two folded pieces of paper which when spread out reveal themselves to be birth certificates, both dated 11 April 1896 but with different names on each. The times of birth in the first column, fifteen minutes apart, show that these are twin boys, born to someone called Annie Louisa Castle a few months before Sholto's brother Archie was born. The father of the twins is written on the certificates as Robert Langton Castle, but it's obvious, given the rarity of the middle name and the fact that these certificates are among the divorce papers, that this is indeed my grandfather Langton. The files also contain Annie Castle's assertion that Langton was the father. Further on in the documents there is a handwritten page of notes penned by Maggie's solicitor summarising what had happened back in 1895.

The notes begin: 'Lived unhappily. Resp[ondent] [Langton] left her [Maggie].' They go on to state that in October 1895, there was a servant, Annie Castle, who was overheard by Maggie whispering with her husband in his study. Langton told Maggie that 'the girl was pregnant'. The statement continues: 'Going abroad after a great deal of persuasion, and promised to take Castle abroad until her child was born. For the purpose of saving scandal.' The solicitor adds that in Paris, on their way to Italy, Langton had shown Annie so much attention that Maggie had returned to the UK with her children.[7]

So it was not simply for the purposes of furthering his studies in Italian art that Langton had made the journey to Italy. Maggie's petition states that for six weeks prior to 26 December, Langton and Annie lived together at Church House in Livorno, no doubt posing as husband and wife and 'habitually committed adultery together'.[8] A short time later, Annie returned to England to have her twins.

That Maggie was prepared to collude with her husband to such an extent in an attempt to save scandal demonstrates how important that was, and that she went out to Italy the following year with her children once Langton had moved to Genoa shows unbelievable forbearance. She must have thought of the poverty that would have been the alternative, and which did eventually follow their separation in 1900. But any hopes that she may have entertained for a true reconciliation were always going to be doomed to failure. Despite her initial physical attractiveness to him, Maggie was of a completely different temperament and background to Langton. She was devoutly Christian, with an overlying severity of character that he would not have found appealing, even though it concealed kindness underneath.

Maggie and Langton were divorced in 1902. He was forced to 'execute a deed of relinquishment under the provisions of the Clergy Disabilities Act', which meant that he resigned from the Church of England just before being defrocked. The scandal that Maggie had so strenuously tried to avoid burst out when the divorce notice was listed in *The Times*, and as a result Langton was dismissed from his posts at Adelaide University. He returned permanently to Europe with Gwendolen.

Following the divorce, Maggie took her children to live in a small terraced house in Foxbourne Road, Balham. Sholto wrote: 'For a good many years after that we led a decidedly impecunious existence.'[9] Although Langton had started to establish his reputation in the art world, this did not seem to earn him much money, or not much that he was willing to share with Maggie and the children. When I was young, Sholto told me that at times his mother could not afford shoes for the boys' feet, so he would take his two younger brothers barefoot on omnibus trips around London, and they jumped on and off the buses like street urchins. A favourite object that Sholto kept from when he was very young until his death, possibly from his time in Italy as a small child, was a little bronze copy of a famous Greco-Roman statue named 'Lo Spinario'. It stood on the mantelpiece in his bedroom beneath his favourite painting, and depicts a barefoot boy withdrawing a thorn from the sole of his foot. This must have had a special significance for Sholto, and makes me wonder what he must have had to remove from the soles of his feet during those barefoot days in London.

Despite the dire nature of their finances, Maggie did her utmost to provide for her three remaining children, devoting herself to caring for them. Sholto remembered how he would take to school each week the ninepence that his mother gave him for his tuition.

Two memories lodged themselves in Sholto's mind more vividly than any others from his childhood. The first was of the night of 18 May 1900, when the news came of the relief of Mafeking after seven long months of siege by the Boers in South Africa. Sholto and his brothers, who shared a bed at that time, sat up listening with awe to the jubilant shouts from the crowds that surged up and down Balham High Road. The second was of the day, about a year later, when the new electric tram service along that same road was opened. All the schoolchildren from St Mary's were lined up on the pavement for the occasion. He wrote later: 'On board the first tram there was the Prince of Wales, who later became King George the Fifth, and it was our task to cheer and to sing in our shrill little voices a song that we had learnt for the occasion: "God Bless the Prince of Wales".'[10] Notwithstanding their impoverished circumstances, the primary education that Sholto and his brothers received at St Mary's School in Balham was a good foundation, and when he went to Emanuel School, Wandsworth, in 1904 as a day boy, he found that he was more than equal to the other pupils in every subject but Latin, which was new to him. Although the school charged fees, many pupils were on scholarships, and given his family's circumstances it is likely that Sholto was in this category.

In that same year, Langton set up on his own as an art dealer, and by 1905 his success led him, after having re-established contact with Maggie, to suggest that their three children should be sent to a public school. There were insufficient funds for them to board, so it was decided that Maggie and the boys should move to Tonbridge, because a large number of the pupils at Tonbridge School were day boys.

On moving to Tonbridge, Sholto and his brothers attended the quaintly named Mr Darling's Preparatory School, occupying Clare House, a large four-storey Victorian villa next to Tonbridge School. Ever ambitious, in a letter to his father in November 1905 at the age of eleven, Sholto wrote that he had read only three of Scott's novels but had made it into the school cricket first eleven. A year later, he reported that he was now head boy of the school, and that he had won two prizes and Archie three. Sholto went on to Tonbridge School in the Lent term of 1908 at the age of fourteen, having done very well in the entrance exam. He wrote to his father in his first term: 'I like the Big School very much, though it is rather strange after Mr Darling's. The boys in my form are a very nice lot of boys on the whole, but of course I get pretty well left to myself, as I am still counted as a "novi".'[11]

He had been at Tonbridge only a short time when he began to realise that, due to his parents' divorce and the family's straitened financial circumstances, his home life was different from that of most of the other pupils. Recognition of this may have prompted in him the first awareness of what he termed 'the inherent self-consciousness which has always bothered me'. His struggle to control this sensitivity, which at that time manifested mainly as acute shyness, led to him adopting a bullish exterior that only made the problem worse. As he said: 'It was hard going having to be always on one's guard.'[12] A photograph of him and his two brothers taken a couple of years later seems to show exactly that, as there is a hint of wariness in his expression beneath the shadow of a smile.

He was plagued by these feelings throughout his life, writing: 'What the psychiatrists would say about that I cannot pretend to know; but I do think that the break-up of my parents' marriage while I was still very young contributed to this wretched shyness.'[13] He said that the problem was limited to his social life and that his work was never handicapped in this way, but it did produce in him, as Bill Simpson commented, a brusqueness of manner that was frequently misinterpreted during his time in the RAF, as well as 'a provocative sense of humour' that led to misunderstandings and offence being taken by others. Of this constellation of psychological kinks that he made enormous efforts to conceal, Sholto wrote: 'But I understand, without people having known it, why the comment has been made that I have succeeded in spite of myself.'[14] He was determined to use intellectual endeavour as a means to fulfil his ambitions, one of which was to win a scholarship to Oxford, his father's university. The letters he wrote to Langton at this time suggest that he was desperate to prove himself, and to gain the regard and respect, even the love, of the father who had previously deserted him, a not uncommon trait in those who have suffered parental deprivation, and one that Churchill clearly shared.

Sholto participated fully in school life at Tonbridge despite his feelings of being different, joining the chapel choir and practising enthusiastically for the schools sports. Due to the good impression that he had made in his entrance exam, he was placed in a form ahead of his age on the classical side, which at that time at Tonbridge was of a very high standard. He was joined by his brothers, Archie doing particularly well and ending his school career by winning an open classical scholarship to Trinity College, Oxford. Sholto said that Archie was the most able of the three brothers, that Bobby was steady and plodding, and that he himself, although not as brilliant as Archie, was ambitious and prepared to work very hard for what he wanted. All three participated vigorously in the debating society, although a report in the school's magazine, *The Tonbridgian*, noted ironically that Sholto 'spoke from the lofty standpoint of his superior knowledge',[15] suggesting that on that occasion at least, he might have been better served keeping certain opinions to himself.

In the summer of 1912, he went on the annual Officers' Training Corps (OTC) camp at Farnborough, and it was there that his fascination with aviation was born. The airfield was much smaller than it is now, and the Royal Aircraft Factory, which subsequently became the Royal Aircraft Establishment, was on the opposite side of the field from the OTC camp. Aircraft were being tested there, which Sholto thought later must have been BE1s and BE2s.[16] He became absorbed with the new phenomenon of flying, spending every moment of his spare time on the camp watching from a distance. He wondered wistfully if there was any way that he 'could indulge in what appeared to be such a wonderful sport'. But as a poor schoolboy, his expectations were not high: 'I felt in my heart that the chance of ever flying was very remote.'[17] He was not aware that the RFC had been formed only a few weeks earlier – nor that he would play such a fundamental part in its development.

Meanwhile Langton achieved increasing success as an art dealer, but his style of living was still relatively modest, largely due to his growing family. At the very least, he was supporting the three boys he had had with Maggie, possibly Annie Castle's twins, and two girls and a boy that he had had with his second wife, Gwendolen. In addition to these, in 1909 and 1912, he fathered two more children, a girl and a boy, with his mistress, Grace Hutchison, who was half Australian and, like the other women in his life, dark-haired and astonishingly beautiful. He had first set eyes on her in 1896 when he was chaplain in Genoa, where she was staying with her sister while on a 'grand tour' of Europe, and he had fallen in love, or perhaps lust, with her. Langton would have a relationship with Grace for thirty years, but he never married her, despite promises to do so. For her part, tragically, she regarded him as the love of her life. In the end, in an utter repudiation of any vestige of his father's Evangelical beliefs, against the strictures of which he had so comprehensively rebelled, Langton's eighteen children would be born to three wives, the last of whom had been Sholto's then current girlfriend, and five mistresses. Sholto's comment later was: 'It will possibly come as a disappointment to some when I reveal that I am one of my father's legitimate sons.'[18]

He was approaching the end of his time at Tonbridge, and being made a prefect brought him face to face with one aspect of school life that he abominated: corporal punishment. He wrote about it at length, feeling that it brutalised those who inflicted it and caused strong resentment in the person upon whom it was perpetrated. He was beaten only once during his time there, and he remembered it all his life, hating the indignity of what he called 'the whole performance', and feeling that he was punished unjustly.

Nevertheless, the incident was not without amusement: during drill of the House OTC squad on one of the playing fields, the non-commissioned officer (NCO) in charge, a prefect from another house, somehow managed to get the boys marching line abreast heading straight for a hedge. He failed to issue the order for them to halt, and whereas the others stopped when they reached the hedge awaiting further orders, Sholto alone continued to force his way through it and marched on across the next field. He reasoned that no order had been given to halt, and it was his duty to ignore the obstacles in his path and press on. This was deemed impertinence, for which he was 'soundly thrashed'.

When he became a prefect himself, he resolved to have nothing whatsoever to do with caning, but many years later, he was accused by someone who had been junior to him at Tonbridge of having beaten him. Sholto was so unhappy about this that he felt compelled to write to the man, by then an Army brigadier, to tell him that he was mistaken. Despite serving in the military for most of his life, there was a strong humanitarian streak in Sholto that considered inflicting any sort of bodily harm on others distasteful to the point of physical revulsion. On the rugby field he was known as a 'safe tackler',[19] and he considered the sport of boxing particularly loathsome, even though its rules were credited to one of his kinsmen, the 9th Marquess of Queensberry.

Despite coming joint top of the Upper Sixth, Sholto failed to get the classical scholarship to an Oxford college that he so wanted, attributing this to anxiety and shyness in the awe-inspiring atmosphere of the university, but was awarded two exhibitions, for £75 and £30 (together worth approximately £8,500 today). In his leaving report in the summer of 1913, his headmaster wrote: 'I have an unlimited regard and respect for him, and confidence in him. His ability and thoroughness are unusually great, and he is entirely trustworthy.'[20] With these two exhibitions, and some financial help from Langton, Sholto went up to Oxford in the autumn of 1913. On arrival in the creeper-covered quads of Lincoln College, he sat the scholarship examination again, and this time he was successful, 'converting his try', and being awarded a classical scholarship of £60 a year. He went on to study Greats – classics and philosophy – but sadly was not to benefit from the hard-won scholarship because it did not become effective until October 1914, and by that time he was 'engaged in pursuits that were less academic'.

But in 1913, for Sholto and his fellow undergraduates, there was no sign of the cataclysm that would come less than a year later. Life in the colleges involved a whirl of social activity. Sholto's ambition was to get a good class in his degree, but apart from that, he had no idea at all about what he was going to do with his life. One irksome aspect of the social life was that college restrictions forbade almost all contact with women, even in the city. To meet his girlfriend of the moment, Sholto would have to take the train out of Oxford, stealing a few hours together at Pangbourne or one of the other villages on the Thames. This state of affairs was, he said, 'not without its own humour'.

With his fine tenor voice, inherited from Langton, Sholto pursued his interest in choral singing by joining the Bach Choir, and continued his habit of reading prolifically. He debated endlessly with his friends, and became interested in the Labour movement, his wide scope of reading taking in Fabian Society pamphlets. He wrote that his interest in socialism 'came more from a personal conviction than from any academic or intellectual interest. It was bred of an innate sense of a need for justice in the relationships between human beings that had started developing in my mind long before I went up to Oxford.'[21]

Perhaps as a means of countering the humiliation that she had suffered at her supposedly more 'upper-class' husband's hands, Sholto's mother had endeavoured to bring up her sons without the consciousness of class that was so prevalent in English society of that time. Of course, Sholto had encountered this when he went to Tonbridge and then to Oxford, realising that for reasons 'so blatantly unjust, opportunities for all men were by no means equal'. This realisation bred in him a strong dislike of any form of snobbery. He knew how it felt to be diminished and excluded, and his childhood poverty compelled him to identify with the disadvantaged.[22] This process led him to become a convinced socialist.[23]

Sholto pursued his sporting activities, playing football, hockey and rugby, both for his college and in trials for the Varsity side, but at eleven and a half stone, he was considered a little too light for a scrum forward in the Oxford team. He was also an enthusiastic rower. He continued with his military training in the Oxford University OTC, joining the signals section of the infantry, but under the influence of a freshman friend from New Zealand, Denis O'Rorke, coupled with his desire to ride a horse, Sholto transferred to the Artillery. In this way he learned to ride and was able occasionally to borrow a mount, which was fortunate as he was always short of money. By the summer of 1914, he had become a driver in the Artillery section, his drill being on the eighteen-pounder gun, which he did not know then was going to be standard ordnance in the coming conflict.

When Sholto finished what would turn out to be his only year at Oxford, amid the magnificent weather he enjoyed the entertainments of the London season, going to the theatre with his mother and brothers. This summer idyll was barely marred by a report on 28 June of yet another incident in the 'tiresome Balkans', as Sholto called them. The heir to the throne of Austro-Hungary and his wife had been assassinated 'in a far off town in Bosnia by the name of Sarajevo'. There were 'vague murmurings' that this might precipitate a war, but hardly anyone outside those involved in international affairs took them seriously, Sholto included.[24]

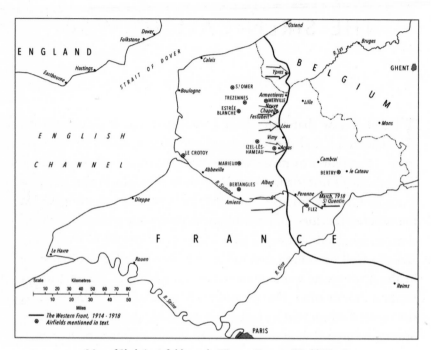

Map of Sholto's airfields on the Western Front in World War I.

CHAPTER THREE

THE SIREN CALL TO WAR

The idyll was shattered when Germany invaded Belgium on 3 August 1914, and the following day Britain declared war on Germany in response to its deliberate violation of our ally's neutrality. The official air historian, Walter Raleigh, wrote: 'The invasion of Belgium by German troops during the first few weeks of the war, and the ordered cruelties inflicted by those troops on a helpless population, set England on fire.'[1] Sholto and most of his fellow students at Lincoln College volunteered for service. Applying for a commission in the Artillery, he was summoned for an interview and referred for medical examination. He was surprised and disgusted when told by the medical officer that he had failed due to his flat feet. Sholto being Sholto, he argued with the examining officer, emphasising his sporting prowess and questioning why flat feet were of concern for the Artillery. He won his argument and was promptly passed fit for active service.

So Sholto received his Royal Field Artillery (RFA) commission as a Second Lieutenant on 15 August. He wrote:

> I find it a little touching to recall that I went into action mounted on a horse with a sword dangling at my saddle-bow. My views then about war were quite unrealistic and far from serious … We who were in our late teens and our early twenties in 1914 did not know that war could produce a depth of misery to which even death would be preferable; and we did not know then anything about the horror that was to be inflicted upon what came to be so well known as the Western Front.[2]

After a short artillery course at Shoeburyness, he was posted to the RFA depot in Newcastle, from where, in early October, he was sent to the Ammunition Column of the Fifth Brigade, Royal Horse Artillery (RHA), part of the Eighth Division. He remarked: 'Quite by chance, I had found my way into the company of the élite of the gunners; and to my delight I learnt that we were due to make an early move to France.' He was given a handsome young black charger named Tommy, of whom, he said, 'I became quite inordinately proud. For his sake as well as my own I tried hard to put up a good show.'³

The Fifth Brigade RHA departed for France in early November and was to support the newly established front line at Laventie, a little way south of the river Lys. At first, the shortage of ammunition was so acute that each gun was rationed to firing just four rounds per day, so the threat they posed to the enemy was minimal. The guns were positioned in revetted pits⁴ just behind the lines, and Sholto's task in the Ammunition Column was to keep them supplied with shells from the depot in the rear. Each day as darkness was falling over the battlefields, when there was still enough light to see where they were going but not enough for the Germans to observe them, the duty officer in charge, sometimes Sholto, led two or three horse-drawn wagons up to the gun emplacements. It was usually dark by the time they arrived. Despite precautions taken, Sholto remarked in a letter to his father that quite a number of officers had been killed or wounded by snipers, and that it was not safe for him to stroll about at night without some means of self-defence, for instance when he was turning out the guard. So he asked Langton to send him a small automatic pistol with ammunition. Snipers were not the only danger with which Sholto and his fellow gunners had to contend. Due to the position of the gun pits, enemy shells were a very present danger, and Sholto remembered being deeply frightened at first, but later on, he became accustomed to the shelling, if that is ever possible.

During that first winter of the war in France, Sholto and his fellow soldiers had to endure almost constant rain, turning the soft ground into vast tracts of clinging, sticky mud, interspersed with bitter cold and hard frosts. He wrote to Langton in December: 'The men are over their knees in water in the trenches largely owing to the fact that the Germans are deliberately trying to swamp us by damming the river and ditches.'⁵ So he asked his father to send him four pairs of gumboots for his sergeants. There is no record of any letters between Sholto and his mother during this period. While one would not expect Maggie to have provided him with a pistol, it was generally mothers who provided the emotional and practical support for their sons at the Front, in the shape of letters and parcels. Of her three sons, however, Sholto was the one with whom Maggie had the least sympathy. He was the most like his father in character, being robustly independent. However, he was sensitive enough to realise that money was still tight for her, so he would not have wished to ask her for anything that would place an extra burden on her.

Langton, meanwhile, was eager to share in his son's experience, despite being over fifty. Though the upper age limit for joining up was thirty-five, those enlisting in the Army as privates were not required to produce a birth certificate, so he lied outrageously about his age, saying that he was thirty-four years and ten months. He had dyed his greying hair so that on the Short Service Attestation form was written 'dark brown'. Being of an exceptionally robust constitution, he wangled his way past the Army authorities without any difficulty and was accepted into the ranks of the Fourth Public Schools' Battalion of Royal Fusiliers as a private on 6 October 1914. So it was that he followed Sholto and his brother Bobby, who had applied for a commission in the same month straight from school, into the war. While training on Salisbury Plain in October and early November, Langton found the unusually harsh weather most definitely not to his taste, so he had his tailor in London line the tunic of his private's uniform with musquash to keep out the worst of the cold. It was a relief to him when his application for a commission in the Royal Army Service Corps was accepted on 11 November, even though the deceit about his age had been discovered.

In October and November 1914, the First Battle of Ypres in the Flemish part of Belgium was the scene of the heaviest fighting on the Western Front. Out of the ferocious hand-to-hand combat as the British Army resisted the German advance, that famous bulge in the Front known as the Ypres Salient was formed. As autumn merged into that first winter of the war, it was not only the situation for the men that was miserable. Sholto was deeply depressed by the conditions the horses were having to endure. The historian Cyril Falls observed that WWI was a war of horses: 'Man had from the remotest times taken his "best friends" to war, but had seldom slaughtered them on such a scale.'[6] A conservative estimate is that eight million horses and countless mules and donkeys perished in the conflict, not only from the horrors of shell fire and gas attacks, but also from the terrible weather and appalling conditions in which they were kept. Some sources rate the total number much higher, at between nine and ten million. Apart from his work in the Ammunition Column, Sholto spent much of his day exercising and looking after them. He felt helpless to alleviate their suffering, but he did try to build up hard ground out of rubble on which they could stand for protection against the traumas of foot rot, although he realised that even that was hopeless.

Soon after joining the RHA, Sholto had begun to have simmering disagreements with his commanding officer (CO), which added to his troubles. Things came to a head one day when he expressed the view that there was an urgent need for a change in ammunition type. He felt that high-explosive was needed instead of the exclusive use of shrapnel, which was of little value in trench warfare. He explained later:

> Having been case-hardened in the traditions of the Royal Horse Artillery, my CO looked upon all subalterns, and in particular his own, as utter non-entities. But I was fresh from Oxford, where the undergraduate has always regarded talking as an important part of his way of life and freedom of speech as an essential.[7]

That Sholto had had the temerity to express his views caused a pronounced frostiness between them thereafter, so when an order was circulated inviting subalterns to volunteer as observers in the RFC, he seized the opportunity. At that time, the main work of the RFC was spotting and ranging for the Artillery, so it was thought that gunners would make the best observers.

Sholto had been in France for just under two months when he

received orders to report for duty with No. 2 Squadron, then operating from a field near Merville, approximately six and a half kilometres from Estaires, where he was billeted. On 11 October 1914, one of the most appalling tragedies of WWI had unfolded in this small French town when forty local civilians were used by the Germans as human shields in their defence of a bridge over the Lys against attack by the French. All of these citizens were killed despite French efforts to avoid shooting them.

Just over two months later, on Boxing Day 1914, three days after his twenty-first birthday, Sholto mounted his treasured charger Tommy, and in the company of his groom, rode the twelve kilometres to the airfield across the flat, highly cultivated farmland that surrounds the Lys. He wrote:

> I cannot believe that there are many Air Force officers, and certainly not of the most senior rank, who first reported at a squadron headquarters for duty in their new service mounted on a charger and accompanied by a groom. I sent my groom back with Tommy to my old unit, and that was the last that I was ever to see of either of them.[8]

The only adverse criticism that he received from anybody on joining the RFC came from his mother, who said: 'You must be mad.'

Even as a temporary aerodrome, Merville had few advantages, but as a permanent base for an operational squadron it was one of the most badly chosen sites in this flat area of France. Where the two L-shaped runways intersected, the ground was very uneven, with a gentle slope down to the river, which certainly added to the excitement of landing. Everywhere there were thickets and ditches, and the canvas aircraft hangars had a habit of blowing down whenever there was a high wind. So Sholto was introduced to the vital part that weather played in the conduct of the air war, most notably the prevailing westerly wind, which was a continual and severe handicap for pilots in the RFC flying into it back to base, but which in turn helped the Germans to slip back over their lines when being pursued by the British.

After the rigid discipline of the RHA, Sholto found the free and easy way in which things were done in the RFC much more to his liking: 'I was now in the company of individualists, some of whom, I was soon to find, could even be regarded as eccentrics if not downright crazy. All that, in itself, held for me a distinct attraction.'[9] Even the official historian noted: 'No one who covets a life of routine, with defined duties and limited liabilities, ever yet took up with aviation as a profession.'[10] Individualism such as Sholto displayed was seen to be an attribute in this new branch of military service.

Due to the shortage of aircraft in the RFC, Sholto's instruction as an observer was 'somewhat meagre'.[11] First, he had to learn to signal in Morse code with an electric lamp. In the bitter winter weather, he spent days sitting in the old barn on the aerodrome learning this new skill. Then one day in January, his CO told him casually that he was to go for his first flight. He and his flight commander made a reconnaissance sortie over the front lines in the direction of Lille on 27 January. Sholto had never flown in an aeroplane, and he had almost no idea at all of where they were from the moment they took off until they landed. To add to the thrill, this first ever flight as an observer was on an operational war patrol under heavy anti-aircraft fire. From that point on, he flew many sorties, teaching himself how to map-read from the air, and through a process of trial and error he became rapidly more proficient. Despite his first reconnaissance flight being recorded in the squadron's work summary as 'unsuccessful', surprisingly, his service record states that he qualified officially as an observer on that date. Just over six weeks after first arriving at Merville, the notification of his permanent transfer to the RFC came through.

The aviation historian John Morrow has written: 'The RFC treated the observer's demanding and essential role casually and encouraged observers to become pilots.'[12] Although the pilot is the captain and in control of the aircraft, Walter Raleigh noted,

> it is equally true to say that a higher degree of cold-drawn courage is demanded from the observer. He suffers with the pilot for all the pilot's mistakes. For hours together he has nothing to do but to sit

still and keep his eyes open. He has not the relief that activity and the sense of control give to strained nerves.[13]

As an observer, Sholto played a pioneering role in the development of aerial photography in the RFC. Soon after he joined No. 2 Squadron, it became known that in his schooldays he had been interested in photography, so he was promptly appointed the squadron specialist. He began to photograph the German trenches, writing to his father that he had taken several snapshots from a height of 5,000 feet. During the period January–April 1915, Sholto made thirty-two photographic reconnaissance sorties with his pilots, almost all of which yielded results, although bad weather sometimes hampered their efforts.

Sholto's early efforts at photography found their way into the official history:

> He cut a rectangular hole in the bottom of his cockpit in a BE2a, and his practice, when the area to be photographed nearly filled the aperture, was to push his camera through the hole and take his snapshot. 'This procedure', he says, 'was not too easy in the cramped space available, especially as the weather was cold and bulky flying kit a necessity. Each plate had to be changed by hand, and I spoilt many plates by clumsy handling with frozen fingers. A proportion of the photographs, however, were successful.'[14]

During one early sortie, when tasked with photographing the headquarters of Crown Prince Rupprecht of Bavaria in a suburb of Lille, Sholto took the first ever air photograph of an enemy airfield.[15]

Before the Allied attack on Neuve Chapelle in March 1915, continuing work by Sholto and C. C. Darley, the photographic officer in neighbouring No. 3 Squadron, led to photography playing its first important role in an infantry offensive. The official history stated: 'For the first time in its history, the British Army went into action with a picture of the hidden intricacies of the enemy defences, and, after the first assault, bombing parties were able to make their way, without loss of time, to their separate objectives.'[16] The historian

Maryam Philpott has noted: 'The value of the maps made by the Royal Flying Corps ensured that not only would aeroplanes have an invaluable role in warfare, but also in Britain's commercial future.'[17] Despite the early capture of Neuve Chapelle and its arterial roads, largely due to the efforts of the RFC in mapping and the increasing use of directing the Artillery by wireless onto the positions of active hostile batteries, the British were not able to exploit their early success. A further advance was prevented by enemy 'strong points', along which the new German lines were built after the battle.

Sholto's work in aerial photography brought him into contact with the Commander of the First Wing, Colonel H. M. Trenchard. Trenchard tried to play Sholto and Darley off against each other, showing them the other's photographs in the hope of encouraging them to better efforts. But they swapped notes, realising what he was up to, and agreed that 'the old boy was wasting his time'.[18]

Trenchard's policy of relentlessly taking the fight to the enemy continues to excite controversy. From the beginning, he viewed the aeroplane as a weapon of attack, not defence. According to Basil Collier, during the Second Battle of Ypres in April 1915, Trenchard pressed his First Wing so hard that 'it suffered losses wholly disproportionate to any good achieved'.[19] However, actual fighting between aircraft at the beginning of 1915 was still an unusual event. Armament in the air was largely a matter of personal choice and consisted of either a Colt automatic or a cavalry carbine. Sholto's account of his first encounter with a German machine at close quarters just prior to the Battle of Neuve Chapelle is included in the official history. His pilot that day was H. D. Harvey-Kelly, the outstanding aviator of No. 2 Squadron and the first RFC pilot to land in France in WWI. They were on a photographic mission when they encountered a hostile aircraft about 100 yards away and just below them. Completely unarmed, all they could do was wave at the enemy, who waved back. Sholto remarked that at the time this did not appear to him in any way ridiculous: 'There is a bond of sympathy between all who fly, even between enemies. But afterwards just for safety's sake I always carried a carbine with me in the air.'[20]

Sholto began his efforts at aerial combat as an observer when a

BE2c aircraft fitted with a Lewis gun arrived in his squadron, but as Cecil Lewis observed in his memoir *Sagittarius Rising*, 'If there was ever an aeroplane unsuited for active service, it was the BE2c,'[21] and Sholto's first attempts ended in failure. Due to the BE2c's 'tractor' configuration, in which the propeller was situated at the front of the aircraft with the observer sitting behind it and in front of the pilot, the aircraft had to be flying away from the enemy in order to strike at him. Sholto observed: 'It soon became apparent that, to attack effectively, one must be able to fire forward in the direction in which one's machine was flying.'[22] This issue was addressed later in 1915 by the introduction of devices for firing a fixed machine-gun through the propeller arc between the blades, so that the pilot could aim his gun by aiming his aeroplane.

Bombing from the air was also a relatively rare occurrence in that spring. It had been tried in the previous year, but in mid-February 1915, RFC HQ directed one flight per squadron to specialise in bombing. Once again, little guidance was given as to how this should be done, only that low flying might be needed to ensure accuracy. During the Second Battle of Ypres in late April, Second Lieutenant William Rhodes-Moorhouse of No. 2 Squadron was detailed to bomb Courtrai. Sholto, who had been flying often with him as his observer, wanted to go up with him, but because of the weight of the bombs, Rhodes-Moorhouse refused, despite his remonstrations. Rhodes-Moorhouse bombed a railway line from a height of 300 feet, releasing his 100lb bomb directly on the target, but he was subject to very heavy rifle and machine-gun fire. He was mortally wounded in the abdomen, thigh and one hand, but managed, who knows how, to fly the fifty-six kilometres back to Merville and insisted on giving a full account of his flight and what he had achieved in Trenchard's hearing. When Sholto helped Rhodes-Moorhouse out of his aircraft, he was horrified to see half a dozen bullet holes in the observer's seat. Rhodes-Moorhouse died of his wounds the next day, but before he died, he was read a message by the Commander-in-Chief (C-in-C) praising his courage. He was awarded the Victoria Cross posthumously, the first to be won by an airman. Sholto wrote to his widow two days after her husband's death:

Dear Mrs Moorhouse

Although I am a total stranger to you I hope you will not consider it a liberty on my part, if I try to express to you my sympathy for the great loss you have sustained. For the last week or two before his last heroic exploit I happened to be your husband's observer and I can truly say that I can wish for no better comrade in any of the work we have to do. He was always so ready to help the observer by every means in his power; and not content with flying the machine superbly he would go out of his way to assist in any observation work that was to be done.

We all admire immensely as you can well believe the wonderful pluck he displayed in his last brave expedition. Very few men could have overcome such pain, and brought the machine back practically unscathed to his starting point. Though it would be a poor consolation, I do hope that such courage will be recognised with a D.S.O. although we all think a V.C. would be none too great a reward for such pluck and endurance.

Once more let me express my deepest sympathy.

I am

Yours Sincerely

W.S. Douglas

2nd Lt. R.H.A.[23]

By the last week of May, activity on No. 2 Squadron's part of the Front decreased. Sholto had made up his mind to become a pilot very soon after he had started flying as an observer, so in this comparative lull in activity, to his delight he was informed by the CO that his request for pilot's training had been successful.

For his initial instruction, which began on 26 May 1915, five months to the day after reporting for duty with the RFC, he went to a small flying school that had been established on the French coast near Le Crotoy for observers who were already on active service. The school had four or five instructors and as many aeroplanes, Caudrons, which according to Sholto were weird and primitive French machines with the gliding angle of a brick. Following a week of dual instruction, his first solo flight came on 2 June and lasted ten minutes. After a further ten minutes flying with his instructor, he had a test lasting one hour, in which he had to do a figure of eight in the air and make several landings on a certain spot marked out on the airfield. On completion of this test, with only five hours forty minutes' flying time, he received Aviator's Certificate No. 1301 from the Royal Aero Club and was sent back to England to complete his training with No. 3 Reserve Aeroplane Squadron at Shoreham Aerodrome before being posted to No. 14 Squadron, based at Hounslow. A week after his arrival, he experienced the first of many crashes that were to punctuate the whole of his career in the Air Force, even during the time that he was an air chief marshal (ACM) in WWII, despite his prowess as a pilot. This first accident occurred shortly after take-off when the engine started to fail. Sholto had to land in an orchard between two lines of fruit trees, which ripped his wings off. However, the engine and he himself came out of the crash intact.

The squadron's stay at Hounslow was short, due to Sholto and his fellow trainee pilots enjoying their proximity to London rather too much and getting into trouble on nights out. The final straw came when the squadron ambulance was commandeered and parked in front of the Piccadilly Hotel until the early hours of the morning while Sholto and his comrades enjoyed their evening. By that time, the Provost Marshal's boys, aka the Military Police, were onto them, so their wing commander ordered the squadron down to Gosport out of harm's way.

Before they left, Sholto was sent to the Central Flying School at Upavon for his final test. He wrote in his logbook for 21 July: 'Passed exam at CFS (80 per cent). Allowed to put up wings.'[24] This was one of Sholto's proudest moments, when he exchanged the half-wing of the observer for the wings of a pilot of the RFC. He had to his credit a total, including dual instruction, of just over twenty-five hours. His sojourn with No. 14 Squadron was brought to an end a month later by him getting into more trouble, although not of the London variety. Doing some practice flying one day, his engine failed and he was forced to land in a field of cabbages, turning the aircraft over. In his logbook he wrote: 'Lost engine and smashed machine.'[25] This number of crashes was not unusual. Arthur Gould Lee, who wrote evocative memoirs of his experiences in WWI as an RFC pilot, observed that during the five months he served as an instructor to trainee pilots in the UK, he became well accustomed to fatal crashes as well as numerous others where the pilot went to hospital or was uninjured. The historian Denis Winter went further, quoting the appalling official statistic that of the 14,166 British pilots killed during WWI, 8,000 died while training at home.[26] The problem was that many of the instructors at RFC training schools were hardened pilots posted back to Britain from the Western Front, most of whom found training duties boring. They wanted to return to their 'real war work' in France and Belgium, and therefore gave somewhat haphazard instruction. The CO of the squadron was not impressed with Sholto's record of crashes, and when he was told to select some of his pilots to send out to France as replacements, Sholto was top of the list.

By the time he received his orders to go, he had flown a total of thirty-two hours and fifteen minutes. This was above the average for pilots being sent to the Front. Nevertheless, he knew that any experience gained in the air was invaluable, so instead of taking the week's leave that he was offered, he asked if he could spend that time with the squadron to increase his flying hours, amassing a total of forty hours and five minutes. In the summer of 1915, the average pilot sent to the Front did not have many more than twenty hours, and Sholto knew of some with only fourteen hours in their logbooks. He and others described that as 'sheer murder'.[27] Some pilots were sent to the Front with as little as five hours of solo flight time, and with this grossly insufficient training they were a liability both to their squadrons and to themselves. It is a salutary statistic that one RFC officer in six was killed during the war, compared to one in seven in the Army and one in twenty in the Navy.

Sholto arrived back in France on 18 August 1915 and was posted to No. 8 Squadron at Marieux. The airfield was situated on the northern edge of a large wood, with the officers' quarters, including some tents that were later replaced by huts, camouflaged among the trees. Today, the place retains its air of secrecy, nestled on the edge of the woods.

About the time of No. 8 Squadron's arrival in France the preceding April, specialisation of aircraft for different duties had already begun to take place, and the aim was to make individual squadrons more homogeneous by operating aircraft of a single type. So a few weeks after Sholto joined the Squadron, it was equipped with only the BE2c. The challenges presented by the Fokker monoplane necessitated a change in tactics: aircraft were now compelled to fight in pairs. In March the following year, a communiqué from General Headquarters (HQ) to the War Office stated that 'it is necessary for reconnaissances to consist of at least five machines flying in formation'.[28] These were the beginnings of formation flying, by which Sholto became much exercised, and which was to prove such a contentious issue for him and others in Fighter Command in WWII.

Meanwhile, in the autumn of 1915, there had been a stalemate for the past few months 'because the more or less exhausted armies on both sides had sunk down into the ever-expanding systems of trenches'.[29] But by the middle of September, there were rumours of a big offensive, to be known as the Battle of Loos. On 21 September, the comparative quiet to the north of the airfield at Marieux was shattered with an artillery bombardment of the German front line that continued for four days. The weather had broken, making flying more difficult, but during the heavy shelling No. 8 Squadron pilots were ordered to follow one another at short intervals and to bomb railway tracks and any trains on the Lille–Valenciennes–Douai lines, as well as junctions and engine sheds north of Valenciennes in order to hinder enemy reinforcements. Sholto made two lengthy patrols over the part of enemy territory that was to bear the brunt of the Allied attack. He thought at first that he had destroyed a train with a 100lb bomb, but later realised that he had been over-optimistic in his assessment – a bomb of that size would not have been sufficient to destroy it, but certainly he had put it out of action. His next efforts hit the brick supports of a railway bridge, cutting a light railway and blocking the main line.

Despite the hard work of the RFC, the Battle of Loos was a failure for the Allies, and in the opinion of Sholto and numerous others, the main reason for this was the Army's 'extraordinary oversight in not providing right from the beginning for the reserves that would be needed'.[30] Reinforcements were kept too far back to be able to secure advances made on the ground. The attack collapsed with fearful losses: the historian J. E. Edmonds quoted a total of 59,247 of the 285,107 British casualties on the Western Front in 1915. Sholto observed that, in case it be thought that generals only ever die in their beds, three British divisional commanders, all major-generals, were killed in the offensive. The acrimonious post-mortem laid the blame at the feet of Sir John French, the C-in-C, who was said to have lost the battle in the initial few hours. French was relieved of his command, and in his place, Sholto wrote, 'we got as our Commander-in-Chief the inflexible Sir Douglas Haig'.[31]

The British Army in the west fought no great action after Loos until the Somme battle in July 1916. However, that did not mean that there was any slackening-off for the RFC. Reconnaissance patrols, bombing logistics targets, aerial photography, and wireless work continued, and towards the end of 1915, activity intensified as 'bombing was carried out on a much larger scale, attacks being made by formations of fourteen to twenty machines'.[32] Furthermore, the RFC pilot had to deal with the increasing menace of the 'Fokker Scourge', knowing that his aircraft was sub-standard. Arthur Lee observed: 'The strain is deepened if his weapon is inferior and he knows he is at a disadvantage even before the fight starts. That is when the most valiant man can reach the stage when his nerve begins to falter, when he realises he is becoming scared.'[33] According to neurologist and consulting physician to the RFC J. L. Birley, flying over enemy territory in WWI with an unreliable aircraft was a rapid route to the acquisition of a clinical anxiety state.

It was against this background that Sholto found himself confronting just such feelings in late December 1915 when he faced what he said was 'just about the most hair-raising experience that came my way in the First World War'. On that fateful day, Sholto and his observer James Child were ordered to make an extensive reconnaissance in their BE2c, with a fellow Scot named David Glen acting as his escort. Sholto wrote in his logbook:

December 29th. BE2c 4057. Observer Lieut. Child. 2 hours 45 minutes. Height 6500 feet. Reconnaissance to Cambrai and St

Quentin. 'Archie' [anti-aircraft fire] very good nearly to Cambrai. Then met six Huns: Glen, my escort, was brought down, followed by two Huns. Child, my observer, downed one Hun. We fought three for half-an-hour. Petrol began to get low, and sump was hit. So, relying on stability of BE2c as against Fokker, came down in steep spiral to 10 feet. Came back Cambrai to Arras just over the trees. Huns shot like mad – Child turned Lewis gun onto one lot by a Farm House. Saw several small convoys, and a staff officer on horseback. Fokkers left us a mile from the lines; climbed to 800 feet and dived over the trenches. Landed among French heavy batteries just S. of Arras. About 100 holes in machine, engine sump pierced 1½ inches from bottom. Recommended for Military Cross.[34]

With characteristic understatement, Sholto wrote that he found the whole experience 'very unpleasant', admitting later that there were indeed adrenaline-soaked moments and that the bare details entered in his logbook by no means told the whole story. Sholto's close friend Glen, who was one of No. 8 Squadron's most able pilots and who had been awarded the Croix de Guerre just two months earlier, had been shot down before his eyes. He watched horrified as Glen's plane tumbled earthwards in a flaming spiral, leaving behind a thick trail of black smoke. Thereafter Sholto's lone aircraft had been pursued determinedly by those three enemy planes. All of this had occurred in the space of a little over half an hour, and at any instant during that thirty minutes he and Child could have been killed. By all accounts, including the one in the official history, they were lucky to have made it back alive. A long and detailed account of the adventure appeared in *The Times* on 6 January 1916, under the heading 'A Risky Air Dive. British Pilot's Fine Exploit. Six Machines to Two'.

Some time after this escapade, Sholto learned that the two Fokker pilots who had attacked him first, and who had chased him to within a mile of the lines, were none other than the two famous WWI fighter aces Oswald Boelcke and Max Immelmann. To have one of them after him would have been more than enough, but to have both of them on his tail was terrifying. Unlike other Fokker pilots, Boelcke sought out his prey by roaming beyond his own lines, reasoning that 'one must not wait until they come but search them out and hunt them'.[35] This he did very successfully until his death in October 1916.

All through the fight, Sholto said that Child had behaved with immense bravery, and had managed to fire some good bursts at their pursuers as they came diving down on their tail. He was not mortally wounded, as Boelcke surmised. Rather, standing in the open cockpit facing backwards and firing his gun over Sholto's head, Child became so physically sick due to the violence with which Sholto was flinging their aircraft around that he fell over finally and threw up all over Sholto's helmet and goggles, temporarily blinding him. Sholto ripped them off and flew back without them, eyes streaming in the bitterly cold air and barely able to see, at one point dodging around a wood in a 'hairpin' left-hand turn below the level of the trees. Paradoxically, he wrote that he had no particular sensation of fear in the heat of combat, although he admitted that he was undoubtedly frightened, and this was an experience that he came to know more frequently as fighting in the air intensified.

The psychiatrist William Rivers, so famous for treating Siegfried Sassoon at Craiglockhart War Hospital, depicted Sholto's experience exactly when he wrote these words: 'Those who escape from danger by the performance of some complex activity bear almost unanimous witness that, while so engaged, they were wholly free from the fear which the danger might have been expected to arouse.'[36] Sholto and his fellow pilots and observers felt the greatest apprehension when they set off and climbed on their way to their offensive patrols, but when an enemy fighter attacked Sholto and tried to get on his tail, he was mostly annoyed, particularly when he knew that his opponent had actually opened fire at him. However, in his case this anger was not translated into a desire to amass a large number of 'kills'. Hannah Arendt in her seminal work *On Violence* observed: 'Soldiers ... are not killers, and killers – those with "personal aggressiveness" – are probably not even good soldiers.'[37] Sholto definitely fell into the former category, and his 'seeing red' seems to have been his defence mechanism for dealing with the challenge to his instinct for self-preservation. On 1 January 1916, his name was mentioned in Dispatches, and from the

Gazette for 14 January he learned that both he and James Child had been awarded the Military Cross (MC).

Boelcke wrote an account in his diary of his duel with Sholto, which was found and later published in his biography:

That was a fine fight. I had to deal with a tough fellow, who defended himself stoutly. But I forced him on to the defensive at once. Then he tried to escape me by turns, etc., and made an effort to get at me on my weak side. He did not succeed, but the only success I scored was forcing his machine even further down – we began at 2,000 metres, and in a short time I forced him down to less than one thousand. Finally he could defend himself no longer, because I had mortally wounded his observer. It was now a comparatively easy job to shoot the fellow down, but when we got to 800 metres I ran out of ammunition because I had previously used some of it on two others. That was his salvation. We now circled round each other, but neither could do the other any harm. Finally Immelmann came to my aid, and the fight began all over again. I kept on attacking merrily, so as to confuse the Englishman. We managed to force him down to one hundred metres and waited for him to land, but he went on flying like a madman all over the place, with the pair of us behind him. I tried to cut off his further progress by flying at him, etc.; then my engine gave out, and I had to land. I could just see my opponent disappearing behind the next row of trees and thought he would land there; I was delighted and, arming myself with a Very pistol – I had no other weapon at hand – I rode across on horseback to take the fellow prisoner. But he had flown on. I made enquiries everywhere and rang up – no definite news obtainable. Then in the evening there came a report that the Englishman actually flew over the trenches at a height of one hundred metres and got home. Smart of the fellow; he won't have many imitators! Immelmann could not go on shooting at him because his gun jammed. That was no victory, but a joyous scrap![38]

That was not how Sholto saw it.

CHAPTER FOUR

FIRST TASTE OF COMMAND

Very soon after his encounter with Boelcke and Immelmann, Sholto was sent back to the UK to become a flight commander with promotion to the rank of captain. Following a week's leave, he was posted as an instructor to No. 18 Reserve Training Squadron at Montrose in Scotland, where pilots were given their final training before they went overseas. He flew a great deal in the process of giving them dual instruction, but in common with many other operational flyers who returned home as instructors, he found he lacked enthusiasm for the work. The only exciting but somewhat careless experience he had was when one of his trainees had to make a forced landing near the Glasgow–Aberdeen railway line, and in flying down in another aircraft to see what had happened to his pupil, Sholto failed to notice twenty or thirty telegraph wires and flew straight into them. Fortunately, he came out unscathed, which he attributed to the slower speed and lightness of those early aircraft. A crash in a later machine may well have been fatal.

While at Montrose he also tried his hand at night flying, which would become a preoccupation of his throughout his military career. All of this helped to round out his experience, and by March he was making up to seven flights a day as an instructor.

Early in April, Sholto's brother Archie went to stay with him for a few days at Montrose during leave from his battery in France. Sholto took him for his first flight in an aeroplane, a BE2c, lasting thirty-five minutes, and marked it in his logbook as 'Joy-ride to Archie'. Archie decided there and then that flying was the life for him and followed his older brother into the RFC in June 1916, initially as an observer.

By the middle of April, Sholto had been a flight commander in a reserve squadron for four months but had not experienced the role on operations. The expansion of the British Expeditionary Force early in 1916 with the addition of a Fourth Army necessitated a corresponding enlargement of the RFC, so Sholto was selected to take two steps forward and was sent as a squadron commander to Stirling to form an entirely new squadron, the now famous No. 43, the 'Fighting Cocks'. He was only twenty-two, and this was his first taste of a command that was entirely his own. His brief was to get the squadron up to operational standard to be sent to France towards the end of the year.

The aerodrome at Stirling was a grass field on Raploch, an open space under the Castle Hill that was once an ancient tilting ground used for jousting. Sholto would have been fully aware of the historical significance of the castle for the Douglas clan. The Battle of Bannockburn, at which his ancestor the Good Sir James commanded the left flank of Robert the Bruce's army, was fought a few miles away in 1314. In 1452, William, Eighth Earl of Douglas, was stabbed in the throat by James II of Scotland in Stirling Castle for failing to give his full allegiance to the King, and his body thrown out of the window by the Captain of the King's Guard.

Sholto wrote of his time in Stirling: 'There were no proper buildings on our new airfield, except for a farmhouse which had been commandeered and in which I lived with my senior officers. The rest of those who joined us there lived in tents ... and we enjoyed a fine open-air and carefree life.'[1] The pilots went bathing in the Teith, or Allan Water, on most afternoons, and in the evenings frequented the respectable hydros at Dunblane or Crieff, their riotous behaviour raising a few eyebrows, but nevertheless they were treated with 'unfailing kindness and hospitality', as one of the trainee pilots attached to the squadron, Robert Money, recorded later.[2]

Following his pilot's exam down south, Money was distracted by a tremendous party and got so drunk that he was absent without leave for forty-eight hours, having been expected back at Stirling two days earlier. Sholto sent for him immediately on his arrival, and it was not until Sholto questioned him that Money realised that two days had elapsed without his being conscious of their passing. Sholto could have reported him as going absent without leave, which would have meant a court martial, but decided not to. Instead, Money was sent at his own request back to France.

Before he went overseas, Money was witness to some high jinks involving his squadron commander. He recalled an incident at a charity bazaar in Stirling, to which the Duchess of Atholl, at that time the Marchioness of Tullibardine but later known as the 'Red Duchess' for her support of and communication with the Republican government of Spain during the civil war, invited Sholto to give a flying exhibition on 22 July 1916. He and two of his pilots flew over the fair in three machines, 'looped in formation, and eventually dived in succession at the party in front of the stand. One of them dived so low that a dear old gentleman, seated on a chair, was frightened and fell over backwards, breaking an ankle. This caused a slight chill in their welcome.'[3] Sholto's low-flying stunts had started in a desperate dogfight as the means of escape, but perhaps he had discovered a feeling of spine-tingling excitement in that incident that he wanted to revisit. Such antics were to become something of a habit, much to the disapproval of his superiors.

Unsurprisingly, the presence of these lively young men attracted the attention of the population of Stirling, particularly its female members, especially when one of Sholto's first acts after arriving was to borrow an aircraft from one of his comrades and fly stunts around the castle. When No. 43 Squadron was given the Freedom of the City in 2005, a current resident, Campbell Chesterman, wrote a charming letter to the then Provost of Stirling, Colin O'Brien:

On Wednesday afternoons, half-day shop closing, my mother, along with many other shop girls, made their way to the cliffs at the top of King's Park, directly overlooking 43 Squadron's flying field. In their long white dresses, they used to wear scarves to attract the attention of the young training pilots. This they did because it became a sport for the pilots to buzz the top of the cliff and thrill the girls … The Commanding Officer of this new squadron was a very dashing 23-year-old army officer who always wore and flew in the kilt. There was much speculation among the shop girls as to what happened to the kilt when he looped the loop in his aircraft.[4]

Sholto was promoted to temporary major in July 1916, and in October, having been on an aerial gunnery course at the Machine Gun School at Hythe, he was sent out to France on a short attachment to No. 70 Squadron. It was the first to be equipped with Sopwith 1½ Strutters, with which aircraft No. 43 Squadron was to be supplied.

No. 70 Squadron suffered unprecedented casualties from August to October 1916. After nine weeks, only nine of the original thirty-six pilots and observers remained. The rest, plus twenty of their replacements, were dead, missing, captured or disabled. They had ranged in age from seventeen to twenty-two.

Tragically, loss was to take on a much more personal aspect for Sholto. His memory of his time at the Front with No. 70 Squadron was rather vague, which he said was due to his distress at learning, just before he left for France in October, that his beloved brother Archie was missing. Their mother was distraught, and Sholto went to see her before he left England. She begged him to do all he could on the spot to see what had happened to her youngest and favourite son. After transferring to the RFC in June 1916, Archie had served as an observer with No. 42 Squadron, arriving in France in August. The squadron was engaged in artillery observation and in bombing of targets well behind enemy lines. As soon as he could, Sholto visited the CO of No. 42, and was given the very sad news that Archie and his pilot, a young man called Valentine Hugill who had been at Tonbridge School with him and Sholto, had almost certainly been killed as their aircraft was seen to disintegrate in the air over the German lines. Archie was barely twenty years old, and Hugill twenty-two.

Sholto was not even granted a funeral for his brother. It was not until decades later that he learned the actual details of the way in which Archie had been killed. They were contained in a letter written to Hugill's father by another pilot who was out on reconnaissance that day and witnessed the tragedy. He confirmed that Hugill and Archie's aircraft had almost certainly been hit by German anti-aircraft fire. Archie was lost on the day that his transfer to the RFC was made official. One of his fellow officers said of him: 'Archie was one of the bravest and best, taking absolutely no notice of anti-aircraft gunfire to make a success of any job he had to carry out – brave even to the point of being reckless.'[5] Was this recklessness a way of overcoming fear as some WWI psychiatrists believed? We shall never know, but another officer said of him: 'He was always so cheery and happy that it did one good to be with him, and we all feel his loss very much.'[6]

In what must have been a cruel twist for Sholto, his parents and his brother Bobby, on 6 March 1917, Archie was erroneously gazetted in the proceedings of the medical board as having been placed on the retired list on account of ill-health contracted on active service. It was a case of mistaken identity, the person to whom that classification actually applied being a Lieut. A. D. Douglas of the RFA. This entry was not corrected until 11 April, when Archie's death was finally confirmed. A letter issued from the War Office on 19 May stated that further official confirmation of his and Hugill's deaths had been received from the *Inspektion der Fliegertruppen*, Berlin, via *Le Comité International* (of the Red Cross) *Genève*. The German report stated that they had been buried together in one of their cemeteries at Capinghem, a small village just to the west of Lille.

Archie's few effects that he was carrying with him when he died were returned to his father by the German government through a neutral embassy and then the War Office on 20 August 1917. They consisted of one gold ring, one pencil case, one receipt, a poem, one cheque for forty-six francs, and German notes and coins to the value of 16.20 Deutsche Marks. These were all that remained of Archie's all too brief incandescent life. In time, he came to be buried in Ration Farm Military Cemetery near La Chapelle d'Armentières in northern France, close to where Sholto had first seen action as a gunner. He visited Archie's grave in 1959, on a tour of WWI aerodromes and battlefields with his former staff officer in WWII, Robert Wright, and noted that Archie was in good company with comrades from the Commonwealth who had fallen. It was a sort of closure, but Sholto always carried the memory of his brother with him, Archie's picture being on his desk until the end of his life.

The close relationship with Archie had been forged in their penu-
rious childhood, when Sholto largely assumed responsibility for his
two younger brothers, and even his mother, after their father's desertion. Many years later he wrote:

> All my life I have been conscious of the way in which I have missed
> the warmth of the relationship that Archie and I had enjoyed. For
> brothers we were unusually close to each other: I was very fond of
> him, and I think that he was equally fond of me. Archie was a very
> nice boy, very clever ... indeed you might say that he was a brilliant
> boy.[7]

Most searingly, he wrote:

> Archie was also the apple of our mother's eye, and his death was
> made all the more unhappy for me through her grief. When I
> got back to England and I told her about what had happened she
> blamed me for it; and with the understandable illogicality of a dis-
> tressed mother, she said: 'It is all your fault. If you had not joined
> the RFC, Archie would be alive today.'[8]

Archie's death was the latest and most severe of many tragedies that
Maggie had suffered in her life, and she poured all her sorrows into
her grief for him, the third of her lost children. Sholto was to carry
that burden with him for the rest of his life and it was there every
time he sent young men out on patrol.

One of the worst aspects of Archie's death with which Sholto had
to deal was that it was precisely the way of dying that quite naturally
he himself feared the most, and that he hated observing regardless
of whether the fatality was on the enemy side or not. Even though
he did his best to hide and suppress it, this was bound to prolong
and complicate his grief, probably contributing to some of the medical disorders from which he suffered in later life, and termed by the
psychiatrist Mardi Horowitz 'Complicated Grief Disorder'. The tor-
turous nature of Archie's demise and Sholto's feeling of responsibility
for it made development of this condition in him almost a certainty,

heightened by the blame that their mother fastened firmly upon him. The powerlessness and shame that Sholto felt epitomise what is termed 'survivor guilt', which is intensified in the combat situation when 'the passion of care' among men who fight alongside each other is comparable to the earliest and most profoundly felt family relationships, and Sholto's deep bonds with Archie embodied both fraternal and comradely love.

Sholto's nemesis, Oswald Boelcke, died shortly after Archie, when his aircraft broke up in clouds and crashed following a collision with another German machine during combat. The RFC dropped a laurel wreath by parachute over the German lines, which bore the inscription: 'To the memory of Captain Boelcke, our brave and chivalrous foe. From the British Royal Flying Corps.'

Although Sholto was in France for only a very brief period at the end of the Somme battles, all of those terrible events, Archie's death and what he witnessed during that fortnight with No. 70 Squadron ensured that the memory of the Somme was for ever engraved in his psyche. During the period between 1 July and 18 November 1916, when the offensive ended in a snowstorm, the RFC suffered heavy casualties: a total of 576 pilots, of which 308 were listed as killed, wounded or missing and 268 struck off the lists from sickness or exhaustion; 592 of 792 aircraft were wrecked, shot to pieces or worn out, and a further 190 were missing. The RFC had lost more planes and pilots than its initial complement of 410 planes and 426 pilots at the start of the battle.[9] Sholto wrote: 'One of the harshest lessons that we all had to learn was to push personal feelings and emotions caused by casualties into the back of our minds, and even, if possible, to forget them.'[10]

He was all too aware that aerial warfare had taken on a much grimmer and more pressing aspect, forcing a change in his attitudes and those of his comrades to the waging of war. That change was exemplified for him in Siegfried Sassoon's poem 'Base Details', written in 1917. Lines in that poem etched themselves into Sholto's mind, and he recalled them when in WWII he became a staff officer with many under his command. Years later, in 1963 Sholto exchanged letters with Siegfried Sassoon, who told him:

I still feel as strongly as ever about what we of the Front Line endured, though life has taught the philosophic mind! And I can claim that all my war poems stemmed from some personal experience. For instance, I wrote 'Base Details' in the Hotel de la Poste at Rouen after hearing that the brass hats were trying to get it put out of bounds for those on their way to the Line ... But in such things one is bound to be unfair to someone; and I was an impetuous and intolerant young man! Time seems to have justified my outbursts, however.[11]

Despite Archie's death and all that Sholto had witnessed in France, he returned to his command of No. 43 Squadron in October 1916 apparently full of optimism. That was to be short-lived. On his arrival at Netheravon where the squadron was now based, he learned that due to heavy losses of pilots and observers during the Somme battles, reinforcements were having to be sent to France as well as to newly formed squadrons about to go to the Front. At a single stroke he lost all the pilots and observers that he had taken such pains to train, including his three flight commanders. Replacements arrived, but most of these were raw from flying school, meaning that he had to start training his aircrews all over again.

In early December, the squadron moved to Northolt, and shortly afterwards its new Sopwith 1½ Strutters began to be delivered. One of the men sent to join Sholto as a flight commander was Captain Harold Balfour, who was to become one of Sholto's closest friends, and who gave the eulogy at his memorial service in Westminster Abbey. In WWII, Balfour was Under-Secretary of State for Air and afterwards served on the board of BEA when Sholto was chairman. In his memoir, he wrote of Sholto:

Leadership is an indefinable quality. As Army Commanders in the last war, Montgomery and Alexander had it in full measure. Likewise Sholto. His seniors could find him difficult; his friends at times might think his conduct bordered on the outrageous, but within the RFC, the RAF, and afterwards as Chairman of BEA those below him admired and respected his moral integrity. Those above might carp and criticise but the men who worked for him knew that he would never fail them and was ever willing to carry their mistakes on his own shoulders.[12]

By the same token, Sholto described the way in which Balfour applied himself to his role in No. 43 Squadron as heroic. He was very young, intelligent and, according to Sholto, 'highly strung',[13] feeling the strain of the large amount of operational flying that he had done already, but he was courageous and strong of purpose, two qualities that were to define his service in both world wars. Like Sholto, he had a rebellious attitude to authority, but this did not mean that the two of them came into conflict, and the friendship between them that began in those early days of 1917 was to stand them in good stead when the squadron went to France soon afterwards.

CHAPTER FIVE

THE FIGHTING COCKS AND
THE WHITE HORSE

At last, in the middle of January 1917, No. 43 Squadron was ready to go to France. Immediately, there was tragedy: Balfour's deputy flight commander, who was leading the first of the flights to take off, stalled and crashed in full view of the rest of the pilots and observers. He and his mechanic were both killed, together with Balfour's small dog, which was being carried in a bag in the rear cockpit of the aircraft. Sholto did his best to keep the rest of the squadron from what must have been deep distress, and he saw them all away before taking off himself.

The aircrew reached their new base, the airfield at Trezennes, two days ahead of the ground party in the freezing cold winter with snow on the fields all around them. Sholto and his fellow aviators had to camp out in empty huts with only their flying kit to keep them warm. He wrote: 'Never in my life have I been so cold as I was during the first forty-eight hours of my longed for return to France.'[1]

However, help was at hand in the form of acts of kindness from the other squadron based at Trezennes, No. 40, whose CO was Robert Loraine, a well-known actor as well as a pioneering aviator. Balfour wrote that Loraine stage-managed the organisation of his squadron with 'a masterly touch', and when he arrived at Trezennes in the freezing cold, wondering where he might get some food, an orderly appeared, saluted and said, 'Major Loraine's compliments. Hot lunch is ready in the mess.'[2]

When No. 43 Squadron had been formed in April 1916, the

Sopwith 1½ Strutter seemed to be a good answer to the threat posed by existing German fighters, but developments in the intervening eight months had rendered it out of date. No. 43's casualty rates were heavy, causing Balfour to observe: 'The use of these obsolete aircraft on the Western Front against new Albatros scouts used by the German flyers in the first quarter of 1917 was a reckless waste of human life, and which, had it not been for red tape and petty jealousies at home, could have been avoided.'[3]

The Strutters were also rather fragile, and when roughly or clumsily handled in the helter-skelter skies above the Western Front, they had been known to break up in the air. However, Sholto, whom Balfour deemed 'a wonderful pilot',[4] knew that if delicately and lightly handled, the Sopwiths were strong enough to perform almost any manoeuvre. To demonstrate this, shortly after the squadron's arrival at Trezennes, he took up an aircraft with the squadron's Recording Officer Tom Purdey as his passenger on Purdey's birthday and performed thirteen consecutive loops. Everything went very well until he landed, when he discovered that he had not warned his passenger about what he was going to do, and Purdey had not been strapped in. Throughout the flight, the poor man had been clinging on to the fixtures in the cockpit and 'grim death had been staring him in the face'.[5] It was not the most welcome birthday gift, and Sholto was annoyed with himself for this omission. Amazingly, Purdey, a cheerful and outgoing character, took it all in good humour.

In the bitterly cold winter, officers, airmen and the engines of their aircraft were all frozen solid, so to thaw out the engines and make everyone more comfortable, Sholto embarked on a programme of getting additional supplies out of the Royal Army Service Corps and Royal Engineers. When this proved insufficient, he decided to take matters into his own hands, and under the cover of darkness squadron personnel raided the nearest dump of the Royal Engineers. Even more serious than the paucity of aircraft and equipment was 'the insufficient training of pilots and the almost complete lack of any training for the observers'.[6] Sholto found himself organising the squadron into a training school in order to bring aircrews up to any sort of operational standard. To lighten the burden for his operational pilots, he did some of the flying instruction himself.

Once again, this state of affairs was largely due to official policy. While Trenchard 'complained vociferously and constantly about inadequate aircraft and poorly trained crews, he persisted in an offensive policy that severely strained those meagre resources, ultimately at his aircrews' expense'.[7] Those same crews of No. 43 Squadron dreaded the sealed envelope that would be brought to Sholto every night from Wing HQ with the orders for squadron operations for the following day. Balfour commented that 'somehow food lost its attraction and spirits sank for an appreciable time after we knew the contents of that envelope'.[8]

To make matters worse, British aircraft had no armoured defence, which was not introduced until 1918 and then only on a particular aircraft designed for low flying. They also had no self-sealing petrol tanks and no parachutes. This left pilots with a constant feeling of fear, especially of fire in the air. Aircrew knew that they could be set alight at any moment, and one of the most harrowing of all experiences for them in WWI was to watch, as Sholto wrote, 'the helplessness of a friend going down in flames'. He had witnessed this himself during his aerial duel in 1915 when his friend David Glen was killed, and also one day in early 1917 as he was leading his squadron in formation and they were attacked by German aircraft. After the initial engagement, he looked across at the aircraft next to him and saw the observer standing up in the back seat, trying desperately to call to the attention of his pilot a glimmer of flame that was starting to appear along the side of their aircraft. 'A moment later there was a violent explosion and the whole aircraft disintegrated.'[9] This was a relatively common sight, and a cause of deep distress to Sholto and his fellow aviators. Conversely, the Germans learned from their Somme experiences 'to develop specialised armour-plated ground attack planes and highly manoeuvrable light two-seaters for trench-strafing'.[10]

At this time, No. 43 Squadron was supporting the First Army along the active front between Armentières and Arras. It was involved in reconnaissance, photography and offensive patrols, the object of the latter being to protect the aircraft of other squadrons engaged upon artillery observation. For this, Sholto and his pilots flew in close formation, but they found that the poor functioning of the Sopwith 1½ Strutter at altitudes above 10,000 feet meant that in order to engage enemy aircraft, they had to fly underneath them and lure them into the attack from below. Sholto felt that this was a miserable way to go on the offensive, and from this point on he was convinced that aircraft performance was of supreme importance. He reflected on this later in a paper that he wrote while on the first course at the RAF Staff College in Andover in 1922. It was no good having the latest armaments if the power of attack, the initiative, was lost through poor performance. It was also bad for morale. This sentiment has been relevant in every aerial battle that has taken place since then.

Despite these problems, Sholto and his fellow fighter squadron commanders in the RFC experimented with formations of ever-increasing size, starting with a flight of five or six aircraft in a wedge pattern. It was clear to Sholto from the beginning that the tighter the aircraft flew in formation, the fewer the casualties, and unsurprisingly, after Archie's death, this seems to have been his abiding concern.

No. 43 Squadron's casualties became even heavier once the Battle of Arras began on 9 April, Easter Monday. No. 43 Squadron adopted its usual role, but weather conditions on the first day were atrocious, with snow showers impeding its operation. Sholto himself went out on a line patrol that day and had to make a forced landing after his engine had been hit by 'archie' well behind enemy lines, where he had been chasing a German aircraft. He managed to struggle back over Allied lines just in time to make a 'pancake' landing on an old trench system, luckily without injury.

Arras lasted for most of what became known as 'Bloody April', and the official air historian wrote: 'In no other month throughout the war was the Royal Flying Corps so hard pressed, nor were the casualties suffered so heavy.'[11] The average life of a scout pilot at Arras was just two weeks. No. 43 Squadron had over 100 per cent casualties. Sholto still had six or seven of his original crews, but the reinforcements sent out to replace them were often shot down only a few days after their arrival. The official strength of the squadron was thirty-two pilots and observers, and during April there were thirty-five casualties. When their losses were at their heaviest, General Trenchard paid them a visit. Balfour wrote:

> We were told to stick it out and that we would continue to suffer casualties, but at all costs the British had to maintain moral, if not actual, ascendancy over the enemy: how our daily task of offensive patrols in obsolete aircraft with heavy losses did this I shall never know.[12]

Balfour, whom Sholto had just recommended for the MC for his gallantry both in aerial fighting and in reconnaissance, was injured badly in this battle when he drifted over the German lines due to stronger than expected westerly winds. Heavy fire from the ground hit his engine, putting it out of commission. He tried to glide back over the lines against the wind, all the time being shot at, and only just managed to limp over the Allied side of the ridge, finally crashing in a mine crater. He was not strapped in, which certainly saved his life, as the impact pushed the engine back to where his legs would have been and would have crushed him 'to a pulp', as he put it, had he still been in the cockpit. However, both he and his observer were thrown out, Balfour landing on his head in the mud and his observer taking a longer dive out of the rear cockpit. They were rescued by Canadians from a neighbouring dug-out and dragged to a first-aid shelter. The Canadians tried to salvage the aircraft, but almost immediately the Germans started shelling the spot and soon nothing was left of it. Simultaneously, Allied howitzers were firing from one of the battery positions nearby, and this was the last straw. By this time, Balfour was in a field ambulance, badly concussed, and had started vomiting. His nerves 'had for the moment gone'. He remembered crying to himself 'with fright and self-pity as these appalling crashes and discharges continued'.[13] Looking back at the end of his career, Sholto wrote of his friend's distress: 'It was a state that any man who makes a claim to honesty would be only too ready to acknowledge.'[14]

For Sholto, the weeks following the Battle of Arras constituted one of the darkest periods of the war. Although advances had been made, the German lines remained firm, and an all-too-familiar stalemate was beginning to supervene. Nevertheless, during the Third Battle of the Scarpe it is recorded that No. 43 Squadron made history when they spent three days shooting up and bombing scattered parties of enemy troops, trench positions and transport. They had tried these tactics the month before at Vimy Ridge, but their success during this Third Battle of the Scarpe 'can be said to have definitely established this novel development in the employment of aeroplanes directly to assist the troops on the ground, operating in fact as "tanks of the air"'.[15] On one occasion, flying very close to the ground, Sholto started shooting at a row of German heads that appeared along the top of a parapet and was a bit shaken when they answered back. He could hear the popping of small arms fire flashing past his ears.

For all its shortcomings, the Sopwith 1½ Strutter was ideally suited to this kind of operation, its performance and manoeuvrability being good near the ground, but the main danger faced by the members of the squadron flying at this height was from friendly artillery fire. When they throttled back their engines for a moment, they could hear their own shells rumbling past them, sounding 'like a succession of trains passing through a tunnel'.[16] Amazingly, the squadron suffered no casualties during the Scarpe battle, which boosted the morale of both pilots and observers, and the results achieved brought congratulations from wing and brigade commanders. From this point on, trench strafing became a more highly organised activity in the RFC, but it was disliked intensely by those who had to do it. There was a distinction between trench strafing and ground strafing, the latter meaning attacking troops behind the lines. In trench attacks the odds were stacked against the aircraft and the possible gains were slight. In these circumstances, as Arthur Lee observed, aviators felt that they were in 'a similar condition of indiscriminate carnage as the infantry',[17] but attacking targets behind the trenches such as marching infantry, transport, airfield hangars or aircraft on the ground was productive, and, dare it be said, even exhilarating.

On 7 May, a few days after the Scarpe battle, Sholto suffered one of the worst aircraft crashes he ever experienced. His squadron was ordered to carry out an offensive patrol, and Sholto detailed one of his flight commanders to lead it. He watched the squadron as they took off by flights to get into formation. However, as they were disappearing into the distance, he noticed that the leader's engine seemed to have failed and that he was making a forced landing in a ploughed field. 'This left the others without a competent leader because the deputy leader was a comparatively inexperienced pilot. Without somebody knowledgeable in charge they could easily have got into trouble, so I decided to get off in a hurry and take command.'[18] Sholto rushed to his aircraft parked in front of the hangars, on the way shouting to a young Canadian observer, who had only joined the squadron the day before, to fly with him. The young man grabbed a Lewis gun and climbed into the rear seat of the aircraft while Sholto started up the engine and took off. Neither of them took time to fasten his safety belt.

As he dashed off across the field, he did not notice what he was told later was a large white horse at work with a plough at the far end of the aerodrome. In order to maintain maximum speed at take-off and to catch up with the rest of the flight as they climbed ahead of him, he kept the nose of the aircraft down to adopt a shallower rate of climb. In so doing, his undercarriage struck the unfortunate animal on its hindquarters. The aircraft crashed beyond it, upside down. Balfour, who must have heard the news later from another squadron member, wrote that the horse was killed and Sholto nearly so. As had happened with Balfour himself barely a week earlier, Sholto was thrown clear through not having fastened his harness, and this is what saved his life since, once again, the engine was slammed back into the pilot's seat. His observer was also thrown clear, landing head first in the plough, and was immediately taken to hospital.

When Sholto was collected from the field, he was found to be concussed, with his nose bent across his severely bruised face, and he had sustained a hard blow to one eye, which was already swelling. When I was a child, he told me that some of his front teeth had been knocked down his throat. Despite all of this, he refused to go to hospital and spent over twenty-four hours in his hut in semi-conscious agony. When his wing commander, Wilfrid Freeman, came to see him, he babbled so incoherently that Freeman decided there and then that he should be whisked off to hospital without delay. The effects of concussion, and what Sholto termed 'the vanity of youth', had made him obsessed with the fear that his face would be disfigured permanently (a not unreasonable anxiety) and that his girlfriends would desert him. He was sent by hospital train to Boulogne, and from there by boat to England. So ended, somewhat ingloriously, his service with No. 43 Squadron. In a kind gesture, Tom Purdey had him credited officially with a wound 'stripe'.

Within about a month, Sholto deemed that his face was back to normal, and fortunately he noticed no falling off in the ardour of his girlfriends. However, from what medical science has revealed to us in the century since then, and from what was manifested in Sholto's later life, the external situation belied the damage that almost certainly had been done inside his head. Recent research has shown that mild traumatic brain injury such as concussion that involves altered mental status, especially loss of consciousness, is strongly associated with the development of PTSD. With repeated concussive episodes, there is an increased risk of neurodegenerative disease, one of the more severe manifestations of which is dementia in later life.

Following Sholto's transport back to the UK, he spent a month in a hospital in London, after which he was given some leave. He received a letter from Wilfrid Freeman with news of No. 43 Squadron, sadly saying: 'There are not many of the old originals left. I only wish there were – they were a good crowd you collected.' The squadron had just moved airfields from Trezennes to Lozinghem, and Freeman wrote that he 'felt somewhat cross at tearing them away from their garden which was just growing to years of discretion and use'.[19] It seems extraordinary that there was time and enthusiasm for gardening amid the intensity of aerial combat at the Front, but No. 43 was by no means the only squadron to go in for plant and even animal husbandry behind the lines. No. 60 Squadron kept a pig while it was stationed at Izel-lès-Hameau next to Filescamp Farm. This large sow had a black cross painted on her nose, a little one on each ear and a large one on each side. Ignoring her gender, the words 'Baron von Richthofen' were painted on her back. An Australian squadron went even further, having obtained two cows more or less legally from the local inhabitants, as well as a spare lorry to transport them, so that while almost everyone else in the RFC in France was surviving on tinned milk, there was always a supply of fresh milk for the Australians.

Sholto spent the latter part of his leave with his father Langton, who by this time was director of the National Gallery of Ireland, having been given special leave from the Army to take up the post. When Langton arrived in Dublin in the summer of 1916, the political situation was tense, the Easter Rising having taken place in the same year. He was in post during the ensuing troubles and the establishment of the Irish Free State in 1921. It was fortunate that Langton was chosen to be director in these difficult years: 'He could so easily have been a hardliner, opposed to independence and hostile to the Irish, but the opposite was the case; he loved the country and its inhabitants.'[20] During his time in Dublin, Langton is said to have given shelter to a wanted man on one occasion, and on another to have hidden guns for the Republicans behind pictures on his way to the gallery in a truck or cab, with the Irish dramatist Lady Augusta Gregory as his companion, although there is no way of verifying this latter anecdote. His deputy at the gallery, James Stephens, was a poet and novelist, and an active Sinn Féiner with whom Sholto frequently passed the time over a Guinness or two and whom he liked a great deal. Although Sholto did not go as far as supporting armed rebellion, he had great sympathy with the cause, feeling that the Irish should have been given the Home Rule that they wanted so passionately much sooner than they eventually got it. He considered that the British did themselves and the Irish a great deal of harm by acting in the way they did.

Following Sholto's leave, at the end of which he felt that he had almost completely recovered from his crash in France, he was passed as fit for light duty by a medical board. He was given a task that turned out to be particularly interesting, and which led him straight back to Ireland. In 1917, it had been decided to enlarge the RFC to 200 service squadrons and ninety-seven reserve squadrons (although, as Arthur Lee commented, this was 'a futile gesture when even existing demands for aircraft and engines could not be met').[21] Nonetheless, a substantial expansion of the training programme was required, and Sholto was given the job of travelling all over Ireland in order to select eight sites for aerodromes on which the RFC could establish some of their training schools. It was a responsible task for such a young officer. There were no airfields in Ireland at all, although the Lands Officer at Irish Command had picked out some suitable locations. Despite the troubles of the previous year, Sholto found no cause for alarm in the way that he was received throughout Ireland. He would fly over the locations that had been suggested to him, and then go and inspect them by car. He found that when he travelled by road, he received scowling looks from boys on street corners and some of them threw stones, so unpopular was the uniform of the British Army. However, when he flew anywhere and landed in a field near a village, the young men would run out cheering and shouting since most of them had never before seen an aeroplane. Sholto wondered whether these were the same youths who had thrown stones at him. New training schools were established for both pilots and observers at most of the sites he had selected. More importantly, many of the principal airfields that exist today on the island of Ireland were selected by Sholto on his trip in 1917, including the main airports for Dublin (Collinstown) and Belfast (Aldergrove), as well as the foremost Irish military airfield at Baldonnel (Casement), a reminder of his fundamental role in the establishment of aviation in Ireland.

CHAPTER SIX

TACTICS AND RETREAT

On Sholto's return from choosing airfields in Ireland for the RFC, he was delighted to hear that he was to take command of a new fighter squadron that was in the process of being formed, No. 84, which was to be equipped with a new single-seater aircraft, the SE5a (Scout Experimental 5a). No. 84 was under orders to get battle-ready as soon as possible: they were needed out in France.

The expertise Sholto had gained from the protracted process of forming No. 43 Squadron greatly enhanced the task of getting No. 84 up to operational efficiency in that summer of 1917, but he had not bargained for one little piece of subterfuge in a prospective posting to the squadron. By late summer, his father Langton had got his work at the National Gallery of Ireland well under control and had returned to England and his job in the Army. He applied for a transfer to the RFC and asked to be posted to No. 84 Squadron as his son's adjutant. When Sholto found out about this, he realised that it would create an impossible situation. He was twenty-three and Langton fifty-three, which alone was enough to cause difficulties without the added complication of the father–son relationship. Furthermore, the adjutant of a squadron often bore the brunt of complaints from all quarters, particularly the CO. So Sholto telephoned the chief personnel officer at RFC HQ to make sure that the threatened posting was cancelled. As would be expected, Langton took a very poor view of his son's action, but the damage to their relationship was nothing to what it would have been had he arrived in the squadron.

No. 84 flew to France in mid-September, landing at the airfield at Estrée-Blanche, only a short distance from the Front, on a broad windswept hill with views all around of gently rolling but scarred and battered countryside. Larger than most, the airfield housed two or three other squadrons as well as No. 84, including the famous and successful No. 56, also equipped with SE5as. The strength of No. 56 had been greatly enhanced by the recent posting to it of James McCudden as a flight commander. He was the most decorated British airman in the RFC, and the squadron was delighted to have him, unlike those in another squadron later in the war who refused him as their CO because he had come from the ranks, which Sholto described as arrant snobbishness that made his blood boil. 'Jimmy', as he was known, made the greatest impression on Sholto of all those that he came to know well in WWI, and he was always proud of their friendship. They discovered that their views on formation flying were very much alike, both of them realising that conducting patrols as squadrons in three flights of five aircraft in each that stuck to each other 'like glue' would minimise losses among new pilots. Sholto and Jimmy's bond was strengthened further when the latter's young brother Anthony, then aged nineteen, joined Sholto's squadron as a pilot. Jimmy was concerned that, only too eager to follow in his illustrious older brother's footsteps, Anthony was exhibiting a dangerous over-confidence for such a young pilot. Sholto promised to keep as sharp an eye on him as he could.

No. 84 Squadron's arrival in France coincided with the Third Battle of Ypres, at the stage known as the Battle of Polygon Wood, a prelude to the assault on the ridge on which the village of Passchendaele was situated. This small Belgian village was to attain hideous notoriety due to its utter destruction. Sholto remarked: 'Well might passion be a part of its name.'[1] He felt that this was the most terrible of all the battles of WWI, worse even than the Somme. The lessons concerning the futility of mass attacks, of which the Somme battles had been a supreme example, had not been learned.

Almost immediately, No. 84 Squadron found themselves confronting that 'most worthy enemy', Manfred von Richthofen and his famous 'circus'. They were to encounter him many times because, having arguably the best aircraft in service, the SE5a, they were sent quickly from one battle to another, as were Richthofen and his gang.

Whenever Sholto and his pilots saw the circus approaching, they would climb as rapidly as they could and then try to take them from above and behind, coming out of the sun if possible. This was facilitated by the superior climbing performance of their new aircraft, but even the SE5a became sluggish and difficult to control at high altitude, so manoeuvres were considerably slower and pilots were hindered by cold and lack of oxygen in their open cockpits. Sholto wore a thick leather flying coat over many layers of clothing, and a muffler round his neck to protect him against the cold, while his comrades used their girlfriends' silk stockings to protect their mouths and faces and smeared anti-frostbite ointment over their cheeks. Without oxygen, any exertion at high altitude left the pilots gasping for breath, and they were often unaware of the extent to which their judgement and mental agility were affected, sometimes making errors in combat that probably they would not have made at lower altitudes, although the more seasoned officers were well aware of these problems.

Due to the inexperience of its pilots, Sholto and his three flight commanders being the only members of the squadron who had served previously in France, No. 84 suffered heavy casualties at first. Later, Sholto expounded his view forcefully to a staff officer at RAF HQ that pilots were not given sufficient training either in air gunnery or in formation flying on the types of aircraft that they were going to fly at the Front.[2] To try to stem the tide of these losses, Sholto insisted on putting into practice the ideas that he and Jimmy McCudden had discussed concerning formation flying. In this he received full support from his young pilots, the most outstanding of whom was A. F. W. Beauchamp-Proctor, a wiry young South African who later was awarded the Victoria Cross (VC). 'Proccy', as he was known, became a very skilled formation leader, and Sholto was content to let him lead the operations and to fly alongside him as his deputy.

On 9 October, when the attack on Poelcapelle was launched by the British, the squadron carried out low-flying attacks against enemy concentrations on the ground. Sholto and his pilots flew at heights of 200–300 feet, and he was horrified at what he saw – a vast sea of mud and destruction, with British troops stuck in an 'appalling morass'.[3] The historian Cyril Falls described the battlefield as having 'the appearance of the moon through a telescope. A number of men were drowned in the water or smothered in the mud. The moral and physical strain tried men to the uttermost and carried many beyond breaking-point.'[4]

These low-flying attacks, for which most of Sholto's young pilots were quite untrained and their SE5as quite unsuitable, were exceedingly dangerous and somewhat ineffective. They could not pick out their targets because everything on the ground, including enemy troops, was the same colour as the mud. When diving into the attack, the pilots found themselves 'unexpectedly peering slap down the muzzles of German machine guns'.[5] From their point of view it was 'grim and bloody and pointless', and Sholto could not see how any progress could be made by the men on the ground in such terrible conditions. Arthur Lee deemed these attacks to be 'a wasteful employment of highly trained pilots and expensive aeroplanes'.[6]

Even when Sholto visited the area forty-two years later, the memories of that awful encounter in 1917 surged up in his mind, and he remembered his outrage about the way in which Haig had insisted on continuing with the battle: 'I wished that Haig and his senior generals and his staff could have been flying with me so that they could have seen for themselves what it was like. That might have made a difference.'[7]

At the end of October, No. 84 Squadron was transferred to the 13th Wing, working with the Fourth Army and taking it southwards to the airfield at Izel-lès-Hameau, which was composed of two halves. No. 84 Squadron occupied one end next to the village of Le Hameau and Nos 46 and 64 Squadrons were ensconced at the other, next to Filescamp Farm. One of the Nissen huts at the farm end was known as 'the Abode of Love' because of its interior made increasingly comfortable by successive squadrons.

When, in November, No. 46 threw a big party in the Abode of Love to say farewell to their CO, who was returning home, all were invited. It was a more sober affair than usual due to the presence of three squadron commanders, but the high point came when Arthur Lee and two others leapt on one of their comrades from behind with the intention of 'debagging' him. They suddenly found themselves being flung all over the ante-room, and discovered that it wasn't their friend at all, but 'Major Douglas', whom they realised then was 'an excessively wiry type'.[8] When Sholto learned that it was all a mistake, he was very sporting about it and the party resumed, but the war had definitely set him on edge and the hypervigilance that comes with combat trauma had taken hold of him.

Perhaps mindful of Izel-lès-Hameau's reputation, he took the opportunity to write of his time there that although life in the RFC was undoubtedly more comfortable than in any other branch of the Army, they had their own traumas with which to contend. He reiterated that the most distressing of these for him was seeing anyone, of whichever side, being shot at and catching fire as they fell to earth. He wrote:

> Whenever I saw that happen I always knew for a moment a feeling of something approaching sickness. A fellow human being had died, or was dying, and it had all happened so quickly. But that reaction was only momentary, and the protective jelly around one's mind that came with experience blotted out any more thoughts about what had happened.[9]

Harold Balfour felt that perhaps it would have been better if the British had behaved more like their French counterparts when dealing with tragedy. He wrote:

> It is the British custom to laugh at French emotionalism and display of feelings, but perhaps had there been a greater outward display of sentiment in some of our British units (which I know is not in accord with our national habits and therefore not possible) there might have been less repression.[10]

He cited an example he had witnessed of a French squadron commander who wept openly when he heard that one of his aircrews had been shot down by the Germans, and as he was sending a replacement out on patrol. Balfour observed that such displays of emotion did nothing to detract from the courage of French aviators.

The airmen of the RFC had to deal with 'the challenge of balancing episodes of combat with long periods of inaction'.[11] The Canadian ace Billy Bishop wrote: 'One minute we were as far removed from the war as if we were in South America, and an hour later we would be fighting for our lives ... [It] somehow made the real fighting, when it came, seem less real and tragic.'[12] He was based for part of the war at the Abode of Love, so knew these extremes all too well. The sudden change from a quiet idyll to the heat of combat had severe effects on the nerves of some, producing stomach ulcers, insomnia and nightmares which 'made a mockery of sleep'.[13] Sholto knew young pilots who broke down in this way and had to be sent home, observing: 'They were casualties not listed as officially wounded, but they were nevertheless still casualties, and some of them were wrecked in health for the rest of their lives.'[14]

Cecil Lewis wrote that no one could stand the strain indefinitely:

Ultimately it reduced you to a dithering state, near to imbecility ... They sent you home to rest, and you put it in the background of your mind; but it was not like a bodily fatigue from which you could completely recover, it was a sort of damage to the essential tissue of your being. You might have a greater will-power, greater stamina to fight down your failing; but a thoroughbred that has been lashed will rear at the sight of the whip, and never, once you had been through it, could you be quite the same again.[15]

Two of the most humane of the physicians and psychologists who dealt with servicemen suffering from 'shell-shock' or war neurosis in WWI were Grafton Elliot Smith and T. H. (Tom) Pear, who worked at Maghull Hospital near Liverpool. Far from being the case that it was the 'weakest' who broke down, the view commonly held by those in High Command, Smith and Pear observed:

First, the most severe and distressing symptoms occur to a surprising extent in the case of those patients whose past history shows that, far from possessing even the normal quota of timidity, they had been noted for their 'dare-devilry' ... Secondly, it is not uncommon for patients to ask to be sent back to duty because they feel that they have been too long with nothing to do, while it is quite obvious to the doctor that they are as yet unfit to bear any great strain.[16]

The purpose of No. 84 Squadron's move to Le Hameau was to take part in the Battle of Cambrai, launched only a few days after the end of the campaign in the Ypres Salient. Although his armies were exhausted, Haig instigated this offensive to prevent the Germans resting their troops and to give them a sense of unease and uncertainty over the winter. He was also aware that, due to the collapse of the Russian campaign in the east, substantial forces were being transferred to strengthen the Western Front, and this flow would increase during the next few months. The squadron's role at Cambrai was to protect, by means of offensive sorties, low-flying and contact patrol aircraft working directly with the Army, but the operations were hampered by fog, mist and drizzling rain. It was not possible to work in groups larger than a flight of five aircraft. At times, Sholto even had to send his pilots off singly or in pairs, contradicting his fine new theories about fighting in larger formations. Casualties were high in the RFC, partly due to enemy action as the German Air Service had been reinforced, but also because of accidents associated with the adverse weather conditions.

As had happened so often before, at the beginning of the battle, the British made spectacular advances, using tanks in full force as a weapon for the first time. They even managed to breach the strongly fortified Hindenburg Line, but yet again, no reserves were available, partly due to a lack of foresight by those planning the operation, but largely because most of the available reserves had been used up 'to no purpose' in the fight for Passchendaele and other strategic points in the Ypres Salient.[17] As a result, before any reinforcements could be gathered, the Germans recovered and launched a counterattack. The overall losses at Cambrai were fearful. One source quotes approximately 45,000 casualties on each side in a two-week period,[18] whereas the *Statistics of the Military Effort of the British Empire during the Great War*, published in 1922, suggests a much higher figure on the

British side of 71,385. A crumb of consolation Sholto gleaned from this offensive was that, due to their experience of low flying over the Ypres Salient, No. 84 Squadron's eventual tally of enemy aircraft shot down was five or six with no loss to themselves. Lessons were being learned, and the strength the RFC had assembled for the Battle of Cambrai had been impressive, with each branch of what had become an increasingly specialised corps playing its part in the offensive.

There were no other actions on No. 84's part of the Western Front that winter of 1917/18. Sholto's command lasted until the end of WWI, and whenever his turn for leave came round, as it did in the final winter of the war, like everyone else in the RFC he was only too glad to get back to England, especially London. Earlier in the year, he had met Gertrude Lawrence, who became very well known for her acting, singing, dancing and musical comedy, and they continued to see each other occasionally over the next three and a half decades until Gertrude's death. During his leave, Sholto often stayed at the Cavendish Hotel in Jermyn Street, owned by Mrs Rosa Lewis, an extraordinary woman who had been the mistress of King Edward VII, who, it was rumoured, had set her up in the hotel. She had a special affection for the young officers of the RFC, and often refused to charge them for their stay if they were short of money, Sholto included. Only rarely did these young men have to pay for the champagne that they almost always drank there. Rosa usually told them that she had charged it to her wealthier and older customers, who she said would not mind, but Sholto always thought that she paid for it herself.

Mindful of the mauling their forces had received during the latter part of 1917, the thoughts of those in the British High Command turned to defensive measures rather than the almost continual attacking strategy that had held sway up to this time, and for which their troops had been trained almost exclusively. This change in thinking did not appeal to Trenchard, who issued a memorandum on 16 January 1918 urging the RFC to maintain its offensive in the air despite the Army's change of stance. Just over two weeks prior to this, on 29 December 1917, No. 84 Squadron had been sent further south to an airfield at Flez on the Somme to form part of the 22nd Wing.

The squadron's task as spring approached was to fly in support of the operations of the Fifth Army, then under the command of General Sir Hubert Gough.

It became clear during February 1918 that the Germans were planning a large offensive to be launched on the Fifth Army's front. Many new enemy airfields were being brought into use directly opposite this sector of the Front. Sholto's wing commander, Lieutenant-Colonel F. V. Holt, a somewhat choleric individual but nevertheless quite an effective leader, organised combined bombing raids on some of these aerodromes. Sholto's pilots were very successful, shooting down ten enemy aircraft on the second of these raids. Nevertheless, Sholto noted that the enemy 'were getting wise to the fact that we were increasing the size of our fighting patrols'.[19]

A day later, on 18 March, something Sholto had dreaded happened. Jimmy McCudden's impetuous young brother Anthony, also known as 'Jack', went missing in action. He had been shot down already on 28 February and had survived, but this time he was not to be so fortunate. Overnight, there was no news, so the following day, Sholto wrote to Anthony's mother:

No. 84 Squadron
RFC
BEF
19 March 1918

Dear Mrs McCudden,

I am sorry to say your son went missing yesterday. I am afraid I can give you no definite news or even a conjecture as to his fate. He went out yesterday with fourteen of our machines on an important patrol about twenty miles over the lines. We ran into a big formation of German scouts, and a mixed fight ensued. Everyone was so busy scrapping they cannot say what happened to your son. All we know is that he did not return. We can only hope for the best – which is quite likely – that a lucky shot hit his engine or radiator. In that case he stood no chance of getting back to our lines, and would have to land and be taken prisoner. His engine may have failed too, one cannot say. I sincerely hope you will get definite news of his safety very soon.

I was exceedingly sorry about your son, as he was quite one of my best pilots; and I am sure that given a little luck he would have emulated the success of his elder brother. He was extraordinarily brave – too brave if anything. He often took risks that ninety-nine per cent of humanity would refuse to take. I most sincerely regret the loss of an exceedingly gallant pilot, and hope he will turn up all right in due course.

Your son had shot down seven Huns since being with this Squadron.

I am yours sincerely,
    W S Douglas (Major).[20]

Shortly afterwards, his death was confirmed by the German authorities, more than one German pilot claiming that they had shot him down. Anthony was awarded the MC posthumously, the citation concluding: 'He has always displayed great courage and determination.'

On 21 March, the Germans launched a crashing, ferocious assault on No. 84's sector of the Front. So began the German offensive in Picardy, known to the British as the March Retreat. The night before, the landscape had become shrouded in thick fog after rain. The official air historian captured the atmosphere: 'With the coming of night on the 20th the mist thickened and gave the illusion that it muffled sound, for the German Artillery fire had ceased. The unusual silence was oppressive, and, with the fog, combined to produce an atmosphere of the macabre.'[21]

Sholto had gone to bed in his hut feeling rather bored, but shortly after 4.30 a.m., he was woken by 'the shattering noise of a colossal and extremely noisy bombardment, with tremendous reverberations of sound'.[22] He leapt out of bed and threw on his uniform, but as he rushed outside, he saw that the airfield was still covered in thick fog. Despite this, it was still clear that the Germans had launched the most intensive artillery bombardment so far in the war, and he and his squadron were right in the thick of it, not realising at the time that they were heavily outnumbered by the enemy. The RFC had a total of 579 serviceable aircraft, whereas the Germans had available 730. They had kept secret the full extent of the build-up of their air force, but in the prevailing foggy conditions, this did not matter much to Sholto and his pilots, who realised that their task was to work in close support of the troops on the ground wherever feasible. When the fog cleared that afternoon, the Germans had advanced so rapidly that No. 84 Squadron was given orders to 'harass the advancing hordes with low flying attacks'.[23] Cyril Falls declared that 'the RFC was displaying magnificent courage and self-sacrifice. It had been told to take "all risks," to fly "very low," and to "bomb and shoot everything they can see on the enemy's side of the line." It did all these things.'[24] This bravery notwithstanding, by the end of the first day, there was an imminent threat of disaster.

The British line on the Fifth Army's front was being held with very few men and guns, and as had so often happened before, the reserves were wholly insufficient. The Fifth Army had to cover sixty-seven kilometres of front line with twelve infantry and three cavalry divisions, against forty-three on the German side. The odds seemed impossible. As dusk was drawing in on that first day, despite all the resistance offered by the British on the ground, and in the air with low-flying machine-gun and bomb attacks to within twenty metres of the ground, orders were given to retreat. Sholto was told to move his squadron quickly from Flez back to an airfield at Champien, to the south-west, away from the rapidly advancing enemy troops.

Before that, he had sent some of his motorcyclists on forward observation duty with instructions to return every hour and report how far the enemy had advanced. Two of these, Air Mechanics Second Class Knight and Alcock, saw British guns and mounted troops being attacked by a low-flying enemy Albatros within a few yards of them. The cyclists dived into a ditch, and as the German fighter flew overhead at a height of around 200 feet, Knight fired back at it with a rifle that he had found by chance at the side of the road. He was astonished when the engine of the aircraft fell silent and the pilot made a forced landing about 640 metres away. He and his companion got back on their motorbikes and raced towards the crash site, noticing that the pilot had climbed out and was running in the direction of Beauvois, some five kilometres to the east. He was captured by British infantry. Alcock rushed back to his CO with the news that Knight, who had remained to guard the aircraft, had shot down a 'Hun' with a rifle. Highly sceptical, Sholto sent a party to investigate. They found the Albatros with a single bullet hole in the aircraft's engine. They set fire to the machine, and Knight was credited with what was believed to be the first instance of an RFC motorcyclist bringing down an enemy aircraft.

By dusk, the last of No. 84 Squadron's motor transport was leaving the aerodrome, and Sholto was just about to leap into his SE5a when the telephone rang. It was his wing commander, Tony Holt, calling from his new HQ several kilometres back from the lines to ask how the evacuation was going. Although Sholto insisted that he could see the last of his vehicles driving away, this did not satisfy Holt, who went on giving instructions that he was to stay at Flez until he was absolutely sure that everyone had left. It was getting dark, and Sholto told Holt that he was not prepared to waste any more precious minutes as the Germans were closing in rapidly. Holt continued to argue, until Sholto ran out of patience and slammed down the phone. He rushed out of the hut and into his aircraft, the only one on the airfield, and a few minutes later he landed at Champien as darkness fell. Just four hours later, Flez had been overrun, with German infantry swarming all over it. Sholto heard nothing more from Holt about the insubordination of which he had been accused over the phone.

The following afternoon, while engaged in low-flying attacks, twelve pilots of No. 84 Squadron found columns of advancing German troops just south of the airfield they had evacuated only the day before. They promptly attacked them until they had run out of ammunition, dropping forty-five 25lb bombs on troops and transport. An hour later when the squadron took off again, the same happened. The Germans were advancing in hordes, but without taking precautions against attack from the air. Too preoccupied with their advance to mount adequate anti-aircraft defences, they proved a surprisingly easy target. One of Sholto's pilots overturned an enemy general's car into a ditch. The aviators were ecstatic, feeling that they were doing something to halt the enemy advance, and Sholto always felt that the low-flying fighters of the RFC were not given sufficient credit for the successful work they did during the March Retreat.

Over the next week, Sholto had to move his squadron back twice more, first to Vert Galand and then to an aerodrome near Abbeville. The British suffered the greatest reverses on the Fifth Army's section of the Front, and along its length the whole line seemed to be crumbling. Although the RFC's losses were increasing due to fierce enemy fire from the ground, No. 84 Squadron continued its ground strafing, attacking relentlessly.

The Fifth Army, grey with fatigue, did eventually halt the German advance on 5 April 1918, but Sholto and his comrades learned to their great surprise that the Army's Commander, Sir Hubert Gough, had been relieved of his command. They felt that he was being made a scapegoat for the lack of planning by those above him in Army High Command, who failed to supply the Fifth Army with sufficient resources even though it was obvious that the Germans were planning an imminent attack.

Later it became clear how close the Allies had been to defeat in March 1918, prevented primarily by the Fifth Army, who had fought over every inch of ground to stop the offensive. The official air historian wrote: 'It may be predicted that when all the facts have been made known and studied, and the last word has been said, the retreat of the Fifth Army will be the subject of a glowing page in military histories.'[25] Gough's reputation was vindicated eventually, and he was awarded a GCB, but not until 1937.

Sholto pondered on what it had been like to be a pilot during what seemed at the time to be a catastrophic retreat. As he 'twisted and turned and dived and zoomed and fired and was shot at', he sometimes found himself shouting absurd battle cries and even singing at the top of his voice, much as his Douglas ancestors would have done as they went into battle against the English. He wrote: 'We who were fighter pilots during the years between 1914 and 1918 knew an emotional experience that was unique, and we lived it to the full. It was the highlight of the most colourful period that flying has ever known.'[26] He reiterated that he was anxious but not particularly scared at the time. The same could not be said of some leading politicians. When, for example, Lloyd George ventured to France on a visit to the Fifth Army, Douglas Haig wrote: 'The PM looked as if he had been thoroughly frightened, and he seemed still in a funk.'[27]

Although the enemy launched fierce attacks to the north of the Fifth Army front, they did not break through either to Amiens or to Arras. Their plan to reach the coast had failed, with huge casualties on both sides. It was an anxious time for the Allies, but Sholto realised that for the Germans it was the beginning of the end.

CHAPTER SEVEN

BIRTH AND TRIUMPH

Almost incidentally in the midst of the bloody battle in France, on 1 April 1918, the Royal Air Force came into being. Its birth had been the result of much argument among politicians, generals and admirals at home. Sholto and his comrades at the Front did not pay much attention to it until a few weeks later when their friends in the Royal Naval Air Service (RNAS), with which the RFC had amalgamated to form the RAF, changed the names of their ranks, which were denoted on the new, rather startling and impractical pale blue uniforms with sparkly gold braid. Then it dawned on them that an entirely separate and independent air force had been formed, a first for any nation.

Towards the end of the March Retreat, on 4 April, No. 84 Squadron moved once again, this time to the airfield on the edge of the village of Bertangles, north of Amiens. Close to the Front, they could see the shells bursting over the lines in the direction of Villers-Bretonneux, where the fighting was still heavy but the British line was holding. Bertangles was a large airfield situated in fine open country surrounded by clumps of trees, and Sholto pitched his tent in a copse full of nightingales. As he lay in his tent their night-time song would keep him awake, but once he had become accustomed to it he found it a great relief from the harsher sounds of war.

On 21 April 1918, the German Air Force lost its most iconic pilot, Manfred von Richthofen. The pilots of No. 209 Squadron, stationed at Bertangles alongside Sholto and his men, took off in their Sopwith Camels for a morning offensive patrol over the lines, and for a change there was an easterly wind, putting the Germans at a disadvantage.

The squadron got into a scrap with Richthofen's circus, and one of its newer pilots, a Canadian named Lieutenant W. R. May, found himself being pursued by a red Fokker triplane, unaware that it was being flown by Richthofen, who by that time had shot down eighty Allied aircraft. May did all he could to get away from the chasing triplane, having been advised by his flight commander, Captain Roy Brown, that due to his inexperience, he should avoid actual combat if at all possible. He flew over the Somme and almost as far as the trenches of the Allied front lines, which at that point were occupied by the Australians, but he could not shake off Richthofen. Brown saw what was happening and came to the rescue, opening fire on Richthofen's aircraft from above while machine-gunners fired from below.

In a direct hit, a bullet passed through Richthofen's chest, after which his triplane plummeted earthwards. The remains of the Fokker and Richthofen's body were taken to Bertangles, where the corpse was laid out in a canvas hangar belonging to Sholto's squadron; many of those based at Bertangles aerodrome went to see Richthofen as he lay there almost in state. The following day, he was buried with full military honours in the village cemetery, next to the airfield. There has always been controversy over the manner of his death: subsequent scholarship indicates that he was shot down by an Australian machine gunner, but at the time, many (including Sholto) believed the fatal bullet had been fired by Brown. The assumption that he had shot down the Red Baron had a severe effect on Brown. In a letter to his mother, he wrote of seeing the dead body of the German ace:

> The sight of Richthofen as I walked closer gave me a start. He appeared so small to me, so delicate. He looked so friendly. Blond, silk-soft hair, like that of a child, fell from the broad, high forehead. His face, particularly peaceful, had an expression of gentleness and goodness, of refinement. Suddenly, I felt miserable, desperately unhappy, as if I had committed an injustice. With a feeling of shame, a kind of anger against myself moved in my thoughts, that I had forced him to lay there. And in my heart, I cursed the force that is devoted to death.[1]

Brown received a bar to his DSC for his supposed feat, the last of ten aerial victories with which he was credited, but he never saw action again as, shortly afterwards, he was admitted to hospital with influenza and exhaustion, where he displayed the hypervigilance so often seen in those with what W. H. R. Rivers called 'war neurosis' but which we now call PTSD. Brown wrote to his mother: 'I do not sleep very well. While I was awake, the nurse came in. When I heard her, I jumped and was as frightened as a baby. After that, every little noise made me jump and frightened me the same.'[2]

Sholto was affected also by Richthofen's death in a way that seemed to surprise him, writing:

> It was with mixed feelings that I watched the burial of the great German ace, for it was impossible not to feel a little emotional about it ... I thought about what he had achieved, and I wondered, as I have many times since, just what sort of a man he was. Richthofen was undoubtedly a gallant pilot, although he always fought with the utmost caution – except for his very last scrap – and he never hesitated to avoid a fight or pull out of one if he thought that the odds against him were too great.[3]

Richthofen always flew with his 'circus' formation behind him, similarly to Sholto's friend Jimmy McCudden, the difference being that Richthofen rarely operated over the Allied side of the lines. In July 1918, McCudden himself was killed, not by the enemy but by a head injury following an accident when his aircraft crashed on take-off in France. Just over two weeks later, another ace whom Sholto knew and respected highly, 'Mick' Mannock, was killed when his engine was hit by enemy machine-gun fire from the ground and his aircraft went down in flames. He had developed an intense fear of going down in a 'flamer', and always carried a revolver in the air with the express purpose of shooting himself should this ever happen to him. The Commonwealth War Graves Commission never recovered his body, so he has no official grave. He is commemorated on the RFC's Memorial to the Missing in Arras. Sholto wrote that many men died in achieving success as fighter pilots, and that the extreme nature of the process must eventually lead to 'burn out', even if it did not lead to death. In Mannock's case, it led to both, as he was known to be suffering severely from war neurosis before he died.

In the summer of 1918, the Front to the south of Bertangles was held by the revitalised French Army, which had recovered after the mutinies and poor morale it had suffered in 1917. It was reinforced by increasing numbers of American troops. The Germans attempted a final breakthrough in July but were repulsed by Allied forces holding the Front around Amiens, including Sholto's squadron. They then advanced on 8 August and caught the Germans completely by surprise.

The RAF's main objective was to target the bridges over the river Somme, although they failed to destroy any. They faced strong opposition from the Richthofen circus, which was commanded now by Hermann Goering. The official air historian wrote:

> Hauptmann Goering, a leader of proved worth, was possibly gifted with a temperament more offensive in quality than that of his predecessor, or it may be that the German air service, sensing that the whole background of the war was changing, was impelled to throw its weight into the battle heedless of cost or danger. There does not seem much doubt that the irrecoverable losses suffered by the enemy air service in the fighting which began on the 8th of August resulted from the fact that the German pilots, for the first time in the war, stayed to fight without calculation.[4]

After four days of intense fighting during which the RAF incurred heavy losses, the first stage of the advance was completed, and the Allied line reached a point just short of where it had been two years before at the start of the Somme battle. There was a lull of ten days before the Second Battle of the Somme started, and Sholto and his squadron were detailed to assist the Army in their advance. He encountered Goering many times in the air during that battle, as they chased each other round the skies, trying to get their gun-sights on each other but never succeeding. Sholto wondered many times over the following decades to what extent the course of history would have been changed if, during one of their aerial encounters, he had been able to 'draw a bead on him long enough to finish him off. It would have saved the world, and me, a lot of trouble many years later.'⁵ But in those last days of August 1918, he could not have known that it would be the start of a long series of hostile encounters that would lead eventually to him rejecting Goering's plea for clemency at Nuremberg.

On 24 August 1918, Sholto and some of his pilots were invited to a cinema show in one of No. 48 Squadron's hangars at Bertangles. The show had been running for a while when suddenly there was a loud explosion as a bomb landed on another of No. 48's hangars nearby, setting it alight. A German night bomber had stealthily flown over the airfield and, perhaps seeing a chink of light coming from somewhere, its crew had taken aim at it. The Orderly Officer rushed into the hangar calling for the fire party, at which point another bomb fell very close by, followed by many more. Sholto, who was sitting in the first row, dived under the piano in front of him as others flung themselves onto the floor. They did not stay there more than a few moments, as other German bombers were attracted by the fire and started bombing and strafing the whole aerodrome. Sholto and a colleague of his, Charles Steele, made a dash for some trenches that had been dug near the mess about 100 yards away. Faster than Steele, Sholto managed to get to the trenches before the next load of bombs was dropped, but although Steele threw himself to the ground, he was hit in three places and had to spend the rest of the war in hospital. No. 48 Squadron had many casualties that night, both wounded and killed, and Sholto lost one of his cheerful American pilots, who was killed by machine-gun fire from one of the bombers as he ran from the blaze.

From the trench, Sholto saw that a hangar of his own squadron had been set on fire at the other side of the airfield. He shouted to others to join him and they rushed across to the blaze, where they did what they could to save their aircraft. Although they suffered no further casualties, they did lose one of their SE5as when the roof of the wooden hangar fell on it. They managed to drag the rest to safety.

To counter the threat posed by the Fokker DVII, a new, highly effective German single-seater fighter, wing and brigade commanders of the RAF instigated the use of even larger formations of aircraft, with two or three squadrons – some fifty aircraft – often flying a considerable distance over enemy territory. This tactic did cause a drop-off in casualty rates, which had started to rise with the appearance of the DVII, and Sholto embraced it wholeheartedly, considering that it meant the difference between life and death. However, an account by the historian Stewart Taylor states that Sholto was unpopular among some of his pilots for his inflexibility over the practice, and also for his behaviour towards two of his flight commanders, a Canadian, Carl Falkenberg, and a South African, Walter Southey, who bridled at his theories and his strict observance of British military protocol. In turn, Sholto had apparently taken an obvious dislike to Falkenberg's laid-back attitude towards his dictums on tactics and squadron discipline in general, supposedly berating him in front of his B Flight pilots.

Sholto's habit each evening was to do the rounds of the aerodrome, inspecting the tented hangars and wooden aircraft sheds for any irregularities. No lights or torches were allowed on the aerodrome lest they attract the attention of German night bombers, so on nights of little or no moon, the narrow passageway between the hangars was dark. Knowing this, some of the pilots of B Flight hatched a plan, and one night in late August 1918 while Sholto was carrying out one of his evening inspections, they ambushed him. Suddenly, out of the darkness, he was assaulted by three or more figures who punched him repeatedly. He staggered back, almost tripping against the C Flight hangar, and fell to the ground. His assailants left him there in the darkness, unconscious.

The next morning, Sholto, flush-faced and bruised, called for his B Flight commander, Falkenberg, who bore the brunt of his CO's accusations. Although Falkenberg denied the charges, he himself sported a beautiful shiner of a black eye. His co-conspirators also denied any involvement despite Sholto's determined efforts to extract a confession, including the threat of a court martial, not unreasonably. He tried for the next few days to identify his attackers, but then handed the job of inquisition to his adjutant. Taylor, who interviewed one of those involved many years later, admitted that 'to the Major's credit he later treated the "B" Flight pilots as if nothing had happened, the sign of a well-adjusted leader'.[6]

Indeed, just before and after the assault, Sholto recommended Southey for the immediate awards of Distinguished Flying Cross (DFC) and Bar, and Falkenberg for a Bar to a DFC awarded already, praising them both for their gallantry and courage in engaging the enemy, especially in low-flying attacks on German troops, guns and transport, which he said they undertook at great personal risk. In one of the citations, Sholto pointed out that Falkenberg had served continuously in the squadron for eight months. Perhaps that was the problem: he had been in the field too long and was becoming 'frayed around the edges'. The neurologist J. L. Birley commented that a pilot's feelings of a CO losing faith in him, or of dissatisfaction with his commander, were indicative of someone whose mechanisms of defence have given way under the strain of war. The psychiatrist J. T. MacCurdy made a similar observation about servicemen ruminating obsessively on friction with brother or superior officers, at the same time noting that homesickness can exacerbate these feelings and that this was much more prevalent among Canadians due to their distance from home. Shortly afterwards, both Falkenberg and Southey were recommended for a return to Home Establishment for a rest by Sholto and his successor as CO of No. 84.

In turn, Sholto was also showing signs of excessive strain. He had lost his normal sociability that had won him so many friends earlier in the war; Falkenberg observed that his CO kept very much to himself, confining most of his limited conversation to his three flight commanders, and his desire for solitude may have been a sign of a deeper malaise. Although Sholto was possessed of a certain amount of psychological and physical toughness, the direct attack on him would only have increased his internal distress, involving as it did not only mental anguish but also another concussive injury accompanied by loss of consciousness. Once again, more recent research has revealed that it is not just combat that is significantly associated with more severe symptoms of PTSD in military veterans but also physical assault other than that sustained as a direct result of warfare. Furthermore, cumulative trauma exposure has been shown to increase the severity of medical problems in veterans.

During the series of Allied offensives that led eventually to the end of the war, the members of No. 84 were being stretched to the limit, and Sholto noted in squadron records that it was quite common for his mechanics during this period to get no more than two full nights' sleep per week, plus an occasional nap when their aircraft were in the air. Nevertheless, everyone was conscious that they were making real progress.

On 29 September, under cover of fog, the ground attack by the Fourth Army was launched. Its objective was to penetrate the strong defences of the German Hindenburg Line, and it succeeded, producing a large-scale enemy retreat. Sholto and his pilots were in the air as soon as the mist and the smoke of the artillery bombardment had cleared, attacking enemy observation balloons, but met strong resistance from Fokker aircraft, one of which they shot down. Sadly, one of his pilots was brought down by ground fire and crashed behind the German lines.

As well as targeting enemy kite balloons, at which 'Proccy', the outstanding pilot of No. 84 Squadron, was particularly successful, part of the squadron's routine work was to look after Allied balloons, and while engaged in that task, Sholto was involved in what he termed 'a most unfortunate misunderstanding'[7] involving that most distressing of wartime situations, friendly fire. He was leading his squadron out on patrol when he spotted a balloon flying in a suspicious way over British front-line trenches. He could not tell whether it was an Allied or a German craft, so he flew down to examine it more closely, and seeing that it was British, he sheered away from it. A few minutes later, he looked over his shoulder and was horrified to see it going down in flames. He turned back and dived towards it at top speed just in time to see a German fighter sneaking back very low over enemy lines. By that time, the balloon was blazing down on the ground. He turned again and chased back over the German lines searching for the fighter but could not find it. When he returned to his airfield, he was informed that the leader of an SE5a squadron had shot down a friendly balloon and it was suspected that he was the culprit.

To make things worse, the observer who had been shot down was Lieutenant-Colonel W. F. MacNeece, the commander of the local Balloon Wing, and he had been badly injured due to baling out at low altitude. Sholto realised that the enemy fighter must have downed the balloon, and fortunately he had not fired his own guns on that patrol, so he was able to obtain a certificate to that effect from his Squadron Armament Officer to prove his innocence to those at Wing HQ. It was much harder to convince MacNeece when Sholto went to visit him at the local hospital, where he was in bed and severely concussed. Sholto tried to explain what had happened, but MacNeece was in no fit state to take it in, and for years afterwards believed that Sholto had shot him down. In the mid-1920s, they served together at the Air Ministry, and Sholto cleared the matter up with him, but was never quite sure whether MacNeece ever really believed him.

Owing to the rapidity of the Fourth Army's advance, and the bad weather, the Army Commander often lacked information concerning the position of his forward troops. It was then that Sholto came to the rescue with a novel form of low reconnaissance, a simple but effective method for locating forward enemy positions. The mist was quite thick and visibility very limited, so he had to fly at heights of only 200–300 feet. When the Allied troops reached the area in front of the town of Le Cateau, Sholto flew along each of the roads running towards the enemy lines in turn until he encountered hostile fire from the ground. He marked the spot on his map, flew back to Le Cateau and repeated this process along the other roads. Having done so, he returned to his own airfield by 'contour-chasing' with his map on his knee. On his arrival, he gave the information to the intelligence staff, who were able then to join up the points and ascertain the position of the German front line.

The work was both useful and exhilarating for Sholto, even as he exposed himself to mortal danger from enemy guns, seemingly with no sense of self-preservation, and he continued with it for three days. For this and other things he was awarded the DFC on 5 November

1918. The citation appeared in the *Edinburgh Gazette* written in a manner that Sholto thought decidedly over-generous:

> A very gallant officer and brilliant leader to whose personal influence and example is mainly due the fine record of his Squadron which, since 21st September 1917, has destroyed 201 and driven out of control 149 aircraft. On 17th, 18th and 19th October last, Major Douglas carried out most successful reconnaissances of the army front at exceptionally low altitudes (at times descending to 20 feet owing to dense clouds) and in face of intense hostile rifle and machine-gun fire.[8]

In view of the rapidity with which the Allies were advancing, in late October, No. 84 Squadron had to leave what Sholto called its 'pleasant nest' at Bertangles, where it had been based for the past six months, and move to the former German aerodrome at Bertry. For the first time in months, the crews were housed in proper billets in the village.

Two days after their arrival, Sholto was set upon by three Fokker DVIIs as he was flying alone on reconnaissance, which took him over the German lines and over the Forêt de Mormal. Immediately, he turned west and flew back as low as he could to Bertry. The three German pilots were shooting at him, but as he reached the Allied lines two of them turned back. The third continued to follow him, but when Sholto turned on him, he did a steep 180-degree turn and headed for his own lines. Sholto chased him back over the forest, closed in on him and fired from a range of fifty yards, hitting him and sending him into a nose-dive to the ground.

On 30 October, only a few days before the end of the war, the German Air Force made a determinedly tough stand in their fight against the RAF. It was a day of heavy losses for both sides, more severe even than the losses during the pivotal day of the Battle of Britain on 15 September 1940. If ever we are tempted to minimise the toll of flying in WWI, it is a salutary thought that only a quarter of all new pilots sent to France between July and December 1917 completed a tour of duty, the rest being killed, wounded, missing or sent home early.

On 4 November, 'the enemy resistance on the ground broke down completely'.[9] Everywhere, the Allies were advancing; the British eastwards and the Americans and French north-eastwards towards the Ardennes. The job of No. 84 Squadron was to attack the retreating columns of German troops with bombs and machine guns, but poor weather prevented what might have been a wholescale slaughter. Germany's position had become untenable. On 11 November 1918, following an uprising in Berlin two days earlier, the Armistice brought the fighting to an end. The combatants had been at war on the Western Front for four years and three months.

No. 84 Squadron reached the end of the war with an impressive record. In the fifteen months it had been on active service in France, it claimed 323 victories, although they could have been as many as 350. It also became the RAF's top balloon-bursting squadron, with fifty being destroyed through fire.

Reflecting on the conflict in later life, Sholto wrote:

> The years of the First World War provided us with an experience that was so extraordinary that it was impossible to understand immediately what it all meant, and so profound that it was to alter the whole course of our lives. We had scarcely more than begun to know what living meant, but we knew all about dying, and for many the experience was so disturbing that it was to leave upon some minds the deepest of scars. It is said of our experience that it was traumatic; but we who went through it have other names for it. We were young in years, and we had learnt to present a front that was high-spirited and apparently carefree; but in other respects we were indeed old before our time.[10]

Nevertheless, he had not lost his enthusiasm for flying. He was part of the strongest, and the first independent, air force in the world at the end of WWI. He had been promoted to Lieutenant-Colonel and was going to command a Wing. At only twenty-five years old, he had been awarded a Military Cross and a Distinguished Flying Cross and had been mentioned three times in dispatches. In 1924, he was awarded a French Croix de Guerre. But having faced death so many times, his own and that of others so close to him, he could not see his future with any clarity, and he did not have the spirit or interest that he had expected would come with the end of the war. Throughout WWI, John Morrow has estimated that more than 50 per cent of British pilots became casualties. As Cyril Falls observed, the generation that fought the First World War was a gallant 'and high-hearted one, and so many of them were dead'. He continued: 'The losses suffered in the ranks of its best were a grave loss to the world, and in some parts of it the effects have still not ceased to be felt.'[11] He wrote that in 1960, forty-two years after the end of WWI.

Sholto left the airfield at Bertry on the morning of 8 November. He caught the boat from Boulogne on 10 November and arrived back in London that evening. He called his favourite girlfriend as soon as he arrived back home, and dined with her at the Comedy Restaurant in Panton Street. That was for them the start of the celebrations that were to erupt with the signing of the Armistice. He woke the next day to the sound of shouting and cheering crowds as they burst into celebration at eleven o'clock on that morning of 11 November 1918. At last, the war had ended.

CHAPTER EIGHT

A TROUBLED AFTERMATH

For Sholto, even the euphoria that came with the end of the war was short-lived, if indeed it ever existed. Everything with which he had been familiar had slipped away in those four long years, causing him to mourn

> the way in which life as we had known it had disintegrated in a curiously silent fashion, for all the noise of the war, leaving us in a void of bewilderment ... Those who had known, as I had, the intensity of the experience of having to find out what fighting in the air meant and demanded of us were in a state of mind that even we could not fully understand. In my own case I was by no means approaching exhaustion, but I was, I realise now, in a confused and unhappy state.[1]

After only two weeks' leave, in which, despite or perhaps because of his mental turmoil, he participated in an endless round of celebrations, Sholto, 'in a state of depletion in every sense of the word',[2] reported for his new job at the airfield at Cranwell in Lincolnshire. A year later, it was to become the site of the new RAF College, but when Sholto arrived it was a sprawling station that had been established by the Navy early in 1916 and used to train large numbers of officers as pilots for the RNAS. It had retained its naval atmosphere, the greater proportion of the officers and men still wearing Navy uniforms, as they resented their integration into the RAF. When they went on leave, the men talked about 'going ashore', and the tender that took them to the nearest railway station was called 'The Liberty

Boat'. Sholto was now in command of a Wing comprising three flying training schools situated at Cranwell and a fourth at Digby, just under eight miles away.

The period immediately after the end of WWI was a difficult time for most servicemen. Although the Armistice had been signed, peace would only come with the signing and ratification of the peace treaty, and the government believed that the armed forces should remain fully in being until this event. Nonetheless, the men felt that the war was over and wanted to return home to their families and their lives as civilians. To add to their difficulties, the 1918 influenza pandemic was taking its toll, unusually affecting young adults such as servicemen more severely. They had been housed in cramped and insanitary conditions, many of them malnourished and traumatised by the war. These individuals were more vulnerable than perhaps they realised, and recent research has shown that those with stress-related disorders such as PTSD, particularly when young at diagnosis, are at increased risk of life-threatening infections.[3]

When the plans for demobilisation were announced finally, they were shambolic and unfair, proposing to release workers in key industries first for the sake of economic renewal, but this meant that those who had served the longest and often suffered the most were likely to be the last to be demobilised. There were several mutinies, the worst being at Southampton when 5,000 soldiers refused to board the ships that were to take them back to France. They had been sent down to Southampton from London Waterloo with the promise that they were to be demobilised there, but on reaching the docks, they were told that they were returning to France. Trenchard himself was sent to defuse the situation. At first, the men heckled and threatened him, so he asked immediately for 250 men armed with rifles to be sent from Portsmouth.

The following day at dawn, in a theatrical show of strength, Trenchard ordered the armed soldiers to stand in a line outside the customs shed where the mutineers were holding out, and there was a loud metallic clicking sound as simultaneously they cocked their rifles ready to fire. Trenchard then stepped forward to address the crowd. A burly sergeant shook his fist at him and told him to 'go to hell'. Trenchard ordered that the man be put on a ship below decks, and then spoke to the crowd once more. When he was sure that they had calmed down, he told them to form into ranks, ordered that a table be brought to him, and for the rest of the day he and his Staff Officer, Maurice Baring, sat at it and heard all of the men's stories individually. He knew that their grievances were genuine, and sent a report to the War Office to that effect.

When the mutiny came at Cranwell, Sholto was minded to take strong action, but using the means available to him in a rather more cunning way, without a show of force. One morning, the men refused to appear on parade and 'skulked' in their huts. Sholto 'harangued them and reminded them of their duty',[4] but like Trenchard, he told them that he would do his best to help expedite their demobilisation. Then he remembered that a pay parade was due that afternoon. He told the men that unless they appeared on parade they would not get their wages. He was not sure of the legality of this action, but it was successful, as everyone turned out on parade and continued to do so without any further trouble.

The officers were unhappy too, but for a different reason: the entire future of the RAF seemed to be in doubt, and many wondered what was going to happen to them. In 1919, the Prime Minister, David Lloyd George, introduced the 'Ten Year Rule', telling service chiefs that they were not to expect a major war within the next ten years and that the military establishment was to be cut accordingly. Trenchard had been re-appointed as CAS in February 1919 by Winston Church-ill, who was the new Secretary of State for War and Air, but for all Trenchard's resolve to hold together the service about which he felt so deeply, 'it was very nearly bled to death'.[5] At the end of WWI, the RAF had consisted of nearly 300,000 officers and other ranks, but now its strength was to be slashed to just under 60,000 – 5,300 officers and 54,000 men – leaving those who wanted to stay in the service with a feeling of deep insecurity. No plan had been produced for the establishment of regular officers with permanent commissions in the RAF, but anyway, Sholto was not sure that he wanted to be part of it in peacetime. Life for him had lost both its lustre and its direction, and he could not apply his mind to plans for the future.

His brother Bobby knew no such indecision. He had served throughout the war in the Royal West Kent Regiment in India and Mesopotamia and was now a captain. As soon as he could, he left the Army and took up his classical scholarship at Christ's College, Cambridge, reading for the Oriental Languages Tripos. He intended to apply to the Indian Civil Service when he had finished his degree. Gordon Alchin, Sholto's closest friend from his schooldays, had survived the war as a pilot and had been awarded the Air Force Cross. Similarly to Bobby, he returned to Brasenose College, Oxford, to continue working for his law degree. Conversely, Sholto felt that he could not settle down to life as an undergraduate after having been a fighter pilot and having held responsibility as a squadron commander for so long. Later, he regretted not going back to Oxford.

In the midst of all this uncertainty, Sholto wondered after many sleepless nights whether he might become a civil pilot, for despite everything, his enthusiasm for aviation was undiminished. The war had assured its future, and here was a chance for him to get in on the 'ground floor' of an entirely new venture: commercial flying. The idea of being a test pilot held some attraction for him, and he made several applications for such posts, but then he heard that Frederick Handley Page was starting a civil air transport company. He went to see Handley Page himself at the company's offices and was offered the post of chief pilot in the newly formed Air Transport Company. Although the job sounded impressive, the salary was 'a somewhat meagre £500 a year' (approximately £18,000 today),[6] but nevertheless Sholto accepted it.

When the opportunity came for him to be demobilised in April 1919, he took it and joined Handley Page in the same month. Civil aviation came into existence officially on 1 May 1919 when the Air Navigation Regulations 1919, published by the Air Ministry on the previous day, came formally into force, and the first thing Sholto did was to get one of the new commercial pilot's licences. He had wanted No. 1, but he was staying with his father Langton in London and became involved in one of their frequent arguments, so by the time he arrived at the Air Ministry, three other pilots had beaten him to it. He was issued with No. 4 of the official licences as a 'pilot of aircraft carrying passengers for hire or reward'. On that very day, Sholto made what has been described as the first transport flight between London and Manchester, taking eleven passengers in a Handley Page O/400 aircraft. The voyage took three hours and forty minutes flying against a vicious headwind. Today, it takes one hour.

Sholto and others who were the first of what were to be known as civil airline captains still lived the same wild, seemingly carefree lives to which they had become accustomed during the war, when they felt it necessary to put up a 'front' to mask their struggles with very difficult conditions. The lack of any daily routine was similar to their experience in France, when they had often to fly at a moment's notice on all sorts of missions. On Rose Day in June 1919, Sholto took off from Cricklewood, where Handley Page was based, with a full load of passengers, and over Hyde Park they dropped a bouquet of roses for Queen Alexandra, who had started this annual appeal for funds for hospitals before the war. He then flew low over Marlborough House, the home of the Queen until her death in 1925, as a result of which Handley Page received a telegram expressing her pleasure and gratitude at this gesture.

In July, Sholto piloted the first commercial cross-channel flight from the UK to Brussels, transporting freight on charter in an O/400. A few days after that, he was asked by Handley Page himself to fly one of his V/1500 bombers to Amsterdam in order that it could be shown at the first ever international aircraft exhibition to be held anywhere in the world after WWI. En route to the exhibition, Sholto had to land at the military base at Soesterberg, south-east of Amsterdam. There, he was excited to meet the famous Dutch aircraft designer Anthony Fokker, whose aircraft had been some of the best flown by the Germans, causing Sholto and the rest of the RFC so much trouble in WWI. He was smaller in stature than Sholto had expected, but he was pleasant in his manner and freely discussed aircraft design and performance with him. When the time came for Sholto to take off from Soesterberg the following morning, he saw Anthony Fokker sprawled out on the ground hundreds of yards ahead of him waiting to check how much of a run he would need to get the aircraft into the air. Fokker seemed content to stay there, lying flat on his stomach and trusting Sholto not to run over him, but Sholto thought that there were probably many who had served in the RFC and RAF who would not have blamed him if he kept the wheels on the ground a little bit longer as he sped along towards Fokker. After the show, Sholto flew the aircraft round Holland and Belgium in the hope of getting orders for Handley Page. Demonstrations of the firm's bombers were being staged by Sholto's pilots in Scandinavia, Spain and Portugal, but no orders were forthcoming, and government contracts were being cancelled. The future for the company seemed far from bright.

However, an agreement negotiated by the British and French governments for commercial flying between their two countries meant that business was brisk on the London to Paris run, with fierce competition from the other company operating at that time, Air Transport and Travel Ltd. To begin with, Sholto had been excited to be in at the start of a new commercial venture. However, lack of consistent government support for aviation meant that he and his colleagues found that they were working with scant resources and without any firm direction or official encouragement. Coupled with what he felt was a meagre salary given the responsibilities of his job as chief pilot, and, more surprisingly, a creeping sense of monotony in his work of civil flying, he decided to give up his job with Handley Page. Even years later, with what he hoped was a more balanced view of himself, he did not comprehend fully why he had done this.

The explanation he gave for his restlessness, which did not seem to be resolving with the passage of time, was that he was suffering from a condition experienced by so many after the end of WWI:

It was a malaise of the spirit that has come to be given such a wide variety of names all the way from downright bloody-mindedness to the mumbo-jumbo that is bandied about by the psychiatrists. The mood that I was in was an extension of the frame of mind that had made me leave the Air Force, and for all that they may say about it today, it then defied analysis. We who had participated so actively and so eagerly in the war over such a long period of time had been subjected to an over-stimulation that was now exacting its toll, and in many different ways we were run down to a state that approached a standstill.[7]

Sholto's anguish and that of others in his situation was heightened by the pangs of 'survivor guilt', rendered particularly acute in his case because of Archie's death and the continual remembrance of it kept before him by his mother: 'If you had not joined the RFC…', propelling him into a terrible sense of remorse. And that was only part of what must have troubled him. There were all those in his squadrons whom he had sent off on patrol or into combat who never returned. This was something from which he was never able to escape his entire life, and which was recapitulated graphically for him in WWII and in post-war Germany.

Today, Sholto and many of his comrades who had experienced the trauma of WWI might well be described as manifesting the first symptoms of PTSD. It is almost certain that Sholto had suffered some of these symptoms in the 'danger zone' during WWI, but they manifested fully when the external turmoil had ceased. So what help was there for those who had not actually been diagnosed with a traumatic neurosis but who were disorientated, unhappy and lacking in enthusiasm at the end of the war? Nothing that was readily accessible, it seems. The American psychiatrist Abram Kardiner in his seminal work *The Traumatic Neuroses of War*, published in 1941, noted that after WWI there was no systematic regime for the treatment of those suffering from traumatic neuroses, and many received no treatment until three to five years after the original trauma.

However, there were some enlightened and compassionate individuals who were indeed providing the analysis of the situation that Sholto said had eluded him, including Grafton Elliot Smith and Tom Pear. They worked with the far-sighted Ronald Rows, the Medical Superintendent at Maghull Hospital, which had been commandeered by the War Office at the beginning of WWI to treat servicemen in the early stages of mental disorder, precisely to avoid the stigma of committal to an asylum, a policy that Rows championed.

Smith and Pear wrote that the suffering of those who had been affected by the war was made immeasurably worse by 'the manner in which we, as a nation, have been accustomed to regard even the mildest forms of mental abnormality ... The shifting and unstable blend of apathy, superstition, helpless ignorance and fear with which our own country has too long regarded these problems is rapidly becoming our exclusive distinction.'[8] Greater progress had been made in Germany in particular, where, despite instances of harsh treatment of servicemen with war trauma, for some years those among the civilian population who were suffering from milder forms of mental illness were treated in the more informal atmosphere of psychiatric clinics. Smith and Pear added: 'Can we be content to treat our sufferers with less sympathy, insight and common sense than Germany?'[9] In the rather polemical style in which their book was written, no doubt this was intended as a goad to prod a few raw nerves and stimulate others in this field in the UK to action. Even today, veterans are expressing their desire for more informal support and 'drop-in' centres that they can use as a first point of contact for an initial evaluation of their mental health and to legitimise their need for support in an atmosphere that is less 'medical'.

One of the many problems was that, as Smith and Pear observed, 'In our own country, mental disorder is seldom treated in its early stages. Nearly all our elaborate public machinery for dealing with this distressing form of illness is devised, and in practice is available, only for the advanced cases.'[10] In other words, one had to be a visible and embarrassing nuisance before treatment was offered, either in one of the specialist hospitals set up by the War Office for treating officers or, if one was in the ranks, in that most stigmatising of all places, the asylum. Many of what could be termed 'mild cases' might recover even if left undiagnosed and untreated, but on the other hand, they could get worse, and there were those with 'incipient mental trouble'[11] who did not seem to be, or indeed feel, ill, like Sholto, walking the streets who never got as far as a physician or psychiatrist. They just squashed the trauma down and got on with their lives as best they could, no doubt expending a lot more energy on the simple everyday tasks of living than their untraumatised fellows. A particularly shocking more recent statistic is that only one in five ex-service personnel with mental health problems receive professional medical help,[12] and although measures are being taken to address this, a continuing difficulty is that many veterans are not able to identify that they have a problem, and even if they can, that it is a mental health problem.

After WWI, a deterrent in seeking help was the wish on the part of the sufferer to 'cure himself by his own unaided efforts'[13] and to conceal his worries, especially from his family, but that only aggravated his distress and made it more difficult to treat when it eventually surfaced. As Kardiner observed, 'One little traumatic neurosis predisposes to another, much more severe.'[14] Those suffering in such a way were also discouraged from talking of their worries by well-meaning but misguided family members, friends, and even some physicians, who thought that it was bad to talk to the men of their war experiences, and that they should be encouraged to forget them. But banishing the memories and the scars that they produced was not that easy: 'In most cases the blood was not running pure again for four or five years; and in numerous cases men who had managed to avoid a nervous breakdown during the war collapsed badly in 1921 or 1922.'[15] Unfortunately, it remains the case that the very character traits that military training fosters so effectively, such as self-sufficiency and resilience, of which Sholto had a plentiful supply, are also those that make it difficult for service personnel to admit that they have a problem and to ask for help.

Sholto knew that he had been unwise to throw away his job with Handley Page, and it was in this troubled state that he had been married only a few months earlier in August 1919 to Beatrice May Hudd, known always as May, who at twenty was five years his junior. May's father was a bricklayer, and other members of Sholto's family, including his parents and some of his siblings, thought that she was most unsuitable for him, although he was only repeating what his father had done some twenty-eight years previously in marrying Maggie.

Sholto was desperately short of money and he had to provide for himself and his new wife, as well as paying the rent on a furnished flat they had taken in the Temple. He asked his father for advice, but Langton was not forthcoming in providing constructive ideas, although he did help Sholto a little financially, for which he was very grateful. Langton had his own preoccupations, having the responsibility of three more children with his second wife, Gwendolen, as well as the three children born to his long-term mistress, Grace, all six of whom were now aged between four and thirteen. Apparently, Langton would contrive to have his two younger families spend the summer holidays near to each other, and he would arrange for the respective nannies and children from each 'camp' to meet. This became too much for Gwendolen to bear, and in 1915 she left him for a Frenchman, although they did not divorce until 1927.

One day when Sholto was talking with Langton about how to resolve his problems, he hit on the idea of joining his father in his work as an art dealer. By this time, Langton was well established, and since Sholto had always been interested in art and pictures, he thought he might enjoy the work. At first, Langton was not enthusiastic about this proposal, but when he saw that his son's interest was genuine, he suggested that Sholto begin with what was in his view the easiest art movement to study, the Dutch school. He read extensively and consulted experts in the field, spending a month in Holland in the winter of 1919/20 visiting the pre-eminent galleries and museums.

Sholto enjoyed his studies in Holland, but when he returned to London, he was compelled to confront the reality that he had absolutely no money and was completely dependent on his father, which he found humiliating. His mind returned to its unending circles of indecision and uncertainty, and he described himself as 'nervy'. Soon he gave up the idea of following in his father's footsteps, and searched around for a job that would enable him to earn his own living. He even thought of emigrating to the United States. Langton had many wealthy clients there, one of whom was J. P. Morgan.

It so happened that Morgan was visiting England in that spring of 1920, and Langton spoke to him about Sholto, who was invited then to meet Morgan at his offices in the City of London. Sholto knew nothing whatsoever about the financial world, but he found Morgan affable and kind during the interview, notwithstanding his imposing appearance. He offered Sholto a job with a company of jute merchants that he had just acquired in India, saying that he would have to settle in Calcutta. If the job had been in the United States, Sholto would have jumped at the opportunity, but the thought of India left him feeling doubtful, and he asked for twenty-four hours to think the proposition through.

After leaving Morgan's office, Sholto went to have a quiet lunch by himself at the Bath Club, where he was a member, in order somehow to address the turmoil in his head. He knew that he had to make up his mind, and he felt that there was no one to whom he could turn for advice. If he went to India, he would be cutting himself off from the world of aviation, which he had to admit now was what he really loved. Even if its employment conditions were precarious and uncertain, flying was the only thing that he felt he could do reasonably well, and where he belonged. With all these thoughts buzzing around inside him, he decided to go for a walk to see if that would help. Then something happened that would set the course of his entire life in an instant.

On the way out of the club, literally on the doorstep, he met 'Boom' Trenchard, who was by now firmly ensconced as CAS. On returning to his desk after months away due to a serious bout of influenza the previous year, he had been horrified at how many brilliant officers, both young and old, had been allowed to leave the RAF in his absence as wartime establishments had been slashed. In his gruff but kindly way, he greeted Sholto and asked him what he was doing now. That was just the cue that Sholto needed to air his troubles. Without hesitation, Trenchard said: 'Oh ... don't go to Calcutta. You come back to the RAF.' Sholto knew at once that that was the answer. Trenchard told him to see his secretary, and that all the necessary arrangements could be made the next day.

Sholto now had to face a further interview with J. P. Morgan, which he did on the following day. On hearing of Sholto's decision to rejoin the RAF, Morgan told him that he was a fool, adding that he would always be poor, whereas if he went to Calcutta, he could retire in twenty years as a rich man. Sholto knew that this was true in financial terms, that service pay was meagre and nothing to compare with what he was being offered by Morgan, but that was by no means his only consideration. As he later wrote:

Money alone is not wealth, and I have never been at all impressed

by the all-consuming pursuit of it which is such a dominant influence in the lives of so many. By returning to the Royal Air Force
I was acquiring a wealth that could never be measured in such
terms.[16]

He did not think that he would rise to any great rank, perhaps air
vice-marshal if luck was on his side, but what was important to him
was that he would be returning to flying and thus to a happy way
of life. The uncertainty he had felt since the end of the war evap-
orated almost instantaneously, and he was determined to seize this
opportunity.

CHAPTER NINE

RETURN TO THE FOLD AND
CLIMBING THE LADDER

In a more settled frame of mind, in March 1920 Sholto rejoined the RAF with a temporary commission as a squadron leader and was posted to the staff of No. 1 Group at its HQ in Kenley, just south of London. He found himself directly under the command of Hugh Dowding, by this time a group captain, whose own path to a permanent commission in the RAF had been tortuous. His position in the service was not helped by his criticism of Trenchard's insistence on an offensive policy in WWI that increased pilot losses. Despite Dowding's difficulties, he made sure that Sholto was given a permanent commission, and in the year that he spent with Dowding, Sholto learned how to be an efficient staff officer.

Trenchard was eager to present the new Royal Air Force to the tax-paying public in as favourable a light as possible, so he instigated the annual RAF pageant, which evolved later into the RAF display. For the first of these shows, at Hendon Airfield, Sholto suggested to Dowding that a small formation of Handley Page V/1500 aircraft, the largest four-engined bomber then in service, might make quite an impression. Dowding agreed immediately, so Sholto arranged that he himself, Keith Park, then station commander at Hawkinge near Folkestone, and one of his pilots would start training in formation flying in these lumbering great machines, no mean feat in those days. Sholto added to the thrill by arranging for a young woman parachutist who had flown with him during his time as a civil pilot to make a jump from his aircraft.

On the day of that first tournament, in July 1920, the wind was blowing directly over the aerodrome from behind the royal box. Although King George V was not, Sholto understood, a fan of aviation, he attended the pageant with Queen Mary. Eager to impress the crowd, Sholto took off in formation with his fellow pilots into wind, as is normal practice, and headed straight toward and over the royal spectators. Sholto decided to add a touch of excitement by holding the formation down to what he called euphemistically 'an intriguingly low height', thundering overhead and blasting the crowd with the noise and stench of burnt oil from the engine exhausts. The pilots executed the rest of their formation flying, ending up with the parachutist making her jump and landing in the middle of the airfield.

When he and the others landed, Sholto was expecting praise for what he felt had been a well-executed and exciting performance, but instead, he was ordered to report immediately to the CAS. Trenchard was waiting for him behind the royal box, incandescent with rage. He accused Sholto of endangering the lives of their royal guests; what would have happened if any one of the three aircraft, taking off as they did in tight formation, had had an engine failure, common enough in those days? It was the first and only time that Trenchard ever went for him, and Sholto realised immediately that he was absolutely right. As his close friend Harold Balfour said, Sholto was only too ready to take the rap for things that went wrong, and that was a lifelong trait.

In 1921, after spending a year at Kenley, Sholto was appointed chief flying instructor of the new No. 6 Flying Training School being formed at Manston in Kent. Sholto was engaged at this time in a heavy diet of flying as part of his instructing duties, and he wrote that in case he was tempted to develop too light-hearted a view of life, 'the fates on one occasion arranged for a court martial to stare me in the face'.[1] One of his flight commanders had been killed when his Bristol Fighter suffered engine failure and crashed. A court of inquiry found subsequently that this was due to faulty maintenance, and that the engineers' instructions were inadequate. Sholto's commanding officer, who was responsible for these orders, was away at the time, and since Sholto was temporarily in charge of the unit, it was decided that he would have to face a court martial.

However, Dowding felt that the charge against Sholto was grossly unfair, so he exercised his prerogative as group commander and refused to take any action. This was a courageous stand on his part as it could have jeopardised his own career prospects in the RAF. But Dowding resented both the injustice of the Air Ministry's determined search for a scapegoat and, Sholto surmised, Air Staff intrusion into the running of his group. Sholto was for ever grateful to him, and despite what has been written about their later relationship, would never have forgotten how Dowding had saved his career. Dowding himself was questioned many years later about the incident and commented: 'I remember it well. As usual, the Air Ministry were being stupid.'[2]

In the early spring of 1922, Dowding put Sholto's name forward to attend the first course of the newly created RAF Staff College at Andover. This was part of Trenchard's effort to give top priority to training following his formation of the RAF Cadet College at Cranwell in 1920. Sholto studied assiduously, writing various papers that won him some valuable prizes. Most notable was a detailed account of his service in the RFC throughout WWI[3] in which he articulated and expanded his views on formation flying, an issue which exercised him throughout his life in the Air Force, bringing him into conflict with others almost from the beginning. He had been impressed with French pilots flying in formation as early as October 1915 and had started himself to fly in tandem later that year, but it was not until his time with No. 70 Squadron in October 1916, immediately following his brother Archie's death, that the vulnerability of isolated aircraft was painfully brought home to him.

After Sholto had completed the Staff College course, he was posted for the first time to the Air Ministry. It was the beginning of a long period of staff work. Dowding had been appointed as Director of Training, and under him Sholto was put in charge of flying training. As a result of WWI and the exploits of pioneers in long-distance flying during the years after the war, aviation had been given a powerful boost in the public imagination, but in the UK it was viewed primarily as a medium for travel or leisure. Although chained to his desk, Sholto himself had 'caught the bug', and over a four-year period he competed in a great number of air races, winning some competitions.

In 1918, a Civil Aerial Transport committee had recommended the expansion of civil aviation after WWI, with state aid if necessary, since a prosperous civil sector would encourage the development of modern aircraft and indirectly benefit military aviation. However, its recommendations were ignored. This was not the situation in Germany where, long before Hitler and Goering came to power, a determined move was made to find some way of evading the limitations imposed by the Treaty of Versailles. Although the Germans were prohibited from constructing military aircraft or having an air force, there was no restriction on the manufacture of civil aircraft, so all through the 1920s they developed these machines, which were designed for rapid adaptation to military use. All that was needed was a mutual understanding between civil and military aviation to convert civilian planes to military ones in case of need. By 1926, the German civil airline Lufthansa had established a network of air routes, becoming the foremost airline in Europe. The Italian air strategist Giulio Douhet had observed: 'To open new air routes is to further the national interest.'⁴ It seems probable that someone senior in the *Luft-fahrtsministerium* was reading his Douhet.

By the end of 1924, Sholto had effectively been at the rank of squadron leader for over eight years. He was too young to be promoted to wing commander, the minimum age for which was thirty-two, and it irked his very ambitious nature that officers who were junior to him in the work they were doing were promoted over his head. His superiors realised that his position was anachronistic, and the matter was raised with the Air Council, whose members took pity on him. So on 1 January 1925, just over a week after his thirty-first birthday, he was promoted to the rank of wing commander, the youngest in the RAF.

Soon afterwards, he was involved in an incident of which he was not at all proud, and which brought him once again under Trenchard's eagle eye. As flying training was Sholto's responsibility, he was asked to accompany Trenchard, who was still CAS, on an inspection of the Flying Training School at Sealand near Chester. The day before

Trenchard's visit, Sholto flew a De Havilland (DH) 9A from Kenley to Sealand with a mechanic as his passenger. In order to leave as much room as possible for landing on the actual airfield, he decided to make his approach between two hangars. What he did not see until it was too late was a wireless mast in the middle of the gap between them, and he was heading straight for it. The aircraft was flung round violently, ending up crashed on the roof of one of the hangars. As the DH9A had a reputation for catching fire in an accident, with the added possibility of sliding off the roof and crashing to the ground, Sholto and his mechanic scrambled out of the aircraft as quickly as they could and were helped to safety.

Badly shaken, Sholto was crestfallen and angry with himself, knowing that, despite his experience, he had been guilty of a bad error of judgement. A crew of mechanics and fitters got to work on the wreckage, managing to remove it from the hangar roof and get it out of the way before Trenchard's arrival the following day, for which Sholto was very grateful. There was a large hole in the hangar roof, which had to be covered with a tarpaulin, and everyone prayed that the CAS would not notice it. He did not seem to, but Sholto could not help wondering whether it was his imagination that Trenchard had a suspicious gleam in his eye as he accompanied him on his tour of inspection.

After nearly four years at the Air Ministry, longer than was usual for a young officer to serve there, Sholto was told that his request for a move to more active service had been granted, but before taking command of the fighter station at North Weald in Essex, he spent eleven months as the youngest officer on the inaugural course at the newly created Imperial Defence College (IDC), now the Royal College of Defence Studies in London.

As Sholto's achievements continued to accrue, he knew that both his father and his mother were proud of his successes, but he realised that there was for them both a lingering element of sadness as a result of their failed marriage. Tragically, of the five children born to them, by 1927 only Sholto remained alive. The last of his full siblings to die was his brother Bobby, in August 1926. He was thirty-one years old, and a rapidly rising star in the Indian Civil Service, having graduated from Cambridge with a first-class degree in Oriental Languages. Bobby was said to have died quickly of cholera, but his widow Gloria, who was pregnant with their second child at the time of his death, was always doubtful that this was the case, suspecting strongly that he had been poisoned by a resentful citizen who had been the recipient of what he deemed to be an unfair judgment, passed down by Bobby in his role as district magistrate in the United Provinces.

So Sholto's mother Maggie had one remaining child, and unlike Langton, she did not marry again. She was left with the son with whom she had the least sympathy. Not only was Sholto the most like his father in character but the remarkable physical resemblance between them no doubt struck Maggie every time she looked at her eldest son. Any affinity that they might have had was thwarted by their extreme differences in religious views. Maggie remained an evangelical Christian while, largely as a result of his war experiences, Sholto had become an atheist. Bobby, in contrast, had remained devoutly religious until the end of his all-too-short life. To Gloria's astonishment, on their wedding night he insisted on kneeling down and saying his prayers before climbing into the marital bed.

In 1928, Langton embarked on his third and final marriage, to a young Scotswoman named Jean Stewart. He was sixty-four and she twenty-six. Although Sholto remarked that it was the most sensible thing his father had done in his life, Sholto himself must have had mixed feelings, because Jean was his girlfriend. His own marriage to May was already in trouble by this time, and he had started an affair with Jean. In 1926, she had needed a job and his father a secretary, so Sholto had suggested that she work for Langton.

Since WWI, Langton had been in thrall to an unusual-looking young woman called Zena Naylor who had turned up at his house in Hill Street one day, claiming that she was his daughter. Generously, he had taken her in, closing his eyes to her faults. Zena was attractive and 'had a Circe-like character', such that many men fell under her spell, including William Walton, the composer, and Eugene Goossens, the conductor and composer, although she possessed a 'demandingly sensual appetite' and had an aggressive vein in her character.[5] Zena became known as Langton's niece, and he was fascinated by her.

In autumn 1927, with Jean now ensconced in her secretarial position, Zena and Langton were leaving for their usual business trip to America, and he attempted to hurry her along, worried they would miss the boat train. This infuriated Zena, who came down the stairs and slapped his face, calling him an old fool. Jean, horrified at this spectacle, sent Langton an unsigned telegram saying, 'Good bye and good luck, I shall miss you.' He received this at Southampton and wrote to Jean asking whether it was she who had sent the telegram, saying that if so, he would take the next boat home. In the same letter, he asked her to marry him. On his return to England, after overcoming her misgivings due to the difference in their ages, she accepted his proposal. This might have been helped by the fact that Langton was now a millionaire, and for all her affection for Sholto, he was only an impecunious RAF officer.

By this time, Sholto was establishing his career in more than just flying. Since his experiences at Staff College and at the Air Ministry, he had become interested in the more academic side of his profession. As was his lifelong habit, he continued to read a great deal, and won a number of official service essay contests during the 1920s. By the summer of 1929, however, the time was coming for a posting overseas. Throughout the 1920s, 'the most pressing duties performed by the RAF were actions against insurgent populations of British colonies'.[6] Sholto wanted to spend as little time away from England as possible, which ruled out India because it was a five-year tour of duty, and besides, it had a reputation for being starved of aircraft and equipment. He did not relish the idea of Iraq either. Finally, there remained the Sudan, which at that time was governed predominantly by the UK together with Egypt. It was a two-and-a-half-year tour and offered more responsibility and freedom, being a long way from the HQ of Middle East Command in Cairo under the aegis of which it came for administration.

But it was still a contentious posting, as the role of the Air Force in the Sudan had been the subject of a tussle between the British Treasury, British officials in Cairo, the Governor-General of the Sudan, the Imperial General Staff and the Air Staff, headed by Trenchard. He believed that air control rather than 'boots on the ground' was the most

economical way of policing so-called 'primitive peoples in sparsely in-
habited territories'.[7] It was also a means of consolidating Britain's grip
on the country and, Trenchard believed, was one way of ensuring the
independent survival of the RAF. However, Dowding had served in
Iraq as Chief Staff Officer in the mid-1920s and had seen the results
of indiscriminate area bombing, realising that although air control
was less costly and caused less damage and loss of life than ground
control, the damage and losses were still heavy.

Despite the arguments that had preceded his arrival, Sholto's posting to the Sudan turned out to be more pleasant than he had anticipated. He lived the typical ex-pat service life in Khartoum, where
his HQ was based, socialising with other RAF and Army officers and
civil servants. He found the climate congenial even in hot weather,
apart from the 'Haboobs' or dust storms, which 'came swirling in
great black clouds across the countryside'.[8] In true Old Testament
fashion, they were also plagued by the occasional enormous swarm
of locusts.

That wasn't Sholto's only biblical encounter during his time in the
Sudan. At a cocktail party one evening, Bishop Gwynne, the Anglican Bishop of Egypt and the Sudan, asked him why he never went to
church. Sholto did not wish to regale the charming old cleric with his
views on religion and cause unnecessary offence, so he said, 'I never
go to church unless I can both read the lesson and sing in the choir.'
The bishop replied, 'Right, my boy, you'll do both next Sunday ...
Choir practice is at six o'clock on Friday.'[9] So the following Sunday
found Sholto somewhat improbably clothed in a scarlet cassock and
white surplice, singing in the Khartoum Cathedral male voice choir.
He had always enjoyed choral and solo singing and turning out each
week gave him a great deal of pleasure.

By contrast, Sholto's work as the most senior RAF officer in Sudan
meant that he was responsible for advising on any air operation that
might be necessary. Within the task of colonial policing, aircraft were
required to penetrate territory little known to European colonis-
ers, mapping hitherto unexplored areas, and – when equipped with
floats – use rivers as routes of access to the interior. As definite air
routes were not yet established, pilots had to navigate using distinctive

features rather than maps, which were hopelessly inaccurate.[10] For these duties, Sholto had only one squadron, No. 47, to cover a vast area. It was equipped with the Fairey IIIF, a large two-seater biplane designed for reconnaissance or bombing. Since the Sudan did not possess an Air Force, there was no need for any fighters, or even for high-performance aircraft. In the rainy summer season, No. 47 converted to seaplanes for six months by adding floats to the fixed undercarriage of its aircraft. The squadron could not be dispersed into flights stationed in different parts of the country, as malaria was endemic throughout and only a very few places were unaffected, Khartoum among them.

Sholto and his fellow pilots would fly either up the Red Sea or along the Nile on their journeys to Cairo. On one trip, he stopped in a gulf on the Red Sea coast almost halfway between Port Sudan and Cairo. Although it was very hot, he found the heat strangely attractive in this coastal part of the desert. Close to the water's edge, Sholto stumbled across the ruins of a temple. He learned later that the inscriptions that they saw there referred to the Roman emperor Tiberius. He and his companion pitched their tent on the beach under the stars, lit a rudimentary fire and cooked their supper. The following day they flew on to Cairo, but he never forgot that isolated and fascinating place, and returned to it later.

The two and a half years Sholto spent in the Sudan opened up for him an entirely unfamiliar world during which he did more flying than ever in a similar time span throughout his career. He felt that he had reached the peak of his efficiency as a pilot. However, that view was not shared by the Air Officer Commanding Middle East, Cyril Newall, later CAS during the Battle of Britain. Sholto flew Newall round the Sudan on his first tour of inspection and, as usual, he did some low flying. Newall reprimanded him afterwards for being altogether too dangerous and taking unnecessary risks, but Sholto thought he was giving him a particularly good view of the wildlife in the region, and found Newall's attitude unadventurous and annoying, like that, he deemed, of most officers of senior air rank. Little did he know that he would be Newall's deputy ten years later, when he himself became a 'brass hat'. Back then he would have greeted the idea with gales of laughter.

While out in Khartoum, Sholto adopted an abandoned female lion cub as his pet, whom he named Belinda. As she grew, she became more boisterous, and one evening in the officers' mess she took rather a liking to the camp doctor's large backside and pounced on it, ripping his khaki shorts and dragging her claws down his bottom, leaving nasty open scratch marks. As if that wasn't bad enough, the final straw came when one afternoon Belinda wandered into the garden of a next-door property, where the young daughter of the house happened to be having her afternoon nap. The lion was found with her 'great paws on her bed, purring like mad! This naturally frightened the small girl, who screamed, and we had to give the lion away.'[11] It wasn't clear whether Belinda was thinking, 'Mmm, lunch,' or whether she was simply being friendly, but she was taken forthwith to Khartoum Zoo, ending her RAF career, much to Sholto's disappointment, although he was pleased that the zoo appeared to be a good one when he inspected it as a new home for Belinda.

The only real trouble Sholto and his pilots encountered during the whole of his time in the Sudan was down in the south-eastern corner of the country. Marauding tribes of Abyssinians, as they were then called, would sweep down from the mountains of what is now Ethiopia, crossing the border and running riot along the western and eastern shores of Lake Rudolf, the present Lake Turkana, which straddles the current borders of South Sudan, Kenya and Ethiopia itself. They attacked the more peaceful tribes of northern Kenya, killing and looting as they went, stealing cattle and abducting women. The government of Kenya appealed to Governor-General of the Sudan, Sir John Maffey, for help. A detachment of the Equatorial Corps of the Sudanese Defence Force (SDF) was sent from Kapoeta in south-east Sudan to Lake Rudolf, to meet up with the Kenya Regiment.

Sholto detailed a flight of five aircraft to go down to the area, appointing an old friend from Bertangles days, Charles Steele, to be the officer in charge of the expedition. Not wishing to miss any of the action, Sholto went along also. His orders were to help chase the Abyssinians back over their own border, but when he and his pilots reached Lake Rudolf, they saw no evidence of them, so they had to be satisfied with being merely explorers. The ineffectiveness of the intelligence system was a perennial problem. Despite Sholto's efforts to improve it, there was a weak link in communication between the civil governors of the provinces and the SDF. Once, for instance, when a raid carried out in a province was reported through civil channels by letter, the SDF did not know about it until fourteen days after it had taken place.

One of the Staff College students listening to Sholto lecture on the air aspect of the military problems of the Sudan in the 1930s asked whether it was even necessary to intervene in tribal fighting on the borders. Sholto's reply was that such fighting caused much distress among the tribes, especially the losers, which meant that action had to be taken, even if it was only to 'stage demonstrations of flying'.[12] He disagreed with Sir John Maffey and his Army colleagues that the use of air and ground forces was more effective than just air forces alone, stating that the sole use of air forces did indeed give the desired results, and that the deployment of land forces resulted in greater loss of life.[13]

Since the end of WWI, Sholto had followed with great interest the career of one of his former opponents, Ernst Udet, who had earned a reputation as a pilot who would take on any sort of flying, the more hazardous the better. Late in 1930, Udet spent three months in Tanganyika, now Tanzania, with a company filming the lives of the local population and the big game. When the rainy season came, Udet and his cameraman Hans Schneeberger flew north, still filming the herds of animals they could see from the air.[14] Though they had intended to stop at Khartoum to pay Sholto a visit, days passed with no news. The world's press heard of Udet's disappearance, and soon there were calls coming into Khartoum from all around the globe. As soon as it became clear that Udet was missing, Sholto sent three of his aircraft down to search for him. They were joined by the pioneering aviator Tom Campbell Black, who knew the area very well.

After three days, a message came that he had found Udet and Schneeberger and their aircraft beside a rough track that ran through the swamp north of Juba. The aircraft itself was undamaged, but they had been forced to land when their fuel had drained away through a leak in the petrol tank. They simply sat and waited, hoping that searchers would find them, but with neither food nor clean water, and with Schneeberger seriously ill with fever, the situation had become desperate. Sholto flew some of his mechanics down with a supply of fuel and beer, and once they had repaired the leak in the tank, Udet continued his flight to Khartoum. He stayed for a few days with Sholto, who found that the reputation Udet had earned during WWI as a decent and likeable man was justified. Sholto admired his honesty and sincerity and was rather attracted by his swashbuckling attitude to life. Udet amused him by saying, 'I never thought that I would know the day when I would be glad to see the roundels of the RAF flying over my head.'[15]

CHAPTER TEN

THE STUNT PILOT, THE RED ALFA AND A CHAIN OF PROTECTION

When Sholto left England in the summer of 1929, the country was still reeling from the after-effects of the war that had ended eleven years earlier. When he returned in the spring of 1932, he felt that it was changing almost imperceptibly 'from a weariness over what was past to an awareness of the future: from a postwar condition to one that was uneasily prewar'.[1] Though glad to be back in England, the pleasure of this was lost to him through the collapse of his first marriage. This was not entirely unexpected since May does not appear to have accompanied him to the Sudan, and during his absence she had fallen in love with Charles Turner-Hughes, a very handsome Pilot Officer in the RAF Volunteer Reserve, who became an accomplished stunt pilot with Sir Alan Cobham's Flying Circus.

Or maybe the writing was on the wall for more reasons than just May's affair and Sholto's infidelity with Jean and possibly others. According to Sholto's half-sister, my Aunt Claire, May was an alcoholic, as were his next two wives. Claire confided to me that, like Langton, Sholto was a 'bad picker of women', not having had a great example to follow. There was also the question of rescue: did Sholto marry women who were vulnerable to act as their protector, much as he had had to do with his mother, who suffered from mental health problems after his father left and after the deaths of her two other sons?

And then, obviously, there was Sholto, who was relentlessly ambitious and willing to subordinate everything to the achievement of his career aims. He said of himself later: 'Not being emotional or easily stirred, I miss the heights of life, i.e. the ecstasies of achievement or even of love,'[2] and that, combined with a two-and-a-half-year absence from May, presumably sounded the death knell for their relationship. It is also probable that Sholto's childhood adversity and his experiences of war had blunted or suppressed his emotional responses. Bessel van der Kolk, a respected trauma expert, has observed that traumatised people are often afraid of feeling because this awakens in them sensations that they would rather put to one side – in Sholto's case, a fear of abandonment by someone in whom he had put his trust and loved, as had happened with his father. In turn, perhaps May felt abandoned when he went to the Sudan.

Sholto, who was living at the RAF Club in London on his return from the Middle East, filed for divorce on 23 May 1932, citing Charles Turner-Hughes as co-respondent. He and May had provided convenient proof of their adultery earlier in the month. The divorce petition rather sadly stated that 'there is no issue of the said marriage now living',[3] raising the question of whether there had been any children who had died in infancy, but if there were, Sholto never spoke of them.

Sholto's second marriage, on 20 September 1933, was to Joan Denny, a West End fashion model eleven years his junior and the daughter of a colonel in the Northamptonshire Regiment. Once again, Sholto's new wife was the subject of his family's displeasure. They rather cruelly called her 'the eternal deb' and thought her giggly and a bit stupid. This attitude towards her persisted right through their marriage, which was to last just over twenty-one years. According to Claire, Joan was probably alcoholic when Sholto married her.

Sholto's arrival back in England marked the end of his time in the RAF as an active operational pilot. Thenceforward, his rise was rapid. He had been promoted to the rank of group captain while still in Sudan, and on his return was posted to the IDC as the RAF instructor. His counterparts from the Army and Navy were Alan Brooke, by now a brigadier, and Captain Bertie Ramsay respectively. Both Brooke and Ramsay were ten years older than Sholto, and the diversity of Brooke's experience especially was 'unrivalled in any of the Services'.[4] It was a sign of the esteem in which Sholto was held in the higher echelons of the RAF that he was appointed to this post with two much more experienced men, and the three of them formed a close friendship that was to endure through the hardships of what was to come.

The staff at the IDC had available to them confidential information about international affairs, so Sholto gained a good picture of what was happening in Germany in the early 1930s, realising that 'something diabolical was afoot'.[5] He learned that two of his adversaries in WWI, Hermann Goering and Ernst Udet, had been given important posts in Hitler's Air Ministry following his appointment as German Chancellor in 1933. Indeed, Goering was its head. Meanwhile, Sholto and his fellow instructors at the IDC were engaged with their students in exercises on paper in how to fight every possible war that might arise.

Sholto noticed that even by the middle 1930s, there persisted in Britain the climate of pacifism in public opinion that had existed ever since the 1920s. He described it as being quite different from the mood in the 1960s when he wrote his autobiography, which he felt was based largely on a fear of nuclear war. Back in the 1920s, it was more the genuine belief that war should be abolished. One of the consequences of this attitude was that the rebuilding of the RAF in particular stalled at a time when it should have been brought up at least to a reasonable strength. Economic considerations also played a part, as the government did not want to upset the import/export balance. By 1932, the RAF had shrunk so much that it was only fifth strongest among the air forces of the world, behind even those of Italy and Japan, when at the end of WWI, it had been the largest in the world. As far as German forces were concerned, Sholto and his fellow instructors at the IDC overestimated their size between 1933 and 1935, but it turned out that their estimates were very similar in numbers and composition to Germany's actual strength in 1940.

They also knew that for a long time, Germany had been sending experienced pilots to Russia to keep their training in military aviation up to date. After Goering insisted in 1933 that this was a temporary expedient and that it would have to end, Germany trained its fighter pilots with the Italian Air Force. Until 1936 and the advent of the

Spanish Civil War, this was done with the greatest secrecy. Even greater subterfuge took place under the cloak of civil aviation and sporting flying, which were used as training schemes for German military pilots. On 9 March 1935, by which time Sholto had been an instructor at the IDC for three years, Hitler stated openly to Sir John Simon, the Foreign Secretary, that Germany had an air force equal in strength to the RAF and was aiming now for parity with the French, though this claim was exaggerated.

Sholto's time as RAF instructor at the IDC lasted a year longer than was usual in this appointment, during which time he was promoted to the rank of air commodore, but he did not object to this extended period because the work they were doing against the backdrop of the political developments in Europe was of intense interest. His next posting, in January 1936, was as Director of Staff Duties (DSD) at the Air Ministry. The title was rather a misnomer, because although his brief included the training of staff officers, the most important element was to take care of the training programme for the entire RAF, including setting up operational training units (OTUs) and organising major exercises.

In this role, in June 1936 Sholto was sent to the picturesque region of Bolzano in north-eastern Italy as the Air Ministry observer of Italian Army manoeuvres. He went with the official representative of the War Office, General Robert Haining, then the Commandant of the IDC, but who became later in the same year, significantly, Director of Military Operations and Intelligence. After three days observing military exercises, they were told that Benito Mussolini had asked that they should spend the next day with him. He duly appeared at their hotel at six-thirty the next morning, at the steering wheel of a bright red open-topped Alfa Romeo with his chauffeur sitting beside him. Sholto and Haining were put in the back of the car, and off they went on a speedy but extensive tour of inspection. Sholto realised immediately that it was going to be an awkward time. Neither man knew sufficient Italian to understand exactly what *Il Duce* was saying, but Sholto noticed that the name of England was invoked frequently in his speeches to the people, among whom Mussolini was enjoying a swell of popularity following his brutal conquest of Abyssinia, completed only a month before.

When the day was over, it seemed the entire time had been consumed by Mussolini in harangues directed to Italian civilians and military with what Sholto termed 'a cunningly varied tempo'. When he addressed the general populace, Mussolini would deliver his speech in the manner of a fiery evangelist, waving his arms and shouting, and taking his audience to a fever pitch of excitement. When he spoke to his troops, however, he was much more restrained in his style, holding himself erect and still and speaking quite differently, seemingly adjusting his persona to what he thought were their expectations of him. Throughout the day Mussolini insisted that Sholto and Haining should stand either side of him while he roared at the crowds of civilians or addressed soldiers. No doubt he intended his hearers to believe that the presence of a senior general of the British Army and an air commodore of the RAF meant that he had England 'eating out of his hand'.

After Mussolini stepped off the rostrum, his demeanour changed yet again, and he became a charming and jolly companion, joking with his two British guests, sitting between them during a hearty official luncheon. In the afternoon, the tour continued and in the evening Sholto and Haining were delivered back to their hotel. Sholto remarked that in addition to his energetic speechifying, Mussolini had done all the driving of that red sports car throughout the day.

Despite Mussolini's charm offensive, Sholto disapproved strongly of the failure of the Conservative British government to press home the implementation of effective sanctions against Italy for her aggression against defenceless Abyssinia, which amounted to an appeasement policy. He wrote that the British could easily have put a stop to Italy's action by refusing her access to the Suez Canal, thus preventing a total of 258,000 Italian troops passing through it, but the British government did nothing to halt this transport. It was not only Italian soldiers who were allowed to pass through the canal: by the end of February 1936, 260 tons of Yperite or mustard gas, which were used to blind and maim civilians including women, children and soldiers alike, had been shipped via this route.[6] Closing the canal to Italian traffic might have been contrary to international agreements concerning its use, and may have precipitated a serious quarrel with Germany, but Sholto felt strongly that it would have been worth the risk. As it was, the British government came out tarnished from the whole affair, and its inertia over sanctions helped to pave the way for the much harsher trouble that followed.

Of course, Abyssinia was not the only front on which the fascist forces were flexing their muscles. Sholto wrote later:

> The year of 1936 was the year during which, having been awakened, we had to get out of bed and go to work. The final act of throwing off the bedclothes, or of having them ripped off, was possibly the march made by the Germans into the demilitarised Rhineland in the early spring of that year ... The immediate reaction of France was to consider forcing the Germans back, and such was the relative military strength of France and Germany at that time that they could have done it.[7]

But the British government would not support the French and, in Sholto's words, 'the whole affair became nothing more than a tortuous argument',[8] from which Hitler, who admitted that he had taken an enormous gamble by this action, even contemplating suicide if it did not work, benefited enormously.

On his return from the Italian manoeuvres, Sholto resumed his position at the Air Ministry, bringing him into much closer contact with all that was going on in the development of the RAF. By this time the four principal commands had been formed that would remain in existence throughout WWII and beyond: Bomber, Fighter, Coastal and Training. Little did Sholto know that he would be appointed C-in-C of two of them. The prototypes of both the Hurricane and the Spitfire had made their maiden flights in November 1935 and March 1936 respectively, and during the spring and summer of 1935 the first practical trials had been made by scientists in the use of Radio Direction Finding (RDF), later to become known as radar.

The utility of radar in detecting aircraft under daylight conditions caused the physicist Watson-Watt, known as the 'father of radar', to predict that a potential enemy would be driven to attacking at night or through cloud. Techniques now had to be developed that would direct fighter pilots to the point of interception with enemy bombers whatever the conditions. In July, Watson-Watt obtained permission for experiments to develop optimum interception capabilities in all circumstances. At the same time, his team set to work on developing airborne radar equipment. Sholto, as DSD, was given the task of implementing the trials. Along with its essential counterpart, Ground Control Interception radar (GCI),[9] aircraft to aircraft radar, or Airborne Interception (AI) as it was known, would be instrumental in ending the Blitz.

Once permission for this research had been given, Sholto wrote to Air Marshal Philip Joubert de la Ferté, AOC of No. 11 (Fighter) Group, the RAF unit to be most involved with the exercises, to inform him of the aircraft and ground facilities needed. Sholto wrote: 'We [in the Air Ministry] are very anxious to do all we can to help Mr Tizard [chairman of the Committee for the Scientific Survey of Air Defence], as these experiments are, in our opinion, most important, particularly from the bearing that they have on the future employment of the RDF system.'[10] Together, Sholto and Joubert de la Ferté decided on the sector station at Biggin Hill in Kent as the optimum location.

The RAF Signals History notes that Sholto sanctioned the continuation of the trials for as long as was necessary, into 1937 if need be, stating that without them

> it is doubtful whether Fighter Command could have been adequately prepared for the Battle of Britain. Apart from their value in developing new interception techniques, the exercises brought other advantages. The sector commander at Biggin Hill was emphatic that one of the benefits of the new system was the great confidence it gave to pilots in the air. They learnt the value of accurate flying. When a method was evolved, primitive at first, to ensure that pilots' positions were always roughly known to their commanders on the ground, they knew that they could always be brought home in difficult conditions. This was an essential part of the new tactics and had an immense moral effect.[11]

To address the problem of coverage all along the coast, plans for a coastal radar chain had been under way since July 1936, and Squadron Leader Raymund Hart, an RAF Signals specialist, was attached to Watson-Watt's team to assist in its development. Watson-Watt later described his contact with Sholto thus:

> Sholto Douglas (Director of Staff Duties when we first met) was imaginative, enterprising, receptive and constructive. We owed him much of our education as amateur air staff officers, perhaps too ready to teach our teachers! He was decisive and vigorous in action, and as he progressed rapidly to Assistant Chief of Air Staff, Deputy Chief of Air Staff, and Air Officer Commanding in Chief of several of the Commands that we hoped to serve most directly, he carried many of our hopes and potentialities with him. If I were given the invidious task of naming the Royal Air Force officer, outside the little group of those engaged wholly on radar duties, who did most to ensure that radar became an effective weapon of war, effectively wielded, I think I should name Air Chief Marshal Sir W. Sholto Douglas.[12]

While it is tempting to accept these accolades wholeheartedly, Watson-Watt had his own issues with other personalities involved, though it is certain that Sholto's directness and at that point sociable character, as well as his technical understanding, would have appealed to his fellow Scot.

Technical leaps forward notwithstanding, Sholto felt the RAF was dragging its feet, especially in the matter of aircraft production, and he was not alone. In 1936, Wilfrid Freeman took over from Dowding as Air Member for Research and Development (AMRD). Sholto's and Freeman's arrival at the Air Ministry within a few months of each other brought about a renewal of their old friendship from their earliest days in the RFC, and they worked very closely together. Sholto supported Freeman in articulating to the technical staff what was wanted in aircraft and armaments, and he asserted later that it was Freeman's work between 1936 and the outbreak of WWII that largely won the Battle of Britain, not Beaverbrook's as Minister of Aircraft Production.

On 17 July 1936 there arrived on the world stage the next cataclysm to propel Sholto out of bed and absorb his attention: the outbreak of the Spanish Civil War (SCW). The rebellion by General Franco's Nationalist insurgents against the elected Republican government of Spain, and the part played in it by the forces of Germany and Italy, illustrated graphically the need for urgency at the Air Ministry in facing the threat of a Europe-wide conflagration. However, its response, and indeed that of the whole British government, betrayed an extraordinary lack of understanding of the extent of fascist ambitions. As the historian Liddell Hart wrote, even Churchill, at that time so vociferous concerning the threat constituted by Hitler, allowed 'his class instincts and fear of the Communist element on the Republican side' to obscure his strategic vision, 'and led him to throw his influence against any effort on the part of Britain and France to check the German–Italian moves in Spain'.[13]

Sholto's interest in the SCW took on a much more personal aspect when his half-brother Donald, born in 1915, whom he met frequently during the 1930s at their father's home, went to Spain to fight on the side of the Republican government. A committed communist, he was wounded in the right wrist at the Battle of Casa de Campo on 9 November 1936 and was found critically ill with septicaemia in a Spanish hospital by the communist writer Hugh Slater and the journalist Kate Mangan.

As the war progressed, the bombing of Guernica on 26 April 1937 made a deep impression on Sholto and his colleagues at the Air Ministry. The reports the Air Staff received from RAF intelligence sought to justify the bombing by observing that there were no fewer than three arms factories in Guernica, as well as main cross-roads and a bridge. However, at least two of these probable planned objects of the bombing, the Renteria Bridge and the Astra arms factory outside the town, were left untouched,[14] as was the Basque Parliament house in front of which stood the remains of a famous oak, the symbol not only of Guernica but also of Basque nationalism. Instead, the centre of the town was left decimated and on fire. Estimates as to the death toll vary from 153, the figure claimed at the time by local historians, to 1,654, the number cited by the Basque government. What is more certain is that 70 per cent of the houses were totally destroyed, 20 per cent seriously damaged, and only 10 per cent left moderately harmed. The buildings in Guernica were predominantly of wooden construction, so burned ferociously until the town was virtually razed to the ground.

Another episode later in the same year in Asturias caught the attention of Sholto and those in the Air Ministry. This time the attack by Nationalist aircraft caused 200 casualties including 100 dead.[15] Then, in October 1937, Adolf Galland and his fellow pilots of the Condor Legion tested the idea of 'carpet bombing' in the same region. Sholto admitted later that for him and his colleagues, the disturbing impression left by the Guernica and Asturias bombing affected their attitude to the Germans at the time of the Munich Crisis.

The years of participation in the SCW proved invaluable to the German armed forces. By contrast, the UK's anti-aircraft defences were in a sorry state. In the preceding summer, to Dowding's extreme dismay when he took over Fighter Command, there had been only sixty usable anti-aircraft guns and 120 searchlights in the whole of the UK. The guns were of an obsolescent design, and their replacements would not be ready in sufficient quantities for some years.

In April 1938, Chamberlain instigated the Anglo-Italian Mediterranean Pact, which accepted the presence of Italian troops in Spain until the end of the civil war 'in return for the imponderable value of goodwill in Central Europe'.[16] Churchill wrote to Anthony Eden, the Foreign Secretary: 'The Italian pact is of course a complete triumph for Mussolini, who gains our cordial acceptance for his fortification of the Mediterranean against us, for his conquest of Abyssinia, and for his violence in Spain.'[17] The pact was also an attempt to obtain Italy's cooperation in preserving the current world order and in preventing Italy's alliance with Germany, which turned out to be a vain aspiration.

In this atmosphere of gathering tension, Sholto and his fellow Air Staff officers at the Air Ministry gradually worked longer and longer hours each day, and after a while, the days of the week melded into one another, weekends off being no more the norm. In the summer of 1938, Sholto had the last good spell of leave that he was to have until 1941, three weeks in Monte Carlo.

One of his main preoccupations in these pre-WWII years, as it had been since WWI, was the study of air tactics. His thinking and that of others on the Air Staff continued to be based largely on what they had learned during that earlier conflict, and they were unsure how far those lessons would apply in the changed circumstances of a future war. The aircraft would be three times faster with more than four times the firepower. There were still many in the Air Ministry and the RAF who were wedded to the idea that the offensive bomber force was the highest priority. In November 1936, the CAS, Air Chief Marshal Sir Edward Ellington, wrote to his deputy, Christopher Courtney: 'Every fighter is a loss to the striking force – the true defence against air attack.' In the same month, Sholto informed Courtney that bombers would not need to be escorted by fighters, with which Courtney agreed. In his biography of Dowding, the New Zealand historian Vincent Orange pointed out, 'They could not have been more wrong, as airmen of all nations would learn during the coming war.'[18]

For the next eighteen months, the Air Ministry continued with the process of RAF expansion schemes that it had begun in mid-1934. Between then and October 1938, thirteen different schemes succeeded one another with 'bewildering rapidity', one plan never being fully implemented before the next was devised, and some not actioned at all. The energy with which these schemes were formulated on paper belied their practical application. Not before time, Hitler's annexation of Austria in March 1938, termed the 'Anschluss', added a new urgency to RAF expansion. Politicians, after their hesitancy of the preceding years, began to urge the Air Ministry to enlarge the RAF, resulting in the unusual situation in which the government was urging expansion while those in the Air Ministry were putting on the brakes. The Air Staff were concerned that expanding too rapidly would dilute both fighting efficiency and morale and were reluctant to go on placing orders for aircraft that were now obsolete albeit still in production, rather than considering new types. Nevertheless, some in the Air Ministry clung to obsolescent types, and Sholto was soon to become embroiled in a debate on precisely this subject.

CHAPTER ELEVEN

FLYING TOWARDS THE CRASH

Despite the sluggishness of RAF expansion, external international events forced the pace, seen in the speed with which senior officers were promoted. At the beginning of 1938, only eighteen months after becoming an air commodore, Sholto was given the rank of air vice-marshal, and with that he hoped that he would be posted to an operational command, having been a staff officer at the Air Ministry for the past five and a half years. Instead, he was appointed to the newly created post of Assistant Chief of the Air Staff (ACAS). He was to serve directly under the CAS, Cyril Newall, and to be responsible for the Directorate of Staff Duties, which he had headed for the past two years, and the Directorate of Operational Requirements. The work of this latter directorate was to make decisions concerning the requirements of and specifications for all the aircraft in the RAF and their equipment, including guns, bombs and especially radar, about which Sholto was well placed to advise after his extensive involvement in its development and application over the preceding two years. He insisted too on being kept abreast of developments in radar methods that would identify friendly from hostile aircraft, known as Identification Friend or Foe (IFF),[1] although the Home Defence Exercise in 1938 revealed that there were still considerable difficulties with this technology.

Meanwhile, Sholto continued to be deeply concerned by what was still happening in Spain, which he described as 'a sacrificial tragedy'.[2] His half-brother Donald had returned there in July 1937 as an International Brigader. He had recovered from his wrist wound, but his right hand and arm were damaged permanently. After brief spells in clerical positions due to his disability, he became bored and, deserting his post, he hopped on a lorry and went to the Teruel Front. He was allowed to join the Transmissions section of the British Battalion of the International Brigades and served in the Teruel sector until his repatriation to the UK in May 1938.

In Spain, the Germans made full use of their new Messerschmitt 109 fighter and their Junkers 87, the dive bomber known as the Stuka. It had a fearsome reputation that would strike terror into people's hearts in WWII and was the culmination of experiments in power-diving by Sholto's erstwhile house guest in Khartoum, Ernst Udet. The use of these aircraft convinced Sholto that Britain was being beaten by the Germans in the race to rearm. He and his fellow senior officers in the Air Ministry became very alarmed over the RAF's un-preparedness should Britain be forced to go to war against Germany in the immediate future. Far from being 'a pack of sabre-rattling war mongers',[3] with only a very few exceptions, senior officers in the services understood very well through their bitter experiences in WWI just what war would mean, and Sholto wrote that they wanted none of it.

This affected the attitude of some of them to the Munich crisis in September 1938, when Chamberlain consented to Hitler's annexa-tion of the Sudetenland portion of Czechoslovakia in order to avoid a pan-European confrontation with him. Sholto viewed this supreme example of failed appeasement in a largely pragmatic way. In no way did he believe in that policy, but for him and his colleagues at the Air Ministry in that summer of 1938, Britain's air defences were not in any shape to be able to bargain with Hitler, let alone to confront him. Unlike some, Sholto did not hold this opinion because he was wor-ried about the costs of rearmament but simply because of the lack of preparedness of the RAF, which was crucial to Britain's military capa-bility. It is well known that neither Winston Churchill nor Clement Attlee concurred with this view. Churchill stated in a speech in the House of Commons on 5 October 1938, five days after Chamberlain and Hitler had signed the Munich agreement:

We have passed an awful milestone in our history, when the whole equilibrium of Europe has been deranged, and that the terrible words have for the time being been pronounced against the Western democracies: 'Thou art weighed in the balance and found wanting.' And do not suppose that this is the end. This is only the beginning of the reckoning.[4]

In Sholto's opinion, prescient though Churchill's words may have been, he and his personal scientific adviser, Professor Lindemann, had interfered unhelpfully in Air Ministry discussions regarding the dire state of the UK's defences, creating 'an extraordinarily political and far from happy atmosphere'.[5] Lindemann consistently pressed his own agenda for such outlandish ideas as 'aerial mines' and undermined valuable work on radar. Sholto wrote that Lindemann never really believed in radar, which was problematic when he had Churchill's ear.

In July 1938, Sholto had been appointed chairman of a new inter-service committee to keep all three services informed of progress in RDF research, development, application and production.[6] In December, he also became a member of the two Tizard Committees, for the Scientific Survey of Air Defence and the Scientific Survey of Air Offence, and used the opportunity to keep his Air Tactics section fully up to date with all developments initiated by these committees. On the Offence Committee, he also worked with Henry Tizard to devise a realistic programme to resolve problems regarding a possible bomber offensive against Germany, especially difficulties with navigation, target identification and bombing by night. Sholto felt that those at Bomber Command were enmeshed in impractical solutions and unnecessary detail. Problems would continue well into WWII, when at first bombing was inaccurate and appallingly costly in bomber crews without being effective.

Sholto expressed his steadily mounting sense of alarm during the summer and early autumn of 1938 as forcefully as he could in an eloquent written plea to support the theory that everything possible should be done to try to postpone the outbreak of war for at least a year so that the RAF might have a chance to reach air parity with the Germans. Newall used Sholto's paper as a basis for his own appreciation that he submitted to the Secretary of State for Air, Sir Kingsley Wood, who oversaw a huge increase in the production of warplanes to bring Britain up to parity with Germany.

Almost immediately after the Munich crisis, Kingsley Wood called for a thorough reappraisal of the situation as it affected the air, and the next RAF expansion plan, which Sholto deemed the most crucial of the numerous schemes that had been proposed since 1934, Scheme M, was the result. It was the last of these to be developed before the outbreak of WWII and attempted to rectify the mistakes and inadequacies of the past, giving the highest priority to the strengthening and equipping of Fighter Command. The next highest priority was the re-equipment of Bomber Command with new heavy bombers.

Sholto's fears concerning the preparedness of the RAF for war were vindicated later by the historian Denis Richards, who wrote:

In September 1938, to oppose the German long-range striking force of some 1,200 modern bombers, Fighter Command could muster, including all reserves, only 93 of the new eight-gun fighters. All the remainder of its 666 aircraft were the outdated biplanes. No Spitfires were yet in the line; and the Hurricanes, being without heating for their guns, could not fight above 15,000 feet, even in summer. A year later, when war came, over 500 of these modern fighters were immediately available for operations.[7]

It may have been Sholto's anxieties about the state of Britain's aerial defences that prompted him to support the supply to Fighter Command of the Defiant, said by some to be one of the most unsuccessful fighters ever to take to the air, although he did not instigate its development, as some historians imply. The success of the Bristol Fighter in WWI caused the Air Ministry to issue a specification in 1935 calling for a similar two-seater fighter fitted with a gun turret. Unsurprisingly, the turret was heavy and unreliable, but the Defiant still seemed like a good idea, especially for attacks on bombers. In January 1938, an order was made for 389 Defiants, and then in April 1938 when Sholto had just taken over as ACAS, the Air Fighting Committee decided to increase the order to 450. Sholto requested that Dowding form nine squadrons of Defiants, asserting that 'for work over enemy territory, a two-seater is best'. He was thinking again of mitigating aircrew losses. Dowding opposed this idea vigorously, and his views prevailed to the extent that when the Battle of Britain started, Fighter Command had only two Defiant squadrons.[8]

However, it seems that some historians have been somewhat unfair in their judgement of Sholto and his views on Defiants. Over the next few months, his opinions altered, so that by August he was advising against increasing the proportion of two-seaters materially.

As if Sholto didn't have enough to be concerned about, his sense of apprehension took a few steps up in the summer of 1939, but in a quite different and more acute way. On 28 June, just over two months before the outbreak of WWII, he experienced the closest encounter that he ever had with death while flying, more serious even than the collision with the plough horse back in 1917. At that time, most of those who had attained senior positions in the RAF had served in WWI and had experienced crashes in aircraft, and Sholto observed that a surprisingly large number were killed even after reaching air rank. On this occasion, he was accompanying Sir Kingsley Wood on an official visit to Belfast along with Air Marshal Sir Christopher Courtney, by now the C-in-C of Reserve Command. They were being flown in a De Havilland (DH) 86 and ran into some foul weather over the Irish Sea, such that by the time the aircraft approached the Irish coast they were flying blind. The pilot became disorientated and allowed the aircraft to go into a spin. Sholto could see from the altimeter in the cabin that they were losing height rapidly with no sight of the ground. Sholto wrote: 'I began to feel with a tightening of the throat and a rather clammy certainty that I was about to face my last moment.'[9] Fortunately, the pilot was able to regain control of the aircraft within only a few hundred feet of the ground, and as he pulled out of the spin Sholto saw the tops of the trees flashing past just beneath them. With his heart in his mouth, he realised then that they were flying straight towards the side of a steep hill, but the pilot managed to pull the aircraft up, narrowly clear the top of the hill and climb above the 10,000 feet thick layer of cloud. He realised that it was no use carrying on to Belfast, so he turned back towards

England, making for Blackpool aerodrome. The aircraft started down through the cloud once again, those on board expecting to find themselves over Morecambe Bay, but when they broke cloud, they found they were at a height of only 2,000 feet among what looked like mountains. The plane was nearly out of fuel, so the pilot decided to put it down on the nearest place that he could, and they landed in a heap on a mountainside. Fortunately, Sholto was sitting towards the back of the aircraft and as soon as it came to a halt, he scrambled out of the wreckage as fast as he could, thinking it might burst into flames. He told my mother later that he was surprised and ashamed at how strongly his instinct for self-preservation kicked in, making him get away from the aircraft rather than staying with everyone else, each of whom had sustained some kind of injury. He did, however, manage to assess the condition of his companions before going for help. Wood had received such a bang on the head that he had been knocked out; his parliamentary private secretary, Sir Edward Campbell, had sustained a broken wrist; the pilot was injured; and the co-pilot had also suffered a head injury and a broken ankle. Sholto realised that his friend Chris Courtney had a leg injury that turned out to be a fractured kneecap. Despite this, he had crawled out of the wreckage almost as quickly as Sholto, realising that there was a danger of fire.

To complicate matters, the mountains were shrouded in thick mist and they had no idea where they were, but being the only one who was unharmed, Sholto set off at random, picking his way through the wet heather that covered the hills. After a quarter of a mile, he found himself at the head of a steep slope that led down into a valley, at the bottom of which was a stone hut with smoke rising from its chimney. Scrambling down the slope, which must have been difficult in uniform without walking boots, Sholto made his way to the hut and banged on the door. When it was opened, he saw three shepherds sitting around a fire, who must have been flabbergasted at seeing a senior RAF officer in full uniform standing in the doorway. It emerged that they were at the southern end of the Lake District, about five miles north of Ulverston. One of the men set off for Ulverston to get help, and the other two climbed back up the slopes with

Sholto to the crashed aircraft. The rain set in and very soon everyone was soaking wet. Sholto and the shepherds managed to get the injured back into the shelter of the broken cabin and a small degree of comfort while they awaited an ambulance. Throughout these events Wood remained calm despite having sustained a bad blow to the head. To Sholto's great surprise, Wood was back at his desk in the Air Ministry the following day.

Sholto and his colleagues there were undeterred in their efforts to increase war readiness. It had been agreed at a meeting he had chaired in September 1938 that work on the radar chain should be stepped up to reach completion by 1 April 1939. Further progress was made also on AI. In early July 1939, following a flight demonstration, Dowding wrote an enthusiastic report to the Air Ministry, recommending further tests. Sholto, who appreciated fully the inadequacies of night defences, initiated a scheme in which a Blenheim was fitted with AI radar so that the tactical use of the equipment could be worked out. This was to be given top priority. Furthermore, he instructed that twenty-one AI sets should be made by hand. Four Blenheims were to be equipped with the sets, which was achieved by 30 August, and these experimental aircraft were attached to a special flight of No. 25 Squadron. A day later, war was declared.

At meetings of the Inter-Service RDF Committee in September and October, Sholto pressed for further progress stressing that every first line Blenheim fighter would need to be equipped with an AI set.[10]

Just before the advent of WWII, the Air Ministry organised a reserve operations and intelligence centre at Garston, to the north of Watford, as a precautionary measure against enemy air attack. Sholto and his staff were instructed to move there on 2 September 1939, and he was put in charge of the entire organisation, codenamed 'Z'. He was to exercise operational control over the RAF should the Air Ministry be bombed to oblivion. There was even a duplicate war room in case the one in Whitehall was knocked out, which the Air Staff thought was a distinct possibility due to the heavy bombing they expected from the Germans.

The Senior Staff Officer in charge of the practicalities of the move was Group Captain R. V. (Victor) Goddard, who had been acting Deputy Director of Intelligence in the Air Ministry at the time of the SCW. He was required to find Sholto a billet in the vicinity, and later wrote of that time:

> Sholto Douglas was one of the ablest, coolest men I have known. Great clarity of mind and independence of thought marked all his Service judgments and actions. If ever his judgment erred more than a little it could have been in regard to his own remarkably powerful metabolism, for he was already showing signs of a future Falstaffian grandeur of figure. Certainly he had excellent judgment of men, wine, and other matters demanding insight and subtle discernment fortified by experience and moral courage. This faculty he applied to air power. He was a spacious man of wide interests and he needed space for living.[11]

I remember from when I was a child that Sholto's excuse for his large girth, which persisted to the end of his life and became increasingly problematic for him, was that his time as a rower while up at Oxford had developed his abdominal muscles, and when he stopped rowing they turned to fat. It seems more likely that his increasingly sedentary life at the Air Ministry in the 1930s, coupled with a large appetite and generous intake of alcohol, to which Goddard alluded also, had contributed to his obesity. However, there is a less parsimonious explanation. Sandy McFarlane, director of the Centre for Traumatic Stress Studies at the University of Adelaide, suggested in a 2017 paper with his colleagues that we should no longer consider PTSD as a purely mental illness but as a full systemic disorder, one of the features of which is abdominal obesity.

It was far-sighted for the times that Goddard linked Sholto's metabolism (and 'Falstaffian' girth) with his judgement, albeit in a humorous way, as relatively recent research has shown that those suffering from PTSD demonstrate abnormalities in working memory, which indicate that the brain has to 'work much harder' in order to maintain concentration and memory, even though an individual's neuropsychological profile may be normal. Certainly, no one, Goddard included, would have realised that there was anything wrong with Sholto – he continued to function at a very high level – but the incipient PTSD from which he suffered would have affected not only his concentration and memory but also his judgement.[12] Despite Goddard's fine assessment of Sholto, especially as a senior officer he made some seemingly inexplicable errors that continue to perplex me (and historians) every time I read about them. Of course, all military leaders make mistakes, notwithstanding the extreme pressure under which they have to work at times, but is one possible explanation for this that they are having to contend with the cumulative effects of the trauma that they have had to endure while climbing the military ladder?

The timing of Sholto's move to Garston could not have been worse, since he and his staff were removed from each other and from their colleagues in the Air Ministry. This had a negative effect on his own work, he felt, and the efficiency of his group as a whole, coming as close as it did to the full mobilisation of the services on 1 September 1939 and the Prime Minister's broadcast on 3 September that marked the start of war with Germany. Decades later, Sholto could remember vividly his thoughts and reactions on hearing that speech. He recalled saying to himself: 'My God ... we've got to take those bastards on all over again ... We finished them off twenty years ago. Why do we have to start off all over again?'[13] Gone were the eagerness and enthusiasm to fight for king and country that had marked the start of WWI for Sholto and many others. They were replaced with a sombre anger at the evil of fascism, Nazism in particular, which had been thrust upon the world and now had to be destroyed.

On that Sunday morning, while Sholto was sitting at his desk in Garston mulling over the Prime Minister's broadcast and even wondering what his former German adversaries in WWI, now at the top of the Luftwaffe, were thinking, the air-raid sirens sounded the first alarm of the war. Sholto's secretary, a civilian, seemed to be in no hurry, and lingered in Sholto's office having listened to the speech, so he told her firmly to get down to the shelter as soon as possible. As they anticipated an immediate enemy attack, he joined his staff there.

They all expected a ferocious aerial onslaught at any moment, but after ten minutes the all-clear signal sounded, and they returned rather self-consciously to their offices. It turned out to be a false alarm, caused by a radar blip indicating an unidentified aircraft, which appeared on the operations room tables of Fighter Command. It was in fact from a French aircraft on its way to Croydon with some French officers on board. No warning of this flight had been passed to Fighter Command, and it was reassuring that those in charge of the UK's air defences were on high alert. This seemingly insignificant event heralded the start of the war.

CHAPTER TWELVE

AN EVIL DREAM WORLD

Despite the Air Staff's anxieties about being bombed and gassed, the war at the start turned out to be quite different from their expectations, and the RAF was left with little more to do than stand guard during what was called the 'phoney war', which lasted until 10 May 1940 when Germany attacked France and the Low Countries. Sholto felt that this period was demoralising for the RAF, which was held back. He had expected that the Air Force would be ordered to start attacking Germany and was convinced that this should have been what happened, even decades later. One of Sholto's contemporaries at the Air Ministry, Air Commodore Jack Slessor, remarked, 'One lived in a sort of evil dream world.'[1] A large part of the Luftwaffe was engaged in the offensive against Poland, and it is entirely probable that the Poles would have held out for longer if the Allies had responded in the air, and perhaps even on the ground, thus exposing Germany to a war on two fronts, as Hitler always feared. Instead, the RAF was, in Sholto's words, 'restricted to the ridiculous and humiliating business of dropping senseless leaflets over Germany',[2] which achieved nothing.

As he had at the beginning of WWI, the indefatigable Langton displayed his eagerness to share once more in his sons' experience, even at the age of seventy-five. In August 1939, he wrote an extraordinary letter to the Under Secretary of State for War explaining that he had already called twice at the War Office to offer his services 'in any capacity' and had been assured that he would be given employment. He added:

I am in excellent health, and am just as fit in mind and body as I was in 1914. I am not a 'retired' officer or a 'retired' civilian: I have never ceased to work hard. In fact, I work just as hard to-day as I did as a young man.

He received a polite but curt reply, thanking him for the offer but regretting that 'there is no direction at the moment in which your services could be utilized'.[3]

Meanwhile, back at the top of the RAF, the conduct of the war continued to be a source of frustration to Sholto and his colleagues at the Air Ministry, who watched with trepidation as the government's inaction enabled Hitler to regroup his forces after he had defeated Poland and prepare them for his attack on France and the Low Countries. Sholto's dismay over British policy had been compounded when he and the CAS, Cyril Newall, had visited the leaders of the French Air Force just before the outbreak of war. They found that once mighty service, which had been such a gallant ally in WWI, depleted beyond recognition.

It was known among the Air Staff that little progress in aircraft design had been made in France in the interwar years, but what Sholto and Newall witnessed on this visit shocked and horrified them. French fighters were not remotely on a par with the Hurricanes and Spitfires now in large-scale production, and the bombers were almost non-existent. On paper, the French had numerical strength in their squadrons, but they were composed of hopelessly outdated aircraft, leading Sholto and Newall to realise that if the war moved west, nothing much could be expected from their ally.

A British Expeditionary Force (BEF), accompanied by an Air Component of reconnaissance and fighter squadrons to work with the Army and an independent Advanced Air Striking Force (AASF) of bombers and fighters, was sent to France as soon as WWII was declared. However, the British Air Forces were stretched beyond measure over the whole of the Allied front in France. Furthermore, the clamour from the French government for additional air support from the UK, including the use of British home-based bombers, started even before they went to war with Germany and grew increasingly desperate over the next eight months. There was no plan on the French side, just 'pathetic pleas'[4] for more air reinforcements. Sholto was given the unenviable task of approaching Dowding in person to discuss sending more of his squadrons to France. Sholto drove over to Fighter Command HQ, a short drive from Garston, and even took with him the Director of Staff Duties, Air Commodore Robin Willock, for moral support, but the mission was doomed to failure from the start. Dowding gave them a smart rebuff, concerned as he was about maintaining his own numerical strength in the face of the possible onslaught to come.

A few weeks later, Sholto and his staff were moved back from Garston to Air Staff HQ in Whitehall, where he pursued one of his particular interests since before the start of the war, the formation of OTUs, initially called Group Pools because of their attachment to individual groups within the commands. The purpose of OTUs was to provide pilots and aircrews with final advanced training on operational aircraft before being posted to fighting squadrons. Sholto was convinced of their importance because of his experiences in WWI, when as a young squadron commander at the Front he had received raw pilots straight out of Flying Training Schools (FTSs) with no more than a few hours' flying to their credit. Despite efforts to give these pilots their final training at the Front, they still went into battle unprepared, and as a result, casualties were high.

Sholto was determined that this should not happen again, so he seized the opportunity as a senior officer to push for the creation of these units. He and his staff also developed equipment that was the forerunner of flight simulators that are so essential today in both military and civil aviation. These pieces of equipment, known then as 'synthetic trainers', were given almost instant Treasury approval. However, it was no easy task to get the OTU scheme started. Due to the rapid expansion of front-line squadrons, there were problems in obtaining enough operational aircraft and experienced crews to make it workable. Eventually, though, sufficient aircraft and personnel were found to begin, despite objections from Dowding, from whom

Sholto least expected opposition. Dowding was more concerned with the building up of his front-line squadrons, and in his opinion, OTUs interfered with that aim.

Knowing Dowding's strong feelings about casualties, which went back to WWI when losses were high, particularly in the Somme battles, Sholto was bemused by his objections, and subsequent events strengthened Sholto's case. Eventually, he was able to convince Dowding of the benefits of the scheme, at least temporarily, and by the time of the Battle of Britain nine months later, three Fighter Command OTUs existed. However, during the battle their output was inadequate to meet the casualty rate, and it was not even possible to supply the necessary intake from FTSs.

During the bitterly cold winter of 1939–40, the 'phoney war' in the west dragged on, and there were few occasions when Sholto could drag himself away from his desk in Whitehall to visit his units in the field. One such opportunity came on New Year's Day 1940, when he set off with his old friend Harold Balfour, by then Under-Secretary of State for Air, to visit the AASF and units of the Air Component of the BEF in France. When they arrived at Hendon aerodrome to begin their journey, it was shrouded in thick fog, with visibility down to less than fifty yards. They were reassured by the pilot of their twin-engined aircraft, an experienced veteran of Imperial Airways, that the weather reports indicated that the fog was local and not actually very thick, so he felt they could proceed. Nevertheless, as soon as the pilot lifted the aircraft off the ground, they found themselves enveloped in dense fog with no visibility at all. Just at that moment, when they needed every bit of power available, there was a loud bang from the port engine and Sholto was horrified to see that the top of one of the cylinder heads was protruding above the engine cowling. At the most critical moment of take-off, the pilot was left with only one functioning engine, and it was all too obvious what might happen next. Once again, Sholto was in a dire situation. Hendon was not a large aerodrome and was surrounded by houses, with the ground sloping upwards in the direction the aircraft was heading. Balfour and Sholto looked at each other and could read each other's thoughts with no difficulty whatsoever.

However, instead of the disaster that could so easily have supervened, the pilot, who was not only experienced but very capable, maintained a slow, steady climb, missing the roofs of the houses that lined the edge of the airfield. By the time they reached 1,000 feet, they were clear of the fog and in bright sunshine. With only one engine, they could not risk turning back and landing in dense fog, but they were told on the radio that Shoreham was clear, so they made their way there, changed aircraft and went on their way to France.

In March 1940, at the instigation of Dowding and Tizard, a Night Interception Committee was formed to coordinate all the efforts being made to solve the problems of defence against night attack. AI was discussed frequently and Dowding was keen to get it into service. At the first meeting, the Fighter Interception Unit (FIU) was formed, commanded by Wing Commander Peter Chamberlain. Early on, Chamberlain met with Dowding who explained the problems of night interception and offered him all the facilities necessary to develop AI into practical usefulness. Thereafter, there was an influx of scientists into the FIU, who quickly bonded with the ninety-two officers and airmen provided by the RAF. They achieved the first airborne radar intercepted 'kill' in history on the night of 22/23 July 1940, when a Blenheim intercepted an enemy Dornier Do17 aircraft and sent it plunging into the sea off the Sussex coast south of Bognor Regis. The German crew was rescued later.

In April 1940, soon after the formation of the Night Interception Committee and just before the end of the phoney war, Sholto was promoted to Deputy Chief of the Air Staff (DCAS), an appointment which brought him closer to actual operations than any other post he had held in the Air Ministry. He was responsible for the day-to-day operations of the whole of the RAF and had under his command the Directorates of Home and Overseas Operations and of Military and Naval Cooperation. An examination of Sholto's correspondence as DCAS provides a picture of a man tireless and unceasing in his efforts to assist and advise in the wide range of areas for which he was responsible. He was worried by the strength of the Luftwaffe and the way it was being used relative to the strength of Fighter Command. Did it have sufficient fighters to defend the UK and its nearest allies, and to combat the challenge of German bombers? Could it face down the fury that Hitler now turned on the west, having disposed so comprehensively of Poland? Sholto's championing of fighters over bombers had run counter to prevailing Air Staff orthodoxy, and because of it, he was surprised that he was able to make such progress in his military career. Few fighter pilots attained high command in the service or served on the Air Council before and during WWII. Now, his concern was the security of the base, and Alan Brooke's words resounded in his ears from when they had served together as instructors at the Imperial Defence College: 'You must make your base secure before you start launching an offensive.'[5]

For Sholto, that meant having adequate fighter defences before even contemplating an effective bomber offensive. Contrary to his earlier stance in 1936, he wrote that now he strongly opposed the prevailing opinion that RAF bombers would be able to bomb Germany in daylight without fighter escorts. It wasn't only the Air Staff who needed to be convinced of the importance of fighter cover. Those in the Army and Navy also had to be persuaded. However, the losses they sustained in 1940, particularly of soldiers in Norway and France, radically changed their opinion, to the extent that the Army went to the other extreme and demanded a 'fighter umbrella' at all times. The RAF was compelled to point out that this could only be realised at the most extravagant cost of keeping constant standing patrols in the air from bases that were reasonably close to the area over which the 'umbrella' was required, and this was impracticable and impossible with the aircraft that were available.

The Stukas, or dive bombers, so feared in Spain were devastatingly powerful against British troops in France in 1940. Their effectiveness was heightened by the terror they struck into soldiers' hearts as they whined down in a horrifying dive onto their targets. Nevertheless, in level flight they were slow and inefficient, and easy prey for British fighters, whose pilots 'almost wept with joy whenever they ran across any Stukas'.[6]

Sholto's appointment as DCAS in April 1940 came in the middle of the ill-fated Norwegian campaign. He was deeply involved in the air side of that operation and learned a great many painful lessons from what was an almost entirely disastrous venture. The Germans attacked Norway on the night of 8/9 April 1940 using their Blitzkrieg tactics and quickly occupied a large part of the country, aiming to secure crucial shipping routes for iron ore and use Norway as a launching place for an attack against the UK. The British Navy launched a counterattack on 10 April.

Two days later, Bomber Command under the leadership of its new C-in-C, Charles 'Peter' Portal, began its largest operation attempted to date in WWII, to find and attack enemy warships in the North Sea. Coastal Command had spotted the German battle cruisers *Scharnhorst* and *Gneisenau* in the northern part of the North Sea, and Portal sent out ninety-two aircraft in pursuit, but they failed to locate the ships. This would cost the Allies dearly as the battle proceeded. Twelve Hampden bombers did attack another enemy warship at Kristiansand on the south coast of Norway, but they were engaged by German fighters and, lacking any fighter escorts, were mown down until only six of them survived. This reinforced the lessons from previous encounters in WWII that unescorted bombers would suffer heavily if sent by day within range of German fighters.

Allied troops were landed at Norwegian ports on 14 April, but from the beginning, as Denis Richards put it, they were 'ludicrously short of anti-aircraft guns' and there was insufficient fighter cover for these ground forces.[7] The Air Staff grossly overestimated the ability of the Navy to get troops and stores ashore, and the RAF found it impossible to establish an air operation in Norway, as the Germans had seized the established airfields right from the start of their campaign.

The task of finding suitable sites for British fighter bases in Norway was given to a young Auxiliary Air Force fighter pilot named Whitney Straight, who was also an enthusiastic civil pilot as well as a racing car driver and who was to become a close friend of Sholto's. He found a landing site in central Norway on frozen Lake Lesjakog, inland from Aandalsnes on the coast where he had landed, and within two hours, he had enlisted the help of 200 Norwegian civilians – a remarkable number in such an isolated place – to clear the two-foot layer of snow on the lake sufficiently to make a runway.

For a single day, No. 263 Squadron flew from this improvised airfield to provide fighter cover for the Army. However, despite the pilots' courageous efforts in the air, and the heroic work of a small party of naval personnel manning two Oerlikon guns near the lake, on 25 April, German air attacks by Heinkel 111s flying over the lake bombing and machine-gunning meant that by the end of that day, only five serviceable British aircraft were left out of eighteen that had landed on the ice, which had been broken up by repeated German bombing and the aircraft set on fire. The next day, only three remained, and the day after that, nil. The surviving pilots were withdrawn by sea in a cargo vessel and, despite numerous attacks from German bombers, reached Scapa Flow safely on 1 May.

The squadron was re-formed and on 22 May, it resurfaced in northern Norway as part of the force intended to capture the port of Narvik, inside the Arctic Circle. Joined by No. 46, over the next exceptionally strenuous fortnight, they played a major part in the operation, the only victory in the Norwegian campaign. The Allied forces managed to destroy the port facilities, and their success was such that no cargo of iron ore left Narvik for Germany until January 1941. However, the immediate victory was short-lived as an all-out German attack meant that they too had to be evacuated. The Gladiators of No. 263 were told to land on HMS *Glorious*, lying off the coast, which they did at midnight on 7 June, but it was thought that the Hurricanes of No. 46 could not be landed on the deck of the aircraft carrier, so the order was given for them to be destroyed. The Hurricane pilots had never made a landing on a carrier, but they pleaded with their CO to be allowed to do so, and in the end, after a day of heavy fighting and nearing exhaustion, every one of the ten pilots managed to land their aircraft safely on *Glorious*.

In a most tragic and cruel twist, however, the following day, the carrier was found and sunk within two hours by the *Scharnhorst*, which was on the prowl off the coast of Norway with its sister ship *Gneisenau*. In total, 1,474 officers and men of the Royal Navy went down in the blazing ship, as well as thirty-nine of the forty-one pilots of both RAF squadrons, and all the aircraft. The two remaining pilots clambered onto a Carley raft, managing somehow to defy 'the Arctic cold, the promptings of despair, and the sight of twenty-five of their fellow survivors on the raft dying before their eyes', before they were picked up by a passing fishing vessel.[8]

Sholto and his colleagues were appalled when news of this disaster reached the Air Ministry. They knew that they had made huge mistakes in their planning for the operation in Norway, and that the Army had been unrealistic in their expectations of being able to land troops and supplies ashore and maintain them there. As Major-General Kenneth Strong, who became Director General of Defence Intelligence after distinguished service as a senior intelligence officer in WWII, wrote:

I find it difficult to understand how any plan can be made in the absence of a professional assessment of an opponent's strength, capabilities and intentions. The Norwegian campaign was neither the first nor last example of this extraordinary syndrome in Britain, and other countries have not been free from it.[9]

For Sholto, the most bitter lesson learned was that 'it was impossible to conduct operations without fighter cover in an area in which the enemy air force could operate freely from secure bases'.[10]

The dismal failure of the operation in Norway propelled Parliament into action to remove 'an ineffectual government that was a hang-over from the days of peace',[11] and on 10 May 1940, the day that Hitler launched his Blitzkrieg in the west, Winston Churchill became Prime Minister. The irony was that it was Churchill, at that point First Lord of the Admiralty, who pressed most strongly for the Norway campaign, as he had for an equally ill-fated but smaller expedition to Antwerp during WWI in October 1914. In both cases, the forces deployed were 'sent to the wrong place too late, too weak and ludicrously ill-equipped'. Churchill's 'predilections for forlorn endeavour in remote places were high among his weaknesses as a war leader'.[12] Chamberlain's departure was hastened by two Labour politicians: the leader of the party, Clement Attlee, and his deputy, Arthur Greenwood. When Chamberlain resigned on 9 May, they supported Churchill in his acceptance of the King's commission to form a government.

In the early hours of 10 May, Sholto was telephoned at his flat in central London with news of the German onslaught on France and the Low Countries by a member of his staff on duty at the Air Ministry. He hurried to his office immediately. At 6.30 a.m., the Dutch Ambassador arrived asking to see the CAS. Since Sholto was the senior officer on duty at the time, he was brought to his office. There followed an acutely difficult conversation in which the Ambassador, who had been up all night and who was obviously distraught, begged Sholto to order squadrons of fighters to be sent at once to the Netherlands.

There was nothing that Sholto could do about this request, and he explained to the Ambassador, with the ongoing Norway debacle to the forefront of his mind, that the RAF had no prepared bases in the Netherlands from which fighters could operate with consistent supplies of ammunition, fuel, oil and everything else that was needed for operations. Sholto felt that it would be cruel to remind the Ambassador that a short time prior to this, the Air Staff had asked the Dutch government if they could discuss proposals for setting up a skeleton organisation for fighter operations in the Netherlands but the Dutch politicians had refused even to talk about it. Sholto assured the Ambassador that the RAF would endeavour to cover the west coast of the Netherlands from fighter bases in England. By this time, the Ambassador was acutely distressed, and to Sholto's dismay, he dropped his head forward on his arms on Sholto's desk and wept. Sholto understood the strain under which the unfortunate Ambassador laboured and felt for him the greatest sympathy. Such emotional scenes were not uncommon in the higher echelons of the service or in government, and in the privacy of their offices at the Air Ministry, some senior commanders were very close to breaking point through stress, anxiety and exhaustion. Sholto described the weeks following this unfortunate incident as 'the most horrible of my life'.[13]

Due to the danger of bombing, Newall ruled that all senior Air Staff officers based in the Air Ministry should sleep on the premises. A series of what Sholto called 'horrible little concrete dungeons'[14] had been equipped as sleeping quarters in the basement of the building in King Charles Street in Whitehall. Newall was unceasingly conscientious and probably worked the hardest of everyone, being in his office until 2 a.m. and then sleeping for only four or five hours in one of the 'dungeons' before returning to his duties in the early morning. He was showing signs of strain, having been CAS since 1937 during the build-up to WWII and subject to the intense pressure that came when war was declared. Sholto saw him following this regime for weeks on end, exercising over himself the most rigid self-control and not leaving the building except to go to conferences elsewhere in Whitehall. Sholto observed that consequently 'Newall became an absolute bag of nerves'.[15]

Although it has never been documented, and certainly, Newall himself would never have admitted this, it is possible that his mental fragility was indicative of covert combat stress or PTSD, as well as simple exhaustion. As Newall became less and less effective, Sholto increasingly took on Newall's duties as well as his own, and was definitely overworked, staying in his office until midnight, but sleeping in the little cells in the basement was not for him. His feelings were shared by the Vice-CAS (VCAS), Richard Peirse, so the two of them took it in turns to sleep on the premises every other night.

The months of May and June flashed by in that early summer of 1940, with one disaster following another. Hitler's forces quickly occupied the Netherlands and most of Belgium, and then came the catastrophe of Dunkirk on 26 May, ending on 4 June. Dowding needed every ounce of his famous single-mindedness to withstand pressure from the Cabinet, and less so from the Air Staff, to surrender his precious forces to the battle that was raging in France, when what he most wanted was to reserve them for the air defence of Britain.

CHAPTER THIRTEEN

MORE CATASTROPHE

As if fulfilling Dowding's worst fears, in the second week of May 1940, Newall received instructions from the War Cabinet to send more squadrons to France. It was then that Dowding made a stand. A crucial Cabinet meeting was called on 15 May to consider the latest request from the French Prime Minister for ten more fighter squadrons. The new Secretary of State for Air, Sir Archibald Sinclair, and Newall were at that meeting, as was Dowding himself at his own request. The RAF squadrons in France had suffered severe losses already, and everyone on the Air Staff knew that sending more of them would be tantamount to throwing them away. At a critical point in the meeting, Dowding, who had the figures of the fighting of the previous few days in front of him, said to Churchill: 'If the present rate of wastage continues for another fortnight, we shall not have a single Hurricane left in France or in this country.' Sholto learned from Assistant Secretary of the War Cabinet Secretariat, his friend Group Captain William Elliott, that the atmosphere was the most highly charged emotionally that he had ever known. Dowding was white in the face with strain, but he made his appeal so ably and sincerely that there was no further room for discussion.

Also at the Cabinet meeting, it was decided to begin the bombing of Germany, and as Sholto put it, 'Bomber Command was let off the leash.'[1] Its C-in-C, Peter Portal, agreed with Dowding that the best way to help the French was to attack Germany. This might also obviate the sending of more fighter squadrons to France, so that evening there began what became known as the strategic air offensive against Germany, which was to continue almost unabated and controversially for the next five years. At a conference in the Air Ministry on 28 April, at which both Dowding and Sholto were present, Portal had suggested that the RAF should not wait until the Germans had occupied the Low Countries before starting the air offensive against Germany, and the VCAS, Richard Peirse, had agreed that intensive air operations should begin as soon as the Germans made their first move. But Sholto had urged caution, saying that with the current delays in the supply of vital equipment, that moment should not be anticipated. He added that an improvement in the fighter situation was a long-term prospect, though events would probably necessitate action before then, but nevertheless, even taking a shorter-term view, he thought the RAF would gain by refraining from major air action until at least June, when equipment difficulties would be on their way to resolution. He obviously realised that an air offensive against Germany would invite retaliation against the UK, and he wanted Fighter Command to be as ready as possible.

On 14 May, the day before the crucial Cabinet meeting, the German bombing of Rotterdam, in which 20,000 buildings were destroyed, 78,000 people rendered homeless and nearly 1,000 inhabitants killed, removed any remaining doubts, and the bombing offensive against Germany was given the go-ahead. However, in thinking that losses at home would force the Germans to scale down their operations in France, Portal was making the same error as Dowding and Churchill, and as Sholto had made and would make in the future. To illustrate this, albeit in a slightly different context, Sholto had demonstrated this misjudgement of German motivation in an extraordinary memo dated 11 August 1938, for which he has been criticised endlessly by historians. He wrote:

I think it is immaterial in the long view whether the enemy bomber is shot down before or after he has dropped his bombs on his objective. The object is <u>not</u> to prevent bombers reaching their objectives – though it would be very nice if we could – but to cause a high casualty rate among the enemy bombers, with the result that the scale of attack will dwindle rapidly to bearable proportions.[2]

Surprisingly, Dowding was guilty of a similar error of judgement, writing to the Air Staff two months after Sholto's memo that 'Home Defence must be brought about by the cumulative effect on the enemy's morale of heavy casualties'.[3] The over-arching misconception to which Churchill and all these senior RAF officers fell prey was that, as Terraine observed:

> The Germans did not regulate their system of war by casualties and damage, they regulated it by objectives. Both wars showed that it requires a very great many casualties indeed to make a German High Command change its mind, and the remainder of the Second World War would show the unbelievable amount of damage that a German High Command would accept without doing so.[4]

Despite repeated attacks on German targets by Bomber Command for the rest of May and into June, the heavy bombers deployed achieved none of their objectives. Industrial damage in Germany was slight, and the delay inflicted on the German Army in its progress across France was negligible. The Germans did not divert a single fighter, bomber or anti-aircraft gun from attacking French armies. Most of all, Bomber Command's assault on the Ruhr, a pet project of the Air Staff, was a failure. Once again, although the conception of the operation was good, poor timing and inadequate forces made it another fiasco, seeming to justify Sholto's concerns about equipment.

In an extraordinary twist of fate, while Sholto in his senior position was mulling over bombing policy in the Air Ministry during that summer of 1940, his half-brother Donald, twenty-two years his junior, was experiencing exactly what it was like flying over Germany as a member of an RAF bomber crew. He had trained as an air gunner (something of which he had had experience in Spain), and on completion of his training he was posted to No. 50 (Bomber) Squadron, equipped with Hampden bombers for sorties across Europe and into Germany. Donald flew as a rear gunner in a Hampden crew of four that also included a pilot, navigator/bomb-aimer and wireless operator. As Max Hastings has written, 'The rear gunner faced the loneliest and coldest night of all.'[5] He was wedged tightly into the freezing cold tiny space at the back of the aircraft that he could not leave for at least the next six or seven hours. He had no parachute – that was behind him in the aircraft – and he could not lose concentration for a minute, as that could mean certain death for him and the rest of the crew. The life expectancy of a rear gunner was incredibly short; estimates vary but suggest that they could expect to be shot down, or killed, within two weeks, or up to five operations.

Donald wrote to his brother Terence in August with a description emblematic of the difficulties in the bomber offensive over Germany. He had been out on two operations, and his crew had encountered neither anti-aircraft fire nor fighters but only searchlights. This he attributed to the cloudy weather with no moon, and to his great disappointment, the crew could not see where they were dropping their bombs or whether they had hit their targets. However, a few days later, Donald completed the letter by saying that his crew had 'visited' the *Flugzeugundmotorenfabrik Junkers* at Bernburg, and this time, they hit their target 'good and proper', being troubled only slightly by inaccurate anti-aircraft fire. He added with ghoulish humour that they had not 'visited' Traben-Trarbach yet, the town where Terence's parents-in-law lived.

Donald flew a total of eight sorties on Hampdens and was promoted to temporary sergeant after the first.[6] He was very pleased about this promotion because, as if the dangers in the air weren't enough, the food in the airmen's dining hall was 'becoming emetic'. Donald's experience near the bottom of the RAF was very different from his half-brother Sholto's at the top.

On 4 June, the day the Dunkirk evacuation was completed, in a letter to Portal that outlined the Air Staff's bombing policy, Sholto wrote, somewhat patronisingly: 'You will no doubt agree that the strenuous and gallant efforts of your squadrons against objectives in collaboration with the land battle since the 10 May have not always had results commensurate with the effort exerted.' In the same letter he reiterated that a major priority for bombing in Germany should be above-ground oil stocks, followed by aircraft factories and on dark nights other self-illuminating industrial targets to interrupt and dislocate the German war industry. However, he stressed that 'in no circumstances should night bombing be allowed to degenerate into mere indiscriminate action, which is contrary to the policy of His Majesty's Government'.[7]

As far as the land battle in France was concerned, Sholto admitted: 'The employment of medium bomber squadrons by day against troop movements again is liable to involve losses quite incommensurate with the results achieved unless the objectives are selected with great care and the attack can be carried out within a reasonably short time of the information being received by reconnaissance.' Importantly, he also stressed the need for adequate fighter support for the bombers, saying that in its absence daylight bombing of German logistics and troop columns 'could only be effected at an almost prohibitive rate of loss'. Once again, he stressed 'the need for avoiding, as far as possible, undue risk to the lives of French, Dutch or Belgian civilians'.

The advent of the Blitz in September 1940 caused Portal to review bombing policy, and to stress the importance of what became known as strategic bombing. He wrote:

Since the enemy's means to fight cannot be decisively reduced in the near future, it seems worth considering whether we might not weaken him more by a temporary change in our policy, directing our offensive primarily against the will of the German people to continue the war.

Widespread hardship and some degree of danger to the population of Germany, which can be brought about by the attack of legitimate military objectives, may be expected not only to induce a positive desire for peace but also to destroy that confidence in their leaders which at present sustains them and must be the sole basis of their desire to continue the war.

He added: 'If bombing is to have morale effect, it must sometimes produce heavy material destruction.'[8] However, despite the adoption of this draconian strategy, it would take another four and a half years to defeat Germany, and the effect on her morale was nowhere near what Portal anticipated. As is well known, the Germans made the same mistake in their assessment of the effect of the Blitz on British morale.

On 16 May, the day after that fateful Cabinet meeting, Dowding wrote a long official letter to the Air Ministry once again reminding the Air Staff of their estimate of fifty-two fighter squadrons needed to defend the UK, and that Fighter Command's strength had now been reduced to thirty-six squadrons. In a dignified but desperate plea, he pointed out that prior to the meeting, the equivalent of twelve squadrons had been sent to France. In the final paragraph he wrote:

> I believe that, if an adequate fighter force is kept in this country, if the fleet remains in being, and if Home Forces are suitably organised to resist invasion, we should be able to carry on the war single handed for some time, if not indefinitely. But, if the Home Defence Force is drained away in desperate attempts to remedy the situation in France, defeat in France will involve the final, complete and irremediable defeat of this country.[9]

Despite Dowding's eloquent plea, both at the Cabinet meeting and in his letter, the following day Sholto had to pass on to him the unpleasant news that the Cabinet had made a complete *volte-face* in the face of information received from the French that the Germans had broken through near Sedan in the north-east of France and French forces were being overwhelmed. The Cabinet requested therefore that four squadrons be sent immediately to France. Sholto had managed to alter the instruction to eight half-squadrons under the impression that the nucleus of eight squadrons would be preserved in the UK, and Fighter Command's strength would not be so severely drained. However, Dowding stated later that this assumption of Sholto's was incorrect because he had 'neither the time nor the personnel available for the purposes of reconstruction, and the remaining half-squadrons had to be amalgamated into composite units with resulting disorganisation and loss of efficiency'.[10] Dowding had now lost the equivalent of sixteen squadrons, and in addition, four squadrons were being sent to fight in France during the day, returning to English bases in the evening.

That same day, Churchill had a meeting with the French Prime Minister in Paris, and when he learned of the extreme disasters that were overwhelming France, he caved in under pressure, at the same time making a grave mistake in the estimate of fighter squadrons needed in the UK. He wired the Cabinet to ask for six more fighter squadrons to be sent to France, in addition to the eight half-squadrons already agreed. To the horror and incomprehension of the Air Staff, Sholto included, it looked at first as though the Cabinet would agree to this, but Newall held out against any further 'frittering away' of British forces and saved the day. He stressed that there were insufficient airfields or facilities to accommodate any extra squadrons, so it was agreed instead that operations over France should be launched from England.

The Air Staff learned later that Churchill, for some unknown reason, was labouring under a most serious misapprehension of the UK's fighter strength, which nearly led to the loss of the Battle of Britain before it had even begun. He was under the impression that Dowding had told him that only twenty-five squadrons would be needed to defend the UK, and this mistake went uncorrected even in his mammoth six-volume work *The Second World War*, first published in 1949, and in other accounts written by those who had been on the Air Staff at the time. Dowding would never have made this statement, and many years later, when Sholto was writing *Years of Command*, Dowding told him he had no idea how Churchill ever came to 'put such an absurd statement' into his mouth.

On 19 May 1940, Sholto pointed out to other members of the Air Staff that Dunkirk was further from the RAF's home bases than either Calais or Boulogne, and that this was a very important factor considering the limited endurance of its fighters. There were very great advantages to be gained by using these ports for embarkation of the BEF. However, Sholto's suggestion was overtaken by events that saw Calais surrounded and then surrendered to the Germans, and the British forces pinned down in a pocket around Dunkirk.

On 20 May, Fighter Command Order of Battle indicates that there were thirty squadrons of Spitfires and Hurricanes, six of Blenheims and one of Defiants, although the numbers of aircraft actually available for home defence were 247 Spitfires and only ninety-nine Hurricanes. So far, Dowding had kept Spitfires out of the battle in France because the supply position was 'poor'. However, on 26 May, the expulsion of British forces from France began with the evacuation from Dunkirk, so Dowding could no longer withhold his Spitfires. At the end of the evacuation, he had only three day-fighting squadrons that had not been engaged in Continental fighting, and twelve squadrons were in the line for the second time after having been withdrawn to rest and re-form.[11] Dowding wrote: 'All this time, it must be remembered, the attack on this country had not begun; with a few accidental exceptions no bomb had been dropped on our soil. I was responsible for the Air Defence of Great Britain, and I saw my resources slipping away like sand in an hour-glass.'[12]

The RAF was strongly criticised by the Army during and after the evacuation of its forces. Why were they subject to so many attacks by the Luftwaffe on the beaches, and *where was* the RAF? Sholto wrote in his autobiography that they did not understand that home-based RAF fighters operating from No. 11 Group airfields were working desperately hard inland and out of sight, endeavouring to hold back a much larger and heavier onslaught that the Luftwaffe was trying to launch at the beleaguered troops on the beaches. A report written in July 1940 by the Air Officer Commanding (AOC) No. 11 Group, Keith Park, stated that the group had provided 'almost continuous Fighter protection for the evacuation and passage across the Channel of the BEF, which lasted from 26th May to the early morning of 4th June'.[13] Despite criticisms from the BEF that the RAF was not much in evidence at the time of Dunkirk, both fighters and bombers played their part, as is amply shown by German records from the time.

Park sent wing patrols of three or more squadrons over France and Coastal Command also flew continuous daylight patrols from 28 May. In the nine days of the Dunkirk evacuation, the home-based RAF lost a total of 145 aircraft (excluding casualties of those aircraft borrowed from the Fleet Air Arm). Despite these losses and against the odds, over 338,000 Allied troops were evacuated successfully from Dunkirk.

Churchill became aware of the accusations against the RAF and defended it staunchly. In Parliament on 4 June, the day the evacuation was completed, he gave his famous 'We shall fight them on the beaches' speech, saying, 'We must be very careful not to assign to this deliverance the attributes of a victory. Wars are not won by evacuations. But there was a victory inside this deliverance which should be noted. It was gained by the Air Force.' In the same statement, Churchill asked the most prescient question: 'May it not also be that the cause of civilisation itself will be defended by the skill and devotion of a few thousand airmen?'[14]

This was indeed about to be proved true, but Britain faced the coming onslaught with severely depleted fighter forces. During six weeks in May and June, the RAF had lost 959 aircraft. Personnel losses numbered 1,382, a low figure in comparison with the Army's 68,111, but contained within the RAF deaths were 915 aircrew including 534 pilots killed, missing or wounded, numbers the RAF could ill afford.[15] In the face of these losses, Sholto wrote to Sir Leslie Gossage, the Air Member for Personnel (AMP), on 29 May, pointing out the growing shortage of fighter pilots, with which the OTUs could not keep pace despite the training course having been shortened. Sholto suggested that stringent steps be taken to 'comb out' as many experienced pilots as possible from non-operational units to make up the shortfall, as the situation was becoming desperate.

During this period, he arranged to meet with his staff in the Air Ministry at 9 a.m. each day for a briefing by their own intelligence services to keep abreast of events. He felt that it was better that his team heard the awful news all together, and it helped him to put a brave face on what were calamitous events, because he had to support his staff. Nevertheless, at this time, the accession of Winston Churchill to the post of Prime Minister and his refusal to accept defeat had an amazing effect on the country's morale. This was in sharp contrast to the despair that was 'eating away at the hearts and minds of the French', which Sholto observed on 3 June when he made his final visit to France until after the war was over. He had been instructed by Newall to fly to Paris with the Assistant Chief of the Naval Staff, Vice-Admiral Sir Geoffrey Blake, to discuss with Admiral Darlan and General Vuillemin, the heads respectively of the French Navy and Air Force, what action should be taken by the Royal Navy and RAF when Italy came into the war, which was expected within the next few days.

When Sholto and Blake landed at the military aerodrome at Villacoublay just outside Paris, they expected that a member of the French military would be there to meet them, but the only person there was Douglas Colyer, the British Air Attaché. Sholto and Blake got out of their aircraft, and just as they did so, a man wearing a tin hat with a gas mask 'bouncing on his backside' rushed up from a nearby dugout and shouted at them to take cover because the Germans would start bombing the airfield almost immediately. They ran to the nearest air-raid shelter, an improvised mound of sandbags and corrugated iron, reaching it just as the first bomb landed on a hangar about thirty-five metres away. This was followed by a whole salvo of bombs that fell all over the aerodrome and the hangars. Sholto was to learn later that that day was the only one in the whole of WWII on which the Germans staged a large-scale raid on Paris.

There were fifty to sixty French fighters parked around the airfield, and Sholto saw a number of them blown up in the raid. Just as he and Blake had landed, he had seen three of these aircraft take off, but as far as he could ascertain, these were the only French fighters that attempted to go into action from Villacoublay on that day. He could see no excuse for such a lack of interest in trying to tackle the enemy, because the British Air Staff had received reports through their own intelligence in the previous twenty-four to forty-eight hours that the Germans were planning a big raid on Paris, and had passed that information on to the French. When the air raid was over, Sholto, Blake and Colyer made their way to the officers' mess and found all the French pilots, with the exception of the three that were airborne, sitting down quietly having their lunch, with no apparent interest in what had just happened. Their attitude contrasted starkly with that of the gallant French aviators Sholto had known in WWI and subsequently the Free French aircrews who would serve under him later in WWII.

After the all-clear had sounded at Villacoublay, Sholto and his companions were driven into the centre of Paris, passing on the way the Citroën factory, which had been bombed and part of which was on fire. Apart from that, they did not see any signs of widespread damage. After lunch they were taken to see Admiral Darlan, who appeared full of fire and spirit and reassured them that when Italy declared war on the Allies, the French fleet would bombard La Spezia and other naval bases on the Italian coast. French torpedo bombers would also attack the Italian fleet. General Vuillemin was similarly reassuring, telling Sholto and Blake that he had given orders for the French Air Force to prepare to bomb factories in northern Italy. Sholto told him the RAF could not do a great deal to help while its bomber bases were in England, but if the French could provide it with the use of a couple of aerodromes in the south of France, somewhere near Marseilles, the Air Staff would send a force of Wellingtons down there to bomb the Italian munition and aircraft factories in Milan and Turin. Sholto also promised a force of Whitleys from English bases that could be refuelled in the Channel Islands for the long flight to Italy and back.

He immediately contacted Air Marshal A. S. 'Ugly' Barratt, the C-in-C of the British Air Forces in France, and arranged with him for a ground party and a Wing HQ from his AASF to be sent down to the two bases near Marseilles that the French had allocated for use by the RAF. He also contacted Portal to organise Wellingtons to be flown to these aerodromes. Barratt and his staff quickly put the arrangements in place for an air attack to be launched against Italy from southern France. The force there, codenamed 'Haddock', was under the command of Group Captain Roger Field, who had been a contemporary of Sholto's in WWI and was an experienced pilot. Italy's declaration of war against the Allies took effect at midnight on 10 June, and a squadron of Wellingtons arrived in the south of France on the afternoon of the following day. Its task was to bomb Turin that night, and the target selected was the Fiat works.

However, as soon as the Wellingtons arrived in the south of France, all the French commanders immediately telephoned Field and told him that on no account should his bombers be allowed to attack Italy because that would invite reprisals against French cities such as Marseilles, Lyon and Toulon. They emphasised that there were no French fighters for defence of that part of the country because all their squadrons had been transferred to the north for the battle that was going on there. General Vuillemin soon waded in, asking Sholto to issue an order that no Wellingtons would bomb Italy that night. Sholto told Vuillemin that he could not possibly give such an order as the operation had been approved by the Prime Minister, but after further protests from him Sholto promised to speak to Newall about it. Churchill was in France at that point, and when he was consulted later that afternoon about the French protests, he gave firm instructions that the operation should continue.

The final orders to proceed were given to Field, who briefed his crews, and they prepared to take off for Italy. Even then, he was being deluged with calls from French commanders, who told him that on no account should he continue with the operation. He handled these calls with skill, having been an Air Attaché at numerous embassies before the war and well used to officialdom. The Whitleys had already taken off from the Channel Islands when the Wellingtons taxied out towards the runway of the airfield in the south of France a little before midnight. Just as they did this, a swarm of French lorries appeared out of the darkness and were driven to positions across the aerodrome that completely blocked their take-off path. It was impossible for the bomber crews to continue, and Field decided to cancel the operation rather than risk a diplomatic incident with the French. Two days later Churchill managed to sort things out, persuading the French government to adhere to the plan that had been agreed. The Wellingtons and Whitleys carried out their bombing operations but with limited success, and nine days later the French capitulated.

Meanwhile, Sholto was concerned with how to get the 'Haddock' force back home. The Wellingtons could be flown back across France at night without fear of attack, but how was he going to get the ground force back? He consulted the Admiralty and found that some British merchant ships were still in Marseilles. They were told to wait there for a short time, and Sholto gave instructions for the RAF personnel in the south of France to make their way as quickly as possible to the port. Unfortunately, they had to leave all their equipment behind, but all of them made it to the ships and thence safely back to England, despite the possible danger of Italian interception on the way to Gibraltar.

A few days after Sholto's visit to France and while he was dealing with the 'Haddock' operation, he was asked by the VCAS, Peirse, to interview Colonel Fournier of the French Air Force, which had at that time some 200 surplus fighter pilots. Visiting Sholto in his office, Fournier put forward the proposal that the RAF give them 100 Hurricanes with which to form fighter squadrons. Sholto explained to Fournier that while the RAF had a small reserve of Hurricanes, this would not be sufficient due to the continual loss of aircraft at that time. He pointed out that the commitment to the French would not end there, as spares and ammunition, of which the RAF was short, would have to be provided and damaged machines replaced. He suggested as an alternative that the French Air Force might be prepared to lend the RAF some of their spare fighter pilots to serve in British squadrons. The RAF would give them a course of training at an OTU before passing them into fighter squadrons. Fournier was not pleased with this proposal but promised to discuss it with General Vuillemin. Sholto put forward his own view to Peirse that the Air Staff should not accede to the French request because the UK was at last building up its fighter production and its reserves. In view of the casualties being suffered by the RAF and those that would be incurred in the future, neither the production nor the reserves could be considered as more than adequate. Sholto suggested that he write to Fournier to decline the French proposal.[16]

On 11 June, the Germans broke through the last French fortified positions on the Marne, Oise and Seine in northern France, and it was clear that the whole of the rest of the AASF, which was providing air cover along this line, was in danger. On 12 June, Sholto sent his personal staff officer to France by air with an urgent letter for 'Ugly' Barratt warning him to prepare for a rapid withdrawal of all his forces. Sholto learned later that there was a letter on the way from Barratt to him requesting instructions on exactly that matter. They could not rely on telephone connections for these important exchanges, since civilian lines were never good at the best of times and were becoming more difficult by the hour. Sometimes Sholto and his colleagues in France came off the phone having hardly understood each other at all. There was however one exception that lodged firmly in Sholto's memory. At around midnight on 12 June, he was at his desk clearing up some paperwork when the phone rang, and at the other end of it, as clear as could be, was the voice of Air Vice-Marshal (AVM) Patrick Playfair, Commander under Barratt of the AASF.

His voice was so clear that Sholto asked him how he had got back from France. Playfair replied that he was still there but was sitting in a chateau while his staff loaded everything onto lorries for their getaway. France was being rapidly overrun, and yet here were Sholto and Playfair talking to one another as though they were in the same room. The chateau from which he was calling was on one bank of a river and the Germans were on the other side. Sholto could even hear the burst of guns and the rattle of machine-gun fire in the background. He asked Playfair: 'Is there anything I can do for you?', feeling at the same time completely helpless. Playfair answered: 'No. I've only rung up because I felt rather lonely and I thought I'd like to talk to somebody at the Air Ministry. I'll be off in my car in a few minutes, and we'll try and get to the coast.' Sholto must have been reminded of that time back in 1918 when he had had to evacuate an aerodrome with the Germans marching along the road towards it.

Churchill was trying desperately to keep the French in the war, even if they had to fight from north Africa. However, the Air Staff knew that what they could not do was send more fighter squadrons to France. Nevertheless, from when the Germans had started their advances to the west on 10 May, General Vuillemin had been on the phone every day asking to speak to the CAS, and if he or the VCAS were busy the general would be put through to Sholto. All he could do was to reiterate to Vuillemin the opposition of the Air Staff to his demands for fighters, trying to articulate the views of Dowding, who was continuing to fight 'like a tiger against anything that would reduce his already limited strength'.[17]

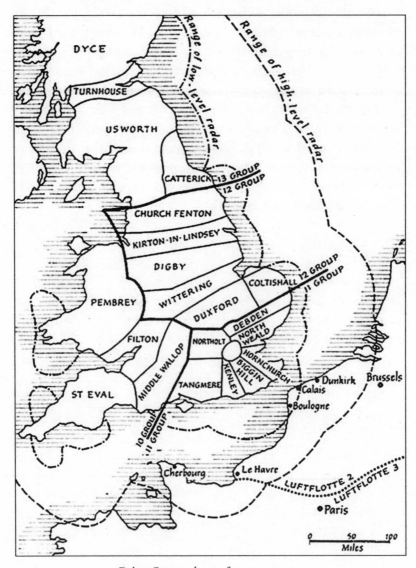

Fighter Command map of group areas, 1940.

CHAPTER FOURTEEN

INFIGHTING CHAOS IN THE BATTLE OF BRITAIN

The final collapse of France came on 22 June 1940, when the French signed an armistice with Hitler. On 10 July, the first large formation of seventy enemy bombers and fighters thundered through the skies over the Channel to attack the British mainland. Prior to this, strikes had been made on Allied convoys, and even on land objectives such as the naval base at Portland. However, this was the first time that the UK's Fighter Defence was brought to battle on a large scale, and these attacks would continue unabated for the next three and a half months. For those involved, such was the battle's intensity that it was hard to see further than the blow-by-blow course of events, and it was not until afterwards that they realised that the greatest air conflict that had ever taken place, or is ever likely to take place, had been fought and won in the skies over England.

During this time, Sholto was involved in some of the most serious controversies of his entire career. The two areas where he has attracted the most criticism were, firstly, his seeming failure to appreciate the severity of pilot losses, and secondly, his part in the bitter row over what is termed by aviation historians the 'Big Wing'. The latter concerned tactical policy, specifically whether incoming enemy aircraft should be met with small groups of fighters, designed to intercept them before the German bombers dropped their load, or whether they should be countered with forces equal or superior to them in numbers, flying in a Big Wing of three to five squadrons (up to ninety aircraft).

The most pressing anxiety both in the Air Ministry and at Fighter

Command was the acute shortage of fighter pilots through casualties as the conflict proceeded. This was of even greater concern than the shortage of aircraft. When the quality of pilots was considered as well as the numbers, the gravity of the situation became even more apparent. The pilots that were sent to replace those killed or wounded, 'though magnificent material, did not match their predecessors in flying experience nor in their knowledge of the technicalities of air fighting'.[1]

During the height of the battle in mid-August, after a week in which Fighter Command had suffered particularly heavy losses, Dowding suggested transferring experienced pilots from Bomber Command squadrons to use them for fighters. At first Sholto resisted this idea, even calling it 'unpalatable' for the reason that bombers would be essential in the event of invasion as they would be needed to deal with enemy troops landing on beaches. The bomber enthusiasts in the Air Ministry strongly opposed this plan too. Later, it seems as though Sholto had second thoughts, but this is where his views as expressed back in 1940 disagreed with the account that he put forward in the 1960s. From this point onwards, telling his story becomes more difficult. The rather sanitised version that appeared in his autobiography, in which one would hardly think that there was any friction between him and Dowding, diverges considerably from others' accounts of their relationship during and immediately after the Battle of Britain.

Dowding's frustration over what he deemed Sholto's lack of appreciation of the dire situation boiled over in a meeting at Bentley Priory on 7 September 1940. He summoned his Senior Air Staff Officer (SASO), Strath Evill, Air Vice-Marshal Keith Park, AOC No. 11 Group, which bore the brunt of the losses, and Sholto, who by this time had become de facto CAS as Newall had faded from the scene. Sholto said that Newall 'knocked himself out when the Battle of Britain started and became quite jittery towards the end'.[2] Much to Sholto's surprise, Dowding announced that this meeting had been called to manage the diminishing resources of Fighter Command caused by the very high pilot attrition rate. He suggested that the squadrons of No. 11 Group, which covered south-east England, should be kept at their present strength and that some operational pilots from other groups could be sent to augment those in No. 11 Group at the forefront of the fighting, allowing inexperienced pilots to be sent away from the battle area to receive further training.

Dowding, Evill and Park took great pains to impress on Sholto the seriousness of pilot losses: 348 in the four weeks to 4 September, and the output from the OTUs during that period was 280, a net shortfall of sixty-eight, not including losses from accidents or illness. In a move that illustrated the widening gulf between Sholto's understanding of the grave situation and Dowding's, Sholto suggested opening another OTU, a not unreasonable suggestion as this had been mooted in a memo from Fighter Command on 2 September. However, this only exasperated Dowding even more, since for him, another OTU would mean a further drain on Fighter Command's resources as pilots and ground crews would be needed to staff it. He felt that Sholto and others at the Air Ministry had failed completely to anticipate the heavy casualties that are inevitable in wartime, and although they were now making 'very great efforts' to address the problem, the bottleneck was the turning of pilots from FTSs and OTUs into operational pilots.[3]

But now Sholto and his Air Ministry colleagues were having to face the grim reality, as was clear from recent Air Council meetings in which desperate solutions were being put forward. Suggestions included waiving the requirement of secondary school education for aircrew, reducing the standard of mathematics for pilots and observers, and relaxing the medical standard for candidates (without prejudice to safety), although the latter two measures were rejected in later meetings. Proposals were made to invite Army personnel of all ranks and people from overseas to volunteer for aircrew, and to scrutinise 'lists of previous "rejects" with a view to re-examining individuals likely to meet the reduced standard to be implemented'.[4] Even pilots who were classified as exhibiting the egregiously named 'lack of moral fibre' and who were disparagingly referred to as 'waverers' were retained for ground duties at airfields, such was the shortage of personnel. These highly dangerous places, frequently subject to bombing, were completely unsuitable for the deployment of those suffering from what would now be called combat stress reaction or PTSD, as some of these servicemen almost certainly were.[5]

Although Sholto said in this meeting that, as he understood it, there was going to be a shortfall of *experienced* pilots, he 'submitted that there should be no question of a shortage of pilots'.[6] But it was lack of experience in some pilots that was leading to the high attrition rate, thereby creating the shortage. Dowding said to Sholto: 'I want you to take away from this meeting the feeling that the situation is extremely grave.'[7]

On 9 September, Evill sent Sholto a copy of Dowding's scheme for preserving his diminishing pilot strength, along with the draft minutes of the conference. It was clear from Sholto's response to Evill on 14 September that he was annoyed with both the meeting and its outcome. In his eloquently angry appraisal of the minutes, he said he was reminded of

> a music hall turn between two knock-about comedians in which one (usually labelled 'Mutt' or some other similar salubrious soubriquet) is made to ask foolish questions or make foolish statements which call down upon his devoted head laughter-making sallies from his more quick-witted partner. I appear to have been cast for the part of 'Mutt'. Frankly, I consider the minutes were drafted by someone with a distinct bias in favour of everything said by a member of Fighter Command. However life is too strenuous in these days to bother about the wording of minutes.[8]

Evill replied to Sholto that the minutes were almost exactly in the form in which they had been recorded at the time.

Sholto hated the idea of grading squadrons in the way that Dowding had suggested at the meeting, believing that it was bad for morale. He was firm in his belief that better use should be made of No. 12 Group squadrons that adjoined No. 11, covering the Midlands. From what Dowding wrote later, it is clear that he was just as much against grading squadrons as Sholto was, calling it 'a thoroughly vicious principle',[9] but had adopted it out of dire necessity.

Coincidentally, on the day of the meeting at Fighter Command,

7 September, the Luftwaffe altered its tactics. Instead of attacking airfields, aircraft factories and the aircraft of No. 11 Group as was expected, some 300 enemy bombers, escorted by double that number of fighters, launched the heaviest raids so far. Their target was London, and for over an hour they bombed areas of Docklands, killing over 400 civilians and starting the largest fires to be experienced in Britain since 1666. A squadron commander described the appearance of one of these raids as like looking up the escalator at Piccadilly Circus.

How were these huge, seemingly unending banks of enemy aircraft to be faced? Intense disagreements between group commanders at Fighter Command as to the most effective tactical method to deal with them bring into focus this most controversial part of Sholto's involvement in the Battle of Britain, the argument over the Big Wing. He wrote that the controversy has been 'regrettably as well as incorrectly over-stressed'.[10] However, this is understating the vehement difference of opinion. A prominent contributory factor was the clash between the personalities of the two principal group commanders concerned: Keith Park at No. 11 Group, who advocated meeting incoming enemy raids rapidly with smaller forces of one or two squadrons, and Air Vice-Marshal Trafford Leigh-Mallory at No. 12 Group, who championed operating as a Big Wing, also called the Duxford Wing. The disagreement reached Shakespearean proportions in the intrigue it generated and the venom expressed both by the participants themselves and by historians taking up trenchant positions on either side for decades thereafter.

Sholto's experience as a commander of fighter squadrons during the latter part of WWI had involved him in the early development of fighter tactics, in which developing ways of fighting with three or more squadrons in wings had played a large part. It was Sholto's opinion that this had led to considerable success, since these big formations were more effective than smaller ones in inflicting losses on large numbers of enemy aircraft, with less damage to Allied air forces. Even so, Sholto did realise that the problem with wings was even more acute in 1940 than it had been in 1918, due to the greater speed of incoming enemy aircraft. Time was too short to get many squadrons airborne and formed into a wing ready for mass attack.

Dowding insisted that to think in terms of wings was out of date and a retrograde step, because the fighter operations in WWI in which wing formations were used were 'free-booting expeditions' over enemy territory, not the kind of disciplined flying that had to be practised by pilots in Fighter Command in 1940, when there was stricter ground-to-air control.

An essential requirement for the operation of the Big Wing was that all the squadrons within it should be able to communicate with each other by radio. This was not possible during the Battle of Britain, as the radio control that was needed to operate a large wing formation was liable to break down. Strenuous efforts had been made to improve communications prior to the start of the onslaught, with a new VHF radio system being introduced throughout Fighter Command. However, the rate of supply was too slow. Dowding had been advised that no further stocks would be available until late summer 1940, so he decided that the VHF system should be suspended indefinitely and the command would revert to using the older High Frequency (HF) radios, as the two systems were incompatible. The problem was that, much to Dowding's frustration, HF was far less effective and did not enable all squadrons to communicate with each other on the same frequency, a point he expressed forcefully to the Air Ministry.

Sholto was largely responsible for the delay in implementing the new system. In what he termed 'a bit of a gamble',[11] but what the historian Peter Flint has called 'a justifiable risk',[12] he cut corners in his haste to get VHF into service. No normal service trials were carried out and modifications to sets and aircraft created delays. VHF was being pressed into use when it was not fully developed and waiting for improved equipment inevitably meant a serious reduction in the command's efficiency.

Sholto's stance on wings had varied over the years. In a 1925 lecture at the RAF Staff College, he had expressed views that were much closer to Park's option of smaller forces than to Leigh-Mallory's Big Wing, illustrating that the flight of five aircraft (six for two-seaters with rearward facing guns) was the ideal fighting unit, although three flights of a squadron could cooperate with one another. The opinion that Sholto expressed back in 1925 was not what he advocated in the summer of 1940. During the Battle of Britain he was found in the opposite camp to Dowding and Park. So what changed?

Wing Commander (later Air Chief Marshal Sir) Kenneth 'Bing' Cross, who had been one of only two members of No. 46 Squadron to survive the disastrous sinking of HMS *Glorious* off the coast of Norway, wrote that the Big Wing idea had been sold to Leigh-Mallory by the newly promoted Squadron Leader Douglas Bader, who capitalised on Leigh-Mallory's resentment at not being able to participate more fully in the Battle of Britain. His own group, No. 12, was sitting on the sidelines while No. 11 Group was in the forefront of the fighting, so Bader found fertile ground in which to sow his theories. Bader was one of the least experienced of the squadron commanders in Fighter Command due to his break in service between 1932 and 1939 as the result of his 1931 accident in which he had lost his legs. He was almost completely ignorant of the air defence system and its capabilities. Nevertheless, he was 'ever ready to tell anyone who would listen how the battle should be conducted',[13] and of course, in the Big Wing of up to five squadrons, he would take the lead. Cross related later that Leigh-Mallory had never been a fighter pilot, nor had he flown the Hurricane or Spitfire, unlike Keith Park, who flew Hurricanes in the battle area and listened to the radio communications. Cross went as far as to say that Leigh-Mallory was never in any way an original thinker, and that it was not unusual for a staff officer to recognise one of his pet ideas retold later by Leigh-Mallory as though it was his own.

Being at heart a fighter pilot, Sholto took the greatest interest in Park and Leigh-Mallory's differences of opinion. As DCAS, he was responsible for the day-to-day operations of the whole of the RAF, so became involved in their argument. Cross, who was the Group Controller of No. 12 Group in October 1940 and spent a lot of time sitting next to Leigh-Mallory on the bridge of the operations room there, wrote in his memoir that Leigh-Mallory was on the telephone to Sholto frequently, and both were critical of the tactics employed by Park.

Sholto reiterated his extraordinary assertion from back in 1938: that the object in stopping an enemy offensive was 'to shoot down such a large proportion of his bomber force that he would be compelled to diminish the scale of his offensive and finally to call it off', even if that meant shooting him down *after* he had dropped his bombs. The way to do that was to engage him with equally large, even superior, numbers of fighters operating in wings of three or more squadrons. However, as we have seen already in the previous chapter, he made the mistake of underestimating the determination of the German High Command to continue with its air offensive despite heavy losses.

Park's tactics as AOC No. 11 Group were not designed to destroy the Luftwaffe, as Sholto fondly hoped they might, because that was beyond his slim resources, but to ensure that there were always aircraft in the sky to meet the invaders, who would be forced to concede that their efforts to defeat the RAF were in vain. On this point it turned out that Park was right. After the end of the war on 7 June 1945, both Generalfeldmarschall Erhard Milch, Inspector-General of the Luftwaffe and Secretary of State for Air, and Generalleutnant Adolf Galland, commander of JG26 (Fighter Wing 26), contended that the German air attack on Britain in 1940 was called off, and with it the invasion, 'not so much because of losses … as because there was no apparent return for them and progressively less prospect of one'.[14]

In a direct riposte to Leigh-Mallory's and Sholto's views, Park expressed his own in a letter in October 1940, explaining his tactics in the most recent confrontation with German bombers:

> We [Nos 10 and 11 Groups] were both using mainly pairs of fighter squadrons as our geographical situation does not afford the time to despatch, assemble and engage with wing formations BEFORE THE BOMBER RAIDS HAVE REACHED VITAL OBJECTIVES. I may be wrong in imagining that our primary task is to protect London, Aircraft factories, Sector Aerodromes, against the enemy bombers, and not merely to secure a maximum bag of enemy aircraft after they have done their fiendish damage [capitals Park's own].[15]

The letter also contained a comparison of the results achieved by each tactical method on 27 September, the day of the last big attack by the German long-range bomber force. The results were unambiguous despite the greater loss of pilots in No. 11 Group, which was almost certainly due to greater engagement with the enemy:

	No. 11 Group (pairs)	No. 12 Group (wings)
Enemy aircraft destroyed	115	13
Probably destroyed	28	6
Damaged	41	3
Own pilots lost	15	2

However, Park was not at all averse to the use of wing formations in the right circumstances, such as over France during the Dunkirk evacuation. As AOC No. 11 Group during that period, he was the only senior commander involved in the wing controversy to have had previous experience of using them in action in WWII.

Due to this expertise, and somewhat proprietorially, Park emphasised in a letter to Evill that the role of No. 12 Group, as had been stipulated by Fighter Command, was to reinforce No. 11 Group when it was called upon to do so, and to protect that group's aerodromes while their squadrons engaged the enemy. However, No. 12 Group squadrons did *not* patrol the areas requested, and as a result, in August two of No. 11 Group's airfields had been heavily bombed. Instead, No. 12 Group wings had roamed into No. 11 Group's area unannounced, causing the Observer Corps to report large raids in the east of Kent, causing immense confusion.

Some responsibility for the breakdown in relations between the two group leaders lay with Dowding, who appeared to do nothing to defuse the clash between them. However, he was by no means unaware of what was happening, as Park and Leigh-Mallory were conducting their argument by proxy through him. A report from Leigh-Mallory to Dowding on 17 September that contained accounts of the Big Wing's operations on 7, 9, 11 and 15 September does not make for impressive reading. He made excuses for its lack of success, the main ones being that the Big Wing could not attain height soon enough to engage enemy fighters and that he needed more aircraft. One notable excuse was: 'The fighters who were attacking the bombers got unduly interfered with by enemy fighters.'[16] What else did he expect German fighter escorts to do?

Sholto continued to watch with irritation from the Air Ministry as the controversy over tactics at Fighter Command continued to simmer, his dissatisfaction exacerbated by Dowding's hesitancy to resolve the conflict between Park and Leigh-Mallory. So he pressed for a conference to address the issues. This meeting, which has been seen by many as a 'carefully staged plot to undermine Dowding and Park',[17] and which has assumed great importance in historical accounts, should have been called by Dowding himself. His failure to deal decisively with the antipathy between his two subordinates had created a vacuum that someone in authority had to fill. Since Newall was at the end of his time, both administratively and psychologically, as his deputy, Sholto had to take the lead, although Portal, the CAS designate, was present.

Surprisingly, as this was a meeting to which only senior commanders were invited, Leigh-Mallory augmented his own position by bringing with him one of his young squadron commanders, a certain Douglas Bader. His views on the Big Wing had much more weight in the controversy than his rank and position warranted, partly because he was an extremely forceful character. The famous aviator Eric 'Winkle' Brown, who was a Fleet Air Arm officer at the time and who knew Bader, later recalled that he was given a great deal of sympathy over his legs and so got away with things that others in his position would not. Eric felt that Bader's disaster, which was of his own making, had not unnaturally affected his entire personality, making him even more determined and belligerent than he had been already. Cross's sentiments were similar, writing that Bader was so headstrong that he ignored the word 'discipline', making him 'a great trial to his immediate superiors and later to those who served under him, but all were prepared to put up with him mainly because of their respect for his courage in overcoming his disability'.[18]

At the conference, held on 17 October, the animosity between the two group commanders was palpable, but the discussion proceeded remarkably quietly in view of the acrimony of previous weeks. Park reiterated his opposition to the use of large formations in his area, but

Leigh-Mallory said he was anxious to use his wing in support of No. 11 Group. Surprisingly, Dowding did not speak up on Park's behalf but said that he could resolve any difficulties of control involved in sending such support. Since he had failed to achieve this up to now, and that was one reason the meeting was taking place, this was an astonishing claim. Sholto summed up by emphasising the advantages of using large wings but added that there need not be a binary choice of *either* pairs *or* wings of squadrons. Forces from the two groups should cooperate, selecting the most suitable combinations for each situation as time allowed.

Park felt when he left the conference that all his assertions over the previous weeks and at the meeting were to no avail, and that henceforward, tactics would change. Dowding had failed to support him and had been outmanoeuvred. Park claimed later that Sholto 'was the public prosecutor' and that he and Dowding 'were condemned – that is the only word'.[19] The draft minutes of the conference were dispatched to the participants with requests for any amendments. Somewhat predictably, those favouring Big Wings were prepared to accept the minutes with minor alterations, whereas Park and to a lesser extent Dowding and Air Vice-Marshal Quintin Brand, AOC No. 10 Group, were dissatisfied with them and requested changes, all of which Sholto rebutted. Three days after the conference, Park wrote directly to Leigh-Mallory, sending a copy to Evill, saying that he would be 'delighted' to have the assistance of the Duxford Wing once a day, provided that it would patrol over the area requested until engaged, and that his group and sector controllers would know the position of the wing at all times so that the Observer Corps and AA (anti-aircraft) units could be informed. However, as could be expected, Leigh-Mallory did not like this idea of waiting on the sidelines and wanted a bigger slice of the action.

Subsequent deployment of the Duxford Wing in support of No. 11 Group did not go well. A report by Group Captain Lawson of the Operations Section of Fighter Command highlighted the continuing failure of the Big Wing to form up in time to patrol the area requested or to intercept enemy raids. The result was that the Charing Cross area of London was bombed and No. 11 Group squadrons had to engage the raids that should have been tackled by No. 12 Group. Due to continuing radio control difficulties, with the two groups operating on different frequencies, Lawson concluded that it was 'almost impossible for No.11 Group, or No.12 Group for that matter, to control effectively the Wing when it passes into No.11 Group's area ... The advantages which have accrued [by operating the Duxford Wing in support of No. 11 Group] seem to be negligible.'[20]

While 'the few' fought for their lives in the skies over England, the controversy and backbiting among their commanders raged on and Sholto's patience ran out. Referring to the differences between Park and Leigh-Mallory so evident at the conference on 17 October, he asked Dowding to act decisively. The quarrel was leading to bitterness not only between the two group commanders but also between the squadrons and their pilots. This situation could not be allowed to continue. Sholto asked Dowding to make 'an authoritative statement of your views'. This would sound much better coming from Dowding himself than from the Air Ministry. Sholto received a somewhat negative reply from Dowding, who felt that Bader had been responsible for much of the ill will between the two groups, saying that he suffered 'from an over-development of the critical faculties', and that it might be better to move him 'to another station where he would be kept in better control'. Instead, it was Dowding himself who was about to be removed from Fighter Command.

In later life, Dowding believed that Sholto had had a big hand in his departure, a view expressed in Robert Wright's biography of Dowding, published in 1969, when Dowding was in his late eighties and his memory was beginning to fail him, and Sholto was very ill in a psychiatric hospital, just two months before his death. Wright wrote that Sholto never told him that he had chaired the meeting on 17 October. However, as Dowding's PA at the time, having taken over from Francis Wilkinson a month before, Wright worked in an inner office between those of Dowding and Evill, so he would have seen the minutes of the meeting and the correspondence that followed it. Wilkinson had warned Wright, 'You'll hear an awful lot and you'll find out an awful lot. The way those boys at the top go after each other, sniping at each other with telescopic sights, is staggering.'[21]

Remaining in his post at Fighter Command when Sholto replaced Dowding, Wright became a close associate and friend of Sholto's in the years that followed, though in the 1960s they had a very painful falling-out over money, the details of which appear later in this story. Thereafter, he was drawn increasingly towards Dowding.

Wright's criticism of Sholto's role in the whole Big Wing affair stood for posterity, influencing historians for decades thereafter and denting Sholto's standing severely. That is not to say that his conduct had been blameless, but as an air vice-marshal, he could not have been responsible for the dismissal of an air chief marshal. There were many other influences and factors working against Dowding, who had arrayed against him two former CASs, Salmond and Trenchard, as well as those on the Air Staff aside from Sholto who thought that he should go. In any case, he had been due to retire a year earlier. He was fifty-eight years old and, like Sholto, he had endured the traumas of WWI as well as the build-up to and start of WWII, having led Fighter Command for over four years. He was exhausted and, importantly, had never had a good relationship with the Air Ministry, many there finding him stubborn and uncooperative. Even Beaverbrook, who had been his supporter, finally colluded with a resentful wing commander at the Air Ministry named Edgar Kingston-McCloughry in the sending of an anonymous memo stating that both Dowding and Newall should go.[22]

Amid this intrigue, Sholto was reported to Churchill for 'talking loosely in a defeatist way' a few days earlier at a dinner party at the home of some friends in Westminster where a senior Conservative MP was present. The Blitz had already begun, but Sholto was angered by the complacency of the assembled company, telling them that they were completely underestimating the effects of further aerial bombardment, and that there was even a possibility that Britain would have to sue for peace. Churchill wrote to Sir Archibald Sinclair, the Secretary of State for Air, about this incident, asking him to make enquiries from someone who had witnessed it, since defeatism would be a particularly unfortunate quality in anyone occupying the post of DCAS. In his reply to Churchill, Sinclair defended Sholto's character and courage, saying that he was 'quite certain that there is no defeatist weakness in him. He is tough, cool, not at all temperamental, and resolute. Phlegm was his characteristic in the critical times we have been through – not jumpiness.'[23] Sinclair convinced Churchill that the whole matter had been blown out of all proportion.

In a chilling fulfilment of Sholto's words at the party a few days earlier, the devastating raid on Coventry took place on the night of 14 November, when more than 4,300 homes were destroyed and around two-thirds of the city's buildings were damaged. An estimated 554 people were killed (the exact figure was never precisely confirmed), with another 865 badly injured. Fighter Command flew 125 night sorties but failed to shoot down a single Luftwaffe bomber, the blame for which was laid at Dowding's door. On 15 November, the day after Coventry city centre was demolished, Sinclair told Churchill in his letter that that very morning he had already given Sholto, after more than one consultation with Churchill, 'an appointment. It has been approved by the King and will be announced on Monday.'[24] Sholto was to be C-in-C Fighter Command.

Sholto arrived at Bentley Priory, Fighter Command HQ, on the morning of 25 November. In the notes for his autobiography, he wrote: 'Stuffy Dowding obviously hated handing over. He was upset at having to be relieved. He was always perfectly polite with me, although rather short and abrupt in manner as he always was. He was however quite reasonable with me about the whole thing.' As for Sholto's thoughts about Dowding as a person, despite the huge difference in their characters and all the clashes that they had had since 1936, he admitted: 'I have a good opinion of him. He had his faults but he had tremendous qualities. I liked him too curiously enough. If you put his qualities down on paper they were not very likeable but he was an honest man.'[25] Portal's biographer Denis Richards interviewed both Dowding and Sholto. He wrote that it was

> ridiculous to present Douglas as just a schemer; he might have been a bit of that, but he was a very clever man, and – if one had been interviewing Dowding and Douglas for a big job – one would have put one's money on Douglas. He was a very clever fellow and a good commander … He might have had ambitions, but he was

basically concerned with the problem of night defence. This Big Wing affair had been blown up out of all proportion.[26]

That debate was reignited in 2020 during the eightieth anniversary of the Battle of Britain. Leo McKinstry in *The Spectator* was critical of Dowding and Park's tactics of putting smaller forces into the air against the Luftwaffe, writing:

> In practice, the reluctance to engage in large-scale attacks allowed too many bombers through, bolstered German morale, and kept Fighter Command on the defensive ... After the war, the senior RAF commander Sir Philip Joubert de la Ferté wrote that Park's 'spoiling tactics' were 'very exhausting for our fighters and it is possible that our losses were greater and our successes not so decisive as would have been the case if we had attempted to throw larger concentrations of our own fighters into the battle.'[27]

Nevertheless, I have often wondered why Sholto espoused the Big Wing in those particular circumstances. Perhaps the cumulative burden of underlying trauma, including Archie's death, was exerting its hidden influence once again, causing Sholto to champion the Big Wing as a means of providing better protection for pilots. It would certainly have been abhorrent to him to see them being put at greater risk when faced with much larger enemy forces.

While researching for this book, I found in Sholto's papers a handwritten page of notes on British European Airways notepaper, which must have been written about two decades after that summer of 1940, when he was writing his autobiography. Echoing others' impressions of him, he described himself in one note as: 'Imperturbable – hence miss heights of life and also depths. Never get really excited about anything, but also never very depressed even when things go wrong. (C.F. Summer 1940).' The note underneath it said: 'Judgment – most important quality of all if you want to succeed.'[28] His own judgement in that summer and autumn had been tested to the limit and has been the subject of considerable controversy ever since, but it would be challenged yet further when he went to Fighter Command.

CHAPTER FIFTEEN

NIGHT TERRORS

Sholto wrote that his appointment as C-in-C Fighter Command came as 'a sudden and rather breath-taking development'. Although everyone in the Air Ministry knew that a change was coming, and some historians have suggested that he had a big part in engineering it, he himself said that this produced in him 'a quite unexpected turmoil of feelings ... To a large extent the fate of the British people would be resting in my hands.'[1] As if to heighten the stakes, the headline announcing Sholto's appointment on the front page of the *Daily Express* blared: 'New chief to meet night bomber problem',[2] bringing into sharp focus his most important priority: tackling the night Blitz.

From the start, Sholto set the tone for his style of leadership over what would turn out to be the next two years. He had kept up with his flying and piloted himself to his numerous stations within the command, even learning to fly the latest model of Spitfire. He tried to keep his visits as regular and informal as possible, dropping in on each base twice a year. He knew his fighter pilots of any length of service individually and insisted that no guard of honour be called out when he arrived, preferring to see the pilots and crews in their dispersal huts and listening to their conversation. He is quoted as saying:

> If you let the boys have their say you find out what they are really thinking. Too much formality prevents a C-in-C getting into the minds of the junior officers and other ranks. A Commander-in-Chief should be able to listen to his own people talking without fear or favour. It's the only way to get at the truth.[3]

Sholto's 'home' for the next two years, Bentley Priory, comprised two parts: the overground part that everyone could see, which was a rambling and historic building designed in the eighteenth century by Sir John Soane, and the huge underground block of operations and filter rooms and offices accessible only to those who were allowed past the heavily guarded entrance. This subterranean complex was known as 'The Hole', and Sholto observed that it 'presented to the newcomer at first sight a picture that was almost Wellsian'.⁴ Sholto knew personally all the senior officers at Fighter Command, some of whom had served with him in WWI, and he was clearly delighted with his team. At last he had his own command and could run things more or less as he wanted, although now being on the 'other side of the fence' from the Air Ministry, like Dowding, he had his own battles with the Air Staff to come. All the problems that had beset Dowding were still there: pilot shortages, aircraft supply and of course, most of all, how to find the solution to those enemy bombers that came across night after night.

Sholto wrote: 'I was sent for by Winston, who told me that I had to concentrate everything on stopping the bombers. Every facility would be placed at my disposal.'⁵ Night defence had long been one of Sholto's preoccupations, but when he took over Fighter Command at the end of November, the situation was desperate. He was tireless in his attempts to solve the problem, writing a detailed report for Churchill's Night Air Defence Committee every month in which the developmental progress of each of the many night interception aids was reviewed. Everyone in the Air Ministry and at Fighter Command knew what the answer was: the Beaufighter equipped with airborne interception radar (AI) manned by a skilled radar operator. Until these aircraft became available, however, his suggested solution was that non-radar-equipped single-engined fighters, called Cat's Eye fighters, should be used at night, and prior to taking over Fighter Command he had criticised Dowding for not deploying enough of these. He wrote later:

> I agreed that it was a primitive effort to throw what were really day fighters into the darkness of the night skies in the hope that they

would be able to see something. But I felt, and in this I was supported by the other members of the [Night Air Defence] Committee and the Chief of the Air Staff, that the effort had to be made.[6]

Fighter Command had been making desperate attempts already to develop a night-fighting capability, but the problem was that the use of day fighters, Hurricanes and Defiants, at night greatly increased the Command's accident rate, and this high price was in no way compensated by success in night interceptions of enemy aircraft. During the month of September, the Luftwaffe had flown an estimated 6,135 sorties at night, yet only four German bombers had been destroyed by fighters.

The official historian, Basil Collier, criticised Sholto for his suggestion of using Cat's Eye fighters, especially in the poor weather conditions that prevailed in the winter of 1940/41, and Sholto himself began to change his opinion on the subject quite soon after taking over Fighter Command, writing to Portal in December 1940 to request six more squadrons of Beaufighters fitted with AI: 'I do not think that Hurricanes, Spitfires or even Defiants will ever be anything but "fine weather" night fighters.' He ended his letter to Portal with an impassioned plea: 'I do feel most strongly about this. It is vital to defeat the enemy night bomber – we may even lose the war if we don't.'[7] Nevertheless, Sholto tried to make use of Cat's Eye fighters by instigating what he called Fighter Nights, when large numbers of these aircraft were sent up in high concentrations on nights of good visibility. But this form of patrol, even in ideal weather conditions, was profitable only in an area of concentrated enemy activity, such as over London on 10 May 1941. Another priority was to have GCI radar sets installed at all the sector stations, especially those near London, which was recognised as 'by far the most important development in the Command'.[8]

For some among the radar scientists, Sholto's appointment as C-in-C Fighter Command was a refreshing improvement. As Professor R. V. Jones, a physicist and military intelligence expert who in 1940 was attached to the Air Ministry, recalled in 1970: 'One senior scientist ... seemed gratified, perhaps because he thought that Sir

Hugh Dowding undervalued scientific aids. Certainly there was a change of attitude after Sir Sholto Douglas took over, and we then found Fighter Command readier to listen to our ideas.' The senior scientist in question was almost certainly Robert Watson-Watt.

Sholto had been visiting fighter squadrons in the south of England, and had identified particular problems with night interception, such as the inaccuracy both of tracking enemy aircraft inland from the coast and of assessing the height of enemy bombers. He welcomed a proposal by General Pile to install a 'carpet' of gun-laying (GL) radar sets along a sixty-mile-wide belt from Kent to Bristol to address these problems. Although this was supposed to be a temporary expedient, it would continue to operate for many more months. All the other devices that had been trialled had yet to prove their worth, including AI.

In his December report, written two weeks after taking over Fighter Command, Sholto asserted that there should be more specialised night fighter squadrons. He had only eleven but wanted at least twenty as soon as possible, including twelve composed of AI fighters. Essential to success in bringing down enemy bombers at night was the most intensive specialist training of personnel involved in that work, and to that end, Sholto had just instigated the first night fighter OTU. Indifferent maintenance was also a problem, and as a result of complaints from scientists, Sholto wanted to allocate an engineer officer and a scientific officer to each of the twin-engined night fighter squadrons. Tizard fully supported Sholto's observations, stating in a note written three weeks after Sholto's report that the disappointing results from AI were due to 'lack of training, maintenance and good engineering, not to lack of science'.[9]

An adjunct to Sholto's report suggested the instigation of Fighter Regional Control Aerodromes specially equipped for night fighters, with facilities for blind landing and homing equipment to guide pilots back at night. To improve radio control at these aerodromes, Sholto advised that specialised air traffic control officers be employed, including, as he had suggested for pilots, transferring professional control officers from civil aviation for war service.

The solution was closer than Sholto realised. Soon after he had settled in to Bentley Priory, he was particularly pleased to receive

Trenchard as one of his many visitors. In one of those reassuring comments that Sholto said was so typical of him, Trenchard said: 'Never mind, Sholto, you take my word for it … a man will arise.'[10] In fact, on the night of 20 November, three weeks before Trenchard's visit, an event had occurred that heralded the fulfilment of Trenchard's prophecy. The Germans staged the second of three nights of heavy raids on Birmingham. One of the night fighters in the skies that night was a Beaufighter of No. 604 Squadron flown by Squadron Leader John Cunningham with Sergeant John Phillipson as his navigator, and they managed to intercept and shoot down a Junkers 88. One month later, the same team shot down another raider, a Heinkel that was part of a heavy force of enemy bombers attacking Liverpool and Birkenhead. Trenchard's prediction was coming true.

During December, the full force of enemy bombing was concentrated on London. At the end of a conference at Sholto's HQ on 29 December, he was told that there were indications that the Germans were planning yet another raid on the capital for that night. The enemy was using an increasingly sophisticated system of radio navigation beams transmitted from the other side of the Channel to guide bombers to their targets for the night. Coupled with this was a special squadron of trailblazers that marked with incendiaries the targets to be bombed.

Following examination of crashed German bombers and a flight by a British aircraft using a special receiver that detected the beams, British scientists had been able to introduce increasingly effective countermeasures to interfere with them, thus confusing the German aircrews and disrupting bombing raids. This was facilitated by the German practice of switching on the beams well before the bombers reached the target area, alerting Fighter Command to the target for that night. The beam system was codenamed *Headache* by the British and the countermeasures *Aspirin*. Despite this and the poor weather that Sunday night, the attack on London was the most spectacular of all raids made on the capital. Due to the use of incendiaries and high explosives, and probably due to high winds, the city burned with a ferocity that none who saw it would ever forget. Churchill called it 'an incendiary classic'.

At that time, Sholto was billeted in Sparrows Herne Hall near to Bentley Priory with other Fighter Command officers. Also living there was the owner of the house, Mrs Helen Margaret Nimmo. Her account of what happened that night was donated to the RAF Museum after her death. She wrote:

> At Sunday night supper the two seniors [Sholto, then Air Marshal, and Air Vice-Marshal Evill] seemed jumpy and distraught, and they both went back to HQ immediately. The noise of the barrage warned little Mrs W. M. and me that something big was going on, but we didn't go out to look for flames. When there is a big noise a jigsaw puzzle helps, so I fetched the one the Air Commodore and I were carrying on, and Mrs W. M. sat and knitted and fretted about her husband out in it [he was an Air Raid warden].

The other occupants of the house came in and finally:

> … The curtains blew in suddenly and the Air Marshal himself barged in, looking as black as any of the 'Black Douglases' [the branch of the clan from which our family comes] could look. He flung his overcoat on a couch and his cap on the table and strode across to us. I can't remember what he said – it was just exclamations and not very consecutive – but I do remember his repeating 'I sent up my fighters, I sent up my fighters.' … Then he caught sight of the puzzle and pounced suddenly on a bit the Air Commodore was just fitting in, with 'No, I can't allow you that one, Sir' and with that he was as deeply concentrated, to all appearances, as the other two.
>
> I took my knitting and noticed that the noise was lessening gradually. Mrs W. M. sitting on the sofa, suddenly giggled and remarked 'All the best brains of the Air Force' but no one took any notice, and she relapsed into silence again.
>
> A bit after midnight the last piece of puzzle was fitted in, and everyone looked up and discovered that the gunfire was practically only distant noises. They seemed to heave big sighs of relief, helped themselves to drinks, and slowly followed each other upstairs.

I stayed and put away the puzzle, with a queer feeling that some nightmare had been going on, and my knees were shaky.[II]

The urgent work on the use of AI at night to combat this threat continued, but John Cunningham and his usual radar operator, C. F. (Jimmy) Rawnsley, had begun to achieve increasing success in making full use of it. Cunningham was only twenty-three years old and with his baby face he looked even younger, but he was an experienced airman and together they formed an expert team. In the new year of 1941, with Rawnsley fully trained and installed as his navigator, Cunningham began to step up his rate of scoring, aided by increased efficiency in GCI and the resolution of problems with AI. Through their infectious enthusiasm and skill, the expertise of aircrews increased, both in No. 604 and in other squadrons. During January, only three enemy raiders were shot down, but by May, the monthly total had increased to ninety-six, not taking into account those enemy aircraft that were damaged or probably destroyed. The sudden progress in the use of AI and GCI in night fighting during those early months of 1941 came as a welcome surprise, but it was the result of years and years of painstaking work with which Sholto had been closely involved and had championed from the beginning.

The radar chain of coastal stations was being greatly expanded, and the scientists of the Operational Research Section at Fighter Command HQ, working in conjunction with No. 60 (Signals) Group, also within Fighter Command, made many improvements to extract the maximum benefit from the radar information available. The success of GCI and AI caused Sholto to receive many requests from both service and civilian officials to be allowed to see how 'this new magic' was being performed. He turned down most of them, but there was one that he could not brush aside. On 7 May, through the unwitting cooperation of the Luftwaffe, King George VI was treated to a ringside seat at what Sholto and his staff called a command performance. That night, Sholto accompanied the King to Middle Wallop in Hampshire to see Cunningham's squadron, No. 604, in action. As dusk was falling, the squadron prepared for the night's operations. When the first aircraft took off, Sholto, the Station CO

Group Captain Elliott and the King drove to a cluster of huts and caravans in a field near Sopley, where a ground radar station was run with consummate skill by Squadron Leader J. L. Brown, who was as much of a genius in operating GCI as Rawnsley was with AI. Brown gave a short explanation before the excitement began. He pointed to a dot that had just come up on the large cathode ray tube of his radar set indicating that an enemy aircraft was on its way in.

That night the Germans sent their bombers for raids on the Midlands. Although their force had been considerably diminished due to withdrawals to the Eastern Front, they still sent 166 aircraft to bomb Liverpool and Birkenhead, and seventy-two to attack Hull. The dot on the screen at Sopley was one of the first to appear. Brown said: 'It's a bandit. John Cunningham's up there. I'll put him on to it.' The approaching enemy aircraft was still well out to sea, giving him time to instruct Cunningham over the radio, manoeuvring him into position. It was all going so perfectly that Sholto wondered whether this was all too good to be true. After a few minutes, they heard Cunningham's voice over the radio, saying tersely that they had radar contact. From that moment, Brown was silent, and everyone on the ground stood around the cathode ray tube watching the two dots on the screen inch closer together as Rawnsley guided Cunningham towards their target.

They were still over the sea when they had picked up the enemy aircraft on their AI radar, and as there was a bright moon behind them shining on the water, Cunningham was cautious in his approach so as not to be seen by any German rear gunner who might be on the lookout. He caught sight of his target but waited until both aircraft were just over the coast and he was less likely to be spotted against the darkness of the ground before closing in for his attack. By then they were not far from where everyone was watching events on the screen at Sopley. Several minutes passed and then suddenly Brown suggested that everyone step outside to see what was happening in the night sky above them. Just as they did so, 'the sound of aircraft engines was interrupted by the thunder of cannon as Cunningham opened fire, and in the sky not far away to the west of where we were standing we saw an aircraft coming down in flames'.[12]

Sholto, Elliott and the King drove the hour's journey through dark country lanes back to Middle Wallop. When they got there, they found an excited gathering, including John Cunningham, waiting for them. Cunningham gave His Majesty a full account of how he had shot down the enemy bomber, a Heinkel III, which was his twelfth victory. Sholto wrote that it was a rare experience for a C-in-C to be able to give his Sovereign such an impressive display.

Three days later, Sholto was back at Bentley Priory, and was told that the German beams indicated that the target for that night was London yet again. This attack would be the last heavy raid London had to face. It was a bright moonlit night, and for seven hours the capital was subjected to a relentless air assault from 500 German bombers. For Sholto, though, his memories of that occasion would be shaped by an event that occurred hundreds of miles away.

From 11 p.m. onwards, the activity in the crowded and busy operations room at Bentley Priory was intense. Soon after nightfall, radar plots began to go down on the filter room table, being passed immediately to the operations room, of the track of an aircraft that appeared to be behaving in a completely different way from all the others. It had crossed the Netherlands coast and was heading in a north-westerly direction across the North Sea towards Scotland. When it was due south of Edinburgh, Sholto requested a report from the Observer Corps in that area. They had already spotted it, saying that it was an Me110. Sholto was sceptical that they had actually identified such a small aircraft at night and he knew also that this aircraft did not carry enough fuel for a long flight from Germany, or even from France, to Scotland and back. He asked for a confirmation on the report, and the Observer Corps replied saying that it was definitely an Me110, and that they had recognised its silhouette against the bright moonlight. They continued to plot its track as it flew westwards across Scotland, and just after 11 p.m., when the main assault started on London, they reported that it had crashed some miles south-west of Glasgow. Two hours later, Fighter Command HQ received a telephone report to say that the crashed aircraft was indeed an Me110, and that the pilot, who had baled out, was being held prisoner.

The heavy raid over London distracted Sholto from what was

happening in Scotland, but after about an hour, his attention was drawn back to events there by a report that, as he said, 'had us all gasping with astonishment'. He was told that the pilot who had baled out of the Me110 was claiming to be Hitler's Deputy Führer, Rudolf Hess, and that he was asking to see the Duke of Hamilton. Sholto could hardly believe what he was hearing, but he got through to the Duke, who was at that time a wing commander in the Auxiliary Air Force serving as the sector commander at Turnhouse, one of Fighter Command's stations near Edinburgh, and asked him if he knew Hess. Hamilton claimed that he didn't but that he had shaken hands with him at the 1936 Olympic Games in Berlin. As an enthusiastic sportsman and aviator, he had been part of a multi-party parliamentary group that had been invited there to observe the Games by the German government. Sholto asked him to drive over to see this man claiming to be Hess and to report back to him. After a long few hours, Hamilton phoned back to say that although he could not be sure, the prisoner did look like the man whose hand he had shaken.

In the early hours of Sunday 11 May, Sholto reported the whole incident to intelligence at the Air Ministry, who in turn consulted an official at the Foreign Office. He advised that Hamilton should fly down to London and report personally to them. This Hamilton did, giving an account to Churchill later that day. For some reason that was never clear to Sholto, the Foreign Office took no effective action for another twenty-four hours. Sir Ivone Kirkpatrick, then Director of the Foreign Division of the Ministry of Information, who had known Hess before the war and who was given the task of interviewing him, admitted that the Foreign Office had been slow to respond to the incident but stated later that 'the Hess episode was comedy from beginning to end', a view shared by Churchill at the time. Kirkpatrick also wrote that 'Hess was a simple, stupid soul with a strong streak of fanaticism and some eccentricity'. This may have been true, but Sholto disagreed with the view that Hess was nothing more than a stupid man, although he observed: 'There can be no doubt that Hess was quite often muddled in his thinking, as well as fanatical in his outlook; and he apparently suffered from more delusions than were normal for even a Nazi leader.'[13] This flight was Hess's fourth attempt to reach the UK, and he believed that he could personally negotiate a peace. The affair caused a great deal of embarrassment to Hitler, who ordered that Hess be shot if he ever reappeared in Germany. Adolf Galland spoke of the event as 'one of the most mysterious affairs of the war'. Apparently, Goering had telephoned him and ordered him to take off with his fighters to intercept Hess, who Goering said 'has gone mad and is flying to England in an Me110. He must be brought down.' Galland commented after receiving this order from Goering: 'I put the receiver down and did not know who had gone mad, the Deputy Führer, the Reichsmarshal, or me.'[14]

Sholto's intimate involvement in the defence against the Blitz took an even more personal turn when his father Langton's house in Montagu Square was bombed, as his daughter and Sholto's youngest sister Claire said, 'into a hole in the ground'. All of Langton's private papers connected with his work were lost. This tragedy was enough for him to decide to move to the United States. Although he was now seventy-seven years old, he set about building another career in the New World, where he already had a sound reputation and a number of influential American clients.

Throughout 1941, Sholto and his team at Fighter Command continued to work on other aids that would increase the likelihood of successful night interceptions and the destruction of enemy night raiders, with varying degrees of success. Airborne searchlights showed promise initially, but Sholto felt that more experiments were needed to judge their effectiveness. Meanwhile the telephone communication network between ground searchlight stations was a top priority, in order that searchlight and fighter efforts could be properly coordinated. One of the greatest dangers in cooperation between fighters and radar-operated ground searchlights, called Searchlight Control Radar (SLC) and nicknamed 'Elsie', was of the searchlights mistakenly illuminating the friendly fighter instead of the enemy raider it was approaching. Eventually, this problem was resolved and the combination of Elsie-equipped searchlights and AI proved to be highly effective.

Sholto expected that the changes to the ground element of radar would be accompanied by the rapid introduction of newer marks of AI that operated on the 10cm wavelength, which was designed to operate at lower altitudes and was much more resistant to enemy jamming. He reiterated that every effort should be made to improve jamming counter measures, particularly those involving ground to air communication. By September 1942, although there was no evidence that enemy jamming aircraft were being used against the UK, their use was being reported in the Middle East and Malta. However, extensive *ground*-operated jamming was being used against Chain Home Low (CHL) and GCI stations in the UK, the Germans having effectively jammed the 1.5m equipment in an area east of a line from Selsey to Gravesend. Sholto reiterated his demands for equipment more resistant to jamming by radio or by the use of metallised leaflets.[15]

Unusually, Sholto begged Portal to abandon the idea of the RAF using metallised leaflets against the enemy, codenamed WINDOW, as experiments that he had instigated within Fighter Command demonstrated that they were highly effective against all forms of AI, GCI and CHL, and that there was no method by which this could be counteracted. If the RAF used the leaflets, the enemy would discover their effects and would use them too to devastating effect, and this would mean that all the hard work on night interception conducted by the Command over the past few years would be nullified. While Portal understood Sholto's concerns and the seriousness of the problem, he felt that Fighter Command should continue to train in ways of overcoming the effects of the leaflets.

The arguments concerning WINDOW simmered on all through the summer of 1942. Professor R. V. Jones disagreed with Sholto's fears over its introduction, observing that 'there was no prospect of the Germans attacking us on anything like the scale that we were now mounting against them',[16] since most of the German bomber force was tied up in Russia. Jones's only proviso was that WINDOW should be introduced when its effect would be greatest, and he felt that this moment would soon pass as the Germans found ways of circumventing the difficulties that it presented for them. In the event, its launch was delayed until July 1943, when it produced spectacular results. In the first RAF night bomber raid over Hamburg in which WINDOW was deployed, it threw the German radar-guided searchlights into confusion as they wandered aimlessly across the sky. The anti-aircraft guns fired randomly or not at all and the night fighters, their radar displays swamped with false echoes, utterly failed to find the incoming bomber stream. Jones estimated that on that first night, WINDOW saved between seventy and eighty RAF bombers.

Notwithstanding the diversion of Hitler's gaze to the East, the determined efforts of Fighter Command in tackling night attacks had eventually yielded rewards, the historian John Ray stating that much credit for this 'must be accorded to its senior officers under the leadership of Douglas'.[17] Sholto wrote of this eventual turn of the tide:

> We worked desperately hard, and by May 1941 we had found the solution. By then the score of night fighters was doubling itself every month. This most significant result was due to increased efficiency through better training and to AI. Even if the Germans had not pulled out in May 1941, and gone for Russia, we had the problem well under control. His casualties would have rapidly become too great and he would have had to desist.[18]

Sholto epitomised the new offensive role assumed by Fighter Command under his leadership, and Ray has summarised beautifully others' impressions of him. Sholto has been described as having 'an unconscious aura of aggression', and as being 'burly, immensely strong and of a commanding presence', and yet 'most friendly and approachable'.[19] All of these impressions I recognise in the father that I knew in my childhood.

CHAPTER SIXTEEN

'FIT TO FLY'

A preoccupation of Sholto's as C-in-C Fighter Command was how to make best use of the exceptionally talented individuals he had serving under him, in whom he seems to have taken a generous personal interest. His experience was that everyone wanted to 'do his bit' by taking to the air and playing his part in defeating the enemy, and he was mindful that all RAF aircrew were volunteers. They were, as he was, individualists, choosing for themselves the path they wanted to follow, and the memory that dominated all others for him was that of the men themselves. Every time he thought about his experiences in his long RAF career, his recollections of these men came vividly to his mind.

One such memory was of a pilot who had served with him in the Sudan in the early 1930s, a real character named Murray Payn. In the spring of 1941, Payn turned up unannounced at Sholto's office in Bentley Priory, bringing with him Prince Bernhard of the Netherlands, for whom he was acting as equerry. Sholto had only just met the Prince informally in London. He had a reputation as a blunt, forthright man and at their first formal meeting at Fighter Command HQ he wasted no time in coming straight to the point, asking Sholto: 'Would you have me taught to fly a Spitfire?' Sholto knew that Prince Bernhard was German by birth, but he had made a gallant stand on behalf of the Netherlands and the Dutch royal family, extending even to personal combat, when the Germans had invaded his adopted country, which, since his marriage to Princess, later Queen, Juliana, had possessed his complete allegiance. Something else Sholto knew about him was that he had accumulated several hundreds of flying hours as a pilot of light aircraft.

Sholto asked Payn whether they had approached the Air Ministry about this, as it was something that only the CAS could decide. Payn 'was not the sort of man who could ever be put off his cheerful, if rather eccentric, stride by any formalities or red tape',[1] but he was forced to admit that they had not consulted the CAS. Prince Bernhard added that the Air Ministry officials with whom they had been in contact had considered it far too dangerous for a member of the Dutch royal family to risk learning to fly a modern fighter, and besides, the Prince's eyesight was a cause for concern as he had to wear glasses. He was charmingly persuasive, however, and, ably assisted by Payn, he made such a strong case that Sholto was forced to acquiesce. His assent was dependent on one condition, though: that the Prince should undergo the full course at an OTU. Sholto said that he was not going to have any 'playing about', and that Prince Bernhard would have to spend weeks studying and flying like all the other trainee pilots. The Prince's utter delight, even at the thought of ground training and lectures, convinced Sholto that he was genuinely eager to become a fully qualified fighter pilot. Both he and Payn went to the Spitfire OTU at Hawarden near Chester, and Prince Bernhard emerged from the course as a competent Spitfire pilot.

Sometimes, due to the insistent way in which they argued their case, Sholto allowed people to take to the skies against his better judgement. One such person who had pestered him to be allowed on operations was his own PA, Bob Wright. Having worked on radar in the filter room at Fighter Command, and then as Dowding's PA before he was Sholto's, Wright wanted to become one of the new breed of night fighter navigators. Sholto felt at first that it was ridiculous for anyone as experienced in a good staff appointment as Wright undoubtedly was to start all over again in something for which he was untrained and possibly unsuitable. Sholto pointed out to him that he had already failed his aircrew medical due to poor eyesight, but Wright insisted on having another attempt, and this time he wangled his way through. This allowed him to increase the pressure, and he explained that he really wanted to experience something of what

Sholto had gone through in WWI. After a year as his PA, Wright was allowed to go for training, and by an extraordinary stroke of luck, or perhaps another wangle, he managed to get posted to No. 604 Squadron, commanded by John Cunningham.

Much to Sholto's distress, occasionally it did not work out as well as this. He wrote:

> It is exacting enough for the hearty, robust, simple-minded en-thusiast to take in his stride the stresses of active service. For the intellectual these stresses become, because of the element of imag-ination alone, much more difficult to cope with. And yet, for all that one might so mistakenly expect of them, we found that the young intellectual was well represented among our air crews in the Royal Air Force.[2]

One such bright young man was Richard Hillary, a former Battle of Britain pilot. He had been severely burned in his stricken aircraft during the battle and appeared as a Flight Lieutenant on Sholto's headquarters staff in 1942. His once handsome face had been seri-ously disfigured and scarred, and his hands were like claws. He had spent over three months at East Grinstead being put back together by the plastic surgeon Archie McIndoe, which entailed four new eyelids and a new top lip. It wasn't only externally that Hillary was a changed man. Sholto wrote: 'By the time that he arrived at Bentley Priory, the whole force and expression of Hillary's character had become rather excessively individualistic.' Some thought that he had a chip on his shoulder due to his physical appearance, but Sholto realised that was not the case. Rather, he found him charming and forthright with an acerbic sense of humour. He wrote that his liking for Hillary might have been because 'I have always preferred that a man should have some bite in his character'.[3]

As soon as Hillary arrived at Bentley Priory, he badgered every-one to be allowed to return to operational flying, but that looked like an impossibility. His fellow officers in the Mess observed that he could barely manage a knife and fork. Sholto and his staff realised that Hillary had been through a very testing time, and although they tried to help him, he could not reconcile himself to having to stay earthbound. He pleaded his case several times with Sholto, who told him that he simply could not recommend a return to the air. Finally, he acquiesced, saying: 'If you can get the doctors to pass you, you can go back on ops,' never for a minute believing that the medics would do so, but they did. Sholto still did not consider Hillary fit for operational flying, but in an attempt to minimise the dangers to him, he told him that he would not allow him to go back to single-seater day fighters. Instead, Sholto proposed that Hillary should go to an OTU to train as a night fighter pilot since the flying was in some ways not as tough as dogfighting during the day, which he accepted, grudgingly.

Sholto heard nothing more until he received the sad news of Hillary's death in January 1943 while on a night training flight in adverse weather conditions. Both he and his navigator were killed. Hillary was only twenty-three years old, and as Sholto wrote: 'So ended a very fine young man and a very promising young author.'[4] Hillary had written a poignant memoir about his experiences during and after the Battle of Britain entitled *The Last Enemy*, first published in 1942. Sholto reproached himself for the rest of his life for allowing Hillary to win him over and for acceding to his requests to return to flying, feeling profound regret for his rash decision.

Notwithstanding the enthusiasm of young men like Wright and especially Hillary, Sholto was also involved in the ongoing discussions throughout the war concerning the optimum length of an operational tour for aircrews and how many could reasonably be expected of them. Central to these discussions, although something with which Sholto seemed reluctant to associate himself, was a concept exclusive to the RAF and egregiously named 'lack of moral fibre' (LMF). This policy was adopted following a series of reconnaissance missions and raids on German naval bases in December 1939 by Wellingtons of No. 5 Group, Bomber Command. Attrition rates of over 50 per cent had caused a crisis of confidence among aircrews, and it was deemed necessary to devise some kind of punitive sanction in order to compel them to undertake hazardous missions.

This was first articulated in a meeting on 21 March 1940 of senior

RAF officers, including Portal, who was to take over shortly as C-in-C Bomber Command, the CAS, Newall, and the newly appointed AMP, Gossage. Following a draft policy document composed immediately after the meeting, LMF was introduced formally in a letter sent on 22 April to commanders throughout the RAF by Charles Evans, Principal Assistant Secretary for Personnel in the Air Ministry, which came to be known as the 'waverer letter', after the name that was given to those deemed to be lacking in moral fibre. Evans wrote that the Air Council had been considering the question of the 'disposal' (in itself an awful word) of members of aircrews in operational units 'whose conduct may cause them to forfeit the confidence of their Commanding Officers in their determination and reliability in the face of danger'.

The instructions issued in the letter were 'not intended to apply to flagrant cases of cowardice which demand disciplinary action by Court Martial, or to cases where flying personnel are exhibiting symptoms of strain as the result of the conscientious discharge of their duties but no question arises of lack of courage or determination'. The cases to which the letter referred were either those of men who maintained a show of carrying out their duties but who had nevertheless lost the confidence of their Commanding Officers, or to those who had not only lost the confidence of their Commanding Officers in their courage and resolution but also who made no secret of their unwillingness to carry out dangerous duties. These cases, in which there was 'no physical disability and no justification for granting a rest from operational employment and, in fact, nothing wrong except a lack of moral fibre' were to be 'disposed of' as quickly as possible.[5]

Another letter sent out by Evans in September 1940 reiterated the policy. Pilots, observers and aircrew classified in this way were to be stripped of their badges. For a man 'lacking in moral fibre',

> there will be no question of his being given an opportunity to rehabilitate himself or given non-operational employment. In the case of an officer, his services will be dispensed with, either by termination of his commission if he is on probation or by calling him to resign if he is not on probation; an airman will be reverted to his

basic trade [while also being reduced to the lowest rank] or discharged, as appropriate.[6]

Furthermore, a large red 'W' was to be emblazoned on the records of personnel classified in this way.

The problem was, how were group, station and squadron commanders and medical officers (MOs) supposed to distinguish between those who were supposedly out-and-out cowards, those 'lacking in moral fibre' and those who were genuinely suffering from psychiatric illness, especially war neurosis? This dilemma remained throughout the war, despite the issuing of more detailed guidance in a 'Memorandum on the Disposal of Members of Air Crews Who Forfeit the Confidence of Their Commanding Officers', also signed by Charles Evans and revised three times during the course of the war.

In 1944, an investigation into psychological disorders in flying personnel examined 'the reliability of psychiatric opinion' in the RAF by looking at the differences between the views of two psychiatrists in the diagnoses they applied to individual patients. It found that they agreed with each other only 44 per cent of the time when one of them made the diagnosis of 'lack of confidence' (a term used later in the war and analogous to LMF), but 88 per cent of the time if one of them posited the diagnosis of an anxiety neurosis (the commonest disorder).[7] This implies that there was doubt and a 'grey area' where it was hard to classify those who were not suffering from an obvious or severe mental health issue.

Although the LMF policy emanated from senior RAF commanders in response to a crisis of confidence in Bomber Command, a conversation on what to do about war neurosis in the next conflict had been stimulated following the Munich crisis in September 1938. At that time, a debate on the policy to be adopted was initiated not by the War Office or even the Air Ministry but by the Ministry of Pensions. The government wanted to avoid the situation that occurred after WWI in which, by 1939, there were approximately 40,000 people in Britain receiving pensions for war-related psychiatric disorders and a further 80,000 cases that had been settled. From the beginning, the Ministry of Pensions took a hard-hearted approach. As far as possible, the invaliding of airmen out the RAF for neurosis attributable to war strain was to be strenuously avoided as it would qualify them for a government pension. Emphasis was placed on 'constitutional predisposition, either inborn or acquired early in life', to nervous illness, not on the level of trauma to which an individual was exposed. The use of such terms as 'shell-shock' or, more appropriate for the RAF, 'flying stress' was discouraged, as these placed the responsibility for breakdown on the strains induced by an airman's activities in wartime rather than on the individual himself.

It appears that some WWI physicians such as William Rivers, Charles Myers and James Birley had shown more compassion on this issue than their WWII counterparts. Although Birley acknowledged that attitude may play a part in breakdown, he was sceptical that there was any such thing as an ideal flying temperament: 'To postulate one temperament and one only for flying, or for any other form of co-ordinated activity, surely implies a too mechanical and stereotyped habit of mind.' He also suggested that the military were culpable for not preparing airmen adequately for what was 'an unnatural and dangerous occupation', and that it was difficult for military authorities to 'realise that will-power like the rest of one's mental faculties was not immune to exhaustion'.[8] For T. A. Ross, a psychiatrist who had also been through the traumas of WWI:

> It is simply true that there are some people who can stand up less well than others to danger and stress. It is also true that no man can stand the stress of warfare for an unlimited time. All of us have our breaking-point. To some it comes sooner than to others.[9]

However, Dr Charles Symonds, the RAF's senior consultant in neuropsychiatry during WWII, took a somewhat different view, writing: 'Curiously the question of predisposition to war neuroses, so called, appears to have obtained relatively little attention in the last war.'[10] Like Birley, he had served in WWI, but his experiences in that conflict had left him pessimistic about human nature. He was convinced that war was essentially a test of character and was concerned that men should not be given any opportunity to evade their duty by any

medical 'back doors'. He outlawed the term 'flying stress' for anything except the external load to which aircrews were subjected and
espoused the LMF policy. If an individual developed a neurosis as a
result of 'overloading or temperamental handicap', recognised psychiatric terms should be used to describe it, such as anxiety or hysteria.[11]

But by the end of 1942, Symonds was having second thoughts
about the LMF policy, largely due to the way in which it was being
applied throughout the RAF. The impression in the service seemed to
be that there were only 'two classes of case to be dealt with, the sick
and the cowards, and that differentiation between those two classes is
all that is necessary. In practice there is a number of cases which do
not fall into either of these categories.'[12] Reports of the brutal treatment of a number of aircrew under this policy, some of whom had
been decorated for bravery in the past, and the lack of distinction between those who had 'done their best' and those who had not, seem
to have caused his change of heart.

Symonds's views on temperament were also called into question
later in the war. The report on differences of opinion between two
psychiatrists issued in 1944 indicated that in 76 per cent of cases of
psychological disorder, the consultants considered that flying duties
rather than temperament had been a factor. When they considered
predisposition to neurosis, they could only agree in half of the cases
whether a man's life experiences and character, as assessed in an hour-
long interview, made him a more likely candidate for that condition.
Symonds and Wing Commander Lawson of Special Disposal and
Releases actually disagreed with the term 'lack of moral fibre' but did
approve of the concept of a label as a deterrent and preferred the even
more condemnatory term 'lack of courage'. Both of these terms were
challenged by the Director General of Medical Services (DGMS), Air
Marshal Sir Harold Whittingham, who wrote in 1944: 'I feel that the
term "lack of moral fibre" is an unhappy one, and that "lack of courage" is worse: I suggest instead the term "lack of confidence to fly".'[13]

Whatever it was called, by 1944, politicians such as Sinclair, the
Secretary of State for Air, who foresaw that the coalition government
would come to a close with the end of the war, realised that the concept of brave airmen, possibly even those who had won a decoration,

being stripped of their rank and badge and pronounced LMF would not go down well either in Parliament or with the electorate. Many MPs had been approached by the parents of those classified as LMF, or sometimes by the individuals themselves, and in the face of criticism Sinclair had promised Parliament that every case which might involve a penalty would be examined by a government minister before any action was taken. This task he helpfully delegated to Balfour, his Under-Secretary, who hated the poisoned chalice he had been handed. He and the AMP looked at each case, and he wrote that no one was more relieved than they were if a medical reason could be found for the person's failure.

Historians disagree about how many men were affected by this policy in WWII, but figures were released each year between 1942 and 1945 by Symonds and his colleague Squadron Leader Denis Williams and summarised by Whittingham. These numbers, which are probably the most accurate, indicate that there were between 300 and 400 cases each year of LMF or 'lack of confidence' and nearly 3,000 cases of neurosis, most of which occurred in Bomber Command, where the attrition rate was highest, and in Flying Training Command,[14] which was a much more stressful environment than it might appear. Pilots accounted for half the cases of neurosis, the preponderance of these occurring among officer rather than sergeant pilots.

The question about how to deal with aircrew who exhibited symptoms of mental breakdown was naturally related to how long they were able to continue on operations before needing a rest. In WWI, Birley realised from careful observation that there was a 'crucial moment' at which pilots needed to be rested once they had reached their 'period of experience', which occurred after about two months of operational flying, but before fatigue supervened and they manifested symptoms of strain. In WWII, Symonds and Williams, after reviewing the scientific literature, concluded that the 'most important single predisposing cause of psychological breakdown in flying personnel was fatigue',[15] and that the main cause of fatigue was fear. Birley had come to similar conclusions, but whereas he concentrated on the universality of fear under extreme conditions and the ways in which men suppressed it, Symonds and Williams continued to assert the primacy of temperament and, similarly to Sholto, imagination. What Birley and Symonds had in common was that they both believed that it was the squadron medical officer's duty to watch his aircrews like a hawk and rest them at that 'crucial moment' in order that they could recover from fatigue and return to duty in a short time.

In February 1940, during the 'phoney war', the Air Staff considered issuing a directive to all Commands on the subject of the relief of tired crews in operational squadrons, and Sholto, who was then ACAS, wrote a memo to Portal, then AMP, suggesting that when full-scale air operations started, there would need to be an established system of relief, which he and the Deputy CAS felt should be considered forthwith. Sholto recalled that in WWI, a regular system was introduced by which pilots were sent home after six to eight months in France for a rest and a change of atmosphere. He proposed that 'personnel withdrawn from operational squadrons for a rest could with advantage be sent to the OTUs and units in Training Command, where their recent operational experience would make them invaluable for instructional duties'.[16] Portal's response, which he sent the following day with Sholto's minute to the DGMS, at that time Air Marshal Sir A. V. J. Richardson, was less than sympathetic to this suggestion:

> I think it would be quite wrong to let it be generally understood that we <u>expect</u> flying crews to display symptoms of war strain after any specified period, e.g., six months ... We must guard against any tendency to over-emphasise war strain just as carefully as we guard against waste of personnel through working them till they are past repair, and I do not see how we can do anything else but rely on the Commanding Officer.[17]

Like Symonds, Portal emphasised individual variability among aircrew in their susceptibility to genuine strain.

Richardson came back with a similar categorisation to Symonds's, and to Sholto's when he became C-in-C Fighter Command, of the two main types of flying personnel: '(a) he who is lacking in imagination, who is self-confident, tough minded and inured to risks, (b) he who is more timid and sensitive, imaginative as to the dangerous potentialities of a situation, and lacking in a firm belief in his own powers to defeat them'.[18] It's not difficult to guess which of these two Richardson deemed would last longer, but even the tough type could degenerate as a result of prolonged physical or mental stress. However, once again, the emphasis was placed on the individual's innate disposition. Like Portal, he was against imposing an arbitrary limit for operational tours.

This attitude did not prepare the RAF for the scale of psychiatric casualties in 1940–41, and even by the end of 1940, it became clear that operational flying should be broken up into manageable portions of time, or tours, and that these should offer a reasonable chance of survival, although the Air Staff continued to argue about this throughout the war. The optimum length of tour was known as the 'datum line', which was to be drawn at a point that offered a 50/50 chance. The number of operational tours was also a concern, two being considered the maximum that anyone could stand.

Sholto, when he was C-in-C Fighter Command, has been characterised, along with 'Bomber' Harris, as being somewhat harsh in his judgement of how much aircrew could endure. The historian John McCarthy wrote that they were both 'quite happy' to see crews come forward for a third operational tour, having to be instructed firmly to submit to the AMP the names of any aircrew whom they wished to serve above the datum line.[19] This contrasts with Sholto's own accounts of both Wright and Hillary, which seem to display a concern for the individual members of his command, but were they simply his favourites, or did he evince similar care for everyone who served under him?

Following his appointment as C-in-C Fighter Command, and in response to a letter in January 1941 from the Air Ministry requesting his opinion on the optimum length of operational tour, Sholto wrote that 'with so many variable factors it is difficult to lay down a hard and fast rule which will meet all conditions'. He stressed the great disparity in stamina between individual pilots, the considerable variability in the strain of operational flying between the different groups of Fighter Command, as well as the differences in performance between types of aircraft, which also contributed to operational strain. He discussed the matter with his group commanders and suggested that 'the best criterion for deciding when pilots and air crews should be rested from operational flying is the number of hours of operational flying performed'.[20] However, he proposed that a certain amount of latitude must be allowed to squadron and group commanders, acknowledging that some pilots would show signs of strain after less than the allotted period while 'tougher spirits' could be permitted to continue for a somewhat longer period of operational flying. This he suggested should be 200 hours. The C-in-C Bomber Command, Peirse, agreed with Sholto's view, but the C-in-C Coastal Command, Sir Frederick Bowhill, wanted greater variation in the length of tour due to the widely differing tasks that pilots in Coastal had to perform.

Later in the year, Portal, now CAS, had to write a corrective letter to Sholto, with a similar letter to Peirse, saying that a number of reports had reached him suggesting that 'some of our most distinguished pilots have been allowed to continue operational flying after they have approached the limit of their endurance'. Contrary to his earlier seemingly hard-hearted attitude when he was AMP in February 1940 during the phoney war, Portal was concerned that those 'who have achieved much' should be 'taken off operational flying before nervous fatigue supervenes'. No doubt the exigencies of continuing warfare and the responsibilities of his position at the top of the RAF had altered his stance. Perceptively, he wrote: 'It is of course useless to rely upon pilots themselves to ask to be taken off operational flying before they approach the danger point. It is little more helpful to ask them, as the majority would say they were fit and anxious to go on.' Portal continued that the responsibility in watching for the first signs of fatigue must rest with station commanders, who were in day-to-day touch with pilots. He advised them also to consult Command medical staff for guidance on the symptoms of fatigue. Finally, he urged Sholto

> to look upon the fixed limit of operational flying as a maximum and to make every endeavour to take pilots off flying before the limit is reached, so that every pilot will know that he has not got to

fly more than a certain number of hours on operational work and may well be taken off some time before.[21]

This letter was followed a few days later by one from the DCAS, Air Vice-Marshal Bottomley, to Sholto concerning the amount of operational flying that should be undertaken by officers in command of fighter stations and requesting his views once again. The Air Staff realised that while these Commanding Officers would be reluctant to cease operational flying, particularly as leaders of formations, they were men 'of considerable professional ability and wide operational and administrative experience', who would be sorely missed if they were lost in battle. On the other hand, they were a great boost to morale on operations and if they ceased to fly regularly, they may lose their skill and eventually fall victim to the enemy.[22]

Once again, Sholto was reluctant to apply any hard and fast rules about 'this delicate question'. He was opposed to issuing an order that prevented station commanders from flying on operations, saying: 'You may occasionally lose a Station Commander that way, but this is more than compensated for by the fillip which is given to the morale of the squadrons on the station ... and indeed, to the Command as a whole.' Sholto cited an order given at one point in the previous war that squadron commanders were not allowed to fly, observing that it was quickly dropped as a bad idea, and that in 1918, almost all squadron commanders (himself included) flew regularly with their squadrons with good results. His final paragraph clearly indicated his desire to guard the independence of his command against interference from the Air Staff, ironically in much the same way as Dowding had done before him in his battles with the Air Ministry. Sholto wrote:

In short, I think that it would be a mistake for the Air Ministry to issue any instructions, regulations or directions in this matter whatsoever. Why cannot you leave these things to the good sense of my Group Commanders and myself? I rather feel that you are trespassing on our preserves.[23]

Over the next six months, Sholto continued to declare his wish to be free of Air Staff interference in the running of his command. He wrote in response to an Air Ministry letter of 22 November 1941 that its provisions, if rigidly applied, would be 'detrimental to the efficiency of Fighter Command'. He asserted that there was as much variability in the strain imposed by flying tasks in Fighter Command as there was in Coastal Command. He had instigated a programme whereby squadrons were exchanged between the quieter groups and those employed more intensively, giving them 'frequent rests from strenuous operational flying'. Individual pilots were also exchanged whenever they showed signs of strain. Conscientious observance of the 200 hours datum line during the previous two months had highlighted considerable problems. There was an overwhelming shortage of experienced flight and section leaders in the Command, and under the 200-hour limit pilots were often taken off operations while they were still quite fresh. These pilots were sent then to OTUs as instructors although they may have had no fighting experience. His request to the Air Ministry was that there should be the same flexibility of datum line for Fighter Command as had been allowed for Coastal Command.

Sholto had a carefully thought-out system of reporting in which operational pilots who had completed 200 hours and instructors who had completed a six-month tour in an OTU were notified monthly to his personnel staff. They also obtained from the Air Ministry a list of vacancies in Flying Training Command. All of these lists were then discussed at a meeting over which Sholto himself presided, and his group commanders recommended suitable posts for each of the pilots. Occasionally, pilots in operational squadrons were kept on for up to a month beyond the datum line, but strict instructions were given for them to be withdrawn immediately they showed any signs of strain, and Sholto felt that this order was being conscientiously carried out by his group, station and squadron commanders. He also observed that Fighter Command would benefit from being sent experienced instructors from Flying Training Command who had completed a twelve- to eighteen-month tour of duty there, something that rarely happened, as their proficiency made them very successful night fighter pilots.

Sholto reiterated these concerns in a letter to Portal at the same time, insisting: 'We are becoming desperately short of experienced pilots and potential leaders in this Command. I am convinced, as is Leigh-Mallory, that this is the main reason for the somewhat heavy casualties we have been suffering lately when we have undertaken large scale offensive operations.' He stressed that he had no desire to keep any pilot on operational flying for one hour longer than he was able to stand, and 'apart from the humanitarian aspect, it does not pay us to do this from the point of view of efficiency'.[24] Sholto made his case so strongly that the Air Ministry acceded to his request for greater flexibility in the application of the datum line over the winter months, but once offensive operations recommenced the following summer, it should be strictly observed once more. However, allowance was made for the different types of flying in Fighter Command and where pilots were involved in less strenuous duties, only half the flying hours would count towards the datum line.

Unfortunately, though, Sholto had another battle with the Air Ministry on his hands. They wanted to reserve for themselves the right to decide whether pilots should be posted for a second operational tour in Fighter Command after a suitable rest and placement as an OTU instructor. Experienced pilots were needed in overseas squadrons, and Sholto was concerned that they would be 'poached' from Fighter Command to fill posts abroad. He also felt that Air Ministry policy, whereby 'no member of an aircrew should be allowed to do a second operational tour if there is available a suitable individual who had not done a first operational tour', meant that certain individuals, particularly sergeant pilots, would be excluded from doing a second operational tour even though they were 'fit and eager to do so'. (He was obviously aware that the incidence of breakdown was lower among sergeant pilots than among officers.) Indeed, he felt that 'pilots of exceptional energy and nerve should be capable of doing a third operational tour in Fighter Command, particularly as Wing Commanders Flying'. However, he issued instructions prohibiting wing leaders from undertaking the most dangerous missions over enemy-occupied France. But this was not enough to prevent the loss of one of WWII's most famous young fighter aces, Paddy Finucane, who went over on such an operation and was lost while engaged in shooting up ground targets, a source of profound regret to both Portal and Sholto.

When offensive operations were few and enemy bomber activity was low, as in the winter of 1941/42, Sholto felt that his pilots had the opportunity to rest and recuperate even while remaining in operational units, so for a few experienced aircrews, greater flexibility should be allowed in the application of the datum line. However, as 1942 progressed and aerial combat increased once more, the Air Staff realised that a re-think was required concerning the length and number of operational tours. The new AMP, Air Marshal Sir Bertine Sutton, minuted the VCAS, Air Vice-Marshal Medhurst:

> Commands are not entirely the best judges of policy in respect of (i) length of operational tour, (ii) number of operational tours and (iii) employment when not on operational tours because first they will be inclined to take merely a front-line view of what is required for aircrew manpower, secondly they tend to try, very wrongly in my opinion, to maintain the 'closed shop.'[25]

These were things of which Sholto could be accused. Finally, due to the changing manpower situation, Sutton wrote that only volunteers need be taken for second operational tours.

There was also a problem in the consideration of the OTU as a 'rest' by those in operational commands. Sutton observed: 'Instructional duties are the reverse of rest for many people. They are disagreeable to many. The long hours produce staleness and fatigue.'[26] The Air Staff suggested that this could be mitigated by giving pilots a rest between the end of their operational tour and the start of their stint as an OTU instructor. Sholto's successor at Fighter Command, Air Marshal Trafford Leigh-Mallory, suggested that the period of leave allowed should be up to a month. But this did not make the prospect of an OTU tour any more attractive to pilots. 'Johnnie' Johnson, an experienced and well-respected fighter pilot, described in his memoir the concept of 'rest' at a training school as 'something of a misnomer', the supposed 'rest' turning into 'a frustrating search to escape. Eventually your stint was over and you went back on ops., far more tired than when you were taken off six months earlier.'[27] Jimmy Rawnsley, John Cunningham's radar operator, experienced at first hand the problems with OTUs when he and Cunningham were posted to one for a 'rest' in July 1942. After a few weeks, Jimmy realised that the whole system had been 'bedevilled by a vicious circle of bad faith'. More often than not, an unscrupulous squadron CO would 'joyfully unload any incapable or ill-disciplined men he happened to have on his hands' who were due for a break from operations onto OTUs as instructors.

> The news got around and to be sent to an OTU came to be regarded as a disgrace, an indication of failure. Those at the OTUs who took their jobs seriously and genuinely tried to run the training programme as it was planned battled on with this sort of misfit material, often despairing, and clinging to such good men as they had until even they began to falter and wonder if they would ever see a squadron again.[28]

OTUs were not immune from attack by many Luftwaffe 'intruders', and this, coupled with all the other hazards connected with training, meant that 'there was far more strain and risk involved in being an instructor on a so-called rest'.[29]

This may explain why Symonds and Williams observed that the incidence of psychological disorder was so high in instructors that it approached the level of that in operational crews. It may have been due in part to the stress of previous operational flying, but the two neuropsychiatrists surmised that it was also the nature of instructing work itself that led to breakdown, caused by boredom, staleness and anxiety. Nevertheless, OTUs were a vital part of the RAF's organisation, and despite misgivings, it was considered that they still provided a respite from operations, provided that OTU crews were not called upon for large-scale operations.

Of course, the problems did not go away when Sholto was posted as C-in-C Middle East Command in January 1943; the length of operational tour continued to be a vexed question until the end of the war. The situation in the Middle East produced different conditions to those of Home Commands, and Sholto had a greater variety of aircraft operating in his squadrons. As he had done during his time at Fighter Command, he made a lot of the fact that the length of operational tour should be tailored to the type of aircraft and the tasks that it had to perform. The Air Staff were proposing a reduction in the duration of operational tours for aircrews on some types of aircraft, as they considered that two short tours were preferable to 'flogging the horse till he drops'.[30] Those on other types might see an increase in their spell of duty, but Sholto put forward a strong case for not increasing the length of tour in his Fighter Reconnaissance (Army Cooperation) and General Reconnaissance Squadrons due to the dangerous work they had to perform. It is not inconceivable that Sholto had his brother Archie at the back of his mind. He had been doing precisely this kind of work when he was shot down in WWI and so Sholto would have been especially conscious of the particular needs of personnel in these types of squadrons.

In his views on the dangers of reconnaissance work, Sholto was echoing those of Symonds and Williams, who observed that the incidence of psychological disorder was as high in those performing these duties as it was in Bomber Command, where the incidence was highest of all, reflecting the amount of hazard involved. Jimmy Rawnsley articulated this perfectly when he wrote:

> But however slight the strain, and no matter how long it took to build up, it was there as a very natural revolt of the human system against repeated exposure to risk, whether present and real or merely potential and imagined. It was there inside each one of us, a secret enemy within. I felt that it was as if each of us started with a certain capital, a sum of something – was it fortitude? – which we spent, sometimes over a short period, sometimes over a much longer stretch of time. But when it was gone life became a torment with the spirit flogging on a bankrupt body. That was what we called the twitch.[31]

As a conclusion to the whole matter, a few months after the end of WWII, Lawson wrote an important memorandum summarising the wartime policy on LMF. Reading the memo today, it sounds like an exercise in self-justification, both of Lawson himself and of the policy, the assertion that it was 'distinctly fair both to the individual and to the Service' appearing near the beginning of the document. Lawson stated that the alternative would have been to court martial everyone suspected of LMF, but even the reason for not going down this route sounds somewhat tough if pragmatic. It would mean that the individual would have to 'remain on his Unit for a considerable time both before and after the court martial and this would have had a most serious effect on the morale of others'. Therefore it was necessary to get rid of these people as quickly as possible. Lawson added that those classified as LMF were not worried about the stripping of their rank but the loss of their badge was of the utmost importance to them. He admitted: 'In such a policy it must always be that a number are harshly treated and it has been our constant endeavour to reduce that to an absolute minimum and I believe that this has been achieved.' However, it was clear as the war progressed that 'some Squadron and Station Commanders were not approaching the subject with sympathy and understanding ... So many [of those labelled as LMF] had been marched in and told they were yellow and marched out, and the requirements of the Memorandum had been carried out in a lot of cases by the NCO in charge of the Orderly Room.'[32]

Lawson did concede that, as Sholto had observed, the type of aircraft and the operations that aircrew were called upon to undertake played a very big part in many cases of LMF. But Lawson was absolutely certain that personnel in training should never be asked to state a preference for the aircraft that they wished to fly, or if they were, no attention should be paid to it. Lawson accused trainees who questioned this approach of a 'spoilt child attitude'. However, he asserted again that he had never been in favour of the term 'lack of moral fibre', and had tried to get it eliminated in 1943 but was strongly opposed by Bomber Command. Due probably to increasingly high attrition rates in Bomber Command in 1943 (33 per cent chance of surviving a first tour and only 16 per cent chance of completing a second), an LMF policy addendum meant that the possibility of being labelled as LMF following completion of a first tour was abolished. However, again because of remonstrations from Bomber Command, this fact was not broadcast in case it caused members of aircrew to give up after one tour and not to undertake a second.

All in all, the relatively small numbers of aircrew classified as LMF, which Lawson quoted as being less than 0.4 per cent of the whole of the RAF, he considered to be 'a grand record', even though men were so frightened of this classification that there were probably many more suffering at least from anxiety if not more severe mental health problems but who were too afraid to come forward.

Lawson considered the final revision of the LMF document, issued in 1945, should be the basis of peacetime procedure. This meant that the policy and its accompanying stigma would continue even if the label was largely dropped; indeed, it pervaded the whole culture of the RAF and its effects were felt for decades thereafter, even up to the present time. In the 1960s, it was used to describe aircrew who might fail in training or once they had become operational. During the First Gulf War in 1991, 'LMF' was used to describe Tornado crews who were quietly sent home when they found it hard to cope with the threat of operations. I have been told that it is still around in the RAF today, usually adopted by those who are nowhere near the sharp end of operations and who feel free to be critical.

One of the hardest things to combat in the recognition and treatment of PTSD among military personnel is this whole question of stigma, and policies such as this are how it is fostered and why it proves so difficult to eradicate. Even the concept of 'resilience', which has gained so much traction in military circles despite considerable confusion around defining and investigating it scientifically, can be a camouflage for stigma and prejudice to flourish. Once again, the responsibility is placed firmly back on the individual, whereas, as Sandy McFarlane observed in a recent examination of how resilience was viewed during the twentieth century: 'Men had to go to war to become ill.'[33] How much have we progressed since Sholto's time?

CHAPTER SEVENTEEN

DAY SWEEPS

When Sholto took over at Fighter Command, although the night threat was in full swing, the heaviest day fighting above the UK had ended, so Trenchard suggested to the new CAS, Portal, that the command should adopt a more offensive policy by operating large patrols over enemy-occupied France. This brought the Big Wing debate into focus once again, reignited by a rather emphatic Leigh-Mallory, who wanted seven wings to be formed across Nos 10, 11 and 12 Groups.[1] As part of Portal and Sinclair's clean sweep after Dowding's departure, Leigh-Mallory was shortly to be made AOC No. 11 Group in place of Keith Park, who moved to Training Command. Although Sholto approved of this change, he did not initiate it, and he realised that Leigh-Mallory was rather self-opinionated, which 'raised the hackles of other people'.[2] The problem was that all the disadvantages of big wings remained.

However, this tactic fed into Trenchard's new strategy for Fighter Command. He advocated a system of offensive sweeps similar to those over the Western Front in WWI. But in Sholto's 1925 Staff College lecture, he had said that he had learned that very large patrols over enemy territory sometimes defeated their own object, in that the hostile fighters turned eastwards and went on doing so *ad infinitum*, only to turn round when the formation turned, attacking its rear as it headed westwards for home.[3] Sholto told Portal that in the present situation in 1940, the severe casualties that they would be likely to suffer in operations across the Channel would offset any results that might be achieved. Portal listened to Sholto and asked him to write a paper expressing his point of view. As he did this, he thought more

221

carefully about it and realised that his arguments were 'pretty feeble', so he informed Portal that he had changed his mind and that he was now in favour of Trenchard's idea, but it did indeed become very controversial due to the pilot losses sustained.

Therefore in the middle of December, Sholto's fighter pilots began 'carrying the war to the enemy'. These operations began slowly with small-scale flights of fighters alone operating at low altitude over France and were codenamed RHUBARB. Between 20 December 1940 and 13 June 1941, 149 RHUBARBS resulted in only eighteen engagements with German aircraft; only seven enemy aircraft were claimed for the loss of eight pilots. During the summers of 1941–43, after which they were discontinued, hundreds of fighter pilots were lost on either small or mass RHUBARB operations.[4]

Larger-scale fighter sorties involving high-flying sweeps, known as RODEOS, were begun in early January 1941. These were ignored by the Luftwaffe since they presented little threat, so CIRCUS operations were introduced, in which a dozen Blenheim bombers, escorted by up to twelve squadrons of fighters, were used as bait, attacking short-range targets in France 'in the hope that the Luftwaffe would oppose this daylight effrontery'.[5] However, as New Zealand's most famous fighter pilot Alan Deere noted, the bombers 'were inadequate, both in numbers and weight of bombs carried, to threaten seriously worthwhile enemy targets'.[6] Fighter Command also made the mistake of allocating too many fighters; sometimes a single Stirling bomber was escorted by as many as 200 fighters, which provided a poor return for the number of enemy fighters destroyed.

Shortly after CIRCUS operations began, the heavy losses incurred by Fighter Command attracted Churchill's attention. As early as 12 February Sholto was voicing his disquiet over the offensive sweeps, reminding Leigh-Mallory that 'our idea was to go over the other side and leap on the enemy from a great height in superior numbers; instead of which it looks as though we ourselves are being leapt on'. Evill agreed and told Sholto in March that the pilots had received insufficient training for the difficult task that they were being asked to perform. He stated: 'It is out of all reason that we should be imposing such a serious handicap on ourselves.'[7]

It was not only on operations that there were difficulties. Shortly after this, Sholto aired his anxiety in a letter to all groups, writing: 'The present high accident rate within the Command is causing me grave concern. During the past three months we have had 89 fatal accidents, which have resulted in 106 deaths.' He asserted that a high proportion of these were avoidable and were due to lack of training for flying in bad weather, practice manoeuvres and insufficient application of flying discipline.[8]

Losses both on operations and due to accidents exacerbated the perennial problem of pilot shortage, something of which Sholto had seemed not to be fully aware during the Battle of Britain when Dowding had been C-in-C of Fighter Command but which now caused him profound angst. He was concerned that he would not have the manpower to deal with any future enemy offensive.

In fact, the Blitz did not return in the way Sholto had anticipated and Portal was considering downsizing Fighter Command following the end of the Battle of Britain, even though he conceded that German night bombing would continue, but for him the solution to defeating night bombers lay in better training and interception aids, not in more pilots or more aircraft.

Between mid-June and the end of July 1941, Fighter Command flew 8,000 offensive sorties of all types, escorting 374 bombers. The RAF claimed the destruction of 322 enemy aircraft for the loss of 123 RAF pilots, but the number of German aircraft actually destroyed was shown later to be only eighty-one, a quarter of the initial estimate. The CIRCUS tactic worked in that it 'stung the Luftwaffe into action, and they came up in strength to oppose the daylight raids', but any element of surprise was lost since the Germans could see the huge 'beehive' formation from a long way off.[9]

Even in June, Leigh-Mallory had changed his tune about sweeps, saying that the casualties were becoming so large as to outweigh any possible advantage that might accrue from them. Nevertheless, Fighter Command continued to conduct offensive operations over the Channel and over France, one variant of which was called ROAD-STEAD, in which fighters acted as escorts for light bombers of Bomber and Coastal Commands in low-level attacks on enemy shipping in the Channel. The Germans mounted a vigorous response and casualties among both bombers and fighters were heavy. Furthermore, the ships were well-protected both by their own fighters and by other ships heavily armoured with AA guns.

On 9 August 1941, Sholto was sitting in his office at Bentley Priory when the door flew open and Bob Wright came rushing in clutching a piece of paper and exclaiming, 'Douglas Bader's missing.' 'Oh God no!' was Sholto's reply. He knew that a fighter sweep over France had been in operation that day and was preparing himself for casualties, but Bader's loss was a severe blow. Despite or perhaps even because of Bader's difficult character, Sholto rated him as one of his best wing leaders, and Wright noted in his diary that Sholto was as upset as he had ever seen him.

Two days later, Fighter Command received the news that he was safe and in the hands of the Germans, having had to bale out of his Spitfire when he was rammed by an Me109 that had chopped off its entire tail, and that he had landed near St Omer. A radio message broadcast by the Germans and picked up by No. 13 Group on 13 August revealed that Bader had been taken prisoner on 9 August and that he had lost his right prosthetic leg while baling out. Bader requested that a new leg be sent, along with his pipe and a better uniform, and the Germans granted permission for these to be dropped by parachute. They asked that the day and time of delivery be communicated by radio, after which they would specify the place. The delivery aircraft would be granted safe conduct.

It was not known, even to higher authority, that a radio SOS channel was kept open between the RAF and the Luftwaffe so that each could tell the other when any of their pilots were floating in the sea off the other's coast, thus preventing them from drowning. Fighter Command did not at first acknowledge the signal, and they had no intention of making any deal with the Germans. Instead, Sholto and Leigh-Mallory planned an operation whereby a spare leg would be dropped by parachute over the airfield at St Omer on one of the normal daylight raids before the bombers went on to their targets for that day.

A large fighter escort for the bombers, including Bader's wing from Tangmere, was planned in the usual way for 19 August. The box containing the leg with a parachute was dropped from a Blenheim flying at 10,000 feet, and Leigh-Mallory had attached a message for the Kommandant of Longuenesse aerodrome at St Omer which read: 'Please accept my thanks, both for your broadcast message and for anything you can do to ensure that this new leg is delivered to Wing Commander Bader as soon as possible.' As soon as a message was received from the Blenheim that the leg had been dropped, Fighter Command sent a signal on the SOS channel informing the Germans that it had been delivered, asking for acknowledgement of its safe arrival, which was promptly received.

As it happened, this gave Bader a spare leg, as the Germans had already repaired his other two, both of which had been damaged when he had been shot down, one more badly than the other. By the time the extra leg had been dropped, only ten days after he had been taken prisoner and was in hospital in St Omer, Bader had already made what was to be the first of many escape attempts by knotting his sheets together and letting himself down from a top-floor window. He was in hiding somewhere in the French countryside but was recaptured almost immediately and remained a prisoner until the war ended in 1945. One of the first to make himself known to Bader after he was admitted to hospital was the German ace Adolf Galland, who wrote in his autobiography: 'This man had terrific will power. He refused to stay in the single room which had been allocated to him. He wanted to be together in one room with the other British pilots in the hospital. He set the tone and upheld the spirit and the comradeship.'[10] Galland even arranged for Bader to sit in his own Me109 but balked when Bader requested that he be allowed to fly one circuit around the airfield, though he wrote later that he 'nearly weakened'.[11]

As soon as Sholto had received the message of safe delivery from the Germans, he allowed the public relations team at Bentley Priory to release the whole story of what had happened. They told of the German radio message and then stated: 'The RAF requires no permission from the Luftwaffe to operate when and where it pleases over the occupied territories of northern France.' The very next morning, Sholto received a phone call and a voice growled: 'You are fraternising with the enemy, Douglas. I won't have it.' Sholto's reply was:

'You may call it fraternising, Sir, but after delivering Bader's leg we managed to shoot down some Me109s and damaged several others. That doesn't sound very fraternal to me.' This elicited a grunt from Churchill, and without another word he hung up. He never again spoke to Sholto about the incident.

Sholto was given the opportunity on several occasions to observe 'at first hand how Winston Churchill filled so dynamically the role of Prime Minister', spending the night as one of Churchill's guests as Chequers. Although these evenings provided Sholto with intense interest, he nearly always regarded them as 'something in the nature of ordeals'. Churchill would come down to dinner in his customary 'siren suit', and afterwards he would add to his ensemble a gorgeous and colourful Oriental dressing-gown. He would show his guests 'with a happiness that was almost a childish glee' presents that had been sent to him, nearly always boxes of cigars or magnums of champagne. These gifts seemed to be of immense importance to him, and Sholto wrote that he found 'very touching the unaffected and warm-hearted delight that he showed in these presents'.[12]

After dinner, there was generally a film, and then late at night the assembled company would get down to discussing the problems they faced. This would go on to the early hours of the morning, with everyone sitting round in armchairs and some trying not to fall asleep. All of a sudden, Churchill would 'electrify' his guests with something he said and would pace up and down the drawing room haranguing them as if they were in the House of Commons. A secretary was always present, taking down everything Churchill said, and later when Sholto and others read the published reports of the proceedings in the House, they would recognise what Churchill had first conceived in that drawing room at Chequers.

While Fighter Command aircraft were attacking heavily defended enemy airfields across the Channel, the defences at its own airfields in the UK were far from adequate. This was brought home forcibly to Sholto by Churchill himself after one of his Chequers visits. During one of these late night/early morning sessions, the discussion turned to the vulnerability of RAF aerodromes in Britain and what would happen if surprise attacks were mounted by enemy parachutists. At the time, airfields were guarded on the ground by Army personnel. It was not a popular task among soldiers, and Sholto was worried about the quality of protection provided. Still, he parried Churchill's rather sceptical questions, perhaps too vehemently, and said he did not think that enemy attacks on airfields would succeed. The next morning, when Sholto was due to leave Chequers, Churchill asked him to drive with him back to London. He raised again the matter of aerodrome defence, and as they approached the RAF station at Northolt he suddenly gave orders to the driver to turn into it. Before Sholto realised what Churchill was up to, they had reached the Station HQ, where he demanded that the alarm be sounded for a parachute raid. He wanted this done immediately so that he could see for himself what would happen.

The response, as Sholto admitted, left him feeling 'rather red in the face'. When the alarm went off there was a lot of aimless running about and no one was at all clear about what they were supposed to be doing. Churchill strode about observing everything, with an embarrassed Sholto accompanying him. At one stage, Churchill went poking around one of the hangars. There, he and Sholto found

a rather scruffy little airman crouching down with a rifle clutched in his hands in a manner that was not at all reassuring.

'What are you doing?' the Prime Minister demanded.

'I'm watching for the parachutists, Sir,' the airman replied.

'What would you do if they came?'

The little man did his best not to be defeated on that score, and he promptly stated: 'I'd shoot them.' But the man's lack of assurance must have caught the experienced eye of the former soldier because Churchill then asked: 'Have you ever fired that rifle?'

'No, Sir,' the airman answered. 'I've never fired a rifle at all.'

The incident was enough to prove Churchill's point about aerodrome defence, but there was more embarrassment to come for Sholto. He and Churchill walked around the perimeter track of the aerodrome towards the dispersal points at which the Spitfires of the Polish Fighter Wing were kept ready. By the time they got there, they found the

Polish ground crews standing right on top of the high embankments that had been built around the dispersal bays. They were eagerly looking up at the sky and paid no attention as Churchill and Sholto approached.

'Come down … come down at once!' Churchill shouted. 'You should never stand on a skyline when the enemy are about!'

The Polish ground crews had not much command of the English language, so Churchill's shouts fell on deaf ears. They stayed where they were, continuing to look intently up at the sky. Sholto observed that as Poles, they hated the Germans far more vehemently than the British did, so they saw this warning of the approach of enemy parachutists as an opportunity to shoot down as many of them as possible, and the shouts of the Prime Minister, even if they realised who he was, were not going to deter them. Seeing that his shouts produced no effect whatsoever put Churchill in a very bad mood indeed, which was not improved by what he saw when he and Sholto walked into one of the dispersal huts. They found the Polish pilots sitting around reading and smoking, with a group of them playing cards. The squadron commander got up as the distinguished visitors entered and came forward to greet them. As Sholto told the story later:

> 'Don't you know that at this moment there is a raid on by enemy parachutists?' Churchill demanded, his indignation beginning to boil over.
>
> It was then that the Prime Minister got what I was beginning to feel was coming to him.
>
> 'Oh, no, sir,' the officer replied, sweeping all such foolishness aside. 'We know it's a false alarm. If it were not we'd have been ordered into the air by now.' Quite unperturbed by the famous Churchillian glower, he then produced a beautifully bound book, and politely he asked: 'Will you please sign our visitor's book?'[13]

Despite his bad temper, Churchill grudgingly signed the book, producing absolute delight on the part of the Poles at having obtained his autograph. This seemed to restore Churchill's good humour, which was boosted by being able to talk with what he knew was such 'a gallant band of fighters' as the Poles were and being able to prove his point to Sholto. He wrote that such was Churchill's magnanimity that, as with their other 'dust-ups', he never mentioned the incident again.

This was not just an amusing episode: it was fundamental in the formation of the RAF Regiment. Dowding, who late in 1941 was given the task of suggesting economies in personnel and equipment within the RAF, was vehemently opposed to the move due to the costs that it would incur. He felt that recruits to the Aerodrome Defence Corps proposed by the Air Council would be engaged in a 'dead end' occupation in which they might never be actively employed and that the responsibility for guarding aerodromes should remain with the Army. He suggested that this duty could be undertaken by young troops under training. The Air Staff disagreed profoundly, stating in a memo to Sinclair that 'Sir Hugh Dowding's arguments are, to a large extent, misconceived' and that 'all existing Commanders-in-Chief are strongly in favour of the Air Council's policy'.[14] They argued that because the organisation of Army personnel employed at present to guard aerodromes was on an *ad hoc* basis, these personnel were in a much greater 'dead end' than they would be in a properly consti-tuted corps. At that point, they comprised under-age infantrymen ultimately destined for the Field Army, and a few who were older and unfit. They were not allowed to handle any specialised weapons such as AA machine guns, or other ordnance used in aerodrome defence, which constituted 'a serious waste of man-power while at the same time our aerodromes are not as well defended as they might be'.[15] Portal asserted that Fighter Command could only operate effectively from secure bases and his arguments won the day.

Unfortunately, this was not the resolution of the problem, since the quality of the personnel released by the Army to serve in the newly formed RAF Regiment was a cause of concern long into the war. Gradually, though, improvements both in the quality of recruits and in training, which was sometimes tougher than anything provided by the Army, meant that the RAF Regiment evolved into a multi-skilled and highly effective force.

As 1941 drew to a close, Sholto had to admit that Fighter

Command's losses sustained for the year were very heavy: 426 of his pilots were killed, missing or taken prisoner, slightly fewer than the 414 fighter pilots and thirty-five other aircrew killed in the Battle of Britain.[16] In a letter to Portal, Sholto questioned the offensive policy that had caused so many casualties, perhaps laced with a hint of self-justification:

> Some people are inclined to be critical of that policy now, but you will remember that during the summer we were being urged by the War Cabinet to be as offensive as possible in order to contain as large a proportion of the German Air Force in the West as possible. Whether the policy was right or wrong however, casualties have been suffered and we have lost a lot of good men as a result.[17]

To add to Sholto's worries, early in 1942, Fighter Command was embroiled in an episode at sea that was the cause of a good deal of confusion and recrimination within the various commands of the RAF, as well as between the RAF and the Royal Navy. This was what has since been termed the Channel dash by the German warships *Scharnhorst*, *Gneisenau* and *Prinz Eugen* on 12 February. Afterwards, no one connected with that affair on the British side could recall it without feeling the most intense embarrassment, Sholto included. He already had chilling memories of the *Scharnhorst* and *Gneisenau* after their sinking of HMS *Glorious* during the Norwegian campaign, which had caused such grievous loss of life to both the RAF and the Navy, and this incident brought those memories flooding back.

Those in senior positions in the RAF and Royal Navy, as well as in the government, had known since the spring of 1941 that these vital German warships, at that time trapped in the French port of Brest on the south coast of Normandy, would eventually have to break out of their enforced imprisonment by making a dash up the Channel in order to reach the safety of north German ports. The Admiralty, however, had assumed they would pass through the Dover Straits under cover of darkness, never imagining they would attempt the journey in broad daylight. The Royal Navy and the RAF made a detailed plan to deal with the break-out, codenamed Operation FULLER, but when it actually happened, what Sholto called the 'twin sisters of blunder and destiny' conspired to frustrate the liaison between the services, causing the operation to fall apart at the crucial moment. This was despite ample warning from reconnaissance reports between 29 January and 8 February 1942 that a break-out was probable.

The German warships started their dash from Brest at 9.14 p.m. on 11 February, following reports of the approach of bad weather conditions that would make it almost impossible for RAF aircraft to detect the ships. Coastal Command had established night reconnaissance patrols, which were sent out on the 11th, but the Air-to-Surface Vessel (ASV) radar failed on the aircraft and no replacements were sent out. Furthermore, the malfunctions were not reported for hours after they occurred. Fighter Command sent out two Spitfires each morning after dawn over the Dover Straits, known as 'Jim Crow' patrols due to their function of acting as lookouts. On the morning of the 12th, although they did not see the battle cruisers because they were too far south, the pilots sighted E-boats travelling both south and north along the Straits, as a result of which a ROADSTEAD operation was ordered by No. 11 Group.

Meanwhile, Sholto had received information from his radar operators that something was brewing. At 8.25 a.m., a single aircraft was seen circling to the south-west, far down into the Channel. Three more plots were received by 9.59 a.m. but were intermittent and only ever showed one or two aircraft. The controllers were struggling to interpret these fleeting appearances. It was not unusual to pick up this kind of activity off the enemy coast and it could have been caused by air-sea rescue exercises, gun-testing or training flights. Sholto later told the Bucknill Inquiry into the debacle: 'I think the Boche kept the numbers down deliberately in order, of course, not to stir us up.'[18]

Suspiciously, intermittent radar interference had begun to be reported at 9.20 a.m., becoming persistent fifty minutes later. It did not occur to anyone at first that this was enemy jamming. This meant that No. 11 Group was slow to order additional reconnaissance, and it wasn't until 10.20 a.m. that two more Spitfires took off. As was compulsory on all Fighter Command reconnaissance patrols, strict radio silence was maintained while the aircraft were airborne, but when they landed, one of the pilots reported sighting a convoy of some twenty to thirty vessels, and the other added that he had seen a ship with a tripod mast and superstructure, which it was realised was one of the battle cruisers.

By that time, two of Sholto's most experienced Spitfire pilots had been on a quick sortie over France as a result of the morning's regular Jim Crow patrols, and had made the first sighting of the warships at 10.42 a.m. On their way back, they attacked two Messerschmitts that they soon realised were part of the air cover for German vessels. The pilots could not believe their eyes when they looked down and saw the huge warships and many smaller escort ships steaming up the Channel, having got as far as the mouth of the Somme. They had not been informed that any movement of these warships was anticipated.

With the weather worsening, the naval authorities at Dover decided to send out what Sholto termed 'six old and pitifully slow Swordfish of the Fleet Air Arm'[19] to attack the ships with torpedoes. Fighter Command committed to providing the Swordfish with five fighter squadrons for top cover and diversionary attacks, but it was all too hurried and in the end only one Spitfire squadron arrived in time to join up with the naval aircraft. As the Bucknill Report observed: 'The task of escorting the 80-mph Swordfish with Spitfires flying at 250-mph proved a difficult one.'[20] The other fighter aircraft arrived on the scene as soon as they could, but by then the Swordfish had tried and failed to attack the German ships, which were through the Straits of Dover and off the French coast near Dunkirk.

Fighter Command's Spitfires were engaged by a far superior force of German aircraft and were so busy fighting for their lives that they were unable to help the embattled Swordfish, which persisted with their torpedo attacks despite 'withering and devastating fire of all descriptions' from both the German ships and the enemy fighters. All six Swordfish were shot down, and none of their torpedoes reached their targets. Only five of the eighteen men survived. Among those killed was their leader, Lieutenant-Commander Eugene Esmonde, who was awarded a posthumous VC for his extraordinary gallantry in leading the attack, the first to be won by the Fleet Air Arm. It was disastrous for the naval pilots, but Sholto observed that 'it was a most

gallant effort and it stands greatly to the credit of the Royal Navy'.[21]
Fighter Command continued to attack the cruisers and their escort
ships, and Coastal Command mounted torpedo bomber strikes. The
total number of fighters dispatched was 398, of which seventeen were
lost for sixteen enemy aircraft destroyed, three probably so and seventeen damaged.

Sholto's close friend Vice-Admiral Bertie Ramsay was intimately
involved with the whole operation as the Flag Officer in command
at Dover. Because of their friendship, it was all the more painful for
Sholto when Ramsay made a strong protest over what he felt was the
failure of Fighter Command to provide the full escort that he considered had been promised for the Swordfish, but time and weather
were against them. Sholto felt that responsibility for the failure to
intercept the German vessels must also lie with the Royal Navy and
with Coastal Command. The aircraft they provided were late in
taking off, wrongly armed and not even aware of what exactly they
were supposed to do because of a failure in communication from
their superiors. The Navy sent destroyers out from Harwich, and although they made a concerted attack, they were easily beaten back
by superior German forces. Bomber Command sent aircraft out to
strike the ships that were by that time out in the North Sea, but the
visibility was so poor that they had absolutely no chance of bombing
effectively. Their attacks led to fifteen aircraft being lost with no hits
on the enemy ships.

So the *Scharnhorst*, *Gneisenau* and *Prinz Eugen* made it through the
Straits of Dover and the North Sea, grazing some mines on the way
that only did the slightest of damage, and reached the safety of their
home ports. On that day, Adolf Galland was in overall command of
the German fighters providing air cover and his assessment of what
happened struck a distinct chord with Sholto when he read it later.
Galland wrote: 'The pilots of the RAF fought bravely, tenaciously and
untiringly, but had been sent into action with insufficient planning,
without a clear concept of the attack, without a centre of gravity and
without systematic tactics.'[22]

The public reaction to what seemed to be an unqualified German
success was predictably harsh. *The Times* stated: 'Nothing more

mortifying to the pride of sea-power in Home Waters has happened since the 17th Century.' But Churchill viewed what had happened in a characteristically unusual way, asserting after the war: 'Viewed in the after-light and in its larger aspects the episode was highly advantageous to us.' Sholto realised then that this view was the right one: pride had been hurt, some searching comments made and worst of all, lives lost, but at the end of the day, the German ships were effectively bottled up in their home ports, and the Allies breathed a sigh of relief that the threat that had stalked the Atlantic for so long was now eliminated since these ships were no longer skulking in Brest harbour.

Over the next few months, Sholto continued complaining to Portal and to the Air Ministry about the drain from Fighter Command of more Spitfire squadrons and experienced pilots to Russia and the Middle East. What annoyed him even more was information from the scientist in his Operational Research Section, who had visited Malta recently, that there was a surplus of 'first-class' Spitfire pilots in Malta for a low number of these aircraft, and this when Sholto was being asked to send yet more pilots and Spitfires there. He reiterated his concerns in a letter to Tedder, C-in-C Middle East Command, who told him not to listen to poison tongues and wrote to Freeman, then VCAS, urging him to see that these rumours be 'scotched'.[23] Portal reassured Sholto that he understood his need for experienced men for future offensive operations and that his commitment to send pilots to the Middle East would be reduced accordingly. Sholto was not mollified, reminding Portal that in the past year, Fighter Command had sent nearly 2,000 fighter pilots to the Middle East and Malta, nearly 100 per cent of his operational strength in pilots, and he had received very few replacements. All of this when he was expected to continue offensive fighter operations over Europe, in which casualties were still high.

Sholto's difficulties were made worse by the appearance of the Luftwaffe's most efficient fighter, the Focke-Wulf (F-W) 190, a formidable opponent. Churchill was alarmed too by losses due to the arrival of this machine. The only solution was to restore technical superiority to the RAF's fighter force with new aircraft. As a result, Rolls-Royce raised the performance of the Merlin Engine, and Fighter Command

Winston Churchill and Sholto in a car at Heathrow Airport, with Katharine, January 1960.

Sholto with Katharine at an airport, November 1963.

Sholto with Errol Barrow, first Prime Minister of Barbados, 1966.

Sholto with his mother Maggie, 1894.

The three Douglas brothers, Sholto (seated on right), Bobby (resting on arm of chair), and Archie, at Tonbridge, 1911.

Lincoln College, Oxford, Torpid crew, 1914:
Sholto seated in the centre, front row.

Sholto's father, Robert Langton Douglas,
around the start of World War I.

Sholto's second brother, Bobby, 1916.

Sholto's youngest brother,
Archie, 1916.

Major Sholto Douglas in a BE2
at Stirling, 1916.

The Campbell family in Stirling,
1912 (the youngest daughter
watched Sholto flying from the
top of the cliffs next to the castle
in 1916).

Stirling Castle and King's Park, where No. 43 Squadron's airfield was situated, taken in the 1900s.

Major Sholto Douglas standing beside an SE5a as Commanding Officer of No. 84 Squadron, 1918.

Wing Commander Sholto Douglas (in the centre of the photo with clipboard) and his pilots standing beside the Nile in Khartoum in 1930, with Belinda, his pet lion cub.

Sholto's half-brother Donald with his wife Anita, 1939.

Air Marshal Sholto Douglas as C-in-C Fighter Command talking with ground crew beside a Spitfire, 1940/41.

Air Marshal Sir Sholto Douglas, C-in-C, Fighter Command, at his desk at his headquarters, Bentley Priory, in 1942.

LEFT Air Chief Marshal Sir Sholto Douglas taking the salute as C-in-C Middle East Command, 1943. The aircraft flying in formation are from No. 219 Group, and the signature is that of Max Aitken, who was out in the Middle East on Sholto's staff.

To The C in C. Middle East and 219 Group. 1943. from Max.

BELOW King Farouk, in centre, accompanied by Egyptian dignitaries, at RAF gala evening in Cairo, 1943. General 'Jumbo' Wilson is standing behind him on the left and Sholto on the right.

The Cairo conference, November 1943. Air Chief Marshal Sir Sholto Douglas, Sir Winston Churchill and Field Marshal Sir Alan Brooke, Chief of the Imperial General Staff.

Air Chief Marshal Sir Sholto Douglas (in centre signing menu cards) as C-in-C Middle East Command with airmen in Cairo, Christmas 1943.

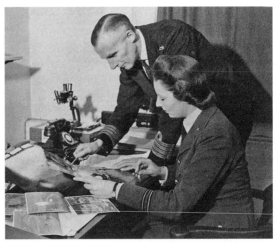

General Dwight D. Eisenhower, Allied Supreme Command, and Air Chief Marshal Sir Sholto Douglas, following the presentation of the Legion of Merit for 'exceptionally meritorious conduct in the performance of outstanding services', 12 December 1944.

WAAF Flight Officer Phyllis Davies with Senior Naval Staff Officer Captain D. V. Peyton-Ward RN (P.-W.), tracking U-boats at Coastal Command, 1944.

Coastal Command, April 1945, left to right: Harold Kerby (Administration, Coastal Command), Sholto (C-in-C Coastal Command), 'Peter' Portal (CAS), Aubrey Ellwood (Senior Air Staff Officer, Coastal Command).

Air Chief Marshal Sir Sholto Douglas as C-in-C BAFO with British Embassy official, viewing the devastation in Warsaw, October 1945.

The bombed-out ruins of the Reichstag, July 1945.

Sholto with his staff at his residence, Schloss Ostenwalde, in 1946. His PSO, Bob Wright, is standing second from right.

MRAF Sir Sholto Douglas, Military Governor of British Zone in Germany, visiting a school with the Education Minister for the Hamburg district, Senator Heinrich Landahl, 1946.

The four Military Governors of occupied Germany: MRAF Sir Sholto Douglas (UK), General Joseph McNarney (US), General Pierre Koenig (France) and Marshal Vasily Sokolovsky (USSR), 1946.

Lord and Lady Douglas of Kirtleside, 1956.

Lord Douglas with Marshal Zhigarev, head of Aeroflot, Moscow, 1958.

Pipers in Red Square, in front of St Basil's Cathedral, as part of a BEA trip to Moscow, 1964.

received the Spitfire IX as well as a completely new fighter, the Ty-phoon, which nevertheless was plagued initially with technical trou-bles following its introduction in 1941. It lacked manoeuvrability, meaning it could not match the F-W 190 on its own terms and was unsuitable for deployment in a wing on sweeps. But it was the only RAF fighter capable of catching the F-W 190 at low altitudes, and as a result it secured a new role as a low-level interceptor, later be-coming a successful ground-attack aircraft with additional armament. Losses during the spring and early summer of 1942 continued to be heavy, with the RAF losing 314 fighters and bombers to the Germans' ninety. Despite Sholto's determined pleas for improvements, 'the new German fighters exacted a serious toll'[24] for British intrusion into their air space, but the pressure had to be maintained.

In February 1942, 'Bert' Harris, whom Sholto called 'that energet-ic, forceful – and at times controversial – character', became C-in-C Bomber Command. Eager to test out new techniques and equip-ment, in March he ordered a heavy attack on the ancient Hanseatic town of Lübeck on the Baltic, causing severe damage to its historic centre. The next target was Rostock, a similarly iconic city, which was almost destroyed. Hitler retaliated with the Baedeker raids on Britain, the response to which fell on the shoulders of Fighter Command. The Luftwaffe attacked cities chosen not for their military value but for their cultural and historical significance. The most severe raids began in late April and finished mostly by the end of May, though towns and cities continued to be targeted for their cultural value for the next two years. However, these raids were an abject failure compared to the original Blitz. Since then, the RAF had made dramatic improvements both in its night fighter capability and in radar, and the Luftwaffe sustained substantial losses. Nevertheless, the attacks resulted in over 1,600 civilian deaths and tens of thousands of damaged homes. Other German incursions included 'tip-and-run' raids by fighter bombers. They would dive in at high speed, having started from a good height, drop their bombs and tear out again at very low altitude. The diving speed alone meant that both day and night fighters were constantly on the alert. One of Sholto's pilots commented: 'We always seem to be going downhill.'[25]

Sholto was promoted to the rank of air chief marshal in July 1942 and was delighted to find himself at what he considered to be the top of the tree. He never imagined in his wildest dreams that he would make it to Marshal of the Royal Air Force, especially since that rank was reserved for those who became CAS, and while he might have entertained ambitions in that direction, it was still a very distant prospect. The British and American governments continued to plan jointly for an attack across the Channel to end the German occupation of France, and Sholto was appointed to the joint Anglo-American committee that was formed to oversee what became known later as Operation OVERLORD. To begin with, the option of going through Normandy was not considered, largely because the range of Fighter Command's aircraft was not sufficient to give adequate fighter cover over the beachheads. Instead, an invasion was planned across the narrow part of the Channel, with possible landings near Calais or Boulogne.

Of all those who were seeking to break the German stranglehold on Europe, no one was more eager for action than Winston Churchill, which meant that, as was often the case, he came up with an impractical scheme. His idea was to invade Alderney as a first stage in gaining a foothold on the Continent, but the island was too stoutly defended by a strong force of German troops augmented by a large number of coastal guns. Alderney was only twelve miles away from the nearest German airfield and any invasion force would be subject to heavy air attacks. Nevertheless, Churchill insisted that Sholto and his colleagues formulate a plan, until he realised eventually that it should be abandoned due to the probability of very heavy casualties. Most importantly, what would the Allies do with Alderney when they captured it and how would it lead to a full invasion of Europe? Sholto and his colleagues were frustrated that so much time and energy had been expended to reach a decision that to them had been a foregone conclusion from the start. Sholto sympathised greatly with Field Marshal Alan Brooke, Chief of the Imperial General Staff (CIGS), who wrote with such feeling in his diaries about the effort he had to waste on detailed planning for Churchill's wild, and in the end fruitless, schemes.

One operation intended as a forerunner to the invasion of Europe that has perhaps attracted more controversy than any other was the Dieppe raid, codenamed Operation JUBILEE, which in August 1942 aimed to capture large German coastal batteries by seaborne assault. Historians have described it as one of the most tragic and costly disasters in the whole history of warfare. It was planned as a result of what Sholto described as 'irrational pressures' brought to bear by the Americans as well as the Russians for a landing on the French coast.

What Sholto did not and probably could not say when *Years of Command* was published in 1966 was that it had been Lord Mountbatten, then a vice-admiral and newly appointed Chief of Combined Operations, who actually commanded the raid, with Churchill's backing. Fighter Command was called upon to provide massive cover, despite its limited scope, and Sholto had at his disposal a larger force of fighters than had fought in the Battle of Britain. The actual air operations were to be handled by No. 11 Group under Leigh-Mallory. A month and a half prior to the raid, Leigh-Mallory had voiced his concerns to Sholto concerning the probability of heavy casualties, citing the failure of fighter sweeps to achieve superiority over the Luftwaffe. Sholto was all too conscious of the political pressures at his back, and responded in a way that indicated he had no intention of changing the plans for the operation:

> I do not know however quite what you expect me to do about it. I
> certainly do not propose to call the operation off. If I may say so,
> I think you are worrying too much about these possible casualties.
> Unfortunately, one cannot often win a battle without considerable
> casualties, however much one would like to do so.[26]

The exigencies of high command had perhaps hardened his heart to the prospect of casualties in a way that he had not demonstrated in WWI, when he had railed against Trenchard's seeming imperviousness to high attrition rates. Now, he was sounding like the man to whom he owed his RAF career, Trenchard himself.

Sholto admitted that he considered the whole action to be a means of 'stirring up the Germans on the ground and keeping them on the hop'. What the Allies actually got in 'stirring things up' was far more than they had anticipated, sustaining disastrously heavy casualties. On that ill-fated morning, over 5,000 Canadian troops made the landing at Dieppe, supported by detachments of British Commandos and Royal Navy landing contingents. By nightfall, only 2,000 Canadians had managed to make it back to England. Aside from its toll of 907 killed and 586 wounded, the Canadian Army lost 1,946 men as prisoners of war, more than in all the rest of the European campaign. Out of 1,000 British Commandos, 247 men were killed, while the Royal Navy suffered 550 dead and wounded.

Sholto spun it that from the point of view of the RAF, the Dieppe raid was a hard-won success, in that lessons were learned about giving air support to a seaborne landing that were to be of great value in the large-scale operations planned for the future. Before the operation, he had thought that the Luftwaffe would be caught at a disadvantage, stretched thin as it was through its commitments both on the Russian front and in the Mediterranean, and that it would be forced to accept the challenge, resulting in significant losses inflicted by the RAF. The Luftwaffe certainly responded, and Fighter Command was not as successful in its scores as Sholto had hoped. Fifty-six fighter squadrons of over 600 aircraft went into battle. RAF losses have been disputed, but in total, 106 aircraft were lost, eighty-eight of which were fighters.[27] Other sources suggest that as many as twenty-eight bombers were lost, and that the overall figure for destroyed and damaged Spitfires was seventy, and seventy-one pilots were killed or missing. Against this, forty-eight Luftwaffe aircraft were destroyed and twenty-four were damaged.

Once again, Sholto painted an upbeat picture, asserting that his fighters 'succeeded in every way in keeping the Luftwaffe away from the battle area'. A report issued later from Combined Operations Headquarters stated: 'The most striking achievement was the success of the Royal Air Force in providing cover...'[28] However, all this meant was that the ships and soldiers in the raid had not been molested from the air, and it is easy to see that this was a way of putting a positive spin on an appalling disaster. In the words of the Canadian historian Eric Maguire, it was 'the blackest day in Canadian military history'.[29] Johnnie Johnson summed up the whole sad affair:

Tactically the Dieppe Raid must be regarded as a complete failure, for none of its stated objectives were achieved in full measure. It is a record of poor security, of faulty intelligence, of inadequate communications between air and ground, of a confused and bloody ground situation over which central coordination could not be exercised. It is a story of great gallantry and heavy loss of life.[30]

As a postscript to this calamitous affair, on the night of 20/21 August, Portsmouth was bombed by fifteen enemy aircraft, which Sholto thought may have been a direct result of the Dieppe raid.

Sholto has been criticised relentlessly by historians over both RHUBARB and CIRCUS operations, largely because of the loss of life they caused without much perceivable benefit. Denis Richards wrote in the RAF history that their chief purpose was to 'force the enemy to maintain strong air defences in the West ... At the same time powerful moral advantages would accrue as our pilots grew accustomed to exercising the initiative, and as the enemy became thoroughly imbued with the idea of our superiority in the air.'[31] However, Sholto felt that Richards was altogether too dismissive of what Fighter Command achieved with his description of 'the completely ineffective mass sweeps at high level by fighters without bombers'. Sholto felt that this ignored the 'tremendous value of the experience alone which was gained by our pilots'.[32] In the official history, Collier also decried any benefits of the early, smaller sweeps of fighters accompanying bombers just across the Channel, partly due to the insignificance of their targets and because at that point the Luftwaffe was not willing to expend forces to defend them. Eric 'Winkle' Brown, however, thought the offensive operations by Fighter Command over the Channel gave a strategic advantage to the Allies. Although they started as a retaliatory gesture, as the British had to make a show of aggression after the fall of France, when these sweeps were continued with later versions of the Spitfire, they paid huge dividends, causing major problems to the Nazis' logistics trains.

Towards the end of 1942, the strength and power of Fighter Command was at its peak. Sholto had been its C-in-C for two years, but once again, machinations at the top of the Air Ministry meant that he was to be posted elsewhere. In September 1942, Sinclair decided, with Portal's agreement, to send Wilfrid Freeman back to the Ministry of Aircraft Production (MAP), which by this time had stagnated under Beaverbrook's leadership. In his earlier stint at MAP, Freeman had been fundamental to the supply of the RAF's most successful aircraft, although Beaverbrook took the credit. Sinclair proposed to appoint Tedder, then C-in-C Middle East, to replace Freeman as Portal's VCAS, largely because Portal declared that he *must* have Tedder, and to send Sholto to the Middle East as Tedder's replacement. Leigh-Mallory would take over from Sholto as C-in-C Fighter Command.

Churchill, writing to Sinclair, was opposed to Tedder's move from the Middle East 'when he is doing so well out there and has a complete mastery of the Command' and strongly disagreed with Sholto's move from Fighter Command,

> which he now knows so thoroughly and has handled so well ... I am sure the interests of the war require both these officers, Douglas and Tedder, to stay in their present posts ... I have only one aim, namely, the effective prosecution of the war, for which I have a great responsibility.[33]

On the same day, Churchill wrote to Portal reiterating what he had said to Sinclair and declaring that Sholto had become Fighter Command's 'complete master, having had two years' experience'.[34] Portal's reply was a surprisingly emotional appeal:

> I feel more than ever in need of your continued help and support now that I have lost the services of Freeman as VCAS ... I do not think we could select a more favourable moment for a change in the Middle East. We are, I hope, in sight of the end of the desert warfare ... and thereafter a series of new strategic and tactical problems will present themselves. I consider that Sholto Douglas is in every way qualified to tackle these problems with the advice and support of the experienced subordinate Commanders and Staff whom he will find in the Middle East ... I regard Tedder as by far the best successor to Freeman in the position of VCAS.[35]

Sinclair also tried to reassure Churchill, writing: 'Portal and Tedder will be a strong team. Douglas will be a fine Commander in the biggest of our overseas theatres.'[36]

However, Churchill was not giving up without a fight. He suggested the appointment of another officer more junior to Sholto, Air Vice-Marshal Coningham, to Middle East Command, writing that this

> would avoid the misfortune which would be caused by removing Air Chief Marshal Sholto Douglas from the Fighter Command. He has made himself a master of the whole intricate technique of night fighting. For two years he has worked under me on the Night Fighting Committee. He knows the whole story and has been in on all the discussions. I am sure that the prosecution of the war will be impeded if he is moved at the present time, just as he has acquired complete mastery of this all-important sphere, and when so many of the plans he has made or presided over are coming into operation.[37]

But Portal was not to be dissuaded, replying that Coningham did not have the necessary experience or capabilities to succeed Tedder, and that Sholto was the best person for the Middle East. In this he was supported by Sinclair. However, Tedder was in no hurry to relinquish his post, not least as it was clear that his expertise and good relationship with the Americans were proving invaluable. In a telegram to Churchill, Lord Moyne, deputy minister resident in the Middle East, reasoned that 'however good Sholto Douglas may be he cannot claim to have Tedder's experience of the Mediterranean air warfare and co-operation with the Americans'.[38]

One would think, given the popular perception of Churchill's dominating personality, that his views on the future employment of both Sholto and Tedder would have prevailed over those of Portal and Sinclair, but as Liddell Hart has observed, 'it is astonishing to find how often he failed to get his views accepted by the chiefs of staff, even when his views were most clearly right,'[39] as they were in this case.

For his own part, Sholto had become deeply attached to Fighter Command, which he regarded as his own. He was also finding the work he was doing on the long-term planning for the air element of the future invasion of France extremely absorbing. More importantly, Eisenhower stated in his memoir that Sholto had been designated as the commander of the British Expeditionary Air Forces for the invasion of Europe. When the time came, though, this post was filled by Leigh-Mallory, Sholto's successor at Fighter Command. Leigh-Mallory's duties were later fulfilled by Tedder, who had been appointed Deputy Supreme Allied Commander for OVERLORD under Eisenhower, and Leigh-Mallory was appointed Air Commander South East Asia, thereby leaving Tedder effectively in command of all the Allied air assets operating in Europe up to the end of the war there.

Sholto's move to the Middle East was to have long-term consequences for him, effectively excluding him from the positions that he most wanted and for which he was fitted. He tried to make the best of it by saying that the appointment was a senior and important one and promised to be interesting because the projected operations along the whole of the north African coast might well yield crucial successes in the war. He also admitted that while serving in the Middle East between the wars, he 'had come under the odd spell that it can exert'.[40] There was no doubt, though, that his career was affected adversely by this move, and he did not know at that point that, even though he had the strong support of Churchill, there was an unseen hand of sabotage working against him by someone he thought was one of his closest friends.

CHAPTER EIGHTEEN

CAIRO: DISAPPOINTMENTS AND SNARES

The start of Sholto's journey to Cairo at the end of December 1942 marked the beginning of a year of military and diplomatic controversy and challenges against his position as a leader that reached as far as the fundamentals of his character, which could only have added to the burden he was carrying already. Even the journey out was difficult: the Air Ministry had decided to select the safest routes for its senior officers on journeys to the Middle East, and Sholto had a circuitous journey, stopping firstly in Lisbon, then at Freetown in Sierra Leone, across the Sahara to Khartoum and finally up to Cairo. There was an enforced delay to the planned stopover at Lisbon, as the aircraft, a BOAC flying boat, was pronounced unserviceable. The British Ambassador invited Sholto to stay with him, but that meant that he was almost under house arrest since he could not venture outside the Embassy precincts. Although Lisbon was supposed to be neutral, it was, as Sholto said, 'crawling with spies',[1] and he had to wear civilian clothes all the time he was there, which he found strange after spending so many years in uniform. One visit he did manage to make, though, was to the airport, where he saw a stream of German transport planes arriving and departing. He found out after the war that these were ferrying vast numbers of stolen works of art back to Germany under the orders of Hermann Goering.

Sholto eventually reached Cairo and looked forward to getting back to work, but when he got there, he realised it was not going to be that simple. Although he thought he knew Tedder and they understood each other, it was quite clear that he was not welcome, and Tedder seemed to resent having to give up Middle East Command. He found all sorts of ways of delaying the handover, including sending Sholto on an introductory tour of inspection of RAF units in Palestine, Syria, Iraq and Iran. He realised Tedder did not want to be VCAS, but he also sensed that there was something else in the air. All became clear a couple of weeks later following the Casablanca conference in January 1943, at which Churchill and Roosevelt met to discuss plans for the future prosecution of the war, and at which Tedder, Portal and Eisenhower were present. Sholto was not invited.

At that conference, it was decided to accept Tedder's suggestion for the establishment of a single, overall command of the air in the Mediterranean, to which Middle East Command under Sholto, Malta under Keith Park, and the North West African Air Forces commanded by the American General Carl Spaatz would all be subordinate. Sholto had heard rumours of these plans, and realised that Tedder would be the ideal person to head the new Mediterranean Air Command (MAC), with a new HQ next to Eisenhower's in Algiers.

Tedder wrote that were it not for the fact that he and Sholto were 'old friends, friction between Cairo and Algiers would have been inevitable. Sholto had originally come out to Cairo to relieve me, but when I was called on to stay in the Mediterranean area and set up a superior headquarters, he was left in an invidious position.'[2] They had almost exact parity in their military careers and had even been promoted to air chief marshal on the same day, but now, Sholto had to accept a subordinate post.

So only a month after Sholto had reached Cairo, Churchill, who appreciated the situation, was writing to Sinclair and Portal:

> I am sure that Air Chief Marshal Sholto Douglas should not remain in the Middle East. The appointment is widely altered from what it has been, first, by the great distances which now separate the enemy from Cairo [the war had moved to the west] and, secondly, by the establishment of Tedder as a Mediterranean overlord. Douglas, who has done such good service, has got a far smaller scope than he had when he was C-in-C Fighter Command. I understood

that you intended to bring him home as your Vice-Chief of Staff. I talked to him in this sense and found he greatly preferred to remain where he is.[3]

This was only because Sholto preferred an operational command than to be back in the Air Ministry, even as Portal's deputy.

Portal had indeed considered Sholto as a replacement for Freeman in the post of VCAS, especially when he realised that Tedder did not wish to leave the Mediterranean. However, Freeman himself strongly opposed this idea in the first of a whole series of poisoned letters to Portal that demonstrably affected Sholto's career thereafter. This was the unseen hand that Sholto always sensed was working against him, and it belonged to someone whom he continued to believe was his loyal friend until the end of his life. In his consideration of whom should replace him as VCAS, Freeman wrote:

> Douglas is at heart a cad – but an able one. He will get on well with the PM and will keep Bert [Harris] and L-M [Leigh-Mallory] in their places. He is a bit inclined to run off early from work – has some very unpleasant friends and is given to favouritism. His judgement of men is bad.

When considering the possibility of staying on in his post as VCAS, Freeman said of himself: 'He doesn't get on well with the PM.'[4] Was there a hint of resentment or even jealousy there? Freeman must have witnessed the whole Big Wing debate and Sholto's criticism of both Dowding and Park at the end of the Battle of Britain. Perhaps it was that which prompted him to describe Sholto as a cad, the incident having left an unpleasant taste in everyone's mouth. As for running off early from work, that could have been simple malice, although Sholto had a reputation, which remained with him up until his retirement from BEA over twenty years later, for dealing with paperwork and clearing his desk with astonishing efficiency while still addressing the matters in hand. And who were the unpleasant friends? Sholto did have an unusual group of contacts, having connections in both the theatre and art worlds, in part through his father and stepmother.

Were those people who might be considered 'unsuitable' as friends of a senior military officer? Did Sholto still have friends among the Irish Republican movement? They would surely invite negative attention.

It is true that while Sholto regarded Freeman as one of his closest colleagues and friends, when Sholto was ACAS, they had had a run-in over Freeman's championing of the Mosquito, the design of which Sholto questioned at first, but which became one of the most successful aircraft of WWII. When Sholto was C-in-C Fighter Command and Freeman himself was VCAS, he was critical of Sholto's reluctance to send experienced pilots from Fighter Command to the Middle East where Tedder needed them as operations there expanded. Freeman complained about this constantly to Portal, writing: 'You and I know quite well that Douglas will not nominate his best and will never do so. This is not fair on Tedder.'[5] Here and in other instances, Freeman's preference for Tedder over Sholto was clear.

Sholto himself wrote a letter to Portal following a meeting with Churchill in Cairo after the Casablanca conference to clarify his position:

> My dear CAS
>
> When the Prime Minister was here, he told me that he thought I ought to return to England and become Vice-CAS. I am of course ready to do whatever you wish, but I would like you to know that I am quite happy here, and that I did not instigate the PM in any way.
>
> While, as is only natural, I am a little disappointed that the operational 'cream' has been skimmed off the job here by Tedder's new appointment, I do not in the least mind serving under Tedder's operational direction. In any case I shall have plenty to do.
>
> As I say however, I am quite happy to leave the matter in your hands to do what you think best.[6]

Despite the changes surrounding his new command that disappointed Sholto, for his first few weeks as its C-in-C he had the exhilarating experience of being in charge of the air forces supporting the Eighth Army under Montgomery in its victorious drive along the coast of north Africa. He had worked before with 'that dynamic little man known to all of us as "Monty"'[7] during the winter of 1940–41 on plans to counter the threatened German invasion of Britain, and although many service leaders, including Tedder, found him difficult to deal with, Sholto admired his incisive thinking and the lucidity with which he approached the problems they faced.

Sholto's Middle East Command still covered a vast area, its forces for a short while encompassing the Desert Air Force (DAF) that was working with the Eighth Army in its victorious fight through Cyrenaica and Tripoli in modern-day Libya, all the Air Force units in Egypt itself, and the air side of the UK's military affairs in Palestine, Lebanon, Syria, Iraq, Iran, the Persian Gulf, Aden, Sudan and east Africa.

Following the formation of MAC, Sholto visited Tedder at his HQ in Algiers and discovered that plans were well under way for the invasion of Sicily, codenamed Operation HUSKY, which was due to start in July. Sholto's own command was required to provide logistics support, but the operational responsibility for HUSKY was MAC's. Despite what was potentially an awkward situation, Tedder acknowledged to Portal all the help that Sholto and his staff had given him in respect of operations in north Africa, but Sholto was less than happy with the arrangement, beginning a missive to Tedder in June 1943:

> I am afraid this letter is going to be rather a moan. But there is a growing feeling here that MAC is, by its recent actions, disturbing the smooth-working organisation of ME Command … I don't think you can accuse us of being unhelpful – on the contrary we are all out to help you in what we realise is a complicated and difficult job. But we feel, broadly speaking, that you should leave us the maximum amount of autonomy. Tell us what you want; and leave us to get on with the job.

Another complaint was that Tedder was 'short-circuiting' Sholto's HQ and issuing orders directly to elements in Middle East Command without informing Sholto or his staff, which was leading to 'confusion and loss of efficiency'. He ended his letter with: 'I am of course quite ready to accept your decisions in these matters, but I ask you to give serious consideration to the points I have raised.'[8] The argument continued to rumble on for another month with Sholto holding his ground and Tedder eventually becoming more conciliatory.

The war having moved westwards, and so much of the operational air forces being removed from Sholto's command, he occupied himself with forming good relationships with his Army and Navy counterparts in Cairo, General 'Jumbo' Wilson and Admiral Cunningham. However, his relations with the British Ambassador in Egypt, Sir Miles Lampson, were less positive. Although Sholto recognised that he was an able and experienced diplomat, they never saw eye to eye, having several run-ins, including over the treatment of the King of Egypt.

A diplomatic initiative in which Sholto played a part involved one of Churchill's preoccupations in the eastern Mediterranean: his desire to bring Turkey into the war on the side of the Allies. In March 1943, he received instructions that Churchill wanted him to go up to Ankara to discuss air defence plans with the Turks.

Sholto and his entourage thought they would have to go to Turkey disguised as civilians, but he was instructed by the Turks to arrive in uniform and was received with a guard of honour. At Ankara, he was welcomed at the British Embassy by the Ambassador, Sir Hughe Knatchbull-Hugessen, who asked whether he had any secret papers with him, to which Sholto replied, 'Yes, I have got in my briefcase a plan for the air defence of Turkey in the event of their coming into the war on the side of the Allies.' The Ambassador said, 'Well, you'd better hand it over to me.' Sholto asked why this was necessary, to which Sir Hughe replied, 'I must go and lock it away in my safe for the night, because my butler is a spy.' When Sholto asked, 'Why don't you sack him?', he received the following charming answer: 'Well, he is a very good butler, and in any case, anyone else I got would probably also be a spy.' It emerged later that this was none other than the famous spy Cicero, and that the contents of the Ambassador's safe were not as secure as he had hoped. Cicero had a wax impression made of the key to the safe, and in the dead of night when everyone in the Embassy was in bed, he went downstairs, took out secret documents and photographed them. Then he handed the films over to the German Military Attaché in Ankara. Later, when Sholto discovered all this, he realised that the plan for the air defence of Turkey would have been in the German Air Attaché's office the next day and in Berlin two days later.[9]

Sholto wrote a full report to Portal of his visit to Turkey, including his meeting with the President Ismet İnönü. The warm welcome Sholto received 'was very much what one would have expected from an Ally who was already in the war',[10] but the Turks had concerns regarding the command structure of the RAF and Turkish air forces working together, equipment including aircraft, and landing grounds. They also feared German reprisals, particularly the threatened bombing of Istanbul. Turkey as a whole was also 'crawling' with German spies, not just the British Embassy. The German Ambassador, Franz von Papen, appeared to have got wind of the visit, as he disappeared from Ankara the day before Sholto arrived, ostensibly to go to the coast for the sea-bathing. However, von Papen made sure that 'a posse of the Gestapo'[11] was present as a chilling welcome for Sholto on his arrival in Ankara.

Although Sholto and his staff returned to Cairo feeling cautiously optimistic, in the event, Turkey did not break off diplomatic relations with Germany until eighteen months later, and it was February 1945 before she joined the war on the Allied side.

As the spring wore on and the realities of his situation in the Middle East became clearer, Sholto was increasingly frustrated. What had been cautious optimism turned to desperation as he wrote to Portal in May lamenting the lack of operational activity in his command.

> ... Please do not think that I am labouring under any sense of grievance. I realise that it is nobody's fault, and that it is merely the turn of fortune's wheel. Nor have I any sort of grouse about Tedder's appointment. It was clearly the right one in the circumstances. Tedder himself is very considerate, and our relations are of the happiest. It is simply that I feel that I would like to have a more active and independent command. In fact, as it has turned out, I would have been better off if I had stayed at Fighter Command.

It may well be of course that there is nothing else in sight, and that I shall have to stay here indefinitely, and grin and bear it. I am of course quite ready to do that if you say so.

Please forgive me for worrying you about personal matters at a time like this, when I am sure you are as usual overburdened with much more important affairs. But I would be grateful for a line from you, telling me frankly how I stand.[12]

In the meantime, Portal had been exploring with the British chiefs of staff a new system of command in east Asia, comprising a British Supreme Commander with an American deputy and three subordinate commanders for each of the three services. They had presented this plan to Churchill, who was strongly in favour of giving the Supreme Command to an Air Force officer. He had considered Tedder for the post, but since he was fully occupied elsewhere, the choice fell between Sholto and Coningham, and Portal advised Churchill that Sholto 'would be in every way better qualified and more acceptable to the other Services'.[13]

Following the final expulsion of the Germans and Italians from north Africa in May 1943 and the successful Allied landings in Sicily, Sinclair arrived in Cairo for a tour of the Middle East, where his presence acted as a much-needed morale-booster both to Sholto and his command. One evening when they were talking quietly together, Sinclair told him in confidence about his possible appointment to east Asia.

This was the first that Sholto had heard of what was to become South-East Asia Command (SEAC). Initially he was delighted with the news that he was to be appointed Supreme Commander of a new tri-service command, but doubts soon started to appear: there would be a lot of teething troubles with such an arrangement, and Sholto had no previous experience of conditions in any of the countries in the Far East. He did not voice any of these concerns to Sinclair, but said simply that he would be prepared to serve in whatever capacity the Air Ministry or the government decided upon.

Despite Sholto's frustrations, life in Cairo was not entirely unpleasant, either from a work or a social point of view. He might have been criticised by Freeman for showing favouritism, but when it had become known that he was leaving Fighter Command to go to the Middle East, various of his subordinates expressed a desire to accompany their Commander-in-Chief.

Sholto also found himself being drawn into the hectic social life in Cairo. The city was at that time a crossroads between east and west, and all sorts of characters, including Sholto's friend Noël Coward, found their way out there. Sholto's PA lined up an endless list of social engagements that occupied altogether too much of his time and he found himself becoming frustrated. In his *Middle East Diary*, Coward seemed to articulate precisely how Sholto felt:

> These uniforms indicated that perhaps somewhere in the vague outside world there might be a war of some sort going on. This place is the last refuge of the soi-disant 'International Set'. All the fripperies of pre-war luxury living are still in existence here; rich people, idle people, cocktail parties, dinner parties, jewels and evening dress.[14]

After volunteering for war service at the outbreak of WWII and working in intelligence, Coward made an exhaustive tour of north Africa, the Mediterranean and what are now Iraq and Iran, entertaining the troops and visiting the wounded in hospital. The most touching comment in his diary was what he wrote following his visit to a desert hospital in the Canal Zone of Egypt:

> Soon, when the immediate necessity for courage has gone; when the physical sufferings are over, and when the will for actual survival has no longer such urgent demands made upon it, these men will come home. That will be the test, not of them, but of us. The spirit of man may triumph in adversity all right but it is putting the hell of a burden on it to demand that it should also triumph over poverty, injustice, callousness and muddled politics immediately afterwards. I wonder how we shall make out this time.[15]

Coward's most horrifying account was that following a visit to RAF El Adem in Libya, where he stopped on his long journey home. The base had been bombed repeatedly by the British, Germans and Italians, and over lunch in the Officers' Mess, the pilots told him 'horrible and obviously quite authentic stories' of 'booby traps' left by the Germans and Italians. Their 'favourite trick' was to mine equipment, including surgical dressings.

> The most dreadful of all was that they fixed mines onto wounded men so that when our chaps came to pick them up they were all blown to pieces. The wounded men who were conscious and aware of what was happening were efficiently gagged so that they were unable to warn their rescuers.[16]

This seemed so far removed from the glittering yet fragile social whirl in Cairo, among what Sholto called 'a plethora of Kings', the most prominent of whom was King Farouk of Egypt. Sholto felt that, since the British forces were in his country, the rules of protocol dictated that Farouk was the most important monarch with whom they had to deal, despite his extravagant lifestyle and his unpopularity with British diplomats, notably Lampson, who attempted to have Farouk deposed on more than one occasion. The worst of these was in February 1942 when Lampson threatened a British military coup in which tanks and armoured cars were parked on the lawns of Farouk's palace in Cairo, and Lampson, accompanied by a general and 'an impressive array of specially picked stalwart military officers armed to the teeth', presented a letter of abdication to Farouk for him to sign.[17] In the end, Lampson climbed down, but the tension that existed between Farouk and the British, Lampson in particular, was palpable when Sholto arrived in Cairo. He wrote that 'our Ambassador and the King seemed to loathe the sight and sound of each other'.[18]

Farouk was courted by both the Germans and the Italians, who attempted to bring Egypt into the war on the Axis side. Sholto observed that they cleverly treated him as an adult whereas the British, and particularly Lampson, treated him 'as if he were nothing but a naughty and rather silly boy. So far as I could make out, Farouk was naughty, and he was still very young, being only in his early twenties;

but to my mind, and taking a hard-headed view, he was also the King of Egypt.'[19]

Sholto decided that it was far wiser to treat Farouk as a friend and ally, no matter how one felt about him personally. He invited Farouk to dine with him at Air House, and soon the King was popping in whenever he felt at a loose end, which turned out to be rather often. Sholto realised that Farouk had taken a liking to him and that it was easy to communicate with him at quite an intimate level. He and Farouk used to go nightclubbing together in Cairo, their favourite haunt being the luxurious *Auberge des Pyramides*. Farouk used to keep Sholto up until 4 or 5 a.m., which was inconvenient when he was supposed to be at work in the morning, fighting a war.

Sholto's trips with Farouk to the *Auberge* did not escape the notice of Lampson, who popped in one night with Noël Coward and found Farouk there 'with Sholto Douglas and his little actress friend'.[20] Sholto's wife Joan had not been allowed to accompany him to the Middle East, and his 'friend' was Constance Carpenter, a very attractive cabaret artist with the Entertainments National Service Association (ENSA) who was out in Egypt, as Coward was, entertaining the troops. Sholto was seen frequently with Connie, as she was known, and it seems that Farouk was equally attracted to her. The gossip was that Sholto was in her room at Shepheard's Hotel (the leading hotel in Cairo) one evening when the King arrived. Sholto had to make a swift and ignominious exit via the service lift. Sholto was also rumoured to have shared Farouk's 'official mistress', Irene Guinle, and to have had an affair with her friend Hélène Mosseri, who was also a close associate of Farouk's. Although unsubstantiated, the whispers swirling around him would not have found favour either with Lampson or at the Air Ministry back in London and they undoubtedly affected his career.

As had happened with his first wife May, Sholto had affairs during his second marriage to Joan, although his relationship with Connie was possibly more serious than most of his liaisons. He was at a particularly difficult period of his life when his job in Cairo had turned out to be disappointing and he was bored. No longer did he have the adrenaline rush that came with heading an organisation as busy as Fighter Command. It was also a time when his competence was being questioned, and he had now as his immediate superior someone whom he had thought was his equal but who had been promoted above him. A risky affair, dangerous because of the attention that it drew, must have seemed the ideal thing to provide the excitement that he was lacking. Risk-taking was a way for Sholto to deal with the danger by appearing not to care, and so in some way to deny it. It's also very much part of the repertoire of behaviours of those who are carrying a heavy, if hidden, burden of trauma.

Despite Farouk's narcissism and insensitivity, Sholto began genuinely to like him, much to the annoyance of the British diplomatic staff. The two men spent many hours discussing religion and politics, and notwithstanding Farouk's flippancy and childish behaviour in public, Sholto found him to be an intelligent young man. Nevertheless, he was, unsurprisingly, 'very right wing in his outlook, and feudal enough not to be able to understand' Sholto's belief in socialism, meaning that in their discussions, Sholto moved further to the left than he actually was, causing Farouk to label him a communist. Sholto warned Farouk that, although he was undoubtedly popular at that point, unless he took measures to address the extreme inequality in his country and, in Sholto's words, 'the poverty and the misery of the masses of Egypt',[21] sooner or later there would be a revolution. Although Farouk appeared to be listening carefully, there was a gap between their understanding that they were not able to bridge. Sholto was not the only person to make this prediction, but no one else was able to approach Farouk with the same intimacy. It was to no avail, however: in 1952, Farouk, who had failed completely to address the yawning chasm between rich and poor, was deposed in a military coup that led to a revolution and thence to the end of the 150-year-old Muhammad Ali dynasty.

Although Cairo had become something of a military backwater, controversies and more botched military operations abounded during Sholto's time there. Not least of these was one that had been discussed at Casablanca: the possibility of further bombing of the nine oil refineries at Ploiesti in Romania. Romania had joined the Axis Powers in November 1940 and Ploiesti supplied them with 30 per cent of their oil. At Casablanca it was suggested that the raid should be in the form of a long-range attack by bombers from the Ninth US Army Air Force (USAAF) in the Western Desert under the command of Major-General Lewis H. Brereton. Both he and Sholto were against the proposed operation, and Sholto informed the Air Ministry that neither he nor Brereton thought that a 'single stunt attack at extreme range' would achieve the desired objective. In the same signal, Sholto wrote that the raid on Ploiesti would be a distraction from the attack on Sicily, Operation HUSKY, on which he felt Allied forces should be concentrating. He finished with the request: 'Let us keep our eye on the ball.' Sholto received a reply from the Air Ministry that agreed with him in principle, but two months later, he found himself chairing a joint UK/US conference to discuss both operations. Sholto and Brereton were informed that the aircraft to be used for Ploiesti would be B24 Liberators flying at the lowest possible level. These heavy bombers were not designed for such attacks, and the thought filled them both with dread.

The raid on Ploiesti took place on 1 August 1943 and involved 178 Liberators carrying 1,751 aircrew. Following an Allied attack the previous summer, the Germans and Romanians had fortified the oil refineries, making them the most heavily defended installation outside the Third Reich. Nevertheless, the USAAF completed its mission, but at a terrible cost: 310 aircrew were killed, 108 captured by the Axis, seventy-eight interned in Turkey, and four taken in by Tito's partisans in Yugoslovia. It was proportionally the most costly major Allied air raid of the war. Only eighty-eight aircraft made it back to Benghazi, of which fifty-five were damaged. With what he described as 'a heavy ache of regret', Sholto sent a signal to Brereton that read: 'The gallantry and dash displayed by your air crews in carrying out the attack at such a low altitude in the face of very strong defences is beyond praise.'[22]

All this for so little return, because although the Allies estimated a 40 per cent loss of the refining capacity at Ploiesti as a result of the raid, some refineries remained largely undamaged. Most of the others were repaired within weeks, after which the net output of fuel was greater than before the raid.

CHAPTER NINETEEN

AN ILL-FATED OPERATION
AND SHOLTO'S NADIR

Shortly after the disastrous raid on Ploesti, Sholto was involved in another ill-fated venture, Operation ACCOLADE, the attempted capture of the Dodecanese islands from the Germans and their occupation by British forces during September, October and November 1943, which was intended as a prelude to an invasion of the Balkans and was a particular project of Churchill's. Eisenhower had considered the possibility of a campaign in the Aegean but had dismissed it as a distraction from the invasion of France and the Low Countries that was to take place the following year in the form of the D-Day landings, behind which the Americans were throwing their whole weight. Brooke called Churchill's plan 'Rhodes madness',[1] and was also opposed to it, fearing it would jeopardise relations with President Roosevelt.

Nevertheless, Churchill was adamant, and with his Army and Navy counterparts, 'Jumbo' Wilson and Admiral Cunningham, Sholto spent months planning ACCOLADE. Right from the beginning he saw clearly that there would be considerable obstacles, which he explained in letters to both Tedder and Portal in May 1943:

> The operation is likely to be a difficult one, as it means transporting an expedition at slow speed across 250 miles of open sea in the face of what may be quite a heavy scale of air attack ... The Prime Minister has told us to plan for the capture of Rhodes and Scarpanto [aka Karpathos] 'with ingenuity and resource'. I hope that this does

not mean that we have got to do it 'on the cheap' from the air point of view. We have had too many lessons in this war of the futility of trying to carry out transpontine [from the other side of a sea] operations in the face of heavy air superiority ... We shall have to make lavish provision of (a) long-range fighters, (b) ship-borne aircraft, and (c) heavy bombers with which to plaster all the enemy air bases within range of our landings. Unless we do this, our losses in ships are likely to be heavy and the expedition is likely to fail.[2]

In the end, the failure of Operation ACCOLADE was due precisely to the lack of those resources and facilities that Sholto said were necessary. He and his fellow Middle East commanders had to watch agonisedly as, firstly, the operation to capture Rhodes, the largest of the Dodecanese islands, failed and then one by one, British forces occupied the other islands, Cos, Leros and Samos, only to have the Germans launch fierce counterattacks and recapture them. What no one, Sholto included, appreciated at the time was that Hitler attached the same importance to the Aegean as Churchill did, but whereas the British were starved of men, ships and aircraft, he ensured that his garrisons there were fully supported.

From the beginning of ACCOLADE, Sholto had felt unhappy with the view of it taken by Eisenhower's HQ, including Tedder, who admitted to Portal that however many aircraft were supplied to Sholto, the fact that they could not operate from bases close to the Dodecanese islands meant that the operation was doomed from the start. Sholto cited as a major flaw the dependence of his own Middle East Command on Tedder's higher command in the central Mediterranean, with Tedder, who was firmly wedded to Eisenhower's strategy, controlling vital air resources.

Perhaps surprisingly, Tedder's view of this situation was not dissimilar:

How could it be that the Air Commander in the Middle East could find himself involved in combined operations in the Aegean with forces quite inadequate for the task, and consequently entirely dependent upon the good will of the Air Commander-in-Chief

Mediterranean? Conversely, how could it be that the Supreme Commander Mediterranean and his Air Commander-in-Chief, responsible for a major campaign in Italy and the Central Mediterranean, could be subject to extreme pressure to divert air forces to operations in the Aegean – operations over which they had no control? If the Command set-up was so irrational, it is not surprising that the operations themselves were equally irrational and, therefore, doomed to failure.[3]

The official RAF historians, Denis Richards and Hilary St George Saunders, were harsher in their assessment, calling the whole Dodecanese fiasco a 'rash experiment' which 'cost the lives of some hundreds of troops and airmen, a large quantity of valuable stores and equipment, a number of naval vessels and 115 aircraft.'[4]

Sholto continued to feel for the rest of his life that he and his service counterparts in the eastern Mediterranean had been hung out to dry, the operation being allowed to fail due to insufficient American support. Churchill was of the same view, writing: 'I remained – and remain – in my heart unconvinced that the capture of Rhodes could not have been fitted in,' adding that it caused him 'one of the sharpest pangs I suffered in the war'.[5]

The last three months of 1943 marked the nadir of Sholto's career. It seemed to him as though he was coming to a complete standstill. He was disturbed and angry over some of the events of the disastrous Aegean campaign, feeling that they ran counter to all that was 'both just and sane'.[6] And as if to twist the knife in the wound, although he had heard previously that he was to be appointed to the new command in south-east Asia, he learned from a press communiqué handed to him in his office in Cairo that Lord Mountbatten had been appointed to the post. As he said, 'That could hardly be described as the pleasantest way of hearing that I was not getting the job.'[7] Although Churchill had put Sholto's name forward to President Roosevelt, he had not been given the appointment because the President had been told that he did not get along well with the Americans. The official reason given was that Roosevelt wanted a naval officer in command, and that American opinion was strongly opposed to an airman being given such a responsible position, though why this was so, and why Sholto was supposed not to have got along with the Americans, he never understood.

Brooke had been entirely supportive of Sholto's prospective appointment and later wrote candidly:

> We had had several discussions with PM concerning selection of a Supreme Commander for South East Asia and had recommended Sholto Douglas to him. Unfortunately we shall see that the Americans objected to him for some reason I have never known. Ultimately the cloak fell on Dickie Mountbatten's shoulders, but I am convinced that Sholto Douglas would have filled the bill better, provided he remained active and did not grow too fat.[8]

An explanation of why Roosevelt was not favourably disposed towards Sholto is contained a lengthy correspondence between him and Churchill, although even then, there is the impression that the President and his generals were holding something back.

Churchill provided a strong defence of Sholto, writing:

> I should like to impress upon you the very strong view which our three Chiefs of Staff all have about Sholto Douglas' qualifications. Both Brooke and [Admiral] Pound assure me that there is no British officer available to whom they would more readily confide the naval and military forces involved and Portal is all for him. He is a man of exceptional physical energy and vigour of mind. I can myself testify to his very high mental ability because as Head of Fighter Command he worked on the Night Air Defence Committee over whose meetings I preside myself. ... Finally I may say that if anything happened to Portal he would be my first choice for CAS, although of course Tedder's growing reputation tends to affect this view ... We have therefore given the most earnest thought to this matter, especially in view of your query. I have been wondering why it is you have these doubts about him and I should be grateful if you would let me know from what they spring. The

only thing I can think of is that he sat on a very large Committee under Eisenhower in the early days of 'Bolero'⁹ and perhaps he could not do himself full justice there. I am sure he is animated by the most friendly feelings towards your people and that he has tact and savoir faire.¹⁰

Roosevelt replied: 'I have been advised that a number of general officers who have been thrown in contact with Douglas all have gotten the same unfavourable reaction', and then implied that Sholto lacked the breadth of vision, moral courage and experience in Combined Allied operations that would be necessary in the post.¹¹

Churchill was not satisfied at all with Roosevelt's explanation, and signalled Field Marshal Dill, chief of the British Joint Staff Mission in Washington, to elicit further information. He replied the same day, throwing more light on the matter. He had not yet questioned Marshall, but he knew about American objections to Sholto, writing that Marshall would

be reluctant to give anything more precise than that Sholto Douglas has been 'contemptuously critical' of American operations on more than one occasion and that this fact is too well known to too many Americans. Marshall feels that Sholto Douglas has created for himself too great a handicap to undertake satisfactorily the difficult task for which he is proposed.¹²

The following day, having spoken to Marshall and senior Generals Arnold and McNarney, Dill sent Churchill the following message:

Marshall said that he knew that on more than one occasion when Sholto Douglas had had a drink or two he had spoken in contemptuous terms of Americans. He could not be more precise than that but the impression had gained ground that Sholto Douglas was unsympathetic towards Americans and by many he was dubbed a 'stuffed shirt' ... Arnold said he knew Sholto Douglas well and in his opinion he was not the man to command the confidence of

Americans. This opinion was based on his general knowledge of the man and of American psychology ... In McNarney's opinion Sholto Douglas was the least suitable British commander whom he had met to command the respect and confidence of Americans.[13]

In the face of all this opposition, there was no possibility of appointing Sholto as Supreme Commander, SEAC. It is easy to see why the Americans viewed him as a 'stuffed shirt': a product of the English public school system and Oxford University, he was always formal in his manner, and perhaps that shyness and easily misunderstood sense of humour that had afflicted him since childhood gave the wrong impression. This is pure speculation, but an additional possibility is that the Americans were aware of Sholto's stance on the progressive side of politics, although in his position it was not something that he could broadcast. American fear of the spread of communism in south-east Asia would have precluded for them the choice of a commander in that theatre who was in any way left-wing.

However, Sholto had his strong supporters. In September, the Minister of State in Egypt, Richard Casey, signalled Churchill with his concern:

> After eight months here as Air Officer Commander-in-Chief Sholto Douglas is anxious to get more active employment than this theatre promises for the future. You know his capability which his work here has borne out ... He has not asked me to approach you but perhaps you would bear him in mind.[14]

Churchill was even more emphatic on where Sholto should be, sending a blistering one-liner to Sinclair that reiterated what he had voiced nearly a year before: 'What a pity you moved him from Fighter Command.'[15] Churchill repeated his insistence on Sholto for VCAS in minutes to Sinclair in October, writing: 'There is only one place for Douglas, namely, that of Vice-Chief of the Air Staff. This post I wish him to have, and the sooner the better. I trust you will meet my strong views in this matter.'[16] At that point, the post of VCAS was being filled by Sholto's former SASO at Fighter Command, Evill. Freeman, whom he had replaced, had said somewhat malevolently that Evill was lacking in character and personality but was nevertheless clever, shrewd and hard-working.

Sinclair replied:

> You and I both know Sholto Douglas and we agree in our estimate of his ability, but you do not know Evill well and you see little of his work. I see it at close quarters, and he fits perfectly into the Air Staff as Vice-Chief and makes a strong team with Portal.[17]

Churchill persisted:

> I remain of the opinion that Sholto Douglas should be made VCAS. This matter affects me very directly as Minister of Defence because of the contacts with the high Cabinet work, especially when CAS is away for conferences. I hope therefore you will meet my wishes in the same way that the other Service Departments do.[18]

Sinclair responded with a subtle but distinct ambivalence towards Sholto and his possible proximity to Portal in that post:

> If Evill were not performing his duties with rare efficiency, loyalty and success or if Portal were indifferent to the choice of his Vice Chief or if the relations between CAS and Vice-CAS were not as important as they are to the working of this Department and the effective conduct of the air war, nothing could please me more than to appoint Sholto Douglas who holds my confidence, respect and friendship. Add to that my desire to meet your wishes which is a big factor in all my work here.
>
> The post of Vice Chief is, however, one of the most important in the Department for which I am responsible. I have, therefore, not formed my judgement without most careful thought – and I find myself convinced that it would be wrong at the present time to replace Evill by Sholto Douglas.

Then Sinclair suggested two posts for which Sholto had 'outstanding qualifications', one of which was to be Tedder's replacement in the

Mediterranean, and the other was to be Allied Air Commander in South East Asia.[19] The latter, though, was really an insult, as Churchill pointed out in his reply to Sinclair:

> I very much regret to receive your letter, and I still hope you will be willing to meet my wishes. The responsibility for these high appointments falls ultimately upon the Minister of Defence who is of course himself responsible to the War Cabinet, by whom if need be a decision must be taken. I may add that there is no possibility of Sholto Douglas becoming Allied Air Commander in the Mediterranean. If Tedder is moved, the Command would have to go to an American officer, almost certainly Spaatz. Considering the unfair prejudice the Americans have expressed about Sholto Douglas, it would indeed be foolish to bring him forward there. Your second suggestion is almost equally inadmissible ... Here also, in this Combined Command, we might meet again the American prejudice and have further difficulties. Besides, it does not seem appropriate to invite Douglas to take the secondary Command in the theatre for which he knows he was our first selection for the Supreme Commander. It would be embarrassing from every point of view, and the Americans would certainly resent it. I think it most important to find for Douglas a purely British position which will assert in a decisive manner our confidence in him and at the same time offer no foothold for American objections. Quite apart from this, I consider Douglas is by far the most highly qualified officer for the post of VCAS, and I desire to have his advice at the centre, especially when the CAS may be abroad. You told me yourself that you regard him as beyond question Portal's successor should a vacancy occur.[20]

No fewer than three times, Churchill had pressed Sinclair for Sholto to be made VCAS, and three times, he had refused to comply. One explanation for this may have been that both Sinclair and Portal regarded Churchill as a poor judge of character, as did his doctor, Lord Moran, who wrote later that this was because Churchill knew so little about those whose causes he championed, including Professor Lindemann (who became Lord Cherwell) and Lord Beaverbrook, neither of whom endeared themselves to chiefs of staff or politicians. Much later, in 1957, when Moran was in the House of Lords waiting to pay his tribute to Lord Cherwell, Portal, who was sitting next to him on the crossbenches, leaned across and whispered: 'Winston was a bad picker.' Moran knew that this was true, although 'not all of Winston's friends were men of straw'.[21]

At the same time as the discussion on who would be VCAS, there was a conversation going on within the Air Ministry about who would be appointed to another very important post, that of AMP, responsible for all personnel matters within the RAF and a member of the Air Council. Sholto's name came up, but once again, even though Freeman had left the Air Ministry for the Ministry of Aircraft Production, his poisoned pen was active to Sholto's detriment as he wrote to Portal: 'You must not have Sholto Douglas at any price – and if you force me to do so I will tell you why.'[22]

In fact, nothing was done immediately about either of these possible appointments and Sholto remained in Cairo, but then he became aware of yet another rumour that early in the coming year, the rank of AOC-in-C Middle East would be downgraded to air marshal, meaning that he would be too senior and would have to return to England. But, he wondered, to what? There was the vague suggestion of an Air Ministry appointment, although Sholto did not seem to be aware of Churchill's recommendation, but what he wanted really was another operational command. However, there was little hope of that unless he went to Transport Command. He felt that he was facing a blank wall just as the important conferences in Cairo and Tehran approached in late November and December 1943. In the face of increasingly divergent views on the part of the British and Americans over the conduct of the war, the Cairo conference, at which Churchill and Roosevelt were present, was used to try to arrive at some agreement over future operations in Europe.

On the way to Cairo, Churchill had prepared an indictment of the mismanagement of operations in the Mediterranean. He wrote: 'One command has the forces but not the responsibilities, the other the responsibilities but not the forces. This can hardly be considered an ideal arrangement.'[23] Those representing the eastern Mediterranean,

Sholto, Wilson and Willis (the latter having replaced Cunningham as Naval Commander), attended a meeting of the combined chiefs of staff at which Churchill was present, with Eisenhower, Tedder and Admiral Cunningham representing the central Mediterranean. The minute Churchill brought up the matter of the Aegean, the Americans were immediately on the offensive, so much so that Sholto witnessed Brooke and the American General George Marshall having 'the father and mother of a row', as Brooke himself described it.[24] All Sholto and his Middle East colleagues could get from the Americans was that they might consider further operations in the Aegean if they could be arranged without disturbing in any way the plans for OVERLORD.

While Roosevelt was in Cairo, he asked for a personal interview with Sholto, who went out to the villa near the Pyramids where the President was staying and was ushered into the sitting room. A few minutes later, Roosevelt was carried in by a bodyguard of US marines, accompanied by several staff officers. Once the chair had been put down, he ordered the bodyguard and all the others out of the room, leaving him alone with Sholto. Roosevelt's opening remarks, which were more akin to a harangue than a conversation, started with: 'Sholto Douglas, one of the most famous names in Scottish history.' He proceeded to lecture Sholto on that subject and on the achievements of the Douglases for several minutes, ending up with his pride in his own Scottish grandmother. Sholto was so touched that he felt tears coming into his eyes, as his Scottish ancestry was fundamental to his very sense of identity. But despite the seeming sincerity of Roosevelt's opening remarks, Sholto realised quite soon that, in fact, he was being worked over by a very skilful actor who had been very well briefed for their meeting.

They proceeded to discuss the war, and Sholto dared to venture the opinion that it was a pity the Dodecanese operation had been so starved of resources and thus unable to be brought to a satisfactory conclusion. Roosevelt dismissed it as a minor skirmish of no importance, but Sholto endeavoured to disabuse him of that view. However, he made no impression whatsoever, and realised that he could not succeed where even Churchill had failed. Nevertheless, Roosevelt and Sholto parted on good terms, and he hoped that he had helped to correct the misconceptions about himself that had been presented to the President.

Meanwhile, it was clear when Churchill arrived at the Cairo conference that he was far from well. Churchill's old friend Field Marshal Jan Smuts was at the second stage of the Cairo conference, and he confided in Brooke that he was very concerned about Churchill's health, even expressing doubts as to 'whether he would stay the course' and saying that 'he was noticing changes in him'.[25]

At this time, it was decided that since Eisenhower, an American, would be the Supreme Commander for OVERLORD, a British officer would be in overall command in the Mediterranean, and Wilson was selected to take Eisenhower's place there. Soon afterwards, in December, MAC became the Mediterranean Allied Air Forces (MAAF), covering all air operations throughout the Mediterranean. Unsurprisingly, given what had transpired recently with ACCOLADE, Sholto continued to argue for greater autonomy for Middle East Command, writing both to Tedder and to the Air Ministry that to place that command entirely under the control of MAAF was not only unworkable but would lead to 'inefficiency and friction'.[26]

As in every other senior post he had held, Sholto was concerned with making sure that pilots were trained properly by building up operational training units or OTUs, which had been neglected by Tedder and were woefully inadequate when Sholto had assumed command in the Middle East. The command was known as 'Muddle East' among servicemen before he took over, but they were confident that 'Sholto will fix it'.[27] In May 1943, he instigated an expansion scheme that placed all training in that theatre under a new umbrella. The programme involved not only operational training but also a big increase in armament, signals and navigation instruction. By December, the system was in full swing and Sholto wanted to be able to communicate directly with the Air Ministry so that the growth of OTUs would not be held up. Tedder replied that he agreed with Sholto in principle but did not wish to intervene. Rather callously, he knew that he was about to become Eisenhower's deputy for OVERLORD, so this was shortly not going to concern him.

Sholto's own future was far from clear. On 23 December, his

fiftieth birthday, he was informed by the Air Ministry that Park was to replace him as AOC-in-C Middle East, but there was still no word about any appointment for him. A birthday party was held at Air House in Cairo that night, and Bob Wright, who was on his headquarters staff there, wrote in his diary that he 'was not in good form at all'. Around midnight, Wright found him standing alone staring out of the window, and when he remarked that his 'chief' did not appear to be enjoying himself, Sholto replied with some disgust: 'Hell, I'm fifty!' However, that was not the real reason for his dejection. Wright had not heard the unofficial news that had been released casually, almost accidentally, that Sholto was to be appointed Deputy C-in-C of MAAF, which was to be commanded by an American, Ira Eaker, in place of Tedder. It bewildered Sholto that he, with all his experience of high command, should be appointed as deputy to an American officer so much junior to him in both rank and experience.

The day after his birthday, Sholto received a copy of a signal sent by Portal to Tedder that said: 'I much regret that Douglas has been kept in the dark about his future.'[28] Portal blamed Churchill for this, saying that Churchill had told him that he was not to discuss the matter with Sholto, so Portal assumed that Churchill would do so himself. Portal urged Tedder, who was still with Churchill in Tunis, to suggest to him that either he would send for Sholto himself or allow Portal to tell him what was in store for him. Sholto got the distinct impression that neither Portal nor Tedder were happy about what someone was going to have to tell him, so they were each passing the buck.

Three days later, Sholto received a signal from Tedder, saying that Churchill had left Tunisia and was going to Morocco to convalesce from a bout of pneumonia. He said he had raised the matter of senior appointments with Churchill before he left, who indicated that they would be announced the following day. Sholto sent a signal to Portal insisting that no announcement be made about any appointment concerning him before he himself was consulted. It seems extraordinary that he should even have to ask this, and unsurprisingly, Sholto finished his signal with: 'I feel that I am being jockeyed into a false position.'[29] The following day, he signalled Portal again, saying that he had led him to believe that there were several alternatives for his next appointment but that now he felt he was being presented with a *fait accompli* that he would not be able to accept. He asked Portal politely for some direct information in order that he could express his opinion on the matter. This signal brought an immediate reply from Portal, saying he was sorry that Sholto should feel this way, and that he quite understood that Sholto had been left in the dark. Once again, he blamed Churchill's illness for this lack of communication. Sholto generously judged Portal's distress at his awkward position as genuine, having known him for many years.

If Sholto took the appointment as Eaker's deputy, he would have no operational functions or responsibilities, and he would become little more than a glorified administration officer of the British Air Forces in the Mediterranean. He realised that officers should not as a rule argue about their appointments, but he felt that he was being sacrificed neither to the good of the service nor to the war effort but to political considerations, Roosevelt having insisted that an American should be given the senior Air Force command.

Sholto became increasingly angry and told Max Aitken, who was visiting Sholto's HQ, that he had a mind to resign. Sholto wrote that Aitken looked at him shrewdly and exclaimed: 'But you can't do that … not in time of war.'

'Oh, yes, I can,' Sholto replied, whereupon 'a broad grin came over Aitken's face. "You'll find yourself a corporal in the Home Guard if you do," he commented.'

Sholto was not the only senior officer who had contemplated resigning during WWII. Brooke had considered it 'during his arduous service as CIGS; Wavell apparently thought about it while serving as the Viceroy of India; at one stage the patient and loyal Pug Ismay [Churchill's staff officer] had even handed in his resignation, only to have it ignored'.[30]

Sholto's long signal brought an immediate answer from Portal, which said that both he and Sinclair had informed Churchill of Sholto's reluctance to accept the post under Eaker but it was Churchill who had put Sholto's name forward to Roosevelt for the job, believing that it was the best post for him. Portal then came in with the punch:

'He [Churchill] does not consider it is for you to say where you will be employed. As I have told you before, I sympathise very much with your feeling of partial frustration since you left Fighter Command.'[31]

Portal's appeal to Sholto's loyalty, which could almost be called emotional blackmail, was backed up with a signal from Sinclair, who repeated Portal's arguments, adding cynically that there was no exact comparison between British and American ranks. Then he came in with his own blow by saying that the British would be working with the Americans for quite some time and that it was important that they should get to know Sholto better. Under such pressure, Sholto accepted the appointment, but in his heart, he was filled with gloom at the prospect of being stuck out in the Mediterranean.

Aware of the machinations that were going on at the highest level behind his back, on 1 January 1944 Sholto wrote a quietly desperate letter to Churchill: '… I will of course accept the appointment with a good grace. You can rely on me to bury any sense of disappointment, and give Eaker full and loyal support. Fortunately, he is a man I both like and respect, so that will not be very difficult.'[32]

In the same letter, Sholto repudiated the stories circulating that branded him as anti-American, and included a very complimentary letter he had received from Lewis Brereton:

> In closing my duty in the Middle East, I wish to express my deep appreciation for your generous support and co-operation and your unfailing courtesy to me, both officially and personally throughout our association. It has been a pleasure and a privilege to serve with you and I sincerely hope that our duties will again throw us together. I feel that the combat operations of the American Air Forces under your direction and my command have accomplished their fair share in the success of our Allied aims in the Middle East. I have great admiration for your leadership and professional attainments, and would ask nothing better than to continue the war in our present relationship.[33]

There was a possibility that the Americans would veto Sholto's appointment to the MAAF post also, but Churchill signalled Portal and

Sinclair that if they did, he would 'protest officially to the President, and ask for a formal inquiry into the facts'.[34] Quite a thing to suggest in the middle of a World War.

In the face of Sholto's reluctance, despite his pledge of loyal support, Sinclair made the following suggestion to Churchill:

> It occurs to me that if Sholto Douglas is unwilling to accept the post of Deputy Commander-in-Chief of the Allied Air Forces in the Mediterranean that post might be offered to Slessor, who is now Commander-in-Chief, Coastal Command … I have no reason to doubt that the Admiralty would be glad to have Douglas at Coastal Command.[35]

Two days later, Churchill replied, perhaps disingenuously, that he had only just learned that Eaker was to be appointed to the senior air post in the Mediterranean, above Sholto, and that Eaker's professional competence would 'narrow Douglas's scope'. Under these circumstances, Churchill suggested that if Sholto would prefer Coastal Command, he would be quite ready to agree to Slessor going out to the Mediterranean to fill the post that Sholto had been offered.[36]

So, in a surprising *volte-face*, only twenty-four hours after Sholto's acceptance of the Mediterranean post, he was now being offered something that he felt was genuinely an honour and with which he was delighted.

The prospect of returning to England and a fully operational and integrated command was to Sholto almost like being wakened from a bad dream, and he was overjoyed to be released from all the political machinations that he had known during his year in Cairo. There was one final irritation, however. Churchill had told him before he left Cairo that the Foreign Secretary, Anthony Eden, had intimated to him that the Foreign Office thought that it would be a good idea to leave Sholto in Cairo because of his positive relationship with King Farouk. When Sholto had looked rather taken aback, Churchill had said to him: 'But don't worry about that.'

As soon as Sholto knew definitely that he was leaving Egypt, he told Farouk, who wanted to present him with the Order of Ismail, one of the highest official Egyptian decorations. Sholto was required by British King's Regulations to obtain official permission before accepting the decoration. However, the Foreign Office declined to give its approval. Farouk was furious, detecting the hand of Lampson in the refusal, probably correctly, and taking it as a personal affront that Sholto had refused the decoration.

Nonetheless, an article in the *Daily Telegraph* of 24 January gave an account of the friendship between Sholto and Farouk, provided by 'an RAF friend recently home from Cairo'. It ended with: 'These unofficial contacts between the Palace and British circles were undoubtedly, adds my informant, highly beneficial to Anglo-Egyptian relations. It is hoped in Cairo that the effort to foster them will be continued.'

CHAPTER TWENTY

VICTORY AT LAST

In January 1944, Sholto made the long journey back from Cairo to take up his appointment as C-in-C Coastal Command at its HQ at Northwood on the outskirts of London. It was the most absorbing and enjoyable of all the senior posts he had held, and perhaps the one where his leadership qualities reached their zenith, but the preoccupations and frustrations with which he had grappled from his time as a squadron commander in WWI onwards remained obstinately present, namely shortages of equipment, including aircraft, and inadequate training of aircrew.

In wartime histories, Coastal Command has received less than its fair share of attention, and yet its aircrews performed heroic work in their long-range sorties out over the Atlantic, the North Sea, the Baltic and the Mediterranean, often lasting up to eighteen hours. The Admiralty had issued a veto on publicity concerning the anti-U-boat operations of the command, fearing that such disclosures would give the enemy a complete general picture of their progress. A thirty-day rule prevented any reporting of U-boat sinkings until after that period. But a far greater problem, certainly from the beginning of the war, was Coastal Command's status as the poor relation in terms of the aircraft supplied to it, having to make do with insufficient numbers, most of which were obsolete. Sholto had a constant battle with the Air Ministry over aircraft provision, particularly for Operation OVERLORD, in which he predicted that casualty rates would be high.

As with Middle East Command, the area covered by Coastal Command was vast, stretching from Gibraltar to Iceland and as far out as the Azores in the mid-Atlantic, and Sholto felt the warmest and deepest sympathy for his aircrews. On the one hand, they had the exhausting and largely unspectacular task of providing very long-range escort duties to convoys, about which almost nothing was made public, and on the other was the work of Coastal Command's Strike Wings, of which there were three when Sholto assumed command. The clue was in the name, as, equipped from 1943 with Beaufighters carrying torpedoes, rockets and cannon, they made hard and swift attacks against enemy surface vessels. The risk of casualties was very high in both types of operation, but the tedium was greatest for the long-range crews. Not only did they have to cope with the longest sorties of any crews in the RAF; they also had the lengthiest tours of duty, normally eighteen months. It is true that an anti-U-boat crew might fly for a whole year without seeing a single enemy submarine, and when they did get a sighting, their chances of making an attack were only about 30 per cent, and of actually destroying the U-boat even less. But the hour upon hour of dogged vigilance over stormy seas meant that Coastal Command's motto, 'Constant Endeavour', which Sholto himself devised along with the command's crest, was well-earned. He was fully aware of the psychological toll on all his aircrews, as right at the beginning of his time at Coastal Command one of the first things he did was to instruct all his senior medical officers to cooperate fully in providing the information required by the consultant in neuropsychiatry who was making a visit.

Sholto inherited an excellent headquarters staff from his predecessor, Air Marshal Sir 'Jack' Slessor, describing them as 'both capable and shrewd'.[1] Two people stood out from all the others in the support they gave him. The first was his SASO, Air Vice-Marshal Aubrey Ellwood, who had been a Coastal Command group commander before joining the staff at Northwood, so was familiar with the operational side of the command. The second was the person Sholto said probably contributed more than anyone else to the smooth running of the command over a long period of time, the Senior Naval Staff Officer, Captain D. V. Peyton-Ward, known to everyone as P.-W. He had served on submarines in WWI and so had a good idea of what was in the minds of U-boat commanders. Between the wars, he developed arthritis and had to be invalided out of the Navy, but rejoined the service on the outbreak of WWII and spent the entire war at Northwood. Sholto could see that P.-W. was often in pain but he never let that interfere with his work, always being in the operations room when he was needed, and performing an excellent job in liaising with the Navy.

P.-W.'s main task, at which he worked exhaustively with his assistant, WAAF officer Phyllis Felton, née Davies, was the tracking of U-boats, the courses of which they deduced with remarkable accuracy. This was of vital importance to the protection of transatlantic convoys. Attrition rates were high on some operations, with the possibility of survival much reduced by an order from the head of the Kriegsmarine, Admiral Doenitz, discovered in surrendered U-boats after the war, which directed their commanders to give priority in their attacks on convoys to the sinking of rescue ships. Each morning, Sholto came into P.-W.'s office to study the board used for plotting the whereabouts of the convoys. He had to make the hard decision of which convoys would receive air cover, as there were not enough aircraft or crews to provide protection for all.

When it came to planning for D-Day, each command HQ had a huge tome containing the orders for OVERLORD, detailed plans with timings, which had to be altered frequently due to factors such as the weather. Phyllis had to ensure that the plans were kept up to date. She shared an office with P.-W. next to the operations room, and an armed guard was posted outside her door if the plans book was in her office. The guard also accompanied her back to the mess. She was not allowed to talk with anyone or go on leave, and although she had shared a bedroom previously with other WAAFs, during the preparations for D-Day, she was given a single bedroom in case she spoke in her sleep and gave anything away.

During a recent interview with her, Phyllis recalled that Sholto came across as arrogant, clever and stern, and that 'he did not suffer fools gladly'. P.-W. and the other junior officers found him slightly difficult and he did not fraternise much with the lower ranks.

Sholto's treatment of Phyllis seems to have been typical of his attitude towards the women with whom he worked and way ahead of his time. Throughout his career, he was ever mindful to promote their interests, realising their vital and equal contribution to the war effort and beyond. When he had been C-in-C Fighter Command in 1942, he marked the third anniversary of the founding of the WAAF with a speech to 500 of its personnel gathered for a parade and march-past at his HQ, at which he took the salute. His words could have been applied to Phyllis directly:

> Without your help, the speedy and accurate work on which the air defence of this country and the safety of our pilots on operations depend, could not be secured. This is only one of the many stations in this Command where your comrades are performing vital duties. At other Commands, you are replacing men in heavy and highly skilled work, releasing them for more active jobs for which they could not otherwise be spared. As Flight Mechanics in the maintenance and repair of the aircraft, you now fly with the pilots who test your work; as nursing orderlies, you fly with the ambulances. Such duties have brought you, deservedly, the status of members of the Armed Forces of the Crown. We of the RAF are proud that you should share this Service on equal terms with us and that the work you are doing has received recognition from the King and Air Council.[2]

In addition to the sterling work of U-boat hunters, convoy escorts and Strike Wings, Coastal Command's other operations included high-flying photographic reconnaissance missions, 'lonely ones performed mostly in unarmed Spitfires',[3] as Sholto wrote. The photographs obtained from these flights were analysed by that most uncelebrated of wartime organisations, the Photographic Reconnaissance Unit, which produced hundreds of thousands of prints, used extensively by all branches of the services. Coastal Command maintained five squadrons at Benson devoted exclusively to this work, which could be as uncomfortable and dangerous as any other form of flying. The command was also required to maintain a fleet of high-powered, fast motorboats and two squadrons of aircraft to provide the Air Sea Rescue Service, sharing this duty with Fighter Command. Coastal Command also provided fifty aircraft for the meteorological service, which had to roam far beyond home shores as the sole source of weather information for military operations by the RAF, Navy and other services, though Sholto felt that the supply of aircraft was never really adequate.

Sholto's return to the UK in January 1944 had coincided with the gathering there of all those who were to be involved in the final planning for OVERLORD. He was disappointed that he was not to have command of the air side of the operation; his posting to the Mediterranean meant that his successor at Fighter Command, Leigh-Mallory, had been appointed Air C-in-C of the Allied Expeditionary Air Force (AEAF), the air force to be used in the invasion. The irony was that Leigh-Mallory's uncompromising, at times even aggressive, manner antagonised the Americans, and Sholto heard rumours that he was not getting on well with Eisenhower or Brereton.

At Coastal Command, meanwhile, Sholto put forward his ideas for the expansion of the Air Sea Rescue Service that would have to take place before D-Day, and by the end of May, its strength had been increased from two to four squadrons, 130 high-speed launches and fifty-two tenders. As part of the preparations for the role Coastal Command would play in OVERLORD, and consistent with his emphasis on the importance of operational training, Sholto also stepped up the intensity of instruction in his command. The introduction of fresh equipment necessitated more specialised training and OTU courses were extended. Andrew Hendrie, who served in Coastal Command from 1939 and flew operationally from 1942 to 1945, emphasised in his book on the command, aptly named *The Cinderella Service*, Sholto's constant preoccupation with ensuring that his crews were supplied with the best aircraft and equipment to do their jobs, including the latest marks of radar. This ran directly counter to Portal's attitude in the months before D-Day, as he planned for drastic cuts to Coastal Command's resources and their resorption into the AEAF, even reductions in training. Sholto criticised this proposal strongly, saying that the advantages accrued by the proposed saving in manpower of 16,000 would be negated by the breaking up of so many now highly trained maritime aircrews.

Once Coastal Command had been able to hold on to its resources, at least for the present, it was allowed to operate as a uniquely independent force during the invasion of Europe. Eisenhower stipulated that all the air forces in Britain would come under his control except Coastal Command, whose function was to operate on the flanks of the main battle area, shielding it from hostile incursions. Although Sholto was delighted with the degree of independence he had been given, Brooke wrote in his diary for 15 May, following a meeting organised by Eisenhower as a final run over plans for the invasion, that Sholto 'seemed disappointed with the smallness of his task, and so was I'.[4] Nevertheless, the task would prove to be vital.

In the run-up to D-Day, intelligence information indicated that the Germans realised something big was about to happen. As they started to concentrate their U-boats in French ports along the Bay of Biscay, Coastal Command in turn began to concentrate its anti-U-boat patrols in the western end of the Channel. These became known as the 'cork' patrols, the bottle being the Channel itself. At its eastern end, for work over the southern North Sea, Coastal Command built up a strike force that could attack all forms of enemy surface craft, being detailed to keep up sweeps and patrols day and night to detect them in the invasion and adjoining areas.

In the early hours of 6 June 1944, D-Day, the 'cork' patrols were in place, as were Coastal Command's anti-ship sweeps patrolling down the French coast of the Bay of Biscay. During the night, there had been reports that upwards of fifty U-boats had set out from the Bay ports heading for the Channel. Some of these were sighted close inshore heading northwards, and three German destroyers were attacked and damaged, having to put into Brest. Altogether during the first four days of the invasion, thirty-six U-boats were sighted by Coastal Command aircraft off the Brest peninsula and in the mouth of the Channel. They did not have the time to make the passage submerged so were easier targets, despite fighting back desperately with their AA guns. Twenty-three were attacked, six were destroyed and four seriously damaged. The First Sea Lord, Sholto's old friend from Cairo Admiral Cunningham, emphasised in his autobiography the importance of Coastal Command in protecting the armada of ships involved in the D-Day landings, writing: 'Our comparative immunity to submarine attack was principally due to the enthusiastic efficiency of Coastal Command.'[5] This is one of the unsung victories of WWII.

From the prisoners of war captured from the stricken U-boats, Sholto and his staff learned that for them, the penetration of the Channel was a nightmare. They could not move without Coastal Command being onto them. This caused Admiral Doenitz to issue an order that only those submarines fitted with the *Schnorkel* breathing device, which enabled them to stay submerged, could operate in the area of the Channel. This made Coastal Command's task much more difficult since all the crews could see were the periscopes and the tops of the tubes. Nevertheless, by the end of July it was clear that the enemy's threat had been beaten. Only a small number of U-boats had got through to the cross-Channel shipping lanes, and in the three months from D-Day to the end of August, of the thousands of merchant ships taking part in the Channel operations, only nine were sunk by U-boat action.

At the other end of the invasion area in the southern North Sea, the U-boats did not make any attempt to break through but patrolled right up the coast of Norway to attack British convoys bound for Russia. Towards the end of the first phase of OVERLORD, Sholto wrote in a report on Coastal Command's activities: 'Invading Europe was bound to be a bloody business, but few realise that the far Northern phase of the invasion operations was in its way as hard as the assault on the Norman beaches.'[6] In the land of the midnight sun, some savage battles were fought between Coastal Command aircraft and U-boats.

While submarines were being defeated in the south-west and north-east, the command continued its attacks on hostile surface vessels. In the early stages of OVERLORD, the enemy deployed his light forces on quite a considerable scale against Allied forces in the assault area. E-boats, heavily armed fast attack craft, were the main weapons. Sholto wrote: 'We know from prisoners of war that hardly an E-boat put to sea without being spotted and attacked from the air,' adding in his dispatch: 'There is no doubt that the menace of the enemy's light forces was held in check by the operations of the Royal Navy and Coastal Command.'[7]

Naturally, the Air Ministry wanted to release to the public news of the RAF's successes in the execution of its role in OVERLORD, and it was planned in a meeting on 10 July that the Cs-in-C of Bomber and Coastal Commands should be invited to give on-the-record talks to the press during the following two or three weeks about the activities of their commands in relation to operations in Normandy and the preparations for them. However, the Admiralty reported that, due to negotiations that were taking place between Churchill and Roosevelt on the amount of information to be made public, a stop had to be put on Sholto's prepared release. The reason given for Roosevelt's reluctance to allow information to be released was that it might prejudice anti-submarine operations in the Pacific. When H. A. Jones, historian and director of public relations at the Air Ministry, learned of this, he was justifiably indignant, arguing that the resultant lack of publicity would be 'discouraging to the gallant crews of Coastal Command who took the maximum risks in the early days of the OVERLORD operations'.[8] The shelving of Sholto's press release would have undoubtedly affected his own morale as well as that of his crews, and as he wrote to Portal: 'What I want is for my anti-U-boat crews to have some public recognition for the fine work that they have done during the past three months.'[9]

By August 1944, the progress of the Allies in north-west France was such that U-boats could no longer use the Biscay ports, and neither could they make their way back through the Channel since Coastal Command had that well corked up at both ends, so they had to go far out into the Atlantic and then back north to their bases in Norway. From there they launched inshore attacks along the British coastline, forcing Sholto to mount patrols around the northern coasts of the British Isles. Meanwhile, the Strike Wings continued their attacks on German convoys along the Norwegian coast. In one attack on an enemy convoy consisting of forty vessels, every one of the ships was hit. Their search for surface craft took the heavily armed Beaufighters and Mosquitoes well into the Norwegian fjords. After the long flight across the North Sea, they had to contend not only with heavy enemy AA fire from both ships and the ground but also, flying as low as they did, with the steep cliffs around the fjords. Their casualties were heavier than in any other flying done by the RAF during the final six months of the war. From July 1944 to April 1945, anywhere from twenty-eight to eighty-six Beaufighters were lost per month, the figures being lower during the winter months when operations were fewer, but nevertheless causing Sholto constant concern, as is clear in his reports to the Air Ministry during this period.[10]

Sholto made further adjustments to the organisation of the Air Sea Rescue Service to increase its coverage and efficiency. In November 1944, the Air Ministry proposed that the Fighter Command element of the service be transferred to Coastal Command, so on 15 February 1945 it became responsible for the coordination of all Air Sea operations around the British Isles, Iceland, Gibraltar and the Azores, and for assisting the Second Tactical Air Force (2TAF) in its Air Sea Rescue operations on the Continent. P.-W. observed that these services, particularly after Sholto's reorganisation, 'were of outstanding value to the morale of all branches of the RAF and saved hundreds of lives'.[11]

Early in 1945, Coastal Command's air reconnaissance revealed that the Germans were still operating more shipping than Sholto expected up the Norwegian coast, meaning there would be no let-up in the activity of the Strike Wings. But there was only one Mustang squadron available for escort duties, necessitating the switching of Mosquitoes to a fighter escort role in support of the less manoeuvrable Beaufighters. A tragic incident on 11 January when Beaufighters and Mosquitoes were set upon by about ten German aircraft with the loss of a Mosquito, a Beaufighter and a British Air Sea Rescue aircraft caused Sholto to press the Air Ministry for a second Mustang squadron, which was provided with unusual promptness. However, this was still not enough. An increasingly ferocious battle was being fought in which Coastal Command was forced to mount a greater number of daytime operations due to German vessels' reluctance to venture out of defended anchorages, even under cover of darkness.

The Strike Wings were met by large numbers of enemy fighters, on one occasion no fewer than forty-five aircraft. Fifteen strike aircraft were lost on these operations, and the particular mark of Focke-Wulf 190 aircraft that the Germans were deploying was at least forty miles an hour faster than the mark of Mosquito used by Coastal Command. In late March, Sholto asked for a third Mustang squadron, realising that his demands conflicted with those of Bomber Command, but arguing that as Germany's defences were weakening, the withdrawal of one Mustang squadron from bomber escort work would not matter a great deal for bomber operations, whereas it would make all the difference to his anti-shipping strikes. Sholto's request was turned down, although Portal's reply was sympathetic.

He had even suggested in a letter to Sholto earlier that month that two of Coastal Command's Beaufighter and Mosquito anti-shipping units be rolled up as part of a reduction in front-line squadrons, due to a manpower crisis within the RAF. Once again, this drew a strong response from Sholto, who said he could not possibly do this, as they were stretched to the limit, both in interrupting transport of enemy troops, equipment and raw materiel from Norway to Germany and in stemming the flow of supplies from Germany to the Norwegian U-boat bases, upon which the continuation of the U-boat campaign was entirely dependent. Sholto felt that any reduction in the effort against the latter traffic particularly would delay the end of the war in Europe. The conclusion reached in a meeting convened on 11 April at the Admiralty was that Coastal Command's offensive should continue. Soon afterwards, Sholto's request for additional fighter protection for his anti-shipping aircraft was granted in the form of not one but two additional Mustang squadrons from Fighter Command. Finally, only three and a half weeks before the end of the war in Europe, Sholto had the resources he needed to conduct the maritime air war.

Coastal Command aircraft continued operations of all sizes and types against enemy shipping right up to the end of the war. Sholto wrote: 'By day and by night, at anchor and at sea, the enemy ships were assailed by our aircraft in a crescendo of activity.'[12] In one incident off the Dutch coast, a dummy attack by an unarmed Air Sea Rescue Anson aircraft on a Molch midget U-boat caused its crew to abandon ship and the submarine to sink.

In those last few months of the war, Coastal Command's aircrews were astonishingly successful, despite bad weather at the beginning of the year and increased opposition that claimed 101 Allied aircraft between 1 January and 7 May. The anti-shipping squadrons sank ninety-two vessels in seventeen weeks, an amazing record even compared with the high figure of 170 for the whole of 1944. In April, there was a general exodus of U-boats from Germany to Norway on the surface, during which many of them were sunk. When in May Mosquitoes were joined by Beaufighters, the score rose sharply.

As the war in Europe drew to an end, there was a general sense of relief, even of jubilation, but Sholto was wary of accepting victory. He sent a signal to all groups and stations on 5 May, two days before Germany's final capitulation, saying that although German forces on the continent of Europe were surrendering, there was no indication that they were contemplating this in Norway, so for Coastal Command, the war went on, especially against U-boats operating from Norwegian bases: 'We started first we finish last. I call upon all squadrons for a great final effort against our old enemy. It falls to Coastal Command to strike the final blow against the enemy's one remaining weapon.'[13] On 8 May, VE Day, there were still some seventy U-boats at sea, and Coastal Command was called upon to continue to give escort to convoys and to carry out operational patrols, ensuring the U-boat commanders were prepared to carry out the orders for surrender. The final anti-U-boat patrol was flown on 3 June 1945.

Post-war analysis showed that the Germans had built 1,162 U-boats, of which 783 were lost through various causes. Coastal Command was responsible for 188 of these unaided, with a share in the destruction of a further twenty-one, and the sinking of 343 enemy ships. The command paid a high price, losing 5,866 pilots and other aircrew, of whom 1,630 were from the Dominions and European Allies, in 1,777 aircraft that either did not return to their bases or crashed on landing. Hilary St George Saunders, the official RAF historian, wrote that the British people 'must for ever mourn' so great a sacrifice.[14]

Despite the undoubted heroism of the crews of Coastal Command, almost unbelievably, the row over Sholto's press release concerning their activities continued even after the end of the war in Europe. His efforts to relate the full story of his command's successes independently from the joint communiqué released with the Admiralty, which was heavily weighted in the latter's favour, were thwarted continually.

Eventually he was allowed to write a separate comprehensive dispatch on Coastal Command's operations during OVERLORD, published in 1947. The Admiralty's efforts to downplay the work of the command may well have affected the number of publications devoted to it, and also its standing with the public, many of whom even now are unaware of how unrelenting and courageous was the work of its aircrews in contributing to victory in Europe.

Dr Christina Goulter, who has written a comprehensive account of Coastal Command's operations,[15] is certain that Sholto saved her father's life. He was a member of the aircrews who flew in anti-shipping operations up the coast of Norway, for which Sholto had pressed Portal so hard to provide escort protection in the form of Mustangs. Dr Goulter told me that if it had not been for Sholto's dogged determination to get the aircraft that were needed, her father would undoubtedly have been shot down and killed.

On the day after VE Day, Sholto received from Portal a personal letter.

> This is just a personal note, written in haste and quite inadequate, to try to express to you a little of the deep gratitude which I feel towards you for your tremendous personal contribution to the achievement of the Service in the war. From my point of view no one in the whole of the RAF has given in fuller measure, personally or officially, the support and loyal co-operation without which I could not have carried on. I am very conscious of the fact that your great talents might have been used more fully, but it is rarely possible to arrange all things for the best. As it is, you have done magnificently every job entrusted to you, and I do most sincerely thank you.

Sholto's handwritten reply is equally affecting:

> My dear CAS
> Thank you very much indeed for your charming letter, which I appreciate more than I can say.
> I know that in some ways things have not worked out particularly

fortunately for me, nor in fact as you yourself intended. All the same I count myself as extremely fortunate to have been selected in time of war for three such fine commands as Fighter, Middle East, and Coastal…

May I say in all sincerity how much I have appreciated working under you as CAS? What I have always felt – and I think all RAF Commanders have felt the same – is that any problem, trouble, or grievance that was put to you would receive calm, cool, and un-biased consideration: and that the answer I got would almost cer-tainly turn out to be right, even if at the time I may not altogether have agreed with it. It is an immense help in one's job to have such confidence in the judgement of one's chief, and indeed it is the inspiration of loyalty.

I need hardly say how grateful I feel to you personally for all that you have done for me – at times, I imagine, in the face of opposition.[16]

Sholto knew he had his detractors, but he may not have been aware that the most vehement of them was so close to him. Now that the war had come to an end, the question of who would replace Portal as CAS resurfaced, and Sholto was one of the contenders. Through-out his time at Coastal Command, Freeman's venomous letters to Portal had continued, and in consideration of who would succeed him, many senior RAF officers were the objects of Freeman's disdain. Churchill had discussed with Sinclair and Portal the possibility of Sholto as a candidate for the post, but Freeman wrote to Portal:

Douglas is well equipped mentally. Socially and morally he is be-neath contempt and I don't suppose any decent parent would allow his son to join the RAF (still less his daughter to join the WAAF) if he was CAS. Anyway you couldn't have him there as long as we were fighting alongside USA.[17]

He continued his attack with: 'Why should Douglas emulate Elling-ton in the number of posts he has held. In my opinion one Com-mand and one seat on the Air Council are enough for any man. And

Douglas has already held three Commands.' Perhaps the real reason for Freeman's contempt for Sholto was manifesting itself: jealousy. Sholto's complicated personal life undoubtedly had a detrimental effect too. Freeman had written in an earlier letter in May 1944, as a result of the continuing discussion over who should fill the post of AMP:

> Douglas has all the qualities except that instinct for preferring the gentleman to the cad no matter in what walk of life. He has a strong character, a forceful personality, but has an unfortunate name for indiscretions in his private life, which cannot be over-looked in an AMP. From the disciplinary point of view he is almost beneath contempt because you cannot discipline others if you yourself are devoid of self-discipline.[18]

And this was from someone whom Sholto always thought his good friend!

Portal's letter to Sholto at the end of the war indicates that he continued to hold him in high regard despite Freeman's comprehensive attacks, but a letter from Portal to Sinclair, in which he continued the discussion concerning the appointment of a new AMP, suggests Freeman may have got through to him after all:

> Douglas is in my opinion ruled out as AMP because of a reputation for serious indiscretions in his private life and because he is personally somewhat undisciplined and therefore most unlikely to be able to maintain discipline in the service. This is a pity, because he is a strong character and has a fine record in command.[19]

In fact, there was a job for which Portal thought that Sholto was eminently suitable, and that was the Air Member for Supply and Organisation, a post that had been filled previously by Dowding in the 1930s, but one that Sholto would have found rather boring after his spells as a C-in-C of operational commands. In the end, he was picked for something far more challenging, although he did not relish the prospect.

CHAPTER TWENTY-ONE

'MISERY AND STARVATION'

On 14 July 1945, just over two months after the end of the war in Europe, Sholto flew out to Germany to take command of the British Air Forces of Occupation (BAFO), formed from 2TAF, which had been commanded by Air Marshal 'Mary' Coningham since January 1944 in preparation for the D-Day landings. Despite Coningham's efforts to make the handover as easy and uncomplicated as possible, after all that had happened in both world wars Sholto felt less like going to Germany than to anywhere else. However, the relationship between Coningham and Montgomery, now Military Governor of the British Zone in Germany, had become strained during the final months of the war. It was known that Sholto was one of the few people who had always worked well with Monty, so he was the obvious person to be appointed C-in-C BAFO.

BAFO HQ was situated in the Fürstenhof (Prince's palace) of the pleasant spa town of Bad Eilsen in Lower Saxony. The town was chosen because it had been the site of the main design office for the renowned German aircraft company Focke-Wulf, and the British wanted to glean as much technical expertise as they could from this leading aircraft developer. Sholto's residence was the manor house of a large historic estate, Gut Rickbruch, out in the countryside approximately sixteen kilometres south of Bad Eilsen. Earlier in 1945 following the end of the war, the manor house, parts of the courtyard and the park of the Rickbruch estate had been requisitioned by the British Army of the Rhine (BAOR), and Monty lived there for a short time before moving to Schloss Ostenwalde, further west in the British Zone.

The owners of the property, the Heidenhain family, had had to vacate it in only twelve hours. In the courtyard a white line was drawn as a demarcation between the British occupiers and owners, who had to move into the estate outbuildings. The new occupiers carried out significant conversions to the house and grounds, digging a pond in case of the need to extinguish a fire, and building a petrol storage facility, power station and guard house. Partition walls were pulled down and bathrooms remodelled. Perhaps the most unwelcome alteration was that many interior doors had a 'slice' cut off the bottom to allow for thick carpets, which the British love but which, today, cause a draught. As a final insult, the house itself was repainted with a poorly chosen paint in an ugly colour, which flaked off extensively and needed renovation after the British occupation ended in 1955. Unsurprisingly in view of these desecrations, the relationship between the Heidenhain family and the occupying forces was very tense at first, but once a system of exchanging cigarettes for eggs was put in place, the situation became more relaxed.

Once again, Sholto's team at BAFO included those whom he had known for many years and in whom he had confidence. His SASO was Air Vice-Marshal Sir Charles Steele, with whom he had endured the bombing raid on Bertangles aerodrome in WWI, and his Air Officer-in-Charge of Administration (AOA) was Air-Vice Marshal F. L. Hopps, who had been one of his group commanders in Coastal Command. The presence of those around him whom he trusted helped to ease the burden that he felt in being out there. His personal assistant was Bob Wright, who had fulfilled the same post in Fighter Command. Sholto's job as C-in-C BAFO comprised what to him were two 'violently opposed tasks': firstly, the maintenance in full operational shape of an effective tactical air force in the British Zone, and secondly the complete disbandment and demolition of the Luftwaffe.[1]

Two days after his arrival in Germany, he was confronted with the full meaning of destruction during his first visit to Berlin, when he was taken on a tour of the city. He was horrified at the utter devastation wrought by the RAF, the USAAF and the street fighting during the Russian capture of the German capital, which was worse than anything he had ever seen. He wrote:

Even the inspired provision of accommodation for me in an undamaged house in a street in Grunewald, on the outskirts of the
city, actually bearing the name of Douglasstrasse did little to lift the
depression that I could not help feeling over what I saw amidst the
ruins of what had once been one of the world's great cities. The task
of rehabilitating a people who had been reduced to such a sicken-
ing level was obviously going to be a formidable one. I did not envy
Montgomery what he was having to face, and I was thankful that
my responsibilities were confined to those of being the Air Force
commander.[2]

Little did Sholto know what lay in store for him.

On 17 July, the day after this visit to Berlin, Truman – the new
US President following Roosevelt's sudden death from an intracere-
bral haemorrhage the preceding April – Stalin and Churchill met at
Potsdam, a few kilometres to the south-west of Berlin, for a major
conference. The meeting was a continuation of the 'struggle' that
had started at Tehran at the end of 1943, and which had persisted
with what would turn out to be irreconcilable differences ever since
then. Whereas Churchill was entirely mistrustful of Stalin's motives,
Truman continued with Roosevelt's mistaken view that he could
handle Stalin, thus grossly underestimating the extent of Soviet ambitions for the partition of Germany and of Berlin, which would have
such dire repercussions for decades. During the conference, it became
known that, following the 5 July general election in the UK, the
British had elected Clement Attlee as their Prime Minister. He also
attended the conference. As a serving officer, Sholto was precluded
from making public his own political beliefs, but it was known to his
friends and close associates that the change to a socialist administration was to his liking, despite his confidence in the wartime coalition
government.

A question that soon confronted Sholto, and which was of great
concern to him, was the repatriation of Czech and Polish airmen who
had served with such bravery in the RAF during the war. One Sunday
at the beginning of August, news reached Sholto that the Czech
squadrons that had started out from England that day on the way

to a triumphal return in their own country had been forced by bad weather to land on airfields in the British Zone. Some had landed at the nearby airfield at Bückeburg. Bob Wright went to meet them, and arranged for Air Marshal Karel Janoušek, the Czech Air Force commander, to stay at Rickbruch. Sholto had known Janoušek from his arrival in England at the beginning of WWII.

When he arrived, Janoušek was very agitated and insisted that, somehow, his squadrons had to get back to Prague on time. However, Sholto ascertained that all the airfields where the Czechs had landed were waterlogged due to the weather. After dinner, Sholto asked Janoušek what news there was of his family whom he had left behind in Czechoslovakia. He was horrified when Janoušek replied, 'quietly and with resignation', that all of them had been killed. His wife Anna and one of his sisters had died in Auschwitz, one of his brothers had died in Buchenwald and two of his brothers-in-law had died in jail in Czechoslovakia.

The following morning, Sholto and his staff did all they could to help the Czechs, and a gap in the weather meant that they could set off once again for Prague after lunch. A week later, Sholto and Evill, still VCAS, and several other senior RAF officers paid an official visit to the Czech capital, where they were decorated with the Order of the White Lion. He saw Janoušek and his pilots once again, and also had a long talk with the President of Czechoslovakia, Dr Edvard Beneš, who told him that he felt that the tide of communism was receding. Unfortunately, his optimism was unwarranted: in June 1948, Beneš was forced to resign after a communist coup and died three months later. Janoušek suffered greatly under the Soviet-backed communist regime. Sholto heard nothing more about him until May 1952, when it was reported that he had died in captivity. Then, in 1965, Sholto found out that Janoušek was actually alive and had been released, leading an impoverished life in obscurity. He retired in 1967 and died in 1971. It was not until 1990, after the fall of the communist regime, that his honours were restored posthumously, and in 1991 he was re-instated as a four-star general.

Shortly after his efforts to help the Czechs, once again Sholto found himself involved in the tortuous diplomatic sphere, this time over the repatriation of Polish aircrew. Sholto had Polish squadrons serving under him in Germany as part of BAFO, who were poised and eager to return to their own country. He was being reminded constantly of their desire to get back home, and only a few days after his arrival in Germany, the Polish C-in-C, Air Vice-Marshal Izycki, came out from England to see what could be done to repatriate his air force. However, the prospects for Poland at that point were uncertain due to the complex political situation. So the Air Ministry decided to stage an exhibition in Warsaw in October 1945 in order to show-case the work of the RAF, with particular emphasis on the impressive contribution of the Polish squadrons stationed in the UK, and asked Sholto to open it.

The Soviet-dominated Polish government officials in Warsaw were strongly opposed, both to the exhibition and to Sholto going there to open it, but he was undeterred, feeling as strongly as he did about the sacrificial service in the war of Polish aircrews who were still in exile. When Sholto and his entourage arrived in Warsaw from Berlin, they were met by the British Ambassador, Victor Cavendish-Bentinck, and several members of his staff, but there was no official welcome from the Polish government or its armed forces. Cavendish-Bentinck warned Sholto that the situation was tricky.

As they approached the centre of Warsaw, the scene confronting Sholto was even worse than in Berlin. The city was almost complete-ly demolished. Even after the German bombing in 1939, Warsaw had remained in relatively fair shape until the uprising of the Polish underground movement in 1944, except for the Jewish ghetto. That had been reduced to rubble following the rebellion in 1943 of its population, after which, following pounding with tanks, artillery, flame-throwers and dynamite squads, the remaining 63,000 Jewish people out of an initial population of 400,000 were either killed or transported to the concentration camps of Majdanek and Treblin-ka. In the uprising the following year, the Poles fought the Nazis for sixty-three days, by the end of which some 200,000 Polish men, women and children had been killed. Sholto wrote of the Nazi anni-hilation: 'After barbarously destroying the city they retreated, leaving the Russians, who were already at hand but who had refused to help, to "liberate" what was left of the Polish capital.'³ A proxy government of Soviet sympathisers was installed, and the legitimate Polish government that had spent the war in exile in London was superseded by the Provisional Government of National Unity, which was dominated by communists and endorsed by the Soviets.

In the ruins of Warsaw there was only one hotel of any size that was habitable, the Polonia, and even then some of the visiting party had to sleep on the floor. The American Embassy was on the second floor of the hotel, and the British on the fourth, the staffs of both working under the most cramped conditions.

After Sholto had been shown around 'the appalling devastation of the city', he was taken to meet the Polish Defence Minister, Marshal Rola-Zymierski, whom Sholto described as 'nothing more than a Communist puppet'.⁴ The marshal, who according to the British Air Attaché, Group Captain Burt-Andrews, was 'somewhat peevish' at the start of the interview, demanded to know why the exhibition was being staged in Warsaw. Sholto explained that exhibitions were being held in most of the principal cities of Europe to show people there the work of the RAF in the late war, and in the exhibition in Warsaw, the Air Ministry wanted to highlight the achievements of the Polish squadrons that had fought so bravely with the RAF. This pleased the marshal, who began to 'thaw' somewhat and, to Sholto's surprise, progressed swiftly to discussing the return of the Polish Air Force to Poland. He seemed to think that the RAF was deliberately preventing them from going back for some obscure purpose of its own. Sholto quickly disabused him of this impression, saying that it was eager for the Polish airmen to return to their country but, as an obligation of honour, it could not send them back without any guarantee as to their subsequent treatment. The marshal was even more impressed by this statement but said he had three conditions: firstly, he wanted the squadrons returned as complete units. Secondly, he wanted the staff officers as well as the squadrons, since they had no staff in Poland competent to organise an Air Force. Thirdly, he wanted to employ some of the Polish Air Force personnel in civil aviation in order to get this on its feet. Sholto agreed to all these points but stalled when the marshal requested that the squadrons would bring their British aircraft with them. Sholto promised that HM government would consider this, but the returning airmen must be given some assurance as to their employment conditions when they returned to Poland, which the marshal seemed to take in his stride. However, a big caveat for him was that there were certain senior officers within the Polish squadrons who were 'politically compromised' and whom the Polish government would not have back in Poland. Sholto parried this adroitly by saying that therefore the marshal might like to accept the return of younger officers only.[5] The whole of Sholto's interview with the marshal had been conducted in French.

Despite being a reluctant diplomat, Sholto persuaded the marshal to accompany him to the opening of the exhibition, which left him thoroughly impressed. Sholto gave a very moving speech, noting:

> It must require a great amount of faith to go on fighting – and fighting superbly – hundreds of miles from your own country, with no knowledge of what is happening in that country, or to your families or wives or friends. Your airmen and airwomen had that faith in plenty. We in the Royal Air Force, and indeed in the whole of Britain, will not forget it.

He ended his speech with: 'I pray that some means can be found, some honourable arrangements made, whereby these gallant squadrons can return to Poland with all the honour that is their due.'[6]

On the front pages of three Warsaw papers the following day were featured Sholto's press conference, his meeting with the marshal and the exhibition itself. To say that it was wildly successful would be an understatement. During the first week, it was visited by 85,000–100,000 people, up to one fifth of the whole population of Warsaw at that time, 35,000 alone visiting in one day.[7]

When the time came for Sholto and his team to return to Germany at the end of their three-day stay, they found a completely different scene at the airfield from that which had greeted them on their arrival in Poland. 'There was lined up a large guard of honour, and some rather villainous-looking Polish Generals were in attendance. A band was playing our national anthem over and over again, and in a way that had to be heard to be believed.'[8] Sholto invited some of these 'villainous-looking' types on board his aircraft since they all looked so miserable. After a whisky-drinking session that left the generals feeling much more friendly, Sholto and his retinue returned to Berlin rather groggy. Robert Hankey, the First Secretary of the British Embassy in Warsaw, wrote to the Foreign Secretary, Ernest Bevin, that the change in atmosphere was 'no mean achievement for which we must thank Sir Sholto Douglas' robust and friendly personality, which carried all before it'.[9] Group Captain Sir Louis Grieg, who was on the personal staff of the Secretary of State for Air and had been one of the party, wrote Sholto a short but effusive letter of thanks, saying: 'I do congratulate you on turning a sticky business into a howling success. Your mixture of suavity and sternness was the medicine they required.'[10]

Despite this seeming progress, nothing improved for the Polish airmen wishing to return to their homeland. Sholto wasted no time in informing Portal, still CAS at this point, of his interview with the marshal and of his suggestion, favourably received, that two Polish group captains on his staff at BAFO travel to Warsaw to discuss informally the return of the Polish squadrons, without any obligation on either side. Although Portal was very much attracted by this idea, when he discussed it with those at the Foreign Office, they insisted on including representatives of the Polish Army and Navy. Unfortunately, this was a step too far for the Polish government, who wanted to consider the Air Force and Navy separately from the Army. Sholto was disappointed, writing to Portal: 'It was a pity perhaps that the Army and Navy were brought into it. If we could get the Polish Air Force to go back more or less as a body, the other Services might follow suit.'[11]

How Sholto informed his Polish Air Force officers in BAFO of the outcome of his Warsaw visit was documented by a Polish wing commander, Marian Duriasz. He was serving in BAFO but unbeknown to Sholto had been recruited as an informer for the Communist intelligence and counter-intelligence services in Poland. He may also have worked as an agent for the British at times. Duriasz was party to discussions between Sholto, Air Vice-Marshal Izycki and Group

Captain Brzezina, who had served in Fighter Command when Sholto was its C-in-C and was one of the BAFO officers Sholto thought would be suitable to send to Poland for preliminary discussions with the Defence Minister.[12]

In the end, of the 15,000 Polish Air Force personnel in exile, only 2,000–3,000 went back to Poland, the rest settling in other countries. Those who returned were dispersed around the country and not allowed to take senior positions. Some were imprisoned or executed and those who weren't lived in poor conditions. In October 1956, when a weakening of the hard-line Stalinist faction in the Polish government led to the 'Polish Thaw', there was a slight improvement in their situation, but this did not last long.

A couple of weeks later, Sholto received a request from Monty to represent him at the opening of the major war crimes trials in Nuremberg. Sholto's abrupt reply was that under no circumstances whatsoever would he consider going to or having anything to do with what was about to take place there. Unfortunately, he could not evade this particular situation indefinitely, and would play a leading part in the outcome.

Sholto found himself unable to escape the other political issues that were intruding on everyone's thinking in Germany, not least due to the Soviets' attempts to establish their position as the dominant power in Europe, the ambitions of whom Roosevelt had underestimated. In November 1945, the Russian Military Governor, Marshal Zhukov, lodged an official complaint with the quadripartite Allied Control Council in Berlin. It accused the British of keeping in their zone quite large units of the German armed forces, in contravention of the Potsdam Agreement. The disbandment of the German Air Force was in the hands of Sholto's deputy, Air Marshal Sir Philip Wigglesworth, and between them they issued a report for Monty that stated unequivocally that Zhukov's accusations were untrue, even though Sholto's Army counterpart, the BAOR C-in-C, did admit that there was some truth to these allegations. In fact, part of the forces that the Soviets said were in the British Zone, the Eighteenth Anti-Aircraft Division, had been captured by the Soviets themselves. Others who were normally resident in the Russian Occupied Zone were awaiting transfer there, although what their fate would be when they reached their homes was uncertain, both from a political and a personal point of view, and many of them wished to stay in the West. Although Monty countered Zhukov's accusations, they were emblematic of the ongoing tensions between the three Western Allies and the Soviets. Those in the West wanted to disarm Germany and render her useless as a potential aggressor while also facilitating her economic recovery, whereas the Soviets wanted to extract the maximum in reparations from Germany, 'not just from their own zone, which they were already busily stripping, but from the western zones as well',[13] despite the Potsdam Agreement that they would not be entitled to any share of the materiel found in countries outside their sphere of influence.

Disarmament was one of Sholto's major preoccupations as C-in-C BAFO, and on assuming command he issued orders forthwith for the destruction of certain arms, bombs and ammunition. The liberated countries (France, Netherlands, Belgium, Denmark and Norway) were beginning to ask for allocations of German air materiel for their own forces, and Sholto deemed that these demands would increase as long as this equipment still existed, expressing the view that 'all warlike items with their related equipment and parts which have no direct application for civil use should be destroyed without further delay'.[14] Monty considered that an exception should be made in the case of France, since 'a cardinal factor in British policy must be the establishment and maintenance of a strong and well disposed France',[15] and in any case, France was one of the occupying powers and therefore had the right to allocate war materiel herself.

Considerable disquiet among the Soviets was generated by the presence in the British Zone of a team of aviators and scientists who had been flown into Germany as soon as the war ended. One of these was Eric 'Winkle' Brown, who was now the chief test pilot and, being a fluent German speaker, interpreter for the Farren Mission. This organisation had been set up by Churchill in January 1945, and its purpose was threefold: firstly, to find and bring back to the UK supersonic wind-tunnels, which were far superior to anything possessed by the British; secondly, to find German advanced jet and rocket aircraft, and test them in Germany or bring them back to the UK; and thirdly, to find as many top German aviation scientists and test pilots as possible and deliver them to Farnborough along with the aircraft. Although officially prisoners of war, the twenty-six that Eric and his colleagues found were given the status of senior scientists. Two of them who were particularly brilliant were offered permanent jobs at Farnborough and stayed there until they died.

When the leader of the mission, W. S. Farren, asked Churchill what he should do if he met any problems in Germany, Churchill told him: 'Don't go to Monty; approach Sholto. He'll sort it out.' This was soon necessary. Following capitulation, RAF pilots were jumping into German piston engine aircraft, and because they were not familiar with them and unable to understand the German instructions in the cockpit, many of them were killed in flying accidents. At one point, there were twenty casualties per month. To discuss this problem, Eric was summoned to Sholto's office at his HQ at Bad Eilsen. He was struck by Sholto's imposing presence but did not feel at all browbeaten by him. He advised Sholto to ban all personnel from flying German aircraft except for official test pilots. When Sholto implemented this policy, the accidents stopped. What Eric liked about Sholto was not only that he was prepared to listen to people of lower rank but that he was very flexible. To the great disappointment of the Royal Aircraft Establishment, the British authorities decreed that even test pilots could not fly the Me163 Rocket Fighter, due to the danger posed by the hydrogen peroxide in its propellant. It was, however, tested clandestinely, to which Sholto turned a blind eye.

Despite being a seemingly fearless pilot, Eric was not left unscathed by his experiences in Germany. Soon after his arrival there, he decided to visit the camp at Belsen, to see for himself what sounded like 'the worst horror fiction', only having read about it. He wrote:

There I saw for myself the piled dead, the still open graves. I tried to speak to some of the silent, shuffling ghosts of men, in their striped rags. They would listen, staring dully at the ground, then step aside and move on … The 2nd Army medical Brigadier Glynn Hughes who was the senior officer at Belsen was surprised to find a naval officer visiting the camp, but when he saw my high-profile pass and found I was German-speaking, he asked me to interrogate the camp commandant Josef Kramer and his female assistant Irma Grese in his presence.[16]

Eric told me that he had never met two more evil and chilling people in his life, particularly the 22-year-old Grese, who had earned the sobriquet 'The Hyena of Auschwitz' as she had already inflicted countless cruelties there before being transferred to Belsen in March 1945.

Until Eric died in 2016 aged ninety-seven, he carried with him the trauma of his visit to Belsen. He experienced olfactory hallucinations (that is, associated with smell) regularly, telling me that he still woke in the middle of the night with the stench of Belsen in his nostrils. Phenomena such as these are not uncommon and occur particularly following past exposure to the smells of blood, burning hair and fuel,[17] but also to decomposition. Such strong olfactory signals are stored and linked to vivid, traumatic and long-lasting memories, of which Eric's of Belsen are typical, and are mediated by alterations in brain regions associated with PTSD.[18]

By October 1945, the Air Ministry wished to put the Royal Air Force on more of a peacetime footing and was considering appointing a chief of staff to serve under Cs-in-C to deal with the day-to-day running of commands. As C-in-C of four RAF commands over a period of five years, Sholto was not in favour of the chief of staff principle, having never had nor ever felt the need for one. He wrote: 'I believe in a Commander-in-Chief actually commanding his Forces and acting as head of his Staff, rather than that he should be a kind of deity stuck up on a pedestal with nothing to do.'[19] The Air Ministry decided to adopt all of Sholto's suggestions for the restructuring of commands.

Despite the respect with which Sholto was regarded in the RAF, and his successes as a commander, by the end of 1945, Sholto himself was feeling that 'somewhere or other there was something that was definitely wrong; but I could not be sure what it was, even when I tried to define it. Was it in my own life, or was it in the times in which we were living?'[20] He was also feeling the inevitable reaction from the long years of unremitting tension under which he had been living through

WWII, adding to 'these after-effects of war in a full measure' following WWI when he was still a young man. He admitted candidly that he recognised in himself 'the symptoms of the same state of mind developing again now that the second war was over. I was becoming restless and unnecessarily depressed.' Once again, there was no help to be had even if he had sought it. Instead, he found solace in a surprising quarter: 'It was then that I possibly came closer to my father, in sympathy and understanding, than at any other period in my life.' Langton, now aged eighty-one, had been living in the United States since 1941 and 'had made a distinct success of his life's work'. He and Sholto had begun to exchange 'longer and more intimate' letters than ever before. Langton wanted to know his son's plans and prospects for the future, and Sholto replied that he did not like the way in which his life was taking shape, which felt beyond his control.

On 13 December 1945, just ten days before his fifty-second birthday, Sholto wrote to his father: 'I think I bear my responsibilities lightly on the whole, but I have been under a continuous strain of responsibility for a long time. The result is that I am tired – tired out.' He emphasised his need for a rest, having had only four weeks' leave in the previous six years, and that he definitely wanted a change of occupation. He continued: 'I don't think you appreciate what an unpleasant life we lead in Germany at the present time. I won't enlarge on this, but I loathe being here. We live in an atmosphere of misery and starvation…'[21]

Ian Buruma in his account of the first year after WWII, *Year Zero*, has written that conditions in Berlin were especially dismal, but cities such as Hamburg in the British Zone were also reduced to rubble, the residents in dire need of food and shelter. He recounts what an American reporter observed on the outskirts of Hamburg: 'One evening, in a marshy plot of land, an elderly German in a business suit takes his cane and clubs a duck to death.'[22] Flying Officer R. M. Williams, who served under Sholto in BAFO, wrote in his diary following a visit to Hamburg opera house in August 1945:

The bomber boys really did their stuff here as there are miles of ruins. The main station still stands but it is disgustingly filthy. A proof of the straits of some of the residents is a man with all his clothes off in the public lavatory having a clean up in the cold water there provided. As we queue for the show Germans wait in the gutter to snatch up the cigarette ends which we cast aside. How are the mighty fallen.'[23]

The historian Ben Shephard has written that the British may have been fortunate in getting as their zone of occupation the industrial area of the Ruhr and northern Germany but, as was acknowledged by a contemporary quip, 'the division of Germany, it was said, had given the Americans the landscape, the French the wine and the British the ruins. The area the British now occupied had never fed itself.' It was largely urban, relying on the rich agricultural land of East Prussia, now divided between Poland and the Soviet Union, and the latter was not in any hurry to share its food resources. In November 1945, the Deputy Military Governor, General Sir Brian Robertson, warned the British government that the rations the Germans were being given did not even meet the statutory requirement of 1,550 calories per day, being nearer to 1,200 calories. At that time, it was thought that the average adult required 2,500 calories daily to stay healthy, whereas for any reasonable manual labour, 2,800–3,000 calories were necessary. Robertson observed that people were 'losing weight noticeably and getting the yellow look that is a sure indication of pronounced under-nourishment'.[24] No wonder Sholto wrote to Langton of 'misery and starvation'.

In his letter to Langton, Sholto went through his options, stressing that he would not accept 'some Governorship or other', a customary option for service chiefs on retirement: 'I have asked not to be considered for this. It would be as bad as being a Commander-in-Chief – worse! To be on one's best behaviour all the time! I couldn't stand it.'[25] As early as the end of August 1945, Sholto had told Charles Steele that what he really wanted to do was to resign from the service and make a new start in civilian life. Steele replied that he had heard that Monty was returning to the UK to take Brooke's place as CIGS, and that Tedder might be coming out to replace him as Military Governor. A month later, Louis Grieg told Sholto that he was in the running to become CAS in place of Portal, but on a visit to London towards the end of October, Sholto was informed that Tedder was to take the post in the New Year. The man who had made a power grab in the Mediterranean at his expense had once again stepped over him to grasp the top prize. The closest members of Sholto's staff were indignant that he had been passed over for this post.

Towards the end of 1945, Sholto started the process of bringing about his retirement, but before anything could be finalised, it was announced in the New Year's Honours List that he was among those created Knights Grand Cross of the Order of the Bath. He and 'Bomber' Harris were also promoted to the highest rank of Marshal of the Royal Air Force, the only two officers in RAF history who have attained that rank without having served as Chief of the Air Staff. As Sholto was digesting this news, he was suffering a severe dose of flu, the after-effects of which left him feeling 'washed out'. That, coupled with his realisation that he was in the same state in which he had been after WWI, gave him a sense of being in a strange kind of limbo. The Air Ministry set the wheels in motion, albeit slowly, for him to relinquish his last command. He began to wind up his connection with the RAF in Germany with heartfelt relief, but it was to be short-lived.

In the first week of January, Sholto went to see Monty at his HQ in the British Zone to inform him of his departure and to say goodbye. As Sholto later recounted, it was a surreal conversation:

> 'Sholto … I'm very glad to see you,' he said. 'I've made all my plans for you to be back here on the 1st of April.'
>
> 'What are you talking about?' I demanded. 'I've just resigned from the RAF and I'm going to be a civilian.'
>
> With that short, sharp laugh of his, which verges on being a snort, Montgomery exclaimed: 'Oh, no, you're not! Hasn't anyone told you? You're taking over from me.'
>
> That caught me completely off balance. 'Like hell I am!' I snapped. 'I'm not coming back to Germany.'
>
> 'You can't say that,' Montgomery replied.
>
> 'Why not?' I demanded.
>
> And then Montgomery played what must have seemed to him

to be his trump card. 'Because I recommended you for the job,' he said; and he proceeded to read me a lecture on my duty to my King, to my country, to the Royal Air Force, and, by no means of least importance, to him.[26]

Sholto took the news with a mixture of humour and despair, and when they parted, albeit politely, there had crept into their relationship a certain coolness that had not been there before.

Simultaneously, pressure was brought to bear on Sholto from many quarters, including Tedder, by this time CAS. A week later, Sholto wrote to both Monty and Tedder, informing them tersely that he would take on the job but only if he could have a couple of months' leave first. A few days after that, news of his appointment was leaked to the press, causing his wife Joan in London, who knew nothing of this development, to send urgent messages asking Sholto what it was all about and how she was to reply to the questions being put to her. She was not at all in favour of the appointment, and no official announcement had been made. Sholto instructed his staff not to make any comment to the media.

He relinquished command of BAFO in Germany at the end of January, handing over to his deputy, Wigglesworth. When he came downstairs on his last morning there, he found the whole staff assembled outside the HQ, and the farewell they gave him as he drove away, he wrote,

was of a warmth that I found unexpectedly touching. I was moved in a way that I had not experienced before in my entire Service career. Perhaps it was that which released the emotions that I had been trying hard to keep under control; but as we drove from Bad Eilsen to the airfield at Bückeburg I felt that it must be the end to my experience of Germany.

He turned to Bob Wright and said, 'Really, you know ... I simply cannot come back to Germany.' Sholto was surprised at his own reluctance to accept what many of his friends told him was 'a most important, and even glittering, appointment', but he was tired out, and felt he could not face 'the strife that, for all the ending of the war, was beginning to torment the former Allies in their running of occupied Germany'.[27]

Sholto returned to London and made it known at the Air Ministry that even though he had said that he would take over from Monty, he was not at all happy to do so. Attlee had also been alerted to Sholto's proposed retirement by a memo from the Secretary of State for Air, now Viscount Stansgate, which stated: 'In my minute of 3rd January I told you that Marshal of the Royal Air Force Sir Sholto Douglas was due shortly to go on half-pay – unless the suggestion I made to you in that minute can be approved.'[28] Presumably, this was a call from Stansgate to spur Attlee into action and prevent Sholto leaving the service. It is not unreasonable to assume that the previous note concerned the post of Military Governor, for which it was known that Monty had recommended Sholto.[29]

A fortnight after Sholto's return, he received a phone call from 10 Downing Street, requesting that he go to see Attlee. Sholto was not looking forward to the interview, having guessed what was going to happen, and was determined to stand his ground. When he reached No. 10, he was ushered into the long Cabinet Room. Attlee was alone in the room, sitting in his usual place at the middle of the long table, 'hunched over it, and sucking away at his curved pipe'.

'I am told, Sholto, that you do not want to go back to Germany,' he said. 'But the Cabinet discussed the matter this morning, and you were unanimously elected to the job. I think you ought to go.'

It was all said in that quiet way in which Attlee always spoke, almost as an aside; and when it was put to me in that way it caused a wilting of my determination. His sincerity and seriousness were so obvious, and from further comments that he made I knew that he clearly considered that it was my duty, if the Government wanted me there, to return to Germany. If he had tried to force me, or to bully me, it would have hardened my determination to refuse; but he did not behave in that way because he was not like that.[30]

Sholto asked how long he would have to stay, to which Attlee replied that it would be eighteen months to two years. Sholto asked then if he could write to him when the time was up to remind him of what he had said, and that he would see to it that Sholto was relieved of his appointment. Attlee replied that of course he would. They agreed that Sholto would take over from Monty on 1 May.

The day after this meeting, a formal announcement was made that Sholto was to become C-in-C of the armed forces and Military Governor of the British Zone of occupied Germany, and the British member of the four-power Allied Control Council in Berlin. Shortly afterwards, he had the first, and what turned out to be the only, meeting with Monty about the actual handover to him. To Sholto's astonishment, he announced that he would come and have breakfast with Sholto at his flat, a time of day that he never considered human, but for which Joan made preparations. When Monty breezed in on the appointed day, he had had breakfast already and wanted to get down to serious discussions straight away. He stressed that food was still one of the biggest problems, the Germans receiving only one third of what the British were having under the UK rationing scheme, which itself was not exactly plentiful. He talked at length about the quantity and range of difficulties that Sholto would face. He was going to have to shoulder a heavier and more difficult burden of responsibility than he had ever done before, which not unnaturally filled him with apprehension.

It is easy to see, though, why Sholto was picked for this most difficult appointment. While he was still C-in-C BAFO, he gave a lecture at the RAF Staff College back in the UK on its role in Germany, demonstrating his acute understanding and detailed knowledge of the problems in the British Zone as a whole, not just those pertaining to the Air Force. He elaborated on the housing situation, which was dire, particularly for Germans but also for British forces, and was complicated by the presence of German refugees from the East, and displaced persons who numbered over 750,000, even though approximately 1,500,000 had been repatriated. He was deeply aware of the inadequacy of public utilities and transport facilities, as well as a shortage of labour and lack of building materials and coal. Most of all, he dreaded the winter, when all these problems would be multiplied.[31] To cap it all, Sholto knew, just as he was being sent back to Germany, that 'acts of an anti-British nature are increasing and that to some extent German opinion is hardening against us'.[32] All this was lying in wait for his return as Military Governor of the British Zone.

The British Zone of occupied Germany, 1946/47.

CHAPTER TWENTY-TWO

IN THE MIDST OF CHAOS

On 1 May 1946, following a three-month gap in which he made a trip to the United States, where he visited his father and had talks with President Truman, Sholto, accompanied by his personal staff, flew out to Berlin to take up his new appointment as Military Governor. He wrote: 'I had an odd feeling of being more alone, or, perhaps I should say, on my own, as a commander than I had ever been before.'[1] As Sholto's aircraft arrived over Gatow Airport on the edge of Berlin, what he saw when he looked down disconcerted him. A full-scale ceremonial parade had been laid on with units from all three Services. Throughout his military career he had always had a strong aversion to pomp and ceremony, but it seems as though on this occasion, his apprehension over the task ahead worsened his disquiet. This was eased as he was greeted at the airfield by one of his oldest friends, Charles Steele, who wore his familiar boyish grin that Sholto had known well ever since they had served together in WWI. He carried off the whole thing, including an inspection of the guard of honour, because that's what he always did, but as he and Steele were driven into Berlin, the car surrounded by 'a gleaming escort of motor-cyclists of the Military Police', they looked at each other with 'astonishment and embarrassment ... The roar of engines and the screaming of sirens were almost deafening,' sounding just the note that Sholto did not want in his role as Military Governor. He told his personal staff officer (PSO) Bob Wright, also in the car, that there should be no more of 'that nonsense'.

Sholto's return to Germany occurred amid what ACM Sir William Elliot, chairman of the Royal Institute of International Affairs (also known as Chatham House), called 'probably one of the most difficult and unhappy periods in the whole of German history, when, as the result of Nazi ambition, the country was overwhelmed by great problems and great misery'.[2]

Unfortunately, things did not get off to a good start. Sholto received no formal handover whatsoever from his predecessor, although he was pleased to be welcomed by General Sir Brian Robertson, who was to serve as his deputy and who was already in charge of the Control Commission for Germany (CCG) in the British Zone. Many years later, Sholto learned from reading Monty's memoirs that he had actually been in Germany at the time of his arrival and was holed up in Schloss Ostenwalde, writing a report for the British government that he handed to Attlee when he returned to London the following day. Sholto knew nothing of this document until he read the memoirs twelve years later, though it would have been of the greatest help to him. The daunting task in front of him included not only that of Commander-in-Chief of all British armed forces in Germany, but also control over the lives of the twenty-two million people in the British Zone. At that point, he did not have any great worry over the armed forces as they 'ran themselves', but the problems facing the CCG were far more taxing and Sholto spent much of his time liaising with Robertson and the heads of its various divisions. Had he seen it, Monty's report would have depressed him even more, since its outlook was bleak in the extreme:

> I consider the general overall picture is sombre, if not black. For the present the food crisis overshadows all else, but it is not by any means the only serious factor in the situation ... We have a sick economy. Coal is short; only the basic industries can be developed ... The present level of production is such that our exports do not pay for our imports.

Monty went on to enumerate the difficulties with the currency and the black market, saying that Germans must know what was to be the future of their country, that they must be given a reasonable standard of living and some hope for a worthwhile future. He added that if these things were not done, 'we would fail in Germany'. The Germans in the British Zone would begin to look East, which would be 'a definite menace to the British Empire'. He warned of the communist propaganda that was coming westwards over the 'green frontier', and he did not feel confident that the Russians ever intended to treat Germany as an economic whole. His solution was to 'get the Germans "in on it" themselves'. Monty's overriding concern was that 'we must not let them starve; if we do, then everything else we do is of no avail'. However, he did not think that the miserable current daily ration could be increased, adding: 'This means we are going to let them starve: gradually.'[3]

Fear of Soviet-backed communist infiltration into the British Zone continued to be a preoccupation throughout Sholto's governorship. In 1947, concerned about the worsening internal security situation, the General Officer Commanding-in-Chief BAOR, Lieutenant-General Richard McCreery, wrote a paper for Sholto and one of his anxieties was that the spread of communism in the zone would be facilitated by the emphasis placed on the development of trade unions and the power given to their officials. Although in agreement with much else that McCreery wrote, Sholto replied:

I do not share your view that the development of Trade Unions is likely to lead to a spread of communism in the Zone. In fact, I believe the opposite to be the case. I have been impressed by the moderating influence which the Trade Unions have, at least up to the present, been able to exercise over the large scale demonstrations which the serious food shortage in the industrial towns has produced.[4]

He reiterated this view in a lecture to the students at the Imperial Defence College, saying: 'The Trade Union organisation is perhaps the most satisfactory aspect of political life in Germany today.'[5] For Sholto, the answer lay in improving material conditions for Germans within the zone, particularly providing them with more food.

The problems that piled in on Sholto's desk included the health of the population (a part of which was the supply of medicines such as insulin and morphine), food and fuel supply, housing, education, including denazification, intelligence information, local administration and politics, disarmament, reparations, displaced persons and refugees, and legal affairs, to name but a few. One of his greatest anxieties was over the deterioration in the relationship between the Western Allies and the Soviets. In this, he relied on his political adviser Sir William Strang, a senior diplomat with the status of an ambassador.

Although Sholto has been portrayed by some as a 'figurehead' who largely handed the administration of the zone over to Robertson, the many documents concerning the British Zone during his tenure as Military Governor give a different impression. Less than two weeks after taking over, Sholto established a monthly conference of the Cs-in-C of the three Services and the Deputy Military Governor that he almost always chaired, in which were discussed questions that affected the security of the British Zone and matters of common interest to all three Services.

After his bad experience with the Soviet Military Governor, Marshal Zhukov, when he was C-in-C BAFO, he was instrumental in instigating an exchange of Missions with the Soviets, a team of their military personnel coming to the British Zone and vice versa.

The Military Governors of the four zones into which Germany was divided were representatives on the Allied Control Council. Sholto wrote that he had the greatest respect for his three counterparts. The first American Governor, General Eisenhower, had been replaced in November 1945 by General Joseph T. McNarney, an airman like Sholto who had served as a pilot in WWI and who was known as a sound administrator. On 3 July 1946, Marshal Zhukov was replaced by Marshal Vasily Sokolovsky, an equally esteemed soldier whom Sholto described as 'an outstandingly handsome man, always immaculately turned out'. He was alternately courteous and tough in manner as the situation demanded and had a very quick mind. Sholto learned rapidly that 'it paid to watch him with an eye constantly on the alert'.[6]

The French were represented by General Pierre Koenig, also distinguished, who had joined the Free French forces after the fall of France. He made only infrequent visits to Berlin as he was constrained by the attitude of his government, which doubted that it would ever be possible to create a German democracy and also mistrusted Soviet intentions – not unreasonably, as it turned out. In common with McNarney's deputy, General Lucius Clay, Sholto felt that with the departure of Monty, Eisenhower and Zhukov and the arrival of their replacements, 'the glamour had been replaced by the daily grind'.[7] That chore became more difficult with every meeting of the Control Council, although the Military Governors and their deputies remained friendly on a personal level.

According to Johnny Kent, a distinguished WWII fighter pilot who replaced Bob Wright as Sholto's PSO in Germany, Marshal Sokolovsky was particularly fond of using parables and sayings to illustrate his points in Control Council meetings, but more often than not they were intended to obfuscate. On one occasion, Sholto recognised immediately what Sokolovsky was up to and expressed the opinion that the marshal 'was trying to drag "a red herring across the trail"'. Kent continued:

> That did it! The whole meeting broke up in confusion – the Russians asking, 'What is a herring and why should it be red?' They seemed to think that this innocent remark of Sir Sholto's was a studied insult aimed at the Soviet Union! The upshot of it all was that the meeting came to a rapid end and we all repaired to lunch. By the time of the next meeting it appeared that the situation had been placed before the Russian experts on Western terminology and it was not referred to again.[8]

In the execution of his duties, Sholto spent three days out of every ten in Berlin, where he had an official residence, as well as travelling back to London frequently for meetings. What was left of the rest of his time he spent either at his residence in the British Zone, Schloss Ostenwalde, or at the CCG HQ at Lübbecke, twenty-five kilometres to the east, where he had offices and staff to help him with all the reports that came in from the services and the various divisions of the CCG. When he was not dealing with these at Lübbecke, he was in Berlin attending meetings and conferences.

Sholto's peripatetic existence between Ostenwalde, Lübbecke,

Berlin and London meant that he was allocated his own personal pilot, Wing Commander Neville Freeman, with the rotation of navigators including Flying Officer Errol Barrow, later to become the first Prime Minister of Barbados. He had made his mark already as a highly competent observer/navigator on forty-five bombing missions over continental Europe. Pilot Officer Bill Scrimshaw from Bolton in Lancashire served on Sholto's staff with Errol, and gave the following account of their relationship:

> He were a grand chap to work for, were Sir Sholto. Tough enough on the job, mind you, but treated all us junior blokes real decent. No bullshit, you know. He would drink a pint with the lads in the Officers' Mess like anyone else. There was no doubt there was a special bond between him and Errol. Always respectful, mind you, but they were a bit like father and son in a way ... [Errol] was a right good pal. Liked an argument all right. But we was all socialists at that time. Going to put the world right when we got home. I never saw Errol again after Berlin. Often wondered what happened to him. You say he got to be Prime Minister? Well he would, wouldn't he? Good on him.[9]

As with his attitude towards the women with whom he worked, Sholto's stance on ethnic minorities was unusual for its time. He had supported Afro-Caribbean service personnel throughout the war, giving an inspiring address that was broadcast to all the people of the West Indies towards the end of 1942. It had not been a recruiting appeal but rather a speech of praise and thanks for all the contributions that those of the Caribbean had made to the war effort in terms of money, materials, machines and, most importantly, men and women 'to fight and give their lives side by side with their British comrades for a common ideal vital to us all. For without freedom, life itself is empty and futile.' Sholto ended his speech with the hope that 'in this great scheme of world shaped nearer to the needs of men, the West Indies will play its part'.[10] His support of Errol was one way of doing his best to realise that dream.

Amid his very busy schedule, Sholto faced a constant flow of visitors to the British Zone and to Berlin, one of whom caused him some embarrassment. On 26 August 1946, almost four months after his appointment as Military Governor, there arrived at Gatow Airport in Berlin, via the diplomatic courier plane from Warsaw, a tall, handsome, fair-haired man, shabbily dressed with a right hand like a claw and a limp. He was described by the British authorities in Berlin variously as 'colourful' and 'an undesirable character'.[11] He had turned up without a military entry permit (MEP). On arrival, he was stopped and questioned by the military police. He told them that he was the Reuters correspondent in Warsaw and that the purpose of his visit was to contact his opposite number in Berlin. Then he shocked his interrogators by claiming that Sholto was his half-brother.

This mysterious man was indeed Sholto's half-brother Donald. His assertion upon his arrest that he was a Reuters correspondent was only partly true, having worked briefly for them in London after the war. During this time, he was also the London correspondent for a left-wing newspaper called *New Poland*, run by the 'Friends of Democratic Poland'. It was through his contact with that organisation that Donald had decided to try to live there. He maintained his connections with Reuters, so when he reached Warsaw, he started sending 'mailers' (news copy from a stringer, or freelancer) back to them, as well as establishing himself as a correspondent for the Polish communist newspaper *Rzeczpospolita* and writing for German communist newspapers that operated in the Russian Zone. However, in a letter dated 17 July 1946, Alfred Geiringer, manager for Reuters in Eastern Europe, wrote to Walton Cole, the editor of Reuters, that although Donald was sending them mailers, the deputy editor was not anxious to make any permanent arrangement with him. He added: 'In any case Warsaw is too delicate and too important a place to be covered by a string correspondent.'[12] Despite Donald's dubious assertions, he was issued with an MEP valid for six months and a report was sent to Sholto, who enquired on whose authority this had been granted. Sholto knew exactly who Donald was, but he did not reveal this to his staff at the time.

On Donald's next visit to Berlin in December 1946, he 'successfully persuaded an RAF accountant officer to accept a cheque, which enabled him to pay his return fare to Warsaw. He did this on the strength of his alleged relationship to the Commander-in-Chief but the cheque was never honoured.'[13] Donald was a thorn in Sholto's side during a very difficult time.

Since the start of the occupation, the CCG had 'grown and grown', in the words of an engineer officer, G. L. Watson, who wrote to the *Manchester Guardian* in September 1946 after spending a year in Germany. At that point, it numbered some 22,500 people at a cost to the British taxpayer of £80 million. Watson was highly critical of the size of the Commission, writing that its upper levels needed urgently to be 'thinned' as they were full of 'high-ranking and largely redundant senior officers', many of whom had 'little or no qualifications' for the posts that they held.[14] These views were echoed by Strang, who wrote to the Foreign Office in October 1946:

> The staff both military and civilian had initially to be constituted before the close of hostilities when the best material was not available. Since then the rundown in the armed services and the progressive changeover from military to civilian staffs have created continuing instability ... At the present moment several key posts urgently requiring men of high calibre to fill them remain unfilled. When one thinks of the chaos in which we found the British Zone when we took over the surprising thing is not that the situation is as bad as it is but rather that it is not very much worse.[15]

No doubt aware of mounting criticisms of the CCG in the British press and in Parliament, at a press conference in Berlin on 9 August 1946, Sholto addressed some of them directly. The CCG had expanded in order to deal with the complex tasks of reconstruction, whereas the military government staff of the invading army had been concerned only with 'immediate troubles and day to day problems'. There were some serious difficulties that were peculiar to the British Zone, not least of which was the administration of a great industrial complex. Sholto accepted that at the beginning of the occupation, due to the rapid recruitment of the large numbers necessary, 'a certain number of "black sheep" found their way into the fold. From their point of view no doubt it is a very tempting fold. I am quite aware of the existence of this element in our organisation and have been aware of it ever since I assumed my present position.' These were the people who were implicated in black market and corruption investigations, some of which Sholto instigated and which are covered later. He drew his press conference to a close with: 'I do say that it is wrong to decry a fine organisation on account of the misdoings of a minority.'[16]

Any shadow of corruption hanging over the CCG would weaken its moral authority when it came to dealing with the difficult issue of denazification, one of the cornerstones of the Potsdam Agreement. Despite Sholto's reservations about the German people, unsurprising in the context of having fought them in two world wars, he felt that he had to approach this matter in as fair-minded a way as possible, stilling the cries for vengeance in order to ease the burden on Britain of having to prop up the German nation. According to Sir Arthur Street, then Permanent Secretary to John Hynd, the Chancellor of the Duchy of Lancaster, Monty had taken the view that three-quarters of the population of Germany were 'hard-bitten Nazis'.[17] Sholto did not know how Monty had arrived at this figure as it did not correspond with those in Nazi Party files captured by the British at the end of the war. A year later, Hynd stated in the House of Commons that the Nazi Party had numbered some eight and a half million for the whole of Germany, with perhaps another four million in what were described as 'dependent organisations'. That meant approximately 20 per cent of the population, but the difficulty that Sholto and his staff had was in finding some way of differentiating between the various shades all the way from Monty's 'hard-bitten Nazi' at one end and what he called 'the merely loyal German' at the other.

In an address to the Zonal Advisory Council (ZAC),[18] shortly after taking over as Military Governor, Sholto said that the matter of denazification had been handed over largely to German institutions, because Germans such as those on the ZAC would know best who were the men who should be punished. They could also advise the CCG regarding those whose record might look black but whose activities were purely nominal. He added: 'We feel also that there may be many men who have been wrongly dismissed or removed. For this reason we gave instructions for the setting up of German Review Boards, to which these men can appeal. The setting up of these Boards is important if we are to right injustice.'[19] Was this an abrogation of responsibility on the part of the CCG or a beneficial change of direction?

The rules laid down for denazification stipulated that the records of all those with any connection to the Nazi Party should be examined. The Americans insisted that anyone who had ever had even the slightest link with the party should be prohibited from working in the country's administration. But the British deemed that while it was necessary to hold for trial all those suspected of criminal offences, it was much more difficult to preclude others who had joined the party 'for inoffensive reasons, and perhaps even under coercion' and who were urgently needed for help in running the country. This may seem shocking to us now, but the times were desperate and so the waters were muddied with compromise. Sholto realised that there were still Nazi influences at work, but the issue for him was how much the 'hard core' had reached down into the fibre of the nation and how it was to be extirpated.

The CCG was criticised for its denazification policy in both directions, some saying that it was too wholesale; others, that it was too half-hearted. From the beginning of the occupation to August 1946, over 120,000 people had been discharged from their employment due to their association with the Nazi Party. A further 70,000 had been refused work because of their Nazi sympathies, and another 55,000 described as 'dangerous Nazis' had to be interned. The problem was, as the Reuters journalist Macfee Kerr articulated: 'Can we get German industry and administration started again solely with the survivors of the concentration camps?'[20]

Professor Mary Fulbrook makes the point well that sometimes the denazification process backfired. Those with Nazi sympathies held in internment camps, many of which were former concentration camps and prisons that had operated during the Third Reich, found their views reinforced by being incarcerated with other like-minded internees, aggrieved at their detention. One occupant of these camps found that the attempts at 're-education' made during her internment were useless. 'It was only after she was released and began to be exposed to the views and sympathies of other Germans, including those who had been opposed to Nazism, that she eventually entered a long, slow process of rethinking.'[21]

As part of the denazification process, plans for educational reconstruction within the British Zone were devised soon after the beginning of the occupation, involving 'prominent educationists who had fallen foul of the Nazis'.[22] These included Heinrich Landahl, the first post-war school senator for Hamburg, who played a leading role in the restoration of the Hamburg school system and the university there. Sholto paid a visit to Hamburg schools in 1946, accompanied by Landahl and Brigadier Armytage, then Regional Commissioner for Hamburg. One of the photos from that visit, which Sholto obviously treasured, shows a classroom of children, with Landahl and Armytage standing either side of Sholto, who is squaring up to a small boy standing very straight in front of him, no doubt reciting something. It might be thought that the boy is terrified, but judging by the way in which Sholto is defensively standing sideways on with his arms folded, it's tempting to suggest that it is Sholto who is awed, in an unfamiliar situation for him. It is clear from the series of pictures that Sholto and Landahl liked each other.

In 1947, the CCG appointed as its education adviser Dr Robert Birley, an educationalist who had been headmaster of Charterhouse during WWII and later became headmaster of Eton, as well as a prominent anti-apartheid campaigner in the 1960s. His moderate liberal politics earned him the nickname 'Red Robert'. He understood well the course some Germans would have had to follow under the Nazis in order to avoid 'loss of employment, poverty, torture, and possibly death for themselves and their families'. One of my strongest childhood memories is of Sholto telling me what had happened when in WWII the Nazis marched into a village or town to subjugate the population, about which he must have heard many times. They would summon the Bürgermeister, or Mayor, and say to him: 'If you do not cooperate with us, we will put your wife and children up against the wall and shoot them.' Sholto explained to me that if they had simply threatened the official, he might well have allowed himself to be killed, but the cruelty lay in the menaces to his family. As Birley wrote:

> Most men and women are not strong enough to solve such a dilemma, and certainly someone who has not had to live in a totalitarian country has no right to condemn them ... It is a sign of the decadence of a civilisation when ordinary men and women must expect to face an impossible dilemma.[23]

I watched my mother Hazel ask Sholto how he would have responded if he had been faced with that 'choice'. His reply was: 'I hope I would have had the strength to do my duty.'

There remained the task of guiding the population to help themselves while at the same time preventing prospective leaders coming forward who were either 'dyed-in-the-wool Nazis' or who were what Sholto called the 'old Prussian Junker type', and were 'merely biding their time before they could again seize power'.[24] Conversely, Sholto was mindful of the imperative not to refer to German guilt for the war in a way that would cause resentment among the people, which had so taken root in Germany after WWI following the Versailles treaty and which contributed to what followed. Even so, those who were responsible for the war and had committed atrocities had to be tracked down and dealt with.

Meanwhile, Sholto was preoccupied with providing the population with the basics of food and fuel in order, as he put it, 'to get them back on their feet'. The support given by the Americans and the British immediately after the war meant that there were no widespread epidemics, but even so, the bare existence of life in Germany was grim. Sholto wrote: 'No humane person can bear to see women and particularly little children starving in the streets obviously suffering from the diseases that go with semi-starvation; hunger oedema etc.'[25] As he told the audience of his Imperial Defence College lecture, 'The Germans themselves say, "It is no use talking to us about democratic ideals unless you first fill our bellies": and, as regards Nazism, some of them are apt to say that "at least under Hitler we were fed".'[26]

In March 1946, during Monty's tenure as Military Governor, the already inadequate food ration had been cut from its nominal value of 1,550 calories to as little as 1,014 calories per day. The situation was desperate, causing the leaders of trade unions in Hamburg to write to the military government: 'The recent cuts in rations are unbearable. The decrease of calories to 1,014 threatens to destroy the life and the capacity to work of our whole nation.'[27] This led Sholto to write a report for the chiefs of staff on the public order implications of further cuts in the German rations, considered in a meeting of that august body on 3 July 1946 at which Monty was present. He dismissed Sholto's concerns in a manner that could only be described as heartless, saying, 'The crisis period is likely to be short, and it may well not arise,' especially since the new harvest would be coming in the next few months.[28] But this would never be sufficient to feed the population.

Macfee Kerr wrote that the food crisis overshadowed all other matters. This was affecting service personnel as well as the German population, as the rations for troops in the British and American Zones were being cut 'to keep the Germans from starving to death'. The food situation was closely allied with the maintenance of law and order, particularly in Hamburg and the Ruhr, two industrial areas most severely affected. Food demonstrations and riots began to spring up, especially in the Ruhr as the Germans laid the fault for the deterioration in their living standards firmly at the feet of their British occupiers.

At Sholto's instigation, the food ration was increased once again in the early autumn of 1946, but in his telegram to the Foreign Office in October, Sholto's adviser Strang wrote: 'Now there comes the threat that even the inadequate ration of 1,550 calories for the normal consumer, recently restored, is in jeopardy again owing to procurement difficulties. This insecurity makes the Commander-in-Chief's problem here almost insoluble.'[29] A memo written by a senior adviser to the CCG, Patrick Dean, at the same time asserted: 'There will be no real progress until we get the ordinary ration up to at least 2,000 calories.'[30]

A Pathé newsreel from 1946, uploaded to YouTube, shows Sholto making a direct appeal to the people of Britain – including no doubt Monty, who, now that he is back in the UK, seems prepared to wash his hands of post-war Germany and leave Sholto with the chaos. 'What is happening in this part of Germany is *very much* your concern,' he tells the viewer. We are then shown distressing footage of a hunger ward in Langenhorn on the outskirts of Hamburg, to which the Red Cross has donated 400 parcels. We see patients with grossly distended abdomens indicative of hunger oedema and severe muscle wasting in their arms, their skin hanging flaccid while the examining physician picks up empty folds of it. The narrator says: 'These people hate us.' Sholto explains that not every German is hungry and that the farmers and those in rural districts get nearly double the ration, largely because they can grow food for themselves and sell the rest on the black market, but then we see a factory where liver sausage is made from wood pulp, beech or pine being the most frequently used. Rather ironically, the commentary then states: 'It is costing you a lot of money to keep the Germans from starving. This is the truth that all of us must face, not because we are sorry for them, but because while we are the occupying power, we are called upon to feed them.'[31]

The problem of food supplies was compounded by the fuel shortage, which exerted its effect in all sorts of ways, such as delaying minesweeping operations around the German coast. This meant that fishing grounds could not be cleared and fished, denying the population a valuable source of nutrition. The food/fuel conundrum also exerted its malign effects the other way round, in that falling coal production in the Ruhr could be explained by grossly inadequate food rations. In April 1946, just before Sholto took over as Military Governor, coal production had fallen below 150,000 tons a day, compared to over 180,000 tons at the end of February. This correlated almost exactly with the drastic cut in food rations in March, exacerbated by a worldwide food shortage. Although miners, being classed as 'very heavy workers', continued to receive over 2,800 calories a day, the fact that their families' rations were cut to just over 1,000 calories a day meant that these men were eating only about 2,000 of their allotted calories, the remainder being given to their relatives. This coincided with an increase in absenteeism, which continued for some months thereafter.

Coal was the most important source of fuel in post-war Germany, but it was being exported to other nations in large quantities. Both Sholto and Monty before him repeatedly urged the retention of more coal in Germany in order to save the economy from collapse. But it was only in October 1946, when, according to Strang, 'economic deterioration' was well under way that a small cut in coal exports was authorised.[32]

A particular problem in the British Zone that, according to Foreign Secretary Ernest Bevin, placed an extra burden on the British Exchequer was the overwhelming number of old people there who were not 'economically productive' and who needed support. Bevin wrote to Attlee from the Council of Ministers of Foreign Affairs in Moscow in 1947 that the repatriation of young German prisoners of war in other countries, a large number of whom were in the Soviet Union enduring extremely harsh conditions, was needed in order to man the Ruhr mines as well as other industries and build up the German economy. However, many of them did not return until 1953. A policy document released during the conference in Moscow said: 'It is essential to remove Germany's potential for war, but it is also essential to maintain her potential for peace.'[33]

Bevin wrote to Attlee again during the meeting:

> The situation in Germany is causing me anxiety. I am informed it is a breakdown of German distribution of food. I spoke to Robertson and Weir [Sir Cecil Weir, economic adviser to the CCG] today and asked Robertson to communicate at once with the Commander-in-Chief that every step must be taken to get this matter straightened out. I understand that there is no real shortage of food, but that the disturbances are due to deficiencies in the German organisation in the zone.[34]

Bevin called for instructions to be issued to Germans to sort out the distribution of food, and that General Clay, who had just been promoted to Military Governor of the US Zone, should be persuaded to issue similar instructions on food distribution in his zone.

Sholto replied to Bevin saying that he should have seen a joint telegram issued by Robertson and Clay in response to Bevin's edict, which showed 'quite plainly how critical the food situation is here'. It wasn't only a question of distribution. Almost exactly two years after the end of the war, there *still* wasn't enough food. The main thing was to get the food out with American help, and Sholto advised that any questions of finance could be left for later. Sholto had himself spoken with the Chancellor of the Exchequer, who 'endorses my recommendations strongly'.[35]

In April 1947, shortly after the Moscow conference, Frank (Lord) Pakenham (later the Earl of Longford) succeeded John Hynd as Chancellor of the Duchy of Lancaster with responsibility for the British Zone. Although the two men had very different personalities, Sholto wrote that Pakenham's

> great heart and integrity and enthusiasm were the qualities about him that appealed to me and which, in turn, provided a fillip to my own flagging spirit. And in addition to his deep compassion for the Germans, he was always so fair in trying his utmost to help those of us who were serving out in Germany during that very difficult time.[36]

Pakenham visited the British Zone five times in two months and wrote in a memo to Bevin that Germany was 'in a shocking condition', asserting:

> It is a complete illusion to suppose that things are getting steadily better. If anything they are worse than six months ago. Everything comes back to food ... The whole thing boils down to obtaining much increased food imports from abroad. The vital decisions here must be taken by Ministers. The administrative arrangements for importing food into Germany are wound round with the most appalling red tape such as I have never seen equalled.[37]

Pakenham suggested a series of measures to alleviate the food crisis, saying that if they were not implemented, he would find it impossible to continue in his post. The day he wrote the paper, 23 June, he gave it to Bevin, but the following day he withdrew it, presumably as a result of pressure to do so. Nonetheless, it was Pakenham's depiction of the situation in Germany that resonated with Sholto rather than anyone else's.

The Moscow conference had heightened the tension between the West and the Russians, who, although much of the capacity for food production in Germany was in their zone, were intent on getting as much out of the Western Zones as possible. This prompted Sholto to say in his Imperial Defence College lecture that 'the Russians would like to use Germany as a cow fed from the West and milked from the East'. The food from the Russian Zone went to support their occupying forces, and some was exported to Russia.[38]

Meanwhile, Sholto was pivotal in attempts to alleviate the food and fuel crisis by boosting the German economy, including a highly successful initiative, the Hanover Export Fair, held first in August 1947 and still going today. The CCG had the idea for a trade exhibition in the British Zone back in the late summer of 1946, but where should it be held? Four cities were investigated as possible sites: Cologne, Düsseldorf, Hamburg and finally Hanover, which was chosen because it was the least destroyed of the four. An article in *Hannoversche Allgemeine Zeitung*, published the week before the thirtieth anniversary of the fair, stated that German politicians were reluctant to hold the event, believing that not much would come of it, but that the British insisted. The article went on to say:

> The decision for the fair matured in the most dreadful winter the Hanoverians had ever experienced. Hungry, freezing, and without work, they sat crammed together in the houses which had been half-spared by the bombs. At the height of the hunger crisis, when in the spring the meagre food rations were cut short once again by the occupation power, and a ragged mass of tens of thousands demonstrated on the Klagesmarkt, Sir Sholto Douglas, Air Chief Marshal and Military Governor of the British Zone, announced that 'Hanover will be the City of the Trade Fair!'[39]

After a Herculean effort over four months, the fair opened on 18

August 1947, and included Germany's first post-war automobile exhibition, of which the Volkswagen Beetle was the focus. In the first three weeks of the fair, approximately 736,000 visitors from fifty-three countries around the world flocked to Hanover. A dollar 'thermometer' was set up at the entrance to the exhibition grounds to show the daily total export turnover at the fair. On the last day, it reached $31.58 million.

Despite this success, another serious problem remained, both for the German population and for British service personnel, inextricably linked to the lack of fuel supply: the shortage of housing. This was a matter about which Sholto felt very deeply. He badgered constantly those with whom he worked to play their part in addressing the dire state of housing in the British Zone, and he had a clear eight-point plan for improving the situation. Two months after assuming command as Military Governor, he wrote to Robertson:

> I am not entirely happy about the answer which I was given about the repair of houses at the Regional Commissioners meeting last Friday. In the discussion it became apparent that we cannot increase the rate of repair without a larger allocation of coal ... It also seemed to be the general opinion that production of consumer goods was of a higher order of priority than the repair of houses. I am not satisfied however that this is correct. Housing seems to me to come next to food in order of importance from the point of view of the contentment of the German population in the British Zone.[40]

Sholto had been informed in this meeting that with the current coal allocation, it would take ten years to reconstruct all repairable houses in the zone, but if the coal supply could be increased to some 250,000 tons per annum, this period could be reduced to three years.

In November 1946, Sholto wrote to the three service commanders and to Robertson:

> The loss of housing accommodation as a result of war and the influx of refugees has created a housing situation in the British Zone which is very grave and probably unparalleled in history. Of

the 23 million inhabitants many are living in conditions which are intolerable. These conditions, coupled with underfeeding and a hard winter (as it may well be), may bring in their train death and disease to many and may justifiably cause serious discontent and even lead to civil unrest.

Priority was to be given to housing for German civilians over that required for occupation purposes or civil functions, and the most economical use made of existing accommodation, whether for Germans or for the occupying power. Sholto had issued instructions to the German authorities to this effect, but the British also had to play their part. This was where the eight-point plan came in, which included a review of all requisitioned property, which must be derequisitioned and used for civilian housing wherever possible. Sholto finished his letter with an appeal to 'common humanity and common-sense', which demanded that everything possible would be done to ease the situation before and during the coming winter.[41]

Sholto visited the areas worst affected by the housing crisis. Addressing the tensions between service demands and civilian requirements, he wrote to General Sir Richard McCreery, C-in-C BAOR, in November:

> I visited Hamburg yesterday and found that the Regional Commissioner [Vaughan Berry] was very exercised about the continued requisitioning of houses and flats for British married families ... The housing position in Hamburg is desperate. Thousands of people are living in the most appalling conditions in cellars, bunkers and air raid shelters. Most German families, even the well to do classes, are living in one room. I myself went and inspected a number of living quarters of the civil population, and I am bound to say that I was horrified by what I saw ... Under these circumstances therefore it seems to me that requisitioning must cease until the situation improves.

Sholto suggested that barracks should be used to 'relieve the appalling housing conditions of the poorer members of the population. We must try to clear the air raid shelters and cellars as quickly as possible, since widespread epidemics are liable under the present conditions.'

He realised that this would cause some discontent among British personnel.[42] The day after Sholto's visit to Hamburg, he went to Düsseldorf and was confronted once again with 'frightful overcrowding'.[43]

The difficulty for McCreery was fulfilling the needs of his Army personnel while still following Sholto's priorities for civilian housing. McCreery was afraid that if Army personnel were not joined in Germany by their families, 'the situation as regards officers and senior NCOs may break down'.[44]

Sholto made two stipulations concerning the allocation of housing in a letter to Vaughan Berry a few days later. Firstly: 'No German civilian must be evicted from his house or flat unless suitable alternative accommodation is found for him.' Secondly:

> that in the last resort the final decision as to whether a house or flat should be requisitioned for married families [of British service personnel] or not rests with you as Regional Commissioner ... I am prepared to accept any slowing up of the arrival of married families in Hamburg which may result from adherence to these principles.[45]

Due to a shortage of building materials, many units in BAOR, particularly those engaged in a timber-felling programme, were living 'under the worst possible conditions', McCreery reported in Sholto's monthly meeting of January 1947. Their living quarters, in a German winter that was the harshest for many years, had no heating, no shower baths and very limited canteen facilities, and there were no materials available for repairs to existing accommodation.

Later, Sholto made his own inspection of BAOR barrack accommodation and he agreed that it was essential to improve the standard as quickly as possible, 'in the interests of the well-being and morale of the troops', and that service demands for building materials should be met in full. On the other hand, criticisms were levelled at the services for their extravagance in the use of accommodation, not only by Germans but also by the British press and in the UK Parliament, causing those in Sholto's April 1947 monthly meeting to instigate more rigorous inspections throughout the zone to ensure that the best use was made of housing.

Perhaps as a follow-up to the meeting, Sholto wrote to Major-General E. P. Nares, General Officer Commanding British Troops in Berlin:

> It has struck me that there are a number of houses in the vicinity of
> my residence which are either empty or very sparsely occupied ...
> I think that it would be a good thing if you sent your Accommo-
> dation Inspection Board to have a look round all the houses near
> my residence, in order to see what accommodation is redundant.
> This should be used for the accommodation of additional married
> families of BTB [British Troops in Berlin] or CCG, or alternatively
> should be derequisitioned and handed back to the Germans.[46]

Once again, the delicate balancing act to satisfy the housing needs of both the Germans and the occupying forces was well-nigh impossible. The crisis was worsened by an influx of large numbers of people of different groups into the British Zone, many of whom were interned in camps under primitive and insanitary conditions. Firstly, there were the German service personnel who had surrendered to the British at the end of the war and who had been retained to work for the British armed forces. Although given the name 'prisoners of war', they were not '*real*' POWs and were therefore not given the rights that would be their due under the Geneva Convention, instead being designated Surrendered Enemy Personnel (SEPs). Many of these men were released after a few weeks or months, but some were retained by the British for the purposes of minesweeping, mine clearance on land, timber felling and other menial tasks, and some of them were given the name *Dienstgruppen* (Service Groups). As Bevin admitted, they were 'really military formations under the command of German officers but under the supervision of the British Military Command', causing him to write to Attlee from the Moscow conference:

> I am faced here with a very difficult situation. We have retained
> in Germany prisoners of war [actually SEPs] to the number of
> over 81,000 ... Nothing I can say can persuade my colleagues that
> these are not a military formation, and it is my weakest point in

the whole negotiations. I understand that there have been talks between the Control Office and the War Office with a view to effect-
ing a change at an early date. But I understand the Admiralty view
is that they cannot clear their work until January 1948, while the
War Office is asking for a period of 18 months, which means that
we are keeping formations in Germany for over three years after the
termination of the war.

Bevin urged Attlee and the Cabinet to make the decision to dissolve
the *Dienstgruppen* by 31 December 1947. If he was able to tell the
Soviets that this was being done, 'one of the nastiest sores as between
Soviet Russia and ourselves can be removed'.[47]

On 29 April 1947, following the Moscow conference, Robertson
confirmed that the UK had agreed to disband the *Dienstgruppen*,
except for a small number of what were euphemistically termed
'minor tasks'. Sholto observed that it would be difficult to civilianise
them by the end of 1947, particularly those who were 'employed in
sweeping mines at sea', and also those (approximately 13,200-strong)
who were 'engaged on important tasks of a skilled nature for which
the provision and training of replacements may not be complete until
the early months of 1948'.[48] The complete civilianisation of the *Dienstgruppen* did not take place until after Sholto had left Germany.

As well as the German service personnel, the second group ex-
acerbating the accommodation crisis was the tide of refugees from
the East, who posed a huge humanitarian problem for the military
government in the British Zone. Some attempt was made to regulate
this flow, but from the end of the war until the end of September
1945, considerable 'unauthorised' movement took place across zones.
Under a quadripartite agreement reached in October 1945, an inter-
zonal exchange was arranged on a 'head for head' basis. Even so, as
many as 12,000 Germans a day were entering the already crowded
British Zone from the Russian Zone. Furthermore, under the aegis of
the Allied powers, at the end of the war, millions of German-speaking
civilians were expelled from Czechoslovakia, Hungary and the parts
of eastern Germany assigned to Poland, in what Professor R. M.
Douglas has described as 'the largest forced population transfer' in

human history.[49] The number of those who were permanently displaced was at least twelve million, possibly as many as fourteen million. At a quadripartite meeting in November 1945, it was agreed that the British Zone would accept one and a half million Germans from the 'New Poland' alone. Most of these refugees from the East were women and children under the age of sixteen and they were subject to disease, ill treatment and starvation while held in transit camps prior to their departure, causing the demise of tens and possibly hundreds of thousands of them. Many of those who did make it to the British Zone died from hypothermia, malnutrition and other effects of their traumatic journey. Sholto inspected the refugee camps where they were housed, no doubt disturbed by what he saw. A photo of his visit to the refugee camp of *Scheerlager* at Kiel Wik in the north of the zone in July 1946 shows barefoot little boys standing by waiting to see him. What must he have thought as, perhaps, he remembered his own childhood, when at times he went without shoes.

Finally, there were DPs, who produced their own humanitarian and public order challenges. In August 1945, the number of DPs in assembly centres in the British Zone was 891,000, some 1,475,000 having been repatriated already. The Yalta Agreement had stipulated that all Soviet citizens liberated after 11 February 1945 should be handed over to the Russian authorities regardless of their wishes, but this proved a difficult commitment to fulfil. Many inhabitants of the Baltic states and eastern Poland refused to be sent back, as did 15,000 Yugoslavs, mainly royalist supporters.

Among the DPs were many Poles who had been forced into slave labour by the Nazis and who, Sholto said, 'had found ways of disposing of their hated German oppressors' after the end of the war. They were brought before military government courts in the British Zone, where they were sentenced to death. The warrants for their execution found their way on to Sholto's desk for him to make the final decisions and sign. They had been brutalised and had lost everything, and now they were condemned, along with their Nazi tormentors. The death warrants presented Sholto, as he wrote, with 'by far the most distressing part of my work while I was in Germany'. And then there was Nuremberg.

CHAPTER TWENTY-THREE

PLEAS FROM NUREMBERG

So much has been written and said about the International Military Tribunal (IMT) at Nuremberg that I do not propose to reiterate every detail here. Instead, I intend to concentrate on aspects of the proceedings that were of greatest concern to Sholto, one of which, consideration of the pleas for clemency from the major Nazi war criminals, has been largely overlooked as being a formality even by some legal historians, but which Sholto took very seriously and in which he played a vital part.

As early as October 1942, a committee had been set up under the Lord Chancellor, John Simon, 'to consider the problem of war criminals in all its aspects'. The matter arose during inter-Allied discussions in October 1943 at the Moscow conference of Foreign Ministers, at which the Soviet Foreign Minister, Molotov, was in favour of 'stern, swift justice'. The British position was equivocal. At one point Churchill favoured summary justice, but then the Foreign Secretary, Anthony Eden, insisted in Moscow that 'all legal forms should be observed', and later in 1943 at Tehran, Churchill appeared to have changed his mind. When faced with Stalin's assertion that at least 50,000 of the German general staff must be physically and summarily liquidated, and Roosevelt's jest that perhaps just 49,000 would do, Churchill said: 'I would rather be taken out into the garden here and now and be shot myself than sully my own and my country's honour with such infamy.'[1] Subsequently, plans for the trial of those responsible for war crimes gathered momentum at the Yalta and Potsdam conferences held in 1945, and were confirmed by the London Charter of 8 August 1945, in which the four Allied powers agreed to 'the

prosecution and punishment of the major war criminals of the Euro-
pean Axis countries'.[2] Nuremberg was chosen as the site for the tribunal not only because it was a city of psychological significance to the
Nazis, being the site of Hitler's political rallies, but also because it was
'the only place in Germany where the necessary facilities remained'.[3]
Even so, the destruction of the city shocked the journalist and writer
Rebecca West, who covered the trial as a correspondent for the *New
Yorker*: 'The Nazi Government had shown a monstrous cruelty to its
own people ... They did not dig out their dead from the ruins after
air-raids. It was for this reason that all German towns stank on hot
days in the summer of 1946.'[4] Nuremberg was no exception.

When Sholto had accepted, reluctantly, the post of Military Governor, he did not appreciate fully that the final 'court of appeal' against
the sentences passed at the trial of the major war criminals would be
the Allied Control Council. This consisted of the Cs-in-C of the four
zones in Germany: Marshal Sokolovsky for Russia, General Koenig
for France, General McNarney for the US, and Sholto. At the last
minute he learned, to his distress, that in company with his three
counterparts, he was to have 'the distasteful duty of sitting in judgment on these appeals after the trials at Nuremberg'.[5] Once he knew
this, he realised that it was of the utmost importance that he should
be clear about his own feelings on the subject.

To begin with, Sholto was troubled as to the legality of the Nuremberg trials, writing:

> International law is a somewhat vague and by no means definitive
> code of law, in fact it can be said that the Western Allies invent-
> ed the law on which they tried the Nuremberg defendants. The
> laws under which these men were tried did not exist in codified
> form before the war. They were laws invented after the commission
> of the offence [termed ex post facto law]. As I say, I felt unhappy
> about the whole set-up. I think that Monty must have felt much
> the same because when he was invited to go and visit the Nurem-
> berg Trials, he declined to go but tried to send me there in his place
> to represent him. I did not blame him for this, but I also declined
> to go at that time out of sheer distaste for the whole business. Later,

when I had taken over as Military Governor from Monty, I was again invited to go, but declined, this time on the grounds that the Control Council, of which I was a member, was to hear the appeals from Nuremberg, and apart from my previous objections I thought that it would be wrong for a member of the Court of Appeal to sit in to the original trials, and listen to the proceedings.[6]

Sholto was not the only one with reservations. There was considerable debate among British academics and in the media regarding the legitimacy of the trials. In one of the files containing the pleas for clemency, there is a scholarly article of July 1946 by H. A. Smith, professor of international law at the London School of Economics, which articulated the difficulties involved in the exercise of international law, in particular 'the lack of any agreed authority which could determine its application to particular disputes'. (At that time, the International Criminal Court did not exist.) Smith also examined the problem of so-called victors' justice, stating: 'Law ceases to be law if its violation can be justified by success.'[7] He cited the unprovoked invasion of Finland by the Soviet Union in December 1939, for which its leaders were not held to account under international law, whereas the Nazi leaders were being tried for almost identical crimes that had begun with the invasion of Poland only three months earlier.

Given the complex issues involved, Sholto was surprised at the brevity of the London Charter. Article Six called for the trial and punishment of those who committed any of the crimes in the following categories, for which there would be 'individual responsibility'. Count One: conspiracy to commit the crimes alleged in Counts Two to Four; Count Two: crimes against peace, namely, planning or waging a war of aggression, or a war in violation of international treaties, agreements or assurances, or participation in a common plan or conspiracy for the accomplishment of any of the foregoing; Count Three: war crimes, including murder, ill treatment or deportation of civilians in occupied territory or prisoners of war, killing of hostages, plunder, wanton destruction of cities, towns or villages, or devastation not justified by military necessity; Count Four: crimes against humanity: namely, murder, extermination, enslavement, deportation and other inhumane acts committed against any civilian population, or persecutions on political, racial or religious grounds.

For the first time in international law, the crime of genocide was enshrined implicitly in Count Three for the protection of groups, whereas the concept contained in Count Four referred to atrocities against individual civilians.

The representatives of the Soviet government, represented by General Nikitchenko, who was later the main Soviet judge at the trial, had had to be persuaded 'that the indictment should include a charge of waging a war of aggression', having initially wanted to 'qualify or limit the charge to a "Hitlerite" war of aggression'.[8] This highlighted one of the problems laid out by Professor Smith: supposing the nations involved in formulating the Charter would be accusing the Nazis of crimes that they had committed themselves? One only has to think of further Soviet incursions in the Baltic states and Poland, and the massacre of 22,000 Polish officers in the Katyn Forest, with which the Soviets wanted the Nazis to be charged but which in 1990 they admitted that they had perpetrated themselves. This point was articulated by Mr Justice Jackson, the chief prosecutor for the US at Nuremberg, in a letter to President Truman on 12 October 1945, writing that the Allies

> have done or are doing some of the very things we are prosecuting the Germans for. You, no doubt, are informed that the French are so violating the Geneva Convention in the treatment of prisoners of war that our command is taking back prisoners sent to them. We are prosecuting plunder and our Allies are practising it. We say aggressive war is a crime and one of our allies asserts sovereignty over the Baltic States based on no title except conquest.[9]

Article Seven of the Charter stated: 'The official position of defendants, whether as Heads of State or responsible officials in Government Departments, shall not be considered as freeing them from responsibility or mitigating punishment.' Article Eight went further still: 'The fact that the Defendant acted pursuant to order of his Government or of a superior shall not free him from responsibility, but may be considered in mitigation of punishment if the Tribunal determines that justice so requires.'

Especially relevant to Sholto was the first paragraph of Article Twenty-Six of the Charter, under Section VI headed 'Judgment and Sentence', which stated: 'The judgment of the Tribunal as to the guilt or innocence of any Defendant shall give the reasons on which it is based, and shall be final and not subject to review.' This meant that the Control Council was relieved of having to make decisions as to the actual guilt of the defendants. Article Twenty-Nine laid out the duties the Control Council would have to perform: 'In the case of guilt, sentences shall be carried out in accordance with the orders of the Control Council for Germany, which may at any time reduce or otherwise alter the sentences, but may not increase the severity thereof.'

In order to fulfil this duty, Sholto found himself confronted with a profusion of documents. British deputy chief prosecutor Sir David Maxwell Fyfe wrote that there had 'never been such a wealth of material for cross-examination as at Nuremberg'.[10] The Nazis had kept meticulous records of their years in power, except, ironically for Sholto, for those of the Luftwaffe, which had been destroyed in one large bonfire. The documents were discovered by Allied armies in German Army headquarters, government buildings, even in underground salt mines and hidden behind false walls. These gave the prosecutors at Nuremberg ample evidence for the charges against the defendants, causing Lord Justice Lawrence, the president of the tribunal, to state in the judgment that the case against the defendants rested 'in a large measure on documents of their own making, the authority of which has not been challenged except in one or two cases'.[11]

The Nuremberg trials began on 20 November 1945. In his opening address, the formidable chief British prosecutor, Sir Hartley Shawcross,

> sought to counter the idea, still quite widely held, that waging war had always been a legitimate form of state policy – 'after all, what is history except wars?' – and that the whole Nuremberg procedure was in truth an ex post facto demonstration of vengeance cooked

up retroactively by the victors but which had no respectable basis in international law. This I think I did by showing that, on the contrary, the Tribunal was administering rules of international law which had been established, with the full outward concurrence of the Germans, many years before the war.[12]

As Rebecca West asserted: 'It was absurd to say that the defendants were being tried for ex post facto crimes when the Briand-Kellogg pact of 1928 had made aggressive warfare a crime by renouncing the use of war as an instrument of policy.'[13]

The chief United States prosecutor, Robert H. Jackson, made it clear in his opening statement that at certain times soldiers can and should be held responsible for the crime of war or crimes against peace. As Jackson put it: 'We recognise that to plan warfare is the business of professional soldiers in every country. But it is one thing to plan strategic moves in the event war comes, and it is another to plot and intrigue to bring that war on.' Jackson went on to say that the leaders of the German High Command were not on trial 'because they lost the war but because they started it'.[14] Nevertheless, the Nuremberg tribunal did reject the argument that *all* military actions undertaken by the Germans were war crimes because they were carried out in pursuit of an aggressive war. As the defence analyst David Fisher has explained: 'That judgment was well founded, however much we may debate whether the tribunal may – for reasons of political expediency or practicality – have been too selective in those it held to account.'[15]

On 10 September 1946, in a meeting that Sholto chaired, the Allied Control Council began to consider the procedure they should adopt in handling any appeals that might be lodged with them. It soon became clear that the four Military Governors were split in their views. General McNarney was in favour of referring everything to the legal directorate and the coordinating committee for their advice before making any decisions. Marshal Sokolovsky was against doing so, saying that the trial 'had lasted a very long time already and every question had been considered in great detail by the most qualified legal experts of the four nations'. Presumably, he had already received orders from the Kremlin to reject any appeals as quickly as possible. General Noiret, acting for General Koenig, suggested adopting a procedure similar to that used in the French legal system of setting up a commission to study the cases before hearing pleas for clemency. Sholto disagreed with the Americans and the French, wanting a direct approach similar to that expressed by Sokolovsky but for different reasons. He 'was not being dictated to by any higher authority'[16] but felt that in all conscience it was 'neither necessary nor proper for the Control Council to examine the legality of the proceedings at Nuremberg', and that the task of the Control Council

> was to determine whether, on humanitarian grounds, they should exercise their power of clemency in the reduction of any sentence which they still regarded as just ... The Council should consider these pleas for clemency not as legal experts but as men of the world. This power of exercising clemency had been vested in the Control Council and it would be dangerous for this power to be delegated to the Legal Directorate.[17]

Sholto stated his case so clearly that McNarney and Noiret were persuaded by his arguments. However, even after this unanimity had been reached, there were repercussions from London prompted by Mr Justice Jackson, who objected to the Control Council's directive that an official record of all the proceedings at Nuremberg should be put at the disposal of the Control Commission's legal directorate. This was because it contemplated a review of the judgment and the sentences due to come from Nuremberg, whereas he felt that 'the petitions for clemency should be dealt with as a matter of policy, and that there should be no review on legal grounds'.[18] Sholto was told that this was also the line taken by the British government, who hoped that the Control Council would follow it.

The trial as a whole finished on 1 October 1946 and the sentences were remitted to the Control Council for appeal against them. Before Sholto attended the council, he received a letter from Ernest Bevin telling him that he should consult Bevin before the council reached any decisions. Bevin was particularly worried about any measures of clemency that might be applied. Although Sholto liked and admired Bevin, on this occasion he took the strongest exception to his instructions. For Sholto, it reignited the question of how far the executive is entitled to interfere with the judiciary, and he felt that Bevin was entirely wrong in attempting to tell him, a serving officer in the execution of his duty, what he should do. Telford Taylor, a lawyer on the US prosecution team who wrote a comprehensive memoir of the Nuremberg trials, described Sholto at this point as 'an outspoken and somewhat explosive man'.[19] (How different from the calm exterior his contemporaries had seen near the beginning of WWII.) In a spirit of defiance, Sholto fired off a cipher to the Permanent Secretary to the Foreign Office, Sir Gilmour Jenkins:

> I appreciate the Secretary of State's natural anxiety about the results of the Nuremberg Trial. At the same time have two comments on your message. First I regard my part in this business as a judicial rather than a political function, and consequently as a question for my own individual conscience to decide. This is also emphatically the view of my colleagues on the Control Council. Secondly I consider that it would be improper for me to hold up the proceedings of the Control Council while I consulted the Secretary of State about each and all of our decisions, and I am sure my colleagues on the Control Council would resent this. I suggest therefore that the Secretary of State should let me have without delay his views on the question of the commutation or reduction of the sentences. I will of course take these views fully into account when making up my mind.[20]

By using the word 'judicial', Sholto was indicating that the overriding purpose of the Control Council was to act on general principles of justice and fairness, but Taylor felt that this was 'certainly the wrong word to use, for the Control Council was not a judicial organ. It was an "executive" power with which the Control Council was temporarily vested.'[21] Sholto's attitude caused Bevin, then attending the peace conference in Paris, to panic. His view was that there were 'no grounds for any weakening of the sentences'.[22] In the end, he did not respond to Sholto's cipher directly, which made Sholto speculate that 'as a very sensible and conscientious man, he really agreed with my point of view in his heart'.[23]

When the Cabinet met on 7 October, its members were faced with two possible responses to Sholto's cipher, the first being Bevin's view that Sholto should receive instructions from the Prime Minister, and the second concurring with Sholto's view that the appeals were a matter of justice rather than politics, and that the Control Council should be free to make its own decisions. The brief for the meeting stated that Article Twenty-Nine seemed 'to show that the Co-ordinating Committee [that drafted the Charter] regarded the matter primarily as one of justice and not one of policy as advocated by the Foreign Office'.[24]

Nevertheless, the meeting decided on the Foreign Office option and it was left to John Hynd to communicate to Sholto what turned out to be the government's view:

> Ministers have considered your telegram No. CCG 45949. They think there is some misapprehension as to your exact position in this matter. They do not regard you as being in the position of a Commander-in-Chief reviewing a court martial sentence, or in that of a Colonial Governor or of the Home Secretary.
>
> The consideration of the reduction or mitigation of sentences was referred to the Control Council as being the organ representing the Four Powers. It was not referred to the personal consideration of those four persons who from time to time might be on it, nor in the view of His Majesty's Government would it be right or fair to place such a heavy responsibility upon any individual.
>
> His Majesty's Government have not seen the petitions for clemency but, on the face of it, their view is that from a political point of view it would be an advantage if there were no alterations of the sentences. If, however, you find that convincing arguments for an alteration are put forward on the Control Council, or that there is a disposition among your colleagues there to make alterations, you should refer back to us so that you may take our instructions.[25]

When Sholto read that signal, he had to stop himself dead in his tracks and ask himself if his official title was not 'Military Governor and Commander-in-Chief'. He felt outraged at the way in which these orders were being given to him. Those in London had not even seen the petitions for clemency, and yet they were already making up their minds, on political grounds, as to the course he should take. One of the major issues Sholto and his colleagues on the Control Council were having to consider in the appeals for clemency was that of the orders given to the German military leaders by the political heads of the Nazi state. He later recalled: 'What part must conscience play in the obeying of such orders? I believed that it must play a vitally important part. Now I was being told that my beliefs and feelings in the matter, my conscience, did not count: I was to accept orders.'[26]

In the end, twenty-one men were tried as major war criminals. Adolf Hitler, Joseph Goebbels, Heinrich Himmler and Robert Ley had all committed suicide, and Martin Bormann had disappeared. Myths about him abounded, but in 1972 his remains were found in West Berlin, confirmed in 1998 by DNA analysis. Of the Nazi leaders arraigned before the military tribunal, three were found not guilty of the charges against them and acquitted. These were Hjalmar Schacht, president of the Reichsbank and Economics Minister under Hitler; Franz von Papen, who had served as Vice-Chancellor under Hitler and then as German Ambassador first to Austria and then to Turkey; and Hans Fritzsche, a broadcaster who worked in the Nazi Propaganda Ministry under Goebbels. Of the remaining eighteen who had been found guilty of one or more of the crimes alleged, three 'seemed to realise that the game was up',[27] as Sholto put it. Ernst Kaltenbrunner, chief of the Reich Main Security Office and the highest-ranking SS official to be tried at Nuremberg, was condemned to death; Baldur von Schirach, leader of the Hitler Youth and Governor of Vienna, and Albert Speer, Nazi Minister of Armaments and War Production, were each sentenced to twenty years' imprisonment. They did not appeal against their sentences.

That left the Control Council with fifteen pleas for clemency. There was enormous ingenuity in the way the defence counsels presented their petitions on behalf of their clients, ranging from attempts to undermine the judgments, to accusations of violation of the Geneva Conventions, to assertions of misunderstanding of the German language, to pleas of the defendant's colourless personality and incompetence, and to the assumption that it would *please* the Control Council to mitigate a sentence, although the latter may simply have been German lawyers' attempts to make a favourable impression by using Anglo-American court phrases. Sholto's outrage at the brazen impudence of some of the arguments presented in these documents is shown by his angry scrawls in red pencil across the pages, as well as more restrained comments in blue biro. He wrote that 'at one time the names of these men whose appeals we had on our hands were known with terrifying familiarity throughout the world'. When *Years of Command* was published, twenty years had elapsed since their trial, and Sholto felt that perhaps the memory of them and the impact of their appalling crimes were blunted in the public mind, but he wrote that 'their names should never be forgotten, and history itself amply records the extraordinary evil that existed in all of them'.[28]

A personal history of Hermann Goering compiled by the Research Department of the Foreign Office asserted:

> Next to Hitler, Goering was probably the most important man in the Nazi organisation, holding more high offices than any other of his colleagues. Goering was one of the earliest and firmest advocates of the methods of violence which the German police and SS formations later perfected, not only in Germany, but also in all the Allied countries which Germany occupied.[29]

He developed the Gestapo and created the first concentration camps. He was also responsible for the deliberate starvation of civilians in the occupied territories. As the supreme head of the Luftwaffe, he demanded from Himmler slave labourers from concentration camps for his underground aircraft factories. He also appeared to sanction the use of rape as a weapon of war, writing in an order to his senior Luftwaffe officers in 1942: 'The circumstances prevailing in war – especially in the East! – demand a different attitude to many questions, particularly in sexual matters, than would be expected in the well-regulated conditions of peacetime.'[30] The final judgment on him stated: 'His guilt is unique in its enormity. The record discloses no excuses for this man.' Indicted on all four counts, he was sentenced to death by hanging aged fifty-three.

Goering instructed his defence counsel, Dr Otto Stahmer, to refrain from submitting a plea for amendment or mitigation of his sentence but, nevertheless, Stahmer felt compelled to present a lengthy petition. He thought that the Control Council 'may be pleased to amend the death penalty proclaimed in the judgment to one of imprisonment', but if it could not bring itself to do so, it might be pleased to alter the mode of execution from hanging to shooting. Stahmer then cited Goering's WWI war record as a brave and chivalrous officer (perhaps even wishing to appeal to Sholto's sensibilities as a former RFC pilot). Stahmer argued that even though Goering had initiated the economic measures against the Jews on Hitler's orders, he had no connection with the carrying out of their biological extermination. Stahmer asserted that it had not been proved that Goering knew of the genocide of the Jews carried out by Himmler. He was at great pains to exonerate Goering from any involvement in the 'Final Solution', saying that Goering had not used those words to mean the destruction of the Jews but only their expulsion from the Third Reich. He claimed that it was Himmler and his circle in 1942 who gave the words their most sinister meaning. The Control Council notified Stahmer that his plea on Goering's behalf was rejected.[31]

Indicted on Counts One and Two, Rudolf Hess joined the Nazi Party in 1920 and became Hitler's closest personal confidant and Deputy Führer until his mysterious flight to the UK in 1941. He was an active supporter of preparations for war and supported Hitler's policy of vigorous rearmament. 'He told the people that they must make sacrifices for armaments, repeating the phrase, "Guns instead of butter."'[32] At the time of Nuremberg, he was a man 'apparently broken in health and in mind'. Sholto's handwritten note on Hess's history read: 'Suggest further mental examination.' Aged fifty-two, he was sentenced to life imprisonment in Spandau Prison.

Hess's defence counsel, Dr Alfred Seidl, presented a lengthy plea for clemency, majoring on the fact that Hess had been indicted only on Counts One and Two and trying to pick holes in the judgment against him, casting doubt on the Kellogg–Briand Pact as a basis for the charge of planning and waging aggressive war. He stated that although war became a violation of international law for the signatories to that agreement, 'it is impossible to conclude from that that the violation of that Treaty would make it a <u>punishable</u> crime. The violation of the Treaty neither makes the <u>State</u> nor <u>the head of the State or other organs of the State punishable</u>.' Seidl moved on to Germany's stance on Poland, in which Hess had played a major part as Deputy Führer, saying that Germany had negotiated with Poland to try to avoid a conflict. However, German demands would actually involve Poland losing maritime access via the Polish Corridor as she ceded territory to Germany and lost the Free City of Danzig, in Nazi Germany's move to connect her territory of East Prussia to the rest of Germany. Seidl thought that this had been quite reasonable, writing: 'It is impossible to deny that the proposal made by Germany was very restrained and contained nothing incompatible with Polish honour or the vital interests of that State.' Seidl continued at great length, using the appeal as an opportunity to air his views, which were unquestionably Nazi. This infuriated Sholto, who scrawled 'Rot!' in red pencil next to Seidl's most outrageous passages and wrote of him: 'An unrepentant Nazi. I can scarcely contain my indignation. Denazify the chap! Irrelevant and dismissive. Political diatribe. Tried to alter finding – not really a plea for clemency.' Further on in the statement, Sholto scribbled: 'This chap should be arrested!'[33]

Joachim von Ribbentrop was Hitler's Foreign Minister from 1938 onwards, an avid agent of Nazi expansionist foreign policy, and was indicted on all four counts. He had been the German Ambassador to the UK from 1936 to 1938, during which time he suggested that the only way Germany could bring about a change in the East was by force. He suggested methods to prevent England and France from intervening in a European war fought to bring about such a change and was one of the two major signatories to the German-Soviet non-aggression pact in August 1939, broken by the Nazi invasion of the Soviet Union in 1941. He was sentenced to death by hanging aged fifty-three.

Von Ribbentrop's defence counsel, Dr Martin Horn, submitted a short plea, accusing the IMT of making statements that were untrue or incomplete and asserting that this warranted a commutation of the sentence. In the statement, which was written in the first person, von Ribbentrop himself denied that he had ever urged a war in Eastern Europe, saying that he spoke of the possibility of a conflict, but that conflict does not necessarily mean war. Sholto dismissed this as 'hair-splitting' in the customary red pencil.[34] He passed no comment on a letter to the IMT from Anneliese von Ribbentrop, who sought to defend her husband's complicity in crimes against peace, war crimes and crimes against humanity by noting:

> I have lived with my husband for twenty-five happy years and am perhaps in the best position to pass judgment on him now when his life is at stake. He is a most decent and most capable man, who was always full of love and solicitude not only for his family but also for Germany.[35]

Chief of the Armed Forces High Command (Oberkommando der Wehrmacht) during World War II, Wilhelm Keitel was indicted on all four counts. Directly responsible to Hitler, Keitel signed a number of criminal orders and directives that led to appalling atrocities. Aged sixty-four, he was sentenced to death by hanging.

In a letter defending himself, Keitel requested that, as a soldier, he should be shot instead of hanged. Sholto was particularly exercised over this. He was in no doubt about the death sentence but wrote in blue biro:

> Only question to be decided is whether to shoot or hang ... Possibly if 'Crimes against Peace' only guilty of, one might accept that as a soldier he was planning strategy under Hitler's orders. But from section 'War Crimes & Crimes against humanity' it is clear that Keitel issued orders not only illegal but of murderous brutality. In view of this I consider he has forfeited any right to be treated as an honourable soldier.[36]

Alfred Rosenberg was the principal ideologue of the Nazi Party, although Sholto described him as a 'muddle-headed thinker'. He was appointed head of the Office of Foreign Affairs, 'whose agents were active in Nazi intrigue in all parts of the world'. Subsequently, as head of the Reich Ministry for the Occupied Eastern Territories, he was responsible for much of the brutality and terror there. He was indicted on all four counts and sentenced to death by hanging aged fifty-three.

It turned out that Rosenberg's defence counsel, Dr Alfred Thoma, shared Sholto's view of his client, describing Rosenberg as 'one of the most colorless personalities among the defendants'. Thoma characterised him as lacking in ideas, passive and weak-willed, but nevertheless brutal and amoral. He even said that Rosenberg wanted good but lacked penetration and vision, and that he consistently advocated the autonomy of the peoples of Eastern Europe, whom he had treated with such savagery. Perhaps Thoma's most outrageous assertion was that Rosenberg recommended the 'quartering of Jews in Ghettos' in order to protect them.[37]

Hans Frank was indicted under Counts One, Three and Four, but the evidence submitted to the IMT did not convince them that he was sufficiently connected with the common plan to wage aggressive war, so he was not convicted on Count One. His personal history, compiled in June 1945 by the Research Department of the Foreign Office, stated: 'The evidence of responsibility for specific war crimes is perhaps clearer in Frank's case than in that of any other Nazi leader at present in Allied hands.'[38] Hitler's personal legal adviser, from 1939 onwards he was also Governor-General of occupied Poland, where he instituted a systematic reign of terror and was directly involved in the mass murder of Jews, setting up concentration camps. He described his policy there thus: 'Poland shall be treated like a colony; the Poles will become the slaves of the Greater German World Empire.'[39] Aged forty-six, he was sentenced to death by hanging.

Hans Frank's defence counsel was Seidl, who also defended Hess. Seidl submitted his plea against the wishes of his client but at the request of Frank's family. Seidl was well aware of the arguments concerning the political versus judicial functions of the Control Council and wrote that the final rulings regarding the executions involved not only a legal judgment but also a political decision, even saying that the Control Council for Germany was exercising the functions of the former German Reich government. But despite Seidl's clever arguments, which Sholto's blue biro noted even involved veiled threats, Sholto was of the opinion that Frank's crimes in Poland were 'more than sufficient to justify sentence'.[40]

Indicted under all four counts, but convicted on the last three, Walther Funk was a German economist who succeeded Schacht as Reich Minister for Economic Affairs, a post he held from 1938 to 1945. He worked with Himmler and was involved in the exploitation of forced slave labour. Aged fifty-six, he was sentenced to life in prison.

Funk's defence counsel, Dr Fritz Sauter, requested a commutation of sentence from life imprisonment to one of ten years 'as an <u>act of mercy</u>', writing that his client 'only participated in the preparations for war during the very last months before the outbreak of the Second World War'. No mention was made of his part in the forced slave labour programme, and Dr Sauter tried to assert Funk's humanity. Sholto's comment was: 'He assisted materially in preparation for aggressive war. The claims made regarding his humanity in the plea are unconvincing.'[41]

Karl Doenitz, Grand Admiral and Commander-in-Chief of the Kriegsmarine, was indicted on Counts One, Two and Three. Doenitz was defended in court by a very able naval judge, Captain Otto Kranzbühler, who argued that Doenitz had not been present at the important war planning conferences because he had been engaged on tactical duties and was therefore not guilty of Count One. The tribunal agreed and acquitted him on this count, but he was convicted of crimes against peace and war crimes, including 'ruthless submarine warfare'. He ordered the sinking of neutral ships without warning, and the prosecution asserted that he ordered the killing of survivors of shipwrecked vessels, whether enemy or neutral. However, the tribunal concluded that the evidence did not establish with the certainty required that Doenitz deliberately made those orders. On 1 May 1945, following Hitler's suicide, he succeeded him briefly as the German head of state. He received a sentence of ten years in prison. Sholto's comment was: 'I think the Tribunal took a very lenient view of Doenitz' conduct of the U/Boat campaign',[42] of which of course, as C-in-C Coastal Command, Sholto had had personal experience.

In his plea for clemency, Kranzbühler argued that Doenitz's offences should be seen in the context of 'a war that was fought for five years with increasing severity and in the course of which serious offences were committed by both sides'. He claimed that the IMT had not followed the Geneva Convention, which gives every officer prisoner of war the right to be judged by a military court composed in accordance with the laws of the country from which he was taken prisoner, in this case Germany. He appealed to the Control Council 'as the military organ of the Allies' and that it was competent to set right the injustice which had resulted from this contravention. Finally, he drew attention to the fact that when Doenitz was arrested, he was the recognised head of the German state, so his sentence and punishment violated 'the principles concerning the immunity of heads of states, which have been acknowledged for centuries'. This assertion was in direct contravention to Article Seven of the Charter. As Sholto put it: 'Hitler would get away with it on this contention.'[43]

Another Grand Admiral and Commander-in-Chief of the Kriegsmarine until 1943 when he was replaced by Doenitz, Erich Raeder was also indicted on Counts One, Two and Three. Found guilty of the planning and waging of aggressive war, he was sentenced to life imprisonment aged seventy. Emphasis was laid on the way in which he 'carried out unrestricted submarine warfare'.[44] Unusually, Raeder submitted his own defence, asking for his life imprisonment to be commuted to death by shooting, 'by way of mercy ... and it would in the long run be a relief for my family'. After stating that in his opinion the judgment against him contained errors, he wrote:

Article 29 of the Charter does not oppose the fulfillment of my application, if I expressly state that I consider this commutation of the sentence an act of mercy and not an aggravation of the judgment in the sense of the Charter. I emphasise that on making this plea for mercy I am in full possession of my mental and spiritual faculties.[45]

Raeder's plea was rejected by the Control Council in a formal letter and he served nine years before his release in 1955, dying in 1960.

Fritz Sauckel was indicted on all four counts but convicted on Counts Three and Four. Head of the Nazi Party in Thuringia, he was responsible for the vast forced slave labour programme instigated by the Nazis, described in the Nuremberg judgment as involving 'deportation for slave labour of more than five million human beings, many of them under terrible conditions of cruelty and suffering'.[46] He was sentenced to death by hanging aged forty-eight.

Sauckel's defence counsel, Dr Robert Servatius, submitted a lengthy plea on behalf of his client. He requested that Sauckel's death sentence be commuted to a term of imprisonment and accused the IMT of misinterpreting 'certain vital facts which are of the greatest importance in the judging of Sauckel's guilt'. The most chilling of these concerned a statement made by Sauckel in a document of 1942 detailing the slave labour programme, in which Sauckel said: 'All the men must be fed, sheltered and treated in such a way as to exploit them to the highest possible extent at the lowest conceivable degree of expenditure.' Servatius argued that this was a mistranslation, and that Sauckel was only talking about economy of *numbers* of workers, but in view of what actually happened, what was meant is very clear. Servatius asserted that Sauckel was not aware of the maltreatment of slave labourers and, emphasising his supposed humanity, he quoted Sauckel's own words: 'It must be remembered, though, that even the effort of a machine is conditioned by the amount of fuel, skill and care given to it. How many more conditions must be considered in the case of men, even of low kind and race, than in the case of a machine.'[47] Sholto's opinion was: 'Nothing here in mitigation. Stretching my credulity too far to expect me to believe that he didn't know. If he didn't know, he should have known. I believe he did.'

Alfred Jodl, a general who served as the Chief of the Operations Staff of the Armed Forces High Command throughout World War II, was indicted on all four counts. He worked under Keitel but reported directly to Hitler on operational matters. Sholto described him as 'completely subservient to Hitler'. Jodl defended himself on the ground that 'he was a soldier sworn to obedience and not a politician

... He said that when he signed or initiated orders, memoranda and letters, he did so for Hitler and often in the absence of Keitel.' But in October 1941, 'Jodl signed an order that Hitler would not accept an offer of the surrender of Leningrad or Moscow, but on the contrary he insisted that they be completely destroyed ... No surrender was ever offered.'[48] He was sentenced to death by hanging aged fifty-six.

As part of the appeal against his sentence, his wife, Luise Jodl, wrote to the Control Council, beginning her letter with: 'You are all soldiers!' and ending with: 'To execute as a criminal a general staff officer who did nothing but fulfil the duties assigned to him will be felt to be unjust by all soldiers in the world.'[49] Luise Jodl also appealed to Monty as her husband's counterpart in the British Army, stating: 'It is the first time in history that a Chief of General Staff is treated as a common criminal for planning strategic operations.' At first, Sholto thought that this might be a possible case for commutation, but in the end, the only issue for him was whether Jodl would be shot, as was his wish, or hanged.

Artur Seyss-Inquart, an Austrian Nazi politician who was appointed Reichskommissar of the Netherlands, was indicted on all four counts. He imposed the Nazi rules that meant that hundreds of thousands of Dutch civilians were subjected to forced labour and over 100,000 Dutch Jews were deported to German concentration camps. He was sentenced to death by hanging aged fifty-four.

Dr Gustav Steinbauer, Seyss-Inquart's defence counsel, tried to appeal to the vanity of members of the Control Council, asserting that although the members of the IMT were 'such good judges', the essential task of a judge was 'only to examine whether and to what extent the law has been violated'. Addressing Sholto and his fellow Military Governors directly, he said:

> Your task, gentlemen, goes beyond that. You are to examine whether mercy is to take precedence over justice ... Through the collapse of the Greater German Reich the sovereignty and with it the right of mercy has been transferred to you. May you exercise this office of yours, to preserve or to destroy human life by your decision, without fear of public opinion, in a truly kingly spirit.

It was 'a clever defence', as Sholto wrote, but he continued: 'The fact is that [Seyss-Inquart] was Chancellor of Austria, Deputy C[onsul]-General of Poland and Reichs Cons. for Netherlands. While he held these posts, horrible crimes were committed in the territories under his jurisdiction. He tried to deny his responsibilities.'[50]

Recognised as chief Nazi administrator and bureaucrat, Wilhelm Frick was indicted on all four counts but found guilty on Counts Two, Three and Four. He was appointed Hitler's first Minister of the Interior in 1933 but was replaced by Himmler in 1943. His next post was as Reich Protector of Bohemia and Moravia. Described by the tribunal as 'an avid Nazi', he signed the documents that led to the mass murder of Jews.[51] He was sentenced to death by hanging aged sixty-nine.

Frick's plea for clemency was submitted by his defence counsel, Dr Otto Pannenbacker, who characterised his client as someone who exercised influence over Hitler only in the early years of his government, between 1933 and 1935, and who was against the methods of violence and terror exercised in the later period. Pannenbacker attempted to exonerate Frick by asserting that Hitler issued orders, especially for the 'liquidation' of those in lunatic asylums, behind Frick's back, and that he was only a figurehead. Nevertheless, Sholto concurred with the IMT that Frick was 'rabidly antisemitic',[52] and the Control Council rejected Pannenbacker's plea.

Julius Streicher was indicted on Counts One and Four, but once again, there was insufficient evidence to charge him with the crime of planning aggressive war. However, a summary for the Control Council stated: 'His persecution of the Jews was notorious.' He was the founder and publisher of the virulently antisemitic newspaper *Der Stürmer*, which became central to the Nazi propaganda machine. 'In his speeches and articles week after week, month after month, he infected the German mind with the virus of anti-Semitism.'[53] In the indictment, he was quoted as saying: 'The sun will not shine on the nations of the earth until the last Jew is dead.'[54] Sholto wrote that 'his general repulsiveness had led to his being ostracised even within the Nazi Party'. Aged sixty-one, he was sentenced to death by hanging, becoming the first person to be held accountable for incitement to genocide.

Dr Hanns Marx, Streicher's defence counsel, submitted his plea for clemency against Streicher's wishes. Dr Marx asked firstly whether the IMT was 'competent' to charge Streicher with crimes against humanity if he had been found not guilty on Count One and had not been charged on Counts Two and Three. Then he made the all-too-familiar assertion that Streicher's actions 'had no real determining influence on the order for the mass killing of Jews, issued exclusively by Hitler'. He went on to say that even if Streicher and *Der Stürmer* had not existed, Himmler and the Gestapo would still have executed Hitler's decree. Marx attempted to circumvent Streicher's part in stirring up violent antisemitic sentiments and stated that he never imagined any such measure as the mass murder of Jews, believing that 'a partial solution, even if on a large scale', was 'not expedient'.[55] Here again, the Control Council rejected Marx's plea for clemency.

Konstantin von Neurath, a German diplomat who served as Foreign Minister of Germany from 1932 to 1938, was indicted under all four counts. He was Reich Protector of Bohemia and Moravia from 1939 to 1943, where it was found that he knew that 'war crimes and crimes against humanity were being committed under his authority'.[56] Aged seventy-three, he was sentenced to fifteen years' imprisonment.

Once again, von Neurath's defence counsel, Dr Otto Freiherr von Luedinghausen, considered it his duty to present a plea for clemency in the absence of his client's request to do so. He cited von Neurath's 'advanced age', 'his poor health – serious heart trouble' and the fact that he had been in custody for approximately sixteen months as reasons to either annul or postpone execution of the sentence. Luedinghausen made the familiar appeal for mercy, saying that von Neurath was not the 'perpetrator' of the crimes with which he was charged, but only the official representative of the regime, and that the inhumane actions committed under his administration were executed without his approval or cooperation.[57] Sholto wondered whether von Neurath's sentence was too heavy and suggested that it be reduced to ten years, but this was rejected by the other members of the Control Council.

Before meeting his fellow Military Governors in Berlin to discuss the appeals for clemency, Sholto received a letter in poorly written English from three retired officers of the Wehrmacht, expressing their outrage at the sentences. Employing the usual arguments against the trials of 'victors' justice' and 'ex post facto law', they wrote:

> Victorious powers condemned in own interest actions which were not punishable at time they were committed both are against valid international law. Utterances in press and radio not opinion of German people referendum would prove therefore we appeal to you as soldier prevent implementation of Nuremberg verdict so that decent Germans and Britons may unite to save the occident. Give German people opportunity to state their views in referendum. This would be beginning of true democracy.

Sholto's opinion, this time scribbled in blue pencil at the bottom of the letter, was expressed candidly: 'Rot – these people will never understand!'[58]

The Allied Control Council sat on 9 and 10 October. Twenty years later, when Sholto was writing *Years of Command*, he could still feel his perplexity over the manner in which the other delegates conducted themselves. It was the turn of the French to take the chair, and General Koenig was in charge. After introducing the name of the defendant whose appeal was under consideration, Koenig turned to Sholto, who had to 'start the ball rolling'. In each case, Sholto offered his opinion and the reasons for his decision. When Koenig asked McNarney and Sokolovsky for their views, they merely agreed, and Koenig agreed in turn. Then they passed on to the next appeal.

It continued like this for some time, and Sholto realised that he was doing all the talking, with nothing more than a formal assent from the others, so after a while he asked Koenig whether he could reverse the order for a change. Sokolovsky and McNarney merely announced their decisions, leaving Sholto to give his comprehensive findings and opinions with the reasons for them. He was the only one who did so in such detail. After two days, the council rejected all the appeals and confirmed all the sentences.

The only point of disagreement arose over the sentence on Jodl. He had been condemned to be hanged, but Sholto wrote that Koenig and McNarney thought that he should be given the privilege of being shot. Marshal Sokolovsky spoke strongly against this and said that he deserved to be hung just as much as the other criminals, and that just because he wore a uniform that was no reason why he should be exempt from the penalty as delivered by the judges at Nuremberg. For my part I voted with Marshal Sokolovsky. My reason for doing so may be thought to be illogical in view of what I have said before, and an element of personal revenge might be said to come into it. But during the war I had been horrified when fifty Air Force Officers, several of them among my friends and acquaintances were, on Hitler's orders, shot for attempting to escape [from Stalag Luft III]. This indeed was an illegal and brutal act since it has always been recognised that prisoners had the right to try and escape. I looked up the evidence in Jodl's case to see in what way he was involved. The evidence as I remember it was that Jodl, who was deputed to sign the order for execution by Hitler, protested to Hitler that the order was illegal. Hitler had told him to jolly well sign the order or else! and Jodl had duly signed. To me, when he signed that order he signed his death warrant. In that he knowingly signed an order which he knew was illegal, simply because he was told to do it by his chief. I do not believe that a man of real conscience and courage would have signed that order, in fact I remember making an impassioned speech aimed at the American Commander-in-Chief, in which I asked him if he believed that if President Roosevelt had suddenly gone mad and told General Eisenhower to shoot fifty German prisoners of war, General Eisenhower would have obeyed the order. He would, of course, rather have resigned, even if his life was involved, rather than sign such an order against his conscience.[59]

Sholto also examined carefully the parts played by Keitel and Goering in the Stalag Luft III murders. Both Keitel's defence of obeying superior orders and Goering's claim that, since he was on leave at the time, he did not know about the executions were demolished comprehensively by Sir David Maxwell Fyfe. He asserted that since the shootings were still going on when Goering had returned from leave, and Goering's deputy knew all about them, it was impossible that he could have been ignorant of them.

Sholto wrote that it was unlikely that he would ever forget the moment when he came to give his views on the appeal lodged in Goering's name. Like Jodl, Goering had petitioned that he might 'be spared the ignominy of hanging and be allowed to die as a soldier before a firing squad'.[60] When Sholto came to the end of his summary and stated that he was rejecting that particular appeal, he felt that he was saying the last word in what had been an intensely personal journey that could not be understood by the other delegates. Sholto remembered all too well the time when, twenty-eight years before as young fighter pilots on the Western Front, he and Goering had fought each other 'in the cleaner atmosphere of the air'. In the Control Council meeting, when Sholto spoke the words that meant for Goering an irrevocable death sentence, he could not help feeling 'for all my loathing of what he had become, the strongest revulsion that I should have to be one of those so directly concerned with it'.[61]

At the end of the second day of the meetings in Berlin, the members of the Control Council considered the way in which the bodies should be cremated after the hangings and the disposal of the ashes. Sholto said he found that the whole 'nauseating discussion' affected his nerves in the most unpleasant way: 'I have seldom, if ever, known a feeling of such distaste as that which I experienced when I found myself having to participate in this last macabre discussion.'[62] It was not only Sholto who found the hangings difficult to bear. Rebecca West observed:

> Though it might be right to hang these men, it was not easy. A sadness fell on the lawyers engaged in the trial. They had all been waiting for this day when judgment would be delivered and the defendants sentenced. They had all surely come to loathe the Nazi crimes and criminals more and more in the slow unfolding of the case. But now this day of judgment had come, they were not happy. There was a gloom about the places where they lived, a gloom about their families.

The trial itself had lasted nearly eleven months and as West reasoned: 'If a trial for murder last too long, more than the murder will out. The man in the murderer will out; it becomes horrible to think of destroying him.'[63]

The executions took place in the prison at Nuremberg early in the morning of 16 October. At approximately 10.45 on the evening before he was due to be hanged, Hermann Goering took his own life by swallowing poison. Sholto admitted: 'When the news was brought to me that he had managed to dodge the hangman, I must admit that I felt a slight relief.'[64]

The Quadripartite Commission for the Detention of Major War Criminals, which was separate from the Control Council and consisted of four officers of slightly lower rank, had determined that the bodies of the executed be removed during the hours of darkness to be cremated, and the ashes then taken under the custody of its members to Nuremberg Airport. Initially, it was proposed to scatter the ashes from an aircraft departing from that airport, but the commission then decided that the bodies would be transported by lorry to Munich, where they would be cremated and the ashes scattered out of one or more aircraft departing from there. Eventually, in order to ensure absolute secrecy, it was agreed that the ashes would be scattered personally by the four members of the commission at an undisclosed location.

A week after the executions, Sholto had one further grim task to perform as a member of the Allied Control Council, and that was to decide finally whether photographs of the executed men should be published. Sholto was definitely opposed to their issue to the press, even though General McNarney and General Koenig thought their release had already been sanctioned unanimously by the Control Council in a previous meeting. Marshal Sokolovsky stated that whatever procedure adopted was immaterial to him. In the end, it was decided to release one photograph of each of the executed men, but Sholto wished to record that he dissented from this and that the photographs would not be issued by him to the British press. Approved photographs were sent to the US, French and Soviet press on 23 October.

Despite its imperfections, the final judgment at Nuremberg was a landmark in international law. With specific reference to the German Bundeswehr (Federal Armed Forces), one of its former officers, Jürgen Rose, has written that ever since Nuremberg,

> service members can no longer appeal to a superior political or military authority in order to avoid responsibility for obeying illegal orders. In accordance with Kant's philosophy of law and morality, the reason for this is the recognition that the conscience of each person sets the standard for any human action. For the service member this means that superior orders alone are insufficient to legitimise any military action. By obeying an order soldiers voluntarily transform the extrinsic will of another person into their own intrinsic determination, and before actualising their own intention through their action soldiers have to scrutinise its legitimacy in relation to their conscience.[65]

In summing up, Shawcross wrote: 'While not excusing the imperfections and deficiencies of the trial, I still feel that it has laid down the law for the future, even if that law is imperfectly applied and still often disregarded.'[66]

Sholto wrote that he was 'only too glad to be finished with the whole sordid business'.[67] This was very much his attitude to the entire matter of Nuremberg, but did it serve him well? Not in the end. The German militarist Carl von Clausewitz warned: 'It is to no purpose, it is even against one's better interest, to turn away from the consideration of the affair because the horror of its elements excites repugnance.'[68] Sholto pushed the anguish generated by these events to the back of his mind until he could no longer suppress it, and of course there was no one who could help him deal with the weight of what he was carrying.

CHAPTER TWENTY-FOUR

'A DIFFERENT KETTLE OF
FISH ALTOGETHER'

The IMT at Nuremberg was not the end for Sholto of having to exercise a quasi-judicial function that meant power over life or death. He wrote that this matter

> was by far the most distressing part of my work while I was in Germany and it rested in the many death sentences with which I had to deal. As Governor I was called upon to make the final decisions about all the death sentences which were passed by the courts in our Zone, either confirming or commuting them as I saw fit; and there is in my memory a deep scar from that odious experience of having to deal with hundreds of these cases.[1]

In addition to the charges against them as individuals, the major Nazi war criminals had also been indicted as members of the groups or organisations the prosecutors at the IMT asserted should be declared criminal. The names of some of these organisations are very familiar, exciting revulsion and fear even today: the Leadership Corps of the Nazi Party, the Gestapo (Secret State Police), SS (*Schutzstaffel*: Protection Squadron) and SD (*Sicherheitsdienst*: Security Service), all of which in the judgment of the tribunal were deemed criminal above a certain level of seniority. It was clear that thousands of German men and women who had been members of these organisations would have to be brought to trial in Germany. Shawcross wrote that at the end of the war, a list had been compiled of around 10,000 'so-called minor war criminals' within the British Zone – 'minor only in the sense that they were not themselves members of the ruling hierarchy, heinous as some of their crimes were'. He continued:

> I had urged strongly that we should bring at least 500 to trial in our military courts by 1946. We did not succeed in approaching that figure. The military, whose task it was, were not keen on organising such trials; they were dilatory in the extreme ... A conspicuously weak War Secretary failed to get anything done. The trials became counter-productive; sometimes derisory sentences were imposed and public opinion turned against their continuance ... In the end Parliament agreed without a single dissentient, Winston Churchill strongly supporting, that the trials should cease as from the end of 1947. All this is history and cannot be rewritten. But it must be admitted that in all zones of occupation, many thousands were left free who had committed often odious crimes which cried out for punishment.[2]

In December 1946, some 27,000 of these individuals were reported to be held in custody in the British Zone. However, as Shawcross had observed, the will and energy within the military government, and back in the UK, for these prosecutions was waning. In a letter to the four regional commissioners within the British Zone that month, Robertson wrote:

> As you are no doubt aware, public opinion in England is tend-ing more and more towards a speedy conclusion of such trials and therefore protracted proceedings extending over a period of years would not be tolerated. Similarly, German opinion is insistent on the immediate disposal of this most difficult matter. These trials have, in many respects, a far greater and more intimate significance for the average German in the British Zone than the more remote trial of a few important Nazis at Nuremberg. The Commander-in-Chief has therefore ordered that the trial of those at present in custody shall be completed by the end of 1947.[3]

It is easy to see how Sholto, exhausted by nearly eight years of war and its aftermath, longed for an end to the trials, especially since, if the death sentence was imposed, he would be the one signing the death warrants.

Despite the obvious need for the reconstruction of Germany, still uppermost in many people's minds was the imperative that those who had committed war crimes and crimes against humanity under the Nazi regime should be brought to justice. An article in the *British Zone Review* clarified the difference between these two crimes: 'To succeed in a prosecution of a war criminal it is necessary to show that the victims are members of an Allied country; in the case of crimes against humanity the nationality of the victims is irrelevant.'[4] This distinction meant that the law afforded German victims of Nazi oppression the opportunity of seeking justice, and that this was not confined to the period of the war but could be applied to crimes committed from 30 January 1933, when Hitler came to power.

In February 1947, Sholto wrote to his regional commissioners that judges in the Courts of First Instance (courts in which legal proceedings are begun or first heard) would be assisted in their task of trying former members of prohibited organisations by lay people whose selection would be the responsibility of the Land (regional) governments. He suggested that trade unions should be consulted in the selection of these lay persons. He ended his letter with an emotive plea:

> Will you also please stress the fact that German participation in these trials must be regarded as a question of duty and that it is only by purging this evil inheritance of the past that it will be possible for us fully to concentrate our energies on reconstruction for the future.[5]

It was not only the 'so-called minor war criminals' who could be sentenced to death. In the turbulent chaos that was the British Zone, the range of those tried for crimes that led to death sentences, in Sholto's words,

> ran all the way from more of the war criminals condemned to death

to unfortunate Displaced Persons – among whom there were many Poles who had found ways of disposing of their hated German oppressors – to a Briton in the forces who had committed a murder such as strangling his German girl friend. Up to that time I had not given a great deal of thought to the problems of capital punishment, although I did have a definite antipathy towards it; but my personal experiences during my time in Germany changed that antipathy into a strong conviction that the death penalty should be abolished.[6]

Sholto's US counterpart from 1947, Lucius Clay, held similar views, writing: 'My responsibility as reviewing officer (there was no court of appeal) and as clemency officer was great, and there was no other which weighed more heavily on me.'[7]

Every few days, a pile of buff-coloured folders would land on Sholto's desk, in which were the particulars of cases tried in general military courts. Crimes that attracted the death penalty included unlawful possession of arms, unlawful use of arms (which may or may not have involved wounding or manslaughter), murder, violence towards Allied and other personnel, and offences against property including plunder, although in practice, the death penalty was only applied to habitual offenders in the latter case. The crime for which the greatest number of death sentences was handed out was that of unlawful possession of arms. This seems incredibly harsh, but the background to this policy was articulated clearly by F. S. V. Donnison in his comprehensive history of the beginning of the occupation, published in 1961:

> In the early months there was a tendency to inflict the death penalty for the unlawful carrying or concealment of firearms on disquietingly flimsy evidence or where the circumstances afforded little justification. The number of weapons in the country was so vast, the risk of their falling into the wrong hands so great, and the resultant danger so real, that this lapse from judicial objectivity can perhaps be understood, if it cannot be defended.[8]

Following the end of hostilities, the availability of hand-held weapons in the British Zone was fuelled by a thriving black market, which meant that almost anyone, including DPs, had easy access to them. The British feared armed insurrection in a society perilously close to lawlessness and so imposed the maximum penalty for possession of firearms.

In his notes for *Years of Command*, Sholto described the procedure for reviewing cases:

These cases used to appear on my desk at regular intervals. There was a thick wad of paper which was the verbatim evidence at the trial followed by the finding of the court. On top of this was a brief account of the case given by my Chief Justice ending with a certificate that, from a legal point of view, the sentence was correct. On top of that were piteous appeals from the man's (woman's) mother, father, husband, wife, Pastor and children; then on top of that was a buff form on which, if I scribbled my name at the bottom, the victim was hanged within a fairly brief space of time. It was all very distasteful and cold-blooded. Some of the sentences I did not mind returning e.g. the Wardens at Belsen or Buchenwald, and men who were responsible for gassing and burning thousands of Jews. But most of the cases were far more difficult to assess than that. For instance, some unfortunate German peasant who had been a Private in the Army had been told by his officer to take [an Allied] parachutist out with one or two of his comrades and shoot him. Probably a poor ignorant boy who would have been shot himself if he had not obeyed his officer's order. How was he to know that his officer's order was illegal in international law? I unhesitatingly commuted the sentence in a case like that to a term of imprisonment. Indeed I commuted the majority of cases that came before me. I am a reasonably humane man although I can be hard-hearted on occasions. It is one thing to kill a fellow human being in the heat of battle, but these cold-blooded judicial murders were a different kettle of fish altogether.

In fact, though he probably did not like to remember this, Sholto signed more death warrants than he commuted sentences, but there was a definite trend from the beginning to the end of his Military Governorship of increasing numbers of commutations as the months passed and no doubt the 'legalised slaughter', as he called it, became unbearable. Just the sort of pitiful appeal that would have distressed Sholto was submitted in a handwritten scrawl to a prison liaison officer by a Ukrainian, part of the Soviet Military Mission, sentenced to death. In it he wrote: 'I salute you, Comrade Officer, I, condemned to death appeal to you, Comrade Officer, that you would be good enough to visit me and help me, as I am here for four months and I beg you to assist me.' The prisoner signed his name, followed by 'Ukrainian (Small Russian)'.[9] As the historians Ralf-Markus Lehmann and Jürgen Balke sensitively observed of Sholto: 'The death penalty drove him into personal conflict.'[10]

The first time I saw Sholto's signature on a death warrant, dated 3 June 1946, I gasped, and then looked round the Reading Room of the National Archives to make sure that I had not disturbed anyone. It was such a shock. 'Sholto Douglas' in my father's fluid, rounded handwriting on the grim buff form that meant the end of someone's life. In the thirty seconds after seeing the signature, I experienced in a rush all the emotions my father must have felt: horror, revulsion, guilt, shame, and yes, even sympathy. It was overwhelming. So often in his old age, I had seen my father distressed over these sentences, and here they were. I read through the records of cases involving 109 individuals, seeing his signature on sixty-six death warrants, and these were not all of them. I found a further 115 names on lists for which I could not find reports. I was interested particularly in my father's signature, 'Sholto Douglas', not 'W. S. Douglas' as he usually signed himself, nor with any formal rank. Here was a human being, fully engaged with this process and not distancing himself from the distressing task at hand. Whatever they had done, these people were fellow human beings, and they deserved the full consideration of another sentient person, not a figurehead. By comparison, Monty's signature on a death warrant he had signed while Military Governor was written in his childlike hand, almost printed: 'Montgomery of Alamein'. Here was a man who concealed himself behind his position.

And so to those individuals. The vast majority of those sentenced to death were DPs of Polish or in some cases Yugoslav or Romanian origin. Although housed in camps, they marauded around the British Zone, holding up mostly Germans in isolated farms in the north of the zone, in the streets of towns and cities, and by entering urban houses and apartments during nocturnal raids to threaten occupants with a firearm, which they did not hesitate to use. There were also cases where British service personnel were murdered by DPs who were attempting to evade arrest. These were people who had been dragged from what were often impoverished homes in Poland or the Balkans, forced into Nazi Germany and degraded and brutalised to an extent that many of us now would find hard to understand. Some of them were former inmates of concentration camps such as Buchenwald.

One case concerned a raid on a farmhouse in which twenty Polish DPs were involved, most of whom carried firearms. They stayed there for three to four hours and stole clothing, jewellery, wine and food. The women occupants of the house were all raped and a man was beaten. In another raid on a farmhouse three days later, the same gang shot and killed one man, wounded his mother in the arm with a pistol and stabbed another man to death, while robbing the house. Although the defence counsel alleged that the evidence connecting the accused with the crimes revolved around identification, which was unreliable, the court reached the conclusion that it was sound and were impressed by the 'obvious reliability of the German female witnesses', who must have seen their attackers at close quarters. The three in the dock produced unsound alibis, and the manner in which their witnesses gave their evidence was 'light-hearted and almost absurd'. Brigadier Lindsay Merritt Inglis, the Controller-General of the Military Government Courts Branch, whom Sholto described as his 'Chief Justice', was a lawyer and magistrate from New Zealand with a distinguished military record in both world wars. He deemed that the sentences were 'proper' and could discover no mitigating circumstances, advising Sholto to confirm the sentences, which, after detailed study, he did.

Soon after this in May 1946, while reviewing the case of a German woman living alone in an isolated house in Schleswig-Holstein who was robbed and gang-raped while being threatened with a firearm by the accused and two accomplices, all Polish DPs, Inglis brought up the matter of their status as Allied nationals, a complicating factor. He wrote:

> Up to a few months ago Allied Nationals were executed for the unauthorised use of firearms only when such use resulted in the death of the person who was shot, that is to say only in cases which were tantamount to murder. The wanton and brutal use of arms, especially by Poles in the course of nocturnal gang robberies of isolated farms, became so frequent that it was felt necessary, in the hope of discouraging actual shooting, to draw, so far as a series of sentences could do so, a clear distinction between those cases where weapons were used merely to threaten and the cases where there was reckless or deliberate shooting. Murders and shootings by Poles are still prevalent; and, in my opinion, it is necessary to continue to apply the policy I have outlined. The Permanent Presidents of General Courts report that capital sentences are feared by this class of criminal, whereas the longest term of imprisonment has little deterrent effect because the convicts hope either to be released for repatriation or, sooner or later, to escape.[11]

Despite this, Sholto commuted the sentence to one of twenty years' imprisonment, perhaps swayed by the petition on behalf of the accused that emphasised his youth (he was twenty-two) and his upbringing. In another case of a Polish DP who had been charged with robbery and unauthorised use of a firearm resulting in the death of a German woman, his plea that he did not intend to kill the woman but fired his pistol accidentally while being attacked by the woman's husband was accepted. Inglis ordered a retrial, emphasising that the accused was only eighteen years old, and in view of this, plus the fact that it could not be proved that he intended to kill the woman, his sentence was also commuted to one of imprisonment for twenty years. Sholto tended to commute sentences anyway for DPs if they had been charged only with plunder and receiving stolen goods, except where the crimes were habitual. When capital sentences were imposed on DPs who were nationals of the United Nations, such as

Poles, Yugoslavs and Ukrainians, they were executed by firing squads composed of members of the Allied Forces instead of by hanging or guillotine, which was the case for German recipients of the death penalty.

Not all Sholto's judgments displayed unalloyed humanitarianism. One case involved a German man accused of unlawful possession of two pistols and nearly 200 rounds of ammunition. He had threatened to shoot his wife with one of the pistols and was sentenced to death. Notwithstanding the judgment of the court, Inglis deemed that 'where there have been domestic disputes, uncorroborated evidence of the parties concerned, particularly the evidence of women, is unreliable: In this case the wife's evidence is entirely uncorroborated and has been flatly contradicted by the accused, who gave evidence on his own behalf.' This evidence was supported by nineteen testimonials of the accused's good character, many of which attacked the character and veracity of his wife. Inglis recommended that the conviction on the charge of threatening his wife should be quashed but asserted that the charge of possession of firearms and ammunition should be upheld, especially since the accused had failed to surrender these weapons despite two arms amnesties well-publicised by the Allies. However, Inglis wrote to Sholto that this was 'a proper case for the exercise of your prerogative of mercy', while maintaining that it was necessary for deterrent effect not to commute the sentence to anything less than twenty years' imprisonment. This was also the opinion of Robertson's stand-in, General Balfour, to whom Sholto wrote: 'I am rather sorry for this chap. His wife must be a bitch of the first water to have given him away as she did! Please tell the Controller-General [Inglis] that I think the sentence of imprisonment should be drastically reduced on review [after three years].'[12]

A crime that, in view of the history of the previous thirteen years of Nazi rule, attracted severe sentencing was membership of fascist organisations, of which two were *Edelweisspiraten* and *Freies Deutschland*. These groups were banned under a proclamation addressed by the Control Council to the people of Germany that prohibited prosecution or molestation 'by the German Authorities or by German nationals on grounds of race, colour, creed, language or political opinions'. Inglis wrote that the principal objectives of *Edelweisspiraten* that contravened this proclamation were:

(1) To rob and beat up DPs particularly Poles, and to make it impossible for them to live in Germany (2) to compile lists of and victimise German women who fraternise with Allied troops and DPs and (3) to combat the 'Black Market'. Their methods of carrying out the last mentioned object, however, appear rather to consist of blackmailing and assaulting black-marketeers in order to profit by the proceeds themselves.[13]

After consultation with the Intelligence Bureau and Public Safety Branch of the CCG, Inglis deemed that both *Edelweisspiraten* and *Freies Deutschland* represented a danger to security, there being definite indications of centralised organisation and direction with a subversive intent. Within *Freies Deutschland* there was also a secret cadre, the *Kampfgemeinschaft* (fighting community), whose intention was to further essentially Nazi ideas and undermine the military government by violent means while operating under the cloak of being a youth organisation. Recruits to *Edelweisspiraten*, which had originally set themselves up in opposition to the Hitler Youth, were drawn from discharged soldiers, sailors and SS men, and women auxiliaries of the services or Nazi organisations. Most of them were armed with knives, truncheons or knuckle-dusters, and some carried firearms. They sang anti-Allied songs and used secret symbols, one being '88'. Since 'H' is the eighth letter of the alphabet, it wasn't difficult to deduce that this meant 'Heil Hitler'. Death threats were made against anyone who gave away any information about the society to the Allies.

Many members were very young; in at least one case, a man of nineteen was sentenced to death. However, Inglis felt that since this youth was not an important member or a leader of any consequence, to confirm the capital sentence passed upon him would 'tend to glorify the institution in the eyes of hysterically inclined young Germans and to risk raising an unimportant youth to the status of a martyr'.[14] Sholto commuted the sentence to one of ten years' imprisonment. He did not do so for the founder of *Freies Deutschland*, a German policeman employed by the military government, who was sentenced to death because of his fundamental role in building an organisation bent on violence and sabotage.

One case of a 23-year-old German, Karl-Heinz Krille, who 'committed an act in support of the NSDAP' (Nazi Party) that involved putting up a poster on which was a photograph of Hitler, the lyrics of the Horst Wessel song (used as an anthem by the Nazi Party since the 1930s) and some subversive, pro-Nazi remarks attracted widespread attention both in Germany and in the UK. The death sentence pronounced on this young man was widely condemned by churches, political parties (including the Communist Party) and citizens of his town. Krille said in his defence that he had been brought up to be anti-communist and had put up the poster not in support of the NSDAP but in anger with the communists. Sholto commuted the sentence to one of two years' imprisonment, prompting an article in the *Manchester Guardian* commenting that if Krille 'deserved two years in prison he could not possibly have deserved to be killed'. The article questioned whether Sholto would have 'interfered so drastically' had the case not been reported to the British press 'and if in consequence there had been no questions asked in the House of Commons'. Its author added, 'One hopes so,' and recommended an overhaul of the military government court system 'so that British justice should not again be made to appear either so harsh or, which is almost as bad, so haphazard'.[15] This case did indeed lead to increasing civilianisation of the British Zone court system, with military government courts replaced by Control Commission courts, and the complete restoration of German courts throughout the zone, where cases involving German nationals were dealt with under German law.

Until these changes came into effect, differences between German and English penal codes provided an extra complication for military government courts when German nationals were being tried. A prime example of this was a case in May 1946 of two Germans who had assaulted and pushed a Polish DP out of a moving train, killing him. The two men were accused of murder and sentenced to death, but the defence counsel had argued that for the crime to be counted as murder under German law, the knowledge and will of the murderer must be directed towards the death of the other person. In the defence's view, the intention was merely to throw the Pole out of the train. The fact that the train was moving clearly negated this viewpoint. The next gambit on the part of the defence was to field the argument that the necessary motive was not present. Section 211 of the German Criminal Code stated that 'a murderer is a person who from murderous passion, or the satisfaction of the sex impulse, from greed or other base motives, insidiously, cruelly, or by means dangerous to the community, or in order to make possible or conceal another offence, kills a man'. Under this law, murder also incurred the death penalty. The defence's argument, which Inglis described as 'typically German', was 'that mere national or racial hatred, such as the hatred of Germans for Poles, is not a base motive'. Inglis added:

> The sooner the German mind is disabused of this idea the better. I have no hesitation in advising that there were base motives within the meaning of the Section [211] … The crime was deliberate, it was a revival of the German notion that they are entitled to take the Law into their own hands where the victim is a member of another nation or race. I submit for your [Sholto's] consideration that this is one of the first ideas which it is our duty to eradicate from the German mind and that in view of this consideration the sentence of the Court was entirely proper.[16]

Sholto confirmed the sentences.

The background of defendants was another issue that received attention. In one case involving three Germans accused of multiple instances of unauthorised use of firearms causing wounding, armed robbery and theft of food, the trial judge remarked that the upbringing and education of one of the defendants, aged twenty, were 'a tragedy. He never really had a decent chance, and, through no fault of his own so far as I can see, he came under the influence of evil persons who made him into the dangerous criminal that he is.'[17] Nevertheless, the judge asserted that he was 'old enough to suffer the full consequences of his criminal acts' and sentenced him to death, but Inglis recommended to Sholto that his sentence be commuted to one of twenty years' imprisonment, to which Sholto agreed.

Likewise, defendants' mental state was given due consideration. One 24-year-old German who had been found guilty of distributing Nazi propaganda and posting threats of death, violence and arson to military government officers and German officials who cooperated with them had his death sentence commuted to one of ten years' imprisonment. Inglis felt that this young man 'played a completely lone hand … His threats were very nasty and disturbing; but there was never any likelihood of his putting them into execution and he had no means of doing so.'[18] The defendant's counsel called a witness who testified that the young man had suffered from fits, and handed to the court a medical certificate that suggested that he was suffering from 'some mental disorder'.

By far the most appalling of all the cases with which Sholto had to deal were atrocities committed by Nazis. In the chaos that marked the end of the war in April 1945, as the Third Reich was being squeezed from both sides and its forces were retreating into Germany, the Allied advance from the West had caused the Germans to force-march a large number of prisoners to penal camps further east. Camp Two at Aschendorfermoor, close to the Dutch border, was therefore crowded with prisoners, both Wehrmacht and civilian. Some of these had escaped and had looted near the line of the march. They were subsequently rounded up and brought into the camp for interrogation. Twenty-year-old Willi Herold, a lance corporal and a straggler from his German Paratroop unit that was being chased out of the Netherlands, had found a Luftwaffe captain's uniform in an abandoned car, and arrived in the camp on 11 April passing himself off as a captain. Since the camp staff had been expecting someone from a Nazi military court to deal with the recaptured prisoners, they thought that Herold was that person and he did not disabuse them, telling them that he had been given the necessary powers to try the prisoners by Hitler himself. However, without any semblance of regular trials, Herold proceeded to order, and in most cases to supervise, the executions of well over a hundred people. The greatest number of murders took place that evening. During the afternoon, a large grave had been dug just outside the perimeter wire of the camp and later the victims were marched out, lined up in front of the pit and shot in three batches. The first batch were shot with an anti-aircraft cannon, but when that jammed, the guards, encouraged by Herold and an accomplice, Karl Schuette, opened fire with rifles and machine pistols. The cannon failed again during the shooting of the second batch and the killing was continued with small arms. No wonder Inglis described the circumstances of the crime as 'cruel and revolting'. He added: 'No pains were taken that the shooting should be accurate and cause instant death. Still living men were finished off in the pit with grenades and pistol shots. No proper examination was made to ensure that all the victims were dead before their common grave was filled in.'

During the trial of Herold and the other thirteen accused, all German soldiers, one of them, Josef Euler, gave a graphic description in his statement of the circumstances of the atrocity:

> Terrible shouting arose and almost all the prisoners fell into the grave. One of the prisoners fell on the side where I stood, and, since the firing had ceased, I went towards it. I saw the prisoner was seriously wounded. He had been shot in the chest and one arm was completely severed, but he was still alive ... I took out my pistol and gave him the coup de grace.[19]

One hundred and thirty-six bodies were later exhumed from this grave. Herold and five of his co-defendants, Karl Hagewald, Bernhard Meyer, Karl Schuette, Josef Euler and Hermann Brandt, all took part in this mass killing.

Two days later, Meyer murdered eight escaped prisoners whom he had rounded up. Once again, without any kind of trial, he had the men marched some distance in their stockinged feet to a heath where, after digging their own grave, they were lined up and shot. It has to be borne in mind that in all these killings, Germans murdered their fellow countrymen, whether servicemen or civilians. Herold stayed at Aschendorfermoor for a week, and 'each day brought new arbitrary shootings and further cruelties'.[20] The camp was then heavily bombed by the Allies and had to be evacuated, so Herold, who by this time had 'gathered a bodyguard of armed thugs around him, set forth to discover fresh adventures'. On 25 April, he and his associates murdered five Dutch resistance members who had been captured by the Germans and imprisoned in a camp at Leer, north of Aschendorfermoor. When their bodies were exhumed and examined by a doctor, the cause of death in four of them was found to be shooting in the neck at close range, but the fifth victim, after being similarly shot, had been buried alive and died from suffocation.

During the court proceedings, Herold seemed to be delighted at finding himself the focus of so much attention, and while his co-accused looked 'stolidly unhappy, Herold was forever bestowing spontaneous, cocky and infectious grins on his Defence Counsel, the prosecutor and other favoured persons, and never showing the slightest remorse or discomfort at the repetition of his calculated and callous cruelty'.[21] One of the most astonishing features of the case was that not one of the senior camp officials whom Herold met ever thought to ask him for his credentials, 'but allowed themselves to be completely overwhelmed by his amazing air of authority, self-confidence and his unbounded zest and enthusiasm'. Here was a lance corporal from an impoverished background, trained as a chimney sweep, who in the most grotesque way transcended his circumstances to achieve his time in the limelight.

Herold was found guilty of both murder and a crime against humanity, and six of his co-defendants guilty of murder. Seven others were acquitted. Those convicted were given death sentences and the case was sent to Sholto for review with comments from Robertson's deputy, General Bishop. Sholto wrote back to him:

> I am not satisfied that all these death sentences are justifiable – or rather perhaps that I should not exercise my prerogative of clemency in regard to some of the sentences. It is obvious, of course, that Herold must hang, and possibly also Meyer and Schuette. It seems to me however, that even in the case of these two men, and certainly of the accused Hagewald, Euler and Brandt, they were under the

genuine impression that they were carrying out the orders of their superior officer. In view of this, and in spite of legal arguments, I am not satisfied that all these men should receive the death penalty. I would therefore like to discuss the case further with yourself and Brigadier Inglis.[22]

Bishop and Inglis persuaded Sholto that, in the words of the report:

All the accused concerned in the mass murder must have known, in fact most of them admit that they knew there had been no proper trial, so that, whether they believed Herold to be a genuine officer or not, they must all have known that the whole business of condemnation and execution was criminal.[23]

One of Herold's six accomplices, Otto Peller, had his sentence quashed as it was found that although he was present at the executions, he fired his rifle only once and then not at the prisoners but in a different direction. The others, including Herold, were executed by guillotine at Wolfenbüttel Prison on 14 November 1946.

Another atrocity trial, involving three SS prison guards, was begun on 25 September 1946. Although the trial was conducted in the British Zone, some of the events had taken place in occupied Poland in late April 1945, and related incidents at Flensburg in Schleswig Holstein, as prisoners from the concentration camp at Stutthof near Danzig were moved west before the advancing Soviet Army. Many prisoners were taken by train from Stutthof to Nickelswalde (now Mikoszewo), and thence by another train to Flensburg, a journey of some 900 kilometres. One trainload included between forty and fifty Jewish women, all of whom were in poor health, some of them seriously ill. Instead of being taken to Flensburg, they were left in two railway trucks in a siding at Nickelswalde in the custody of a group of SS men under the command of one of the accused. According to witnesses, including both camp guards and prisoners, the women were taken to some bomb craters nearby, many being beaten on the way, and were shot. Several women had been too ill to walk to the pits and had to be carried there. Before some of them were dead, their bodies were covered with earth. A camp guard described shooting a woman in one of the craters who was moaning: 'I fired a shot at her and then everything was quiet.'[24] Another of those killed was only fourteen years old. Gruesomely, she attracted the attention of one of the soldiers, who said he was 'interested in her', but nevertheless she was killed.

The rest of the prisoners from the camp arrived at Nickelswalde and were made to embark on a huge river barge by means of a gangway consisting of two planks, one of which was only fifty centimetres wide. There was no handrail and some of the prisoners slipped off the gangway into the water, where they were shot at by the other two defendants. All three of the men accompanied the prisoners on the voyage to Flensburg, during which they murdered an unknown number of them, throwing them overboard, where they drowned. Most of the prisoners taken on this long journey were suffering from malnutrition, disease or both, but the SS men compounded their misery by failing to supply them with food, water, sanitary facilities or medical attention. Some of the prisoners had been forced to jump into the holds on the barge, or been thrown into them, for the journey. It seems that three such barges were used, transporting 1,000 prisoners each. A. T. Williams in his recent book *A Passing Fury* records one of the prisoners telling a British investigator that they had been forced to drink sea water to survive. Half of the prisoners on the barge on which she was transported died.[25] Sholto signed the death warrants on 13 December 1946, and less than twenty-four hours later, the three men were hanged.

As he had done when reading the pleas for clemency from Nuremberg, Sholto did not treat these numerous cases lightly and allowed the weight of responsibility to rest on his shoulders, which it did, for the rest of his life.

CHAPTER TWENTY-FIVE

THEFT AND CORRUPTION

Allegations of widespread corruption in the Control Commission and British forces during Sholto's time in Germany added to his burden. The highest-profile of these concerned what became known as the Schaumburg-Lippe case. It did not show the RAF in its best light and was a source of accusations against Sholto himself. What follows is something of a detective story.

Though today it is less well known than the SS and Gestapo, the SA (*Sturmabteilungen*) was the paramilitary wing of the Nazi Party, one of whose first commanders was Goering. It was not judged to be criminal by the IMT, largely because, although its members, described as 'ruffians and bullies', were undoubtedly involved in the violent spread of Nazi ideology, it diminished in importance after 1934 and was not engaged in a systematic plan to wage aggressive war. Nevertheless, at the beginning of the occupation following the end of the war in 1945, before the start of the IMT proceedings, all those who were thought to be members of the SA were arrested. These included Prince Wolrad of Schaumburg-Lippe, the owner of Schloss Bückeburg, an impressive honey-coloured castle dating back to the fourteenth century, later to become the administrative HQ of BAFO. Although he was described by the curator of the schloss, Dr Wolrad Schwertfeger, as 'a harmless Nazi'[1] (if such a person existed), the Prince had been a member of the Stahlhelm (literally 'Steel Helmet'), a paramilitary organisation formed after WWI. It was absorbed into the SA in 1933 when Hitler came to power, and Prince Wolrad was made a Sturmführer in the Reiter-SA, the mounted branch of the organisation. The SA ceased to exist officially following Nazi Germany's collapse in May 1945.

At the end of WWII, under military government law, management of the Prince's estate should have been transferred to the Property Control Branch of the military government, and later the Allied Control Commission, pending denazification proceedings against him. However, this is not quite what happened. The RAF took charge of the schloss and its contents when its forces arrived in April 1945. The Prince was not allowed to continue overseeing his large estate, comprising not only the schloss and its outbuildings but also several houses in the town of Bückeburg, the New Palace (usually housing the mother of the current Prince), the whole of the town of Bad Eilsen and a large quantity of valuable objets d'art, silver, porcelain, jewellery and coins. The schloss had been included in the official list of monuments declared by General Eisenhower to be of exceptional cultural importance, and the Monuments, Fine Arts and Archives (MFA&A) Section (think the British equivalent of George Clooney and *The Monuments Men*) wanted it included in that list not so much because of the schloss itself as for the collections it housed. Nevertheless, it contained an eccentrically ornate chapel dating from the early seventeenth century, as well as the *Goldene Saal*, or Golden Hall, considered to be 'the most important existing monument of German Mannerist art',[2] which was used by the RAF as an office – much to the distress of the MFA&A Section, who were not allowed oversight of the estate when it was most needed.

Prince Wolrad was placed under house arrest at his summer residence, Schloss Hagenburg, until June 1947 when his denazification was completed. He was able to visit Schloss Bückeburg only once. Dr Schwertfeger was given nominal control over the schloss and its contents.

On 8 April 1945, the day after German armed forces withdrew from the town of Bückeburg, an advance party of 2TAF, shortly to be renamed BAFO, occupied nearby Bad Eilsen, which was to become its operational HQ. Schwertfeger, who lived there, was instructed by the RAF to furnish offices and living accommodation. He requested that he be taken to the schloss to check on its condition and contents, which he did four days later, accompanied by a group of RAF officers, including Flt Lt Barkay, personal staff officer to the C-in-C, Air Marshal Coningham (from whom Sholto took over on 15 July). It was obvious that 'unauthorised persons' were entering the schloss, so it was arranged for a guard of the RAF Regiment to be quartered there to protect it. So far, so good, but Barkay was given authority by Coningham to requisition from the schloss considerable furniture, linen, cutlery and other table silver to equip RAF messes and offices at Bad Eilsen and Bückeburg. He was also detailed to find a residence for Coningham, and that is how the farmhouse at Almena Rickbruch became the residence of the C-in-C BAFO. Although the keys of rooms in the schloss where valuables were stored were kept supposedly safe, many officers and other ranks furnished their messes and billets with them without permission.

As the farmhouse was completely empty and cleared of furniture apart from six carpets, Barkay suggested to Schwertfeger that as much as possible of the most costly objects should be transferred from the schloss to the farmhouse, so that Coningham could have use of them and the remainder to be stored there in safe custody, to which Schwertfeger, amazingly, agreed. To this end, thirty-eight chests of family silver that had been assembled already were sent to the farmhouse on 25 May. Of these, two had already been opened and some small items taken. Also sent to the farmhouse were paintings and twelve Gobelin tapestries. Shortly afterwards, Coningham moved in. Barkay used to take visiting RAF and Army officers down to the cellar to show off the silver stored there that was not in daily use. The staff supervisor, Helmut Riepe, observed that 'the various officers had silver articles in their hands as they went upstairs … I did notice that the number of silver articles in the cellar decreased little by little.'[3]

On 1 July, an MFA&A officer, Squadron Leader Gould (usually employed at the National Gallery), raised concerns about what was happening to the Bückeburg valuables with his immediate superior, Major Ellis Waterhouse (an art historian and fellow of Magdalen College, Oxford), who wrote in his diary for that day that Coningham had an 'unfortunately Goering-like attitude' to the property at Bückeburg. In this context, Gould thought that it was rather unusual that all the servants at the farmhouse were dismissed two days before Coningham left for France on 15 July when he completed his tour in Germany.[4]

When Coningham left, he told the RAF Welfare Branch, based at Bückeburg, that they could collect from the farmhouse any spare silver for distribution to senior officers and their messes for their use, as nothing was to be left for the new C-in-C, Sholto. Accordingly, sixteen chests of silver were taken to Welfare House pending distribution. A day or so prior to Coningham's departure, after the servants had left, he instructed that certain silver, china, pictures, carpets and three Gobelin tapestries be packed and flown to a house in Cannes, the Villa Rosalia, which had been given to the RAF by the French government and which Coningham intended to use as a rest centre for senior officers. At this point, not a single inventory had been made of the property removed from Schloss Bückeburg, despite pleas to do so from Schwertfeger and the schloss warden, Herr Gottschalk, and urgent representations by the Property Control Branch of the CCG to control the property. The RAF refused these, asserting that it was properly requisitioned by them. When Coningham arrived in Cannes, he found that he had more silver than he needed, so he had some of it repacked and sent to his house in Brussels in his official Rolls-Royce that he was returning, along with his driver.

Shortly afterwards, having arrived to replace Coningham as C-in-C BAFO, Sholto was installed in the farmhouse. He was issued with silver from the collection at Welfare House, which was properly signed for. Subsequently, when attempts were made to catalogue the items that had been at the farmhouse, Coningham was contacted as to their whereabouts, but failed to mention that he had taken a quantity of silver to Cannes and that most of it was still in his possession. In September 1945, Gottschalk made an inventory in German of the rest of the items transferred from the farmhouse to Welfare House, and these were taken back to the schloss and placed in a locked room. Nevertheless, somehow, people could still gain access to it, and by the time the list was checked in April 1946, a number of articles mentioned in it could not be found. In June 1946, the items were removed again to the mausoleum at the schloss for safe keeping.

When Sholto returned to Germany as Military Governor, his official residence, Schloss Ostenwalde, was refurbished and seventy-two items of silver and furniture were requisitioned by his wife Joan from the mausoleum at Bückeburg in September. This happened in the presence of Gottschalk and a list was compiled, which is in the National Archives files. However, Schwertfeger voiced his concerns about the property to Joan when she visited the mausoleum and afterwards in a letter, in which he requested that he be given a certificate of authority to prevent anyone taking further items from the mausoleum. He thanked Joan for the interest she had taken in his case. Shortly afterwards, Sholto's personal staff officer wrote to the Property Control Branch requesting that the promised letter be issued to Schwertfeger 'in order to be sure that the contents of the Mausoleum are frozen and that he does not have trouble with people endeavouring to remove any of the items'.[5] Joan informed Schwertfeger that this was on Sholto's direct orders.

In July 1947, an article concerning the Bückeburg case appeared on the front page of the *Daily Mail*, written by Richard Greenough, an accredited correspondent of the paper who had visited Germany and interviewed, among others, Mr Haworth, the Property Control Officer for Land Niedersachsen (where Bückeburg was situated), Schwertfeger, Prince Ernest Augustus, Duke of Brunswick, and his son Prince Ernst August of Hanover, to whom Prince Wolrad had aired his concerns about his property. Greenough told his interviewees that he had been sent to Germany specially by Lord Rothermere, the *Daily Mail*'s owner. Greenough knew that Prince Ernest Augustus had written to his distant cousin King George VI, and the whole affair was set to be 'one of the biggest stories ever to come out of Germany'. The article named Coningham, Tedder, Wigglesworth (now AOC-in-C BAFO) and Sholto, who were said to be 'assisting inquiries' into the disappearance of property from Schloss Bückeburg.

Haworth wrote an interim report arising from his investigations, which had begun before the article was published, and in a meeting Sholto immediately ordered that a full report be completed and a comprehensive inquiry made, at the same time surmising that after such inventories as there were had been checked, 'quite probably there would be some property found to be missing'. He observed that when he had been AOC-in-C BAFO, 'there were numerous packing cases of property which were laid out, sorted and inventories made, and that not required was put in the Mausoleum at Bückeburg'.[6] However, both he and Wigglesworth could see that the newspaper report implied that they were involved 'in the matter and that the report as such was libellous'.[7]

Following the meeting, an official inventory was made of all Schloss Bückeburg property in the hands of various RAF officers and messes. Once again, it was revealed that a number of RAF personnel proceeding on leave or demobilisation took with them goods that they had acquired in Germany, and this practice was widespread among all ranks, including senior officers. One air commodore took back to the UK items originally from Schloss Bückeburg that had been issued to another senior officer as part of a total of 1,800lb of luggage, transported in two aircraft. When it was examined, it was found to contain a quantity of Bückeburg silver. However, the officer in question received only a reproof from the Air Ministry and the articles were returned to the schloss.

Three months after the *Daily Mail* article, Sholto also sent for Mr Hayward, a former Metropolitan Police officer who was Assistant Inspector General, Special Enquiry Bureau, Public Safety Branch, stationed at Bünde in the British Zone, and instructed him to conduct a comprehensive investigation. As Hayward wrote later, Sholto told him that

he was confident that neither Lord Tedder, Sir Philip (Wigglesworth) nor himself had ever had any of the property other than that lawfully requisitioned in their official residences which had been, or would be, handed to their successors on termination of appointment. He felt, however, that Sir Arthur Coningham had laid himself open to criticism by causing some of the Schloss Bückeburg property to be sent to his residence at Cannes which he had used as a holiday home for senior RAF personnel. Sir Sholto was sure that it had been taken in good faith and that it had now all been returned, although that was not done until he, Sir Sholto, had approached Sir Arthur after the publication of the newspaper reports. Sir Sholto asked that my enquiry be as thorough and detailed as possible in order to completely refute the imputations contained in the newspaper reports.[8]

Underlying Sholto's apparent generosity to Coningham was a clear hint as to the direction that Hayward's investigations should take.

In fact, following his letter to Coningham in July, Sholto received a reply asking for his help in moving table silver, ornaments, crockery and rugs back to Bückeburg from Cannes, saying that a thirty hundredweight truck would be needed for the purpose. Coningham's life ended tragically only six months later. He retired from the RAF in 1947, and in January 1948, the aircraft in which he was travelling on a business trip to South America crashed into the sea near Bermuda and no trace of it or any of the crew or passengers was ever found. Hayward's final report on the Bückeburg case was published in June 1948, after Sholto had left Germany, and in it, he wrote: 'My enquiries have not disclosed a shred of evidence that either Sir Sholto or Sir Philip [Wigglesworth] have ever removed a single article of Bückeburg property from Germany.'[9]

My own very careful study of the Bückeburg documents revealed that on the two occasions when items were issued to Sholto for his use, first at the farmhouse and then at Schloss Ostenwalde, inventories were made and everything was signed for. Perhaps needless to say, there were never any valuables in our house either before or after my father died that could possibly have come from Germany. Sholto had inherited some pieces of Italian Renaissance art from his father, but I discovered after my mother died that most of these were nineteenth-century copies, and others were damaged. Sholto was presented with gifts when he was chairman of BEA, but the provenance of these was clear.

Undoubtedly, the Bückeburg affair tainted Sholto's governorship, and even an assertion in a recent book that he and Joan had 'a taste for grand living that was in contrast with the dislike for pomp and ceremony he later claimed in his memoirs'[10] casts an unwarranted shadow. In fact, these are two entirely different things. One relates

to comfort in personal accommodation and the other to official ceremonial. I remember that Sholto was relatively simple in his personal
tastes but, as someone who had endured extreme poverty in childhood, he was anxious not to run short of what he felt was needed to
maintain his position, and Joan was very eager, possibly more so than
Sholto, that their standard of living should equate with their status.

Sholto also had a dislike of red tape, so a Berlin-based designer,
Herr Dohler, was approached directly for work in Schloss Ostenwalde and in Sholto's official residence in Berlin. It is also possible that
Sholto wished to encourage German businesses. When Herr Dohler
presented his bills to the Control Commission, the delay in payment
that ensued caused him to be in 'financial straits', as Sholto wrote to
Paul Chambers, head of Finance Division.[11]

This drew a 'rap on the knuckles' from Chambers to the effect that
Sholto should have followed official procedures for the procurement
of services. He wrote:

> We could not allow everybody in the BAOR and in the Control
> Commission to order what work they wanted to be done and then
> just pass the bills to some cashier for payment. If we did many
> junior officers would have a grand time [they were anyway] ... In
> your case, and that of Sir William Strang [who had also commis-
> sioned work from Dohler], there is of course no question of any
> interference with your wishes. If I may say so, however, even in
> your case, it is convenient for the normal channels to be followed.[12]

Not only did Sholto's style of living at Schloss Ostenwalde raise eyebrows. Nicola, daughter of Nicholas Macaskie, the British Chief of
the Legal Directorate at the Control Commission in Berlin, commented that Sholto's official residence there was full of wonderful
paintings. These he was 'widely rumoured' to have acquired from
local Germans in 'somewhat dubious circumstances', who had in
turn often seized them 'in equally if not more dubious circumstances
from the pre-War Jewish population of Berlin'.[13] The first part of this
assertion was also untrue, although other senior officers were indeed
involved in the illegal trade in stolen art.

The issue of widespread fraud, of which the looting of the Bückeburg property formed part, was raised in the House of Commons by the Conservative MP for Farnham, Godfrey Nicholson, on 10 May 1946, only a few days after Sholto had taken over as Military Governor. In a dramatic speech, he told of 'alarming allegations of corruption in the military government in the British Zone' that caused him 'the greatest possible disquiet'. They had been relayed to him by someone in 'a subordinate position in the British Military Government' whom he described as a friend. He urged the Chancellor of the Duchy of Lancaster, at that time John Hynd, to consider how the matter could be investigated. The friend in question was a man called Ralph Tarlton, a junior military government officer who had known Nicholson for five years and who had met him for lunch on 6 May, when they had discussed the 'misuse of powers by Military Government officers for personal gain'.[14]

Sholto and Robertson met to discuss the matter on 25 May and agreed that the problem should be investigated. Robertson wrote to Sir Arthur Street at the Control Office for Germany and Austria (COGA): 'I do not think that any trouble which may exist is generally in the form of ordinary peculation [the theft of money from public funds]. It is more likely that officials are tempted by various offers of consideration in kind by Germans.' Robertson emphasised what Sholto would reiterate in a press conference on 9 August, that the CCG staff had been recruited rapidly, and that it was 'inevitable that in such a flock there should be some black sheep. The degree of temptation in some cases is very high.'[15]

The problem was that when Tarlton was asked to name names, at first he would not do so, saying only that there were German firms in the British Zone that were manufacturing luxury goods 'for the benefit of the individuals of the Control Commission' and that as a result these companies received regularly a very liberal supply of coal, some of which should have gone to hospitals. Furthermore, there were those in the CCG who were using pre-war business connections in Germany to 'reap gains unheard of in the normal business'.[16] As a result of Tarlton's allegations, Robertson suggested to Sir Gilmour Jenkins, also at COGA, that a skilled CID force be sent out from

Scotland Yard to examine the problem. Tarlton was at last induced to submit the names of certain German firms that should be investigated, but when these firms were questioned by CID personnel from the Public Safety Branch, there was little found to substantiate Tarlton's allegations. Robertson was convinced that 'the majority of the allegations made by Tarlton are based on chatter and groundless rumour'.[17] The Deputy Secretary to COGA, Maurice Dean, wrote to Street:

> Generally speaking, I think the enquiry has shown that Mr Nicholson's original statement was seriously exaggerated but that there have been (and no doubt still are) irregularities on a modest scale. The moral is to press on with strengthening the special police branch which is to take on enquiries into this kind of case.[18]

The large-scale corruption throughout Germany involved deposits of precious stones and metals that had been held by the Nazis at the time of Germany's collapse. An internal report by the Economic Information Section (EIS) of the CCG into the whereabouts of these items estimated them to have a value of £250 million. The report stated: 'No co-ordinated action was taken by the Allies to collect these deposits and place them at the disposal of appropriate authorities.' Intelligence on behalf of the EIS revealed that 'a large number of illegal trading groups existed in Berlin, in which many Allied officers appeared to participate'. The involvement of these officers constituted, in the opinion of the EIS, 'a threat to Allied prestige and morale, and may eventually lead to political repercussions'.[19] It was not only industrial- and jewellery-grade diamonds and precious metals that were traded on the black market but also currency, narcotics, works of art, bonds, shares and patents. Following this report, a joint British–US investigation, Operation SPARKLER, was launched on 10 September 1946. It targeted sixty-eight addresses in the British Zone and sixteen in the British Sector of Berlin, as a result of which finds valued at £463,771 were traced out of an estimated £1,909,607.

Corruption within the British Zone was so extensive that Julian Simpson, an Australian who was appointed Chief of the Internal Affairs and Communications Division of the Control Commission in May 1946, resigned his post 'disillusioned and frustrated' in May 1947. Although it was stated in the House of Commons that Simpson was due to resign anyway at the end of his agreed period of service, he told the Adelaide *Advertiser* that he was going to tell Prime Minister Attlee that he had

> failed to cleanse the Control Commission of major British racketeers, because of opposition and passive resistance by high officials; therefore, he and Scotland Yard racket-busters were wasting their time in Germany ... He told Lord Pakenham, the British Minister in Germany, much of this on Saturday night [three days before an article was published], when they dined with Sir Sholto Douglas.[20]

The documentarist and BBC producer Patricia Meehan suggested in her book *A Strange Enemy People* that Sholto's involvement in the corruption investigations nearly brought about his premature resignation, but this is not the case, although in May 1947 several British newspapers printed statements to the effect that Sholto intended to resign his position as Military Governor. Sholto was compelled to send a handwritten letter to Bevin stating that in no way had the reports been inspired by him, and that he had denied them emphatically. He wrote that he was prepared to relinquish his post in the autumn if that was what the government wanted, and in some ways would be glad to do so, but, as he said:

> I don't want to go when (as now) things are tough, like a rat leaving a supposedly sinking ship! Nor do I want to embarrass you or anyone else by a premature or spectacular resignation. I am in fact quite prepared to stay on in Germany as long as I am wanted ... I would like to leave the matter entirely in your hands. Meanwhile you can rely on me to do my damnedest to make a success of the British Zone.[21]

In a letter to Attlee in June 1947, Bevin wrote that Sholto had told him more than once that he would like to resign when his term had expired on 1 November. He suggested therefore that Sholto should be informed that he would not be required to stay on longer than his eighteen months' tour of duty. Bevin also recommended that, despite Sholto's desire to enter civilian life, his 'capacities and experience would fit him well for the post of Governor of a colony or for other work under the Government', and proposed that Sholto be given a peerage, the announcement for this to be released at the same time as that of his retirement as Military Governor, without waiting for the 1948 New Year's Honours List.[22]

Obviously aware of the newspaper reports concerning Sholto, Attlee was not in favour of announcing the barony independent of the Honours List since the post of Military Governor would continue, and he did not want the announcement of the honour to be construed as a way of concealing an undeserved lack of confidence in the administration as a whole. He pointed out to Bevin that Sholto had held the office of Military Governor 'rather longer than is common in such appointments' and he did not see

> why a change at this stage should be specially open to a sinister construction. Moreover, it would be very embarrassing in the future to have a precedent for taking the view that it is necessary to gazette an Honour immediately, in order to make it clear that removal from a senior post is in the course of honourable retirement, and not by way of criticism of the work done or of the organisation in question.[23]

Sholto had undoubtedly had his run-ins with Bevin, but in another memo to Attlee less than a month before Sholto's departure from Germany, Bevin wrote:

> We discussed my suggestion that Sholto Douglas should be given a peerage ... A short record of Sholto Douglas's service is given in the enclosed note, but I should like to add to that my very strong personal recommendation. I ought to say frankly that, until I took over direct responsibility for the affairs of the Control Commission, I did not realise fully the contribution which the Commander-in-Chief personally was making to the carrying out of the extremely difficult

task with which we are faced in Germany. I found, however, – and experience since has more than confirmed the discovery – that we had, in Sholto Douglas, a man of exceptional qualifications for his job. He has proved a most wise counsellor to me and a dignified, able and successful representative of his country, not only in his relations with the other occupying powers, but also in his capacity of Military Governor of the German people in the British Zone. He has shown a wide human sympathy in everything he has done, and his staff have the highest admiration and affection for him.

Bevin finished by saying that Sholto would be of great assistance to him in the House of Lords, adding: 'His political sympathies lie in our direction and it would, in my view, be a material strengthening of our team there to have a man of his standing and quality supporting our cause.'[24]

The short biography that accompanied Bevin's memo stated that Sholto's military governorship had been 'undertaken at a time of extreme difficulty', citing the reduction in rations just prior to the start of Sholto's time in Germany and his work through one of the worst winters in living memory, as well as the complexity of setting up the German constitutional structure and the transfer of power to the German authorities. It finished with: 'By his resolute and skilful handling of these grave problems Sir Sholto Douglas has earned the respect of his Allied colleagues and of the Germans and the warm admiration of the British authorities both in the United Kingdom and in Germany.' The announcement from Downing Street of Sholto's replacement as Military Governor stated that he was relinquishing the appointment at his own request on the completion of his tour of duty on 1 November 1947, and that Robertson would succeed him.

A measure of the esteem in which Sholto was held by his staff in Germany is provided by two touching entries in the log book of his pilot, Neville Freeman, the first dated 31 October 1947:

Official farewell of MRAF Sir Sholto Douglas on retiring from Military Governor & C-in-C of the British Zone of Germany. Guards of honour by British and American Forces, & escort of

Tempests of No.3 Squadron RAF from Gatow [Berlin] to Melle. After take off the Marshal told me to beat up the assembled party, as this consisted of Air Marshals, Generals, & many VIPs, I really enjoyed the opportunity.

An even more poignant account is contained in Freeman's log book entry for the following day:

Unofficial departure of MRAF Sir Sholto Douglas for UK. Even so quite a crowd turned up to see him off. Just before entering the aircraft he addressed the airmen of the Military Governor's Flight, which they much appreciated. When nearing the English coast we were met & escorted to Northolt by Mosquitoes of Fighter Command. It was not easy to say farewell to the Marshal after having been his pilot for well over a year, a period from which I shall retain many pleasant memories.[25]

Despite the esteem in which he was held, Sholto was inexpressibly relieved when his time in Germany came to an end, writing almost two decades later: 'It is still impossible for me to think of the time that I spent as Military Governor and Commander-in-Chief in Germany as anything but the unhappiest period of my entire official life.'[26] Frank Pakenham was able to articulate more clearly than anyone else besides Sholto himself his relief at leaving Germany and ending his military career:

After seven years as Commander-in-Chief he longed to cast off official harness for a time; as he put it himself, to ride a bicycle down the street in grey flannels without anybody looking at him. And in every good sense of the word he is so completely human that many features of the occupation life caused him distress: the semi-starvation, the bitterness it generated and, to mention only one other thing, the number of death warrants he had to sign. But he stuck to the job until he could be released. He seemed to keep a moral reserve available to deal with crises, and the staff of the Control Commission, flung far and wide across Germany, were much attached to him and Lady Douglas.[27]

CHAPTER TWENTY-SIX

'AND ALL THE TRUMPETS SOUNDED'

Sholto's last day of active duty with the RAF was 16 November, although he was not placed on the half-pay list (usual for marshals of the RAF) until the following February. In the New Year's Honours List for 1948, it was announced that Sholto had been made a hereditary peer. For his title, he selected a name with a Scottish flavour, linked with a place that had provided him with, as he put it, 'many pleasant memories'.[1] In the south of Scotland, there is a small river, Kirtle Water, which flows into the Solway Firth, in the heart of an area that has been associated with the Douglas clan for centuries. So, after an amusing exchange of letters with Sir Thomas Innes of Learney, the Lord Lyon King of Arms, Sholto chose the title 'Douglas of Kirtleside'. This was not before the Lord Lyon had suggested other possible titles, including 'Douglas of Dornock Shore' (Dornock is one of the nearest villages to that part of Kirtle Water). However, Sholto pointed out that if someone chose to put an apostrophe between the s and h of shore, people might think that he was the son of the local 'lady of easy virtue'. The Lord Lyon told him not to be flippant.

The peerage was a fitting recognition for Sholto's distinguished, and in some ways unique, military career, which had begun on a wet August day in 1914, but he felt dissatisfied. He admitted himself, and Vincent Orange felt compelled to point out in his account of Sholto for the *Oxford Dictionary of National Biography*, that in WWII, he had arrived at his commands after their 'glory days' had passed. He took over Fighter Command *after* the Battle of Britain, Middle East

Command *after* the Battle of Alamein, Coastal Command *after* the Battle of the Atlantic, and Germany *after* the defeat of Hitler. What Orange doesn't say – besides the obvious fact that, by definition, all British Military Governors took command *after* the fall of Hitler – is that Sholto's appointment as Military Governor came at the time of greatest challenge in the occupation.

Sholto finished his service career absolutely exhausted and at a low ebb. Unsurprisingly, his marriage to Joan was under considerable strain after being tested to the limit during their time in Germany, and she had started a relationship with an Army general. It was in this far from ideal state of mind that, early in 1948, Sholto met my mother, Hazel. She was sitting on a bar stool in a nightclub, where she had gone with another RAF officer with whom she was having an affair. Her first husband, a captain in the Royal Artillery, had been killed during the war, although she was separated from him already when she was widowed, and she was enjoying a career as an haute couture mannequin, having been employed by several top fashion houses. The sight of Hazel, slim, elegant and youthful (she was twenty-four years Sholto's junior), was just what he, tired and possibly even aware of his own mortality, felt he needed. He had gone to the nightclub without Joan, and at the end of the evening, he offered to give Hazel a lift to her mother's house in Mill Hill (what had happened to Hazel's companion at this point I do not know). On the way, Sholto asked her, 'Do you have a boyfriend?', and when she replied, 'No, not really,' he enquired whether he could be her boyfriend. For Hazel's part, this man was one of her heroes. She had seen posters of him up all over London during the war, saying: 'This is one of the men who is saving our country', but the thought of him as her boyfriend was inconceivable. Even so, Sholto was persistent. Hazel's mother told her: 'He has a reputation with women, and if you go with him, you'll get a bad reputation too,' not realising that Hazel had made a name for herself already, principally with American generals during the war. Nevertheless, the way in which Sholto pursued her could be considered stalking. He was infatuated with her, finding out where she lived and waiting outside her flat, interrupting her if she was at lunch or dinner in a restaurant with a companion (she had many admirers) and writing her what I have to admit are the most beautiful love letters. In the first of them that I have, dated 20 February 1948, he wrote: 'I haven't met anyone so nice as you since – I don't know when!' Needless to say, he wanted to see her again as soon as his busy schedule permitted. At first, she was reluctant, but gradually, Sholto wore her down, and I think also that she realised the advantages that a relationship with him might give her.

At last, having left the service, Sholto was able to make known fully his political views and, as he wrote,

> to declare where I stood, and how I had felt all my life. I joined the Labour Party, and I took my seat on the Labour Benches in the House of Lords. I did not believe in merely sitting on the crossbenches and thereby avoiding having to declare one's political convictions. That way out has always seemed to me to be a rather cowardly one. While I have always been a convinced Socialist, I am not by any means a fanatical one, and my associates in the Labour Party have always known that; and the hustings have never held any attraction for me.[2]

One of those associates was Frank Pakenham, who became Minister of Civil Aviation shortly after Sholto's return to the UK. He and Sholto spent many hours discussing the problems associated with the burgeoning field of commercial aviation. Attlee had suggested to Sholto previously that there was work for him to do, and in March 1949, after a period on the board of BOAC, he was appointed chairman of BEA.

What Pakenham called 'a discreditable cry of "jobs for the boys"' ensued from the Conservative side of the House as well as from the press.[3] This negativity filtered through to staff at BEA, compelling Sholto to make a speech to its departmental and branch heads on his first day as chairman, reassuring them that he did not want to politicise the organisation but to make it the most efficient and profitable airline in the world. He also encouraged anyone with any grievance to come and talk to him, however junior, at the same time reassuring managers that he would always discuss any complaints from their sections with them. The criticism in Parliament and in the press ignored the fact that Sholto was an experienced professional airman who had been in at the beginning of civil aviation back in 1919. Pakenham commented that Sholto's 'leadership, technical knowledge and humanity soon killed that nonsense, and when I came to extend his period as chairman from three years to five years I met with unanimous approval'. For his part, Sholto regarded Pakenham as probably the best Aviation Minister of the nine he served in his fifteen-year tenure at BEA, telling an interviewer on his retirement: 'I say this not because he is a Socialist, but because he did something which other Ministers did not always do. He always did his homework, and I respected him for that.'[4]

Sholto's time at BEA was one of hard-won but undoubted success. Aside from the exhaustion involved in running a pioneering nationalised industry, and his complicated personal circumstances, he managed to keep his distress from all the traumatic events in his life at bay during this period, at least so it appeared to most people. There were professional controversies, including over the choice of aircraft to be supplied to BEA, but Sholto won most of his battles, and ten years later had turned it into 'Europe's biggest, most efficient airline', even according to the *Daily Mail*, not usually his strongest supporter.[5]

This was a dramatic reversal of fortunes from when Sholto took the helm on 14 March 1949, when the financial statement for the previous year reported a loss of over £3 million. Sholto wrote in BEA's 1949 report and accounts: 'The objective of the Corporation is to eliminate the deficit entirely, while maintaining its standards of safety and service to the travelling public. The energies of the Board and Staff are devoted to this end.' It would take another six years to achieve this goal, although from July 1949 for the next three months, BEA made a profit for the first time in its history.

As Sholto had done with his RAF commands, he embarked on a regular tour of stations throughout the BEA network, ensuring that 'the feeling of team spirit spread throughout the Corporation', and this continued throughout his chairmanship. One of his first moves was to appoint as his chief executive Peter Masefield, until then director-general of long-term planning and projects at the Ministry of Civil Aviation and only thirty-five years old. He had had a wartime career as a co-pilot and gunner with the US Air Force and then as an aviation journalist. Afterwards, he became secretary of the War Cabinet committee on post-war civil air transport and was the first Civil Air Attaché to the British Embassy in Washington, prior to his return to London as a senior civil servant. Other young men were appointed to the board as executives, including two future chairmen, Anthony Milward and Henry Marking. The air correspondent of the *Evening News*, Garry May, wrote in his history of the corporation: 'Such was the spirit of BEA at this time that some of the board members gave up part of their salaries to help the financial crisis and Mr Masefield cut his own earnings.'[6]

For the next six years Sholto and Masefield proved to be an unstoppable team. Between them, they determinedly introduced innovations that would make BEA profitable. Masefield said of his association with Sholto:

> I always look on my chief executiveship and his chairmanship as one of the ideal relationships. We really worked hand in glove. I liked him very much and I think he liked me. We always maintained, right to his death, a very close relationship. We never had a cross word. The rest of the staff were suspicious of him to begin with because here was an Air Marshal coming in to tell them how to do things and they hadn't realised that Sholto had been in civil aviation before some of them were born. The way we worked was he looked after ministers and I looked after running the airline.[7]

Masefield was allowed to get on with this work because Sholto protected him from Whitehall interference, which for all but two of his fifteen years as chairman was under Conservative control. As a committed socialist, Sholto was determined that BEA, a state-owned corporation, should and must pay its way, but this involved some tough decisions. To begin with, he and Masefield made drastic reductions in staffing levels from 7,500 to 6,000 in five months, mostly through natural wastage, but there were some redundancies, inviting opposition from the unions. Tighter financial controls were introduced, meaning that each department and station had to draw up an annual budget of proposed expenditure to which they had to adhere, and which was vetted by head office. On top of that came a vigorous sales drive, the most significant launch being off-peak night fares on the London–Paris route from 29 July. In October, the servicemen's fare was introduced, providing cheaper flights for servicemen and their families wishing to visit the UK from European postings, something that would have been close to Sholto's heart. The improvements began to be reflected in the financial results for the year 1949/50, which showed that BEA's deficit of the previous year had been more than halved, and the corporation's profitability would be dramatically enhanced by the introduction on 29 July 1950 of the world's first scheduled gas turbine-powered service.

The year 1951 contained both sadness and celebration: sadness in that Sholto's father Langton, by this time eighty-seven years old, had become increasingly infirm and was suffering what was thought to be vascular dementia. As Sholto would be later in life, Langton was prone to outbursts of anger, and was frustrated at his growing incapacity. Despite his colourful personal life, he had converted to Roman Catholicism and had decided that he wanted to spend whatever life he had left in the place he loved best of all, Italy. On his journey there from the United States, he passed through London Airport and Sholto arranged a family lunch, gathering as many of Langton's considerable family of children, grandchildren and their spouses as he could. This was the last time that father and eldest son were to see each other. Langton spent his last few months at the Convent of the Poor Clares, San Girolamo, in Fiesole, just outside Florence, where the sisters looked after him with kindness and forbearance, although he could be incredibly rude.

Langton died on 14 August 1951. The city of Siena, on which Langton had written a seminal history, asked his widow Jean for permission to bury him. She wrote to Gloria, the widow of Sholto's brother Bobby:

I knew he loved the Sienese and on the day of his funeral I realised how sincerely they returned his love. The entire populace lined the long funeral route kneeling as we passed. The Misericordia [Brotherhood of Mercy], in their black hoods and garments, carrying lighted torches, surrounded his hearse. The Mayor, Rector of the University, President of the Academy of Fine Arts, the Chief Magistrate made speeches. Some of the soldiers and policemen on guard wept like true Sienese. Then amid the fluttering banners of the representatives of each ward of Siena, who wore their medieval Palio costumes, Langton was put to rest ... His tomb is in the centre of a beautiful cemetery, one he loved, and from it one can see the Lily Tower of Siena and in the other direction, the rolling hills of Chianti.[8]

Celebration came in the form of professional success, as it almost always did for Sholto: the first yearly total of one million passengers carried by BEA. The following year, the airline's premium Silver Wing service was launched on the London–Paris route. Tourist fares were introduced throughout Europe in April 1953, to cater for passengers with all levels of resources. Shortly afterwards, the world's first scheduled Viscount service was started on the London–Cyprus route. Sholto had fought hard to get the Viscount for BEA. It had its faults, being small and underpowered at first, but his board members agreed that it had potential for the short-haul routes on which BEA operated. Whitehall backed other, even smaller aircraft, but as Garry May wrote: 'Face to face with the warrior from two wars, the opposition wilted. Lord Douglas would fix his keen blue eyes on an unfortunate minister's face, light his pipe and then softly but firmly put his case. Resisting him seemed to be a waste of time.'[9]

Sholto continued a frenetic schedule of trips abroad, travelling to the US and Canada in 1952 and 1953 to learn from those nations' experiences of commercial aviation and, as he put it, to 'pick up some money-saving tips for BEA'. Rationing was still in place in the UK, so on each trip, Hazel gave him a list of quite exacting shopping commissions to fulfil, which he tried to do in between business meetings. As well as her expensive requests, Sholto also chose things himself that he thought she might like. He wrote her letters, ending one rather outrageously with: 'I love you, darling. Be faithful to me. I don't know why, but that means a lot to me this time.' For someone who was quite shy outwardly, he was remarkably affectionate in these letters, always writing that he loved and missed her dreadfully. Unfortunately, none of her letters to him from this period have survived, but by 1953, it seems that she was beginning to reciprocate. Just as well, as the shopping lists were getting longer and ever more complicated, and Sholto was having to try even harder to find everything. It was almost as though she was putting him to the test.

Sholto continued his efforts to bring innovation to BEA. He was a great champion of helicopters, and the first scheduled helicopter passenger service between Heathrow, Northolt and Eastleigh Airport was inaugurated on 15 June 1954. Three weeks earlier, he had spoken in the Lords about the importance of the helicopter to aviation in general, saying that 'the civil and military requirements of helicopters broadly coincide, so that the development of one assists the other'.[10] He emphasised that the advancement of the helicopter in the UK lagged behind that of the US, and that an important opportunity would be missed. His prediction came true: even now, the US is the major manufacturer of helicopters used by the British military.

By late 1954, Sholto had told Joan that, what with her relationship with the general, and his with Hazel, their marriage was a mockery and it would be best if they ended it. Joan did not want to be the guilty party, so Sholto and Hazel provided the necessary evidence with a weekend at the Spread Eagle at Midhurst, during which the inevitable private detective in mackintosh gathered the incriminating information. A few months later, on 28 February 1955, Sholto and Hazel were married at the registry office in Wareham in Dorset, near the waterfront and town quay. It was a bright day and the sea sparkled in the sun. The room where they were married was decorated with bright spring flowers. They had chosen Wareham for their wedding because it was where Hazel's best friend and her husband lived. Sholto turned to Hazel after the ceremony and said, 'Thank you, darling, that's the nicest wedding I have ever had,' whereupon she replied, 'I've got news for you, chum, it's going to be your last!'

In April 1955, BEA was officially out of the red, having accomplished its first ever whole profitable year through a 'rigorous control of expenditure combined with a highly successful sales drive',[11] which in 1953 had also involved a fare reduction to the lowest point in the history of the corporation. However, Sholto saw that this hard-earned profitability was under threat from the Conservative government, which wanted to introduce competition by giving increased opportunity to 'a limited number of major independent operators'. John Boyd-Carpenter, the Minister of Transport and Civil Aviation, wrote in a memo that the Conservatives had stated in their manifesto for the election in May 1955: 'Air transport gives us new highways. Experience has shown that a blend of public and private enterprise is best for this service,' bemoaning the 'near monopoly' of BEA on European and internal routes.[12] Independent air operators had lobbied him to allow them to run scheduled services on remunerative routes. Sholto was opposed to this move, on the grounds that it risked undermining the nationalised industry he had striven so hard to make a commercial success. This was one battle he would eventually lose.

At the end of October, Masefield resigned to take up his new appointment as managing director of Bristol Aircraft Ltd, and for the next six months, Sholto fulfilled the duties of both chairman and chief executive, departing on 11 November for Moscow to negotiate a reciprocal agreement with Aeroflot for air services between Britain and the Soviet Union. They had expressed interest in a direct air route between London and Moscow in July, after which a Foreign Office cipher to the British Embassy in Moscow stated that hitherto it had opposed regular Soviet flights into UK airports on security grounds, but 'from the political angle we should not wish to appear to rebuff a Soviet approach on the subject. Nor should we like to see BEA forestalled by other Western airlines ...We may also need to consult the United States Government before entering into any commitments.'[13]

A week later, the British Air Attaché in Moscow met with Marshal Zhigarev, Chief Marshal of Aviation, who proposed a London–Moscow air service operated to a common timetable, the eastern portion to be flown by Aeroflot, the western portion by BEA, connecting at Schönefeld Airport in East Berlin. This would be a prelude to direct London–Moscow flights by both Soviet and British aircraft. In what could be seen as an incentive for the UK to accept the proposal, Zhigarev noted that Aeroflot was being approached by other airlines, including Sabena and KLM. Sholto's discussions with him were successful, and by 19 December air tickets to Moscow and other Soviet cities could be bought at BEA booking offices. By April 1956, BEA was carrying more passengers than any other airline in the world outside the United States, including, on the 23rd of that month, Mr Khrushchev and Marshal Bulganin, who travelled on a London–Birmingham Viscount.

Sholto was performing a delicate balancing act. While playing his part in bringing about some kind of rapprochement with the Soviets, he remained in favour of a nuclear deterrent as a bulwark against the outbreak of WWIII, saying in the House of Lords: 'The results of using these weapons are so catastrophic and so horrible to contemplate that I do not believe that any nation would willingly start a war which would involve these weapons.' Nevertheless, he did agree with Lord Beveridge (the author of the report that provided the basis for the welfare state) that the elimination of the nuclear threat would be advantageous if it was accompanied by a general disarmament in conventional weapons. He quoted Beveridge, who had written in *The Times*: 'The abolition of war with any weapons is the only rational aim the scientists have left us.'[14] Sholto was making his own efforts to mitigate any threat, but a relentless schedule was taking its toll on him, and in photographs from this period, he looks as tired as I have ever seen him.

Unfortunately, he had continued to gain weight, particularly around his girth, and this was noted even in the House of Lords. His old friend Harold Balfour, who had known him since 1917 and was now a director of BEA, spoke before him in an Air Estimates debate. He referred to 'skating on very thin ice' due to his position in BEA and therefore not being a disinterested party in the debate, but he said of Sholto as chairman of BEA: 'He weighs more (I mean in words of course) and therefore has to be even more careful than I do.' This did not escape Sholto's notice, who in the speech that followed referred to Balfour's 'somewhat unkind reference to my present figure'.[15] This did not stop him from regaining his pilot's licence aged sixty-two. Hazel had decided that she wanted to learn to fly, so Sholto arranged for her to receive instruction at Croydon aerodrome and went along intending to watch, but the sight of the little Auster Aiglet training aircraft was too much for him to bear.

At the beginning of May 1956, one of the board members, Anthony Milward, was appointed as the new chief executive. The relationship between him and Sholto was not as close as it had been with Masefield, but they continued together for eight years until Sholto retired. Garry May observed: 'Both men tempered aggression with tact and became friends despite being poles apart politically.' Milward remarked later that Sholto was 'a very good chairman in every sense. Everyone trusted him. He was forthright, able, with a very good brain. He had the confidence of people around him. I worked with him for fifteen years and I don't think we ever quarrelled.' Milward also got to the heart of Sholto's character, remarking:

> Sholto was a contradiction in dozens of different ways, but he got on well with the rest of the staff ... But if you are running a nationalised industry you have to be extremely tough because politicians and civil servants will walk over you if you will possibly let them. You have to say 'I'm sorry, I am running this business and not you.'[16]

In September, BEA issued their specification for a short-haul jet aircraft to four British aviation manufacturers on the same day Sholto assumed office as the president of the International Air Transport Association (IATA) for one year. It was to be a crowded year, in the middle of which I was born on 26 July 1957 by caesarean section. It was not customary in those days for fathers to be anywhere near the birth, so Sholto was informed of my arrival at 11.15 a.m. in the middle of a BEA board meeting. Hazel had had a tumultuous pregnancy, and actually weighed less at the end of it than she had done at the beginning. She had suffered from anorexia prior to this, as well as being addicted to alcohol, with both of which she continued to struggle, and had then suffered from extreme sickness, known as hyperemesis gravidarum, throughout the nine months, so I was probably lucky to be born at all. Sholto came to visit in the afternoon and again in the evening. The following day Hazel was back on the champagne, and this was a daily event that was noted in her diary until she left hospital on 12 August. Nevertheless, she resumed her public role as the chairman's wife on 27 August when she opened the first London home of BEA's Silver Wing Club, its staff association, formed the previous year.

In 1959, Sholto's ten-year anniversary with BEA was celebrated throughout the airline. The economist on the board, Steve Wheatcroft, wrote to him:

> It is difficult to say what I want to say in making this gesture without seeming presumptuous. But I would like you to know how very highly I regard your stewardship of BEA's affairs in the past ten years. The stability which you have given the organisation is an invaluable asset. We have learned from you how to recognise the major objectives and to keep them constantly in sight.[17]

Despite his success and that of the corporation, Sholto stuck to his principles. For example, he did not believe that being chairman of BEA automatically entitled him to first-class travel. Returning from Rome with Hazel and me in 1960 in the economy section of the aircraft, he explained that the first-class seats had all been taken, saying: 'I put our names on the first-class list a month before, but there wasn't room for us. You can't displace people who have booked before you.'[18]

However, his relationship with Hazel was not going well. I did not realise until my mother died that things had almost fallen apart entirely when I was four years old.

In August 1961, Hazel discovered that Sholto was probably having a liaison with Lorna Snow, a well-known and flamboyant rally driver and furrier and a close friend of one of my godmothers. Sholto liked buying fur coats for Hazel, and that is probably how they met Lorna. My parents did spend a lot of time going to social events at which both she and the godmother in question were present, and bizarrely, I found a letter from Lorna to Sholto in Hazel's handbag after her death in 2010, in which Lorna wrote of 'us' and of the collusion of my godmother in the affair. How much actually happened I do not know since there is no evidence from Sholto's side, but Hazel had kept the letter in whatever bag she was carrying for nearly fifty years, where it acted as a focus for her resentment against Sholto, dripping constantly into her psyche like a poison. Sholto had pressed Hazel into a relationship with him, and now he was having an affair, so she thought, although Sholto's PA Sheila Brough told me that she was sure most of the 'running' came from Lorna, and this is certainly the tenor of her letter.

In the years since my birth, as well as before, it is clear from Hazel's diaries that her drinking was out of control. She referred on numerous occasions to getting 'sloshed', 'high' or 'whistled' and feeling fragile the next day. She embarrassed Sholto many times in public, most notably during a stay at Government House in Hong Kong, where she was so drunk that she fell up the steps to the entrance, either side lined with a Gurkha guard of honour. She found it funny, but for Sholto it was mortifying. Sheila told me that those in BEA felt that, although Hazel was a 'trooper' and appeared to be up for anything, her fondness for alcohol spoiled things, which sapped away the admiration that they might have felt for her. Although she relished the limelight, she found the constant flow of public engagements when she was expected to be on her best behaviour overwhelming. According to one of her friends, she was very conscious of the disparity between Sholto's social standing and hers and lacked the confidence to deal with it, so covered up her feelings of inadequacy with alcohol. What I did not know until after Hazel's death was that she had had affairs with at least two business associates of Sholto's, which had also started when I was about four years old.

It was around this time that an old rumour resurfaced: that BEA and BOAC would be merged by the government. Sholto had always been against such a merger and dismissed the idea publicly in the chairman's page of an edition of the BEA magazine in 1963. He asserted that the interests of BEA and BOAC were too diverse, and that the profits by this time being made by BEA could not offset the losses that were made generally by BOAC. Moreover, the savings accrued by the union of the two airlines would be very small. The single airline thus produced would be too large, employing 38,000 staff. Sholto felt that this would decrease efficiency, the whole concern becoming too impersonal and staff losing any sense of belonging or pride in the company. He ended his article with the suggestion that BEA staff in the new airline may be regarded as junior to those already in BOAC. They did merge eventually in 1974, and in his 1989 history of BEA, Phil Lo Bao concluded that: 'much of what Douglas predicted occurred and he almost deserves the title of Prophet'.[19]

Once again, bad weather hampered BEA's success at the beginning of 1963, but the innovative introduction of stand-by fares on certain domestic routes at one third of normal rates meant that losses were recouped. In April, the airline made a very unusual staff appointment, no doubt a reflection of Sholto's pride in his Scottish ancestry: an honorary bagpipe player. Pipe Major Robert Crabb, formerly with the Second Battalion Scots Guards, was enlisted to play on special occasions, making his debut on 20 April when he piped passengers aboard the first Comet service to Venice.

The newly completed West London Air Terminal in the Cromwell Road was opened by the Duke of Edinburgh on 6 November 1963. In all the photographs from this time, Sholto looks exhausted, and in his Christmas message to staff, he announced that he would be retiring on 31 March of the following year and that his successor would be the current chief executive, Anthony Milward. Sholto congratulated everyone on a highly successful year and announced that he had arranged for all BEA staff not on operational duty to have an extra day off for Christmas. So it was that the first 'Chairman's Day' was inaugurated.

Sholto's work was not finished, however: the New Year of 1964 saw the formation of BEA Helicopters Ltd, something he had worked to achieve from the start of his chairmanship. It was the continuation of civil helicopter operations that had been started in 1947 by BEA's helicopter unit. The first Trident to enter service, named by Hazel at a ceremony on 28 February, made its initial passenger-carrying flight between London and Copenhagen on 11 March. Most satisfyingly of all, on 31 March, the day of Sholto's retirement, he was able to announce a profit of £3 million, BEA's highest to date and the equivalent of approximately £25 million today.

So ended Sholto's time as the longest continuously serving chairman of a nationalised industry. He was given an unusual retirement present from BEA's staff of 17,000. Garry May wrote:

> The Government had allowed him to keep the eight-year-old Bentley that he had used as Chairman of BEA. He had mentioned casually in his office one day that his garage was too small for the car which was usually kept in one of BEA's garages after a chauffeur had driven him home. To his delight, the parting gift was a new garage – planned and built at the expense of BEA's employees.[20]

The tribute to Sholto in the BEA magazine for March 1964 stated:

> During the past fifteen years we have survived many difficulties and achieved much. That we have done so has often been attributed to our 'team spirit' – but no team, however good, can accomplish anything without a leader. BEA has had such a man in Lord Douglas, who is not only a born leader but 'one of the boys' and there can be no nicer compliment.

Vaughan Berry, the regional commissioner for Hamburg during most of Sholto's Military Governorship in Germany, wrote to Sholto on his retirement from BEA:

> You will have received so many letters on your retirement that I hesitate to add another but I feel I must tell you how greatly I have admired your leadership of BEA all these years. I think perhaps my interest was so keen because I always understood that you had been practically a life-long socialist, as I had...[21]

Sholto's socialism was a theme in all the newspaper reports of his retirement, an article in *The Observer* remarking: 'For a Socialist in command of a State-owned corporation, he has shown a remarkable enthusiasm for making money.'[22] But its writer did not assert that Sholto's socialism was anything other than genuine, referring to his impoverished childhood circumstances. It was the only article anywhere, including those in BEA's monthly magazines and in its final tribute to Sholto, to mention that he had had a stroke. This is undoubtedly the way he would have wanted it, but as I wrote in Chapter One, he had had two strokes prior to his retirement and had begun to suffer considerable ill health.

An addition to Sholto's workload during his tenure at BEA, and a source of some strain for him, was that he had started to write his autobiography, assisted by his former personal staff officer at Fighter Command and in Germany, Bob Wright. This would have stirred up many traumatic memories for him. He spent hours dictating his reminiscences and checking the transcripts. Bob had helped considerably with *Years of Combat*, which had been published to great acclaim prior to Sholto's retirement, but his assistance in the second volume, *Years of Command*, and on the US edition, was even more substantial. This was reflected on the front cover of *Years of Command*, where Bob's name appeared under Sholto's, and in the fact that the proceeds of the book were to be split fifty–fifty between them. Work on the book had been delayed already due to Sholto's second stroke, more severe than the first, at the end of 1963. He was slow in returning Bob's drafts, and although both he and Sholto's literary agent, A. D. Peters, urged Sholto not to overdo things, Peters writing: 'It is time that you thought a little more about yourself,'[23] the delay meant that by July 1964, Bob's financial situation was desperate. He wrote to Sholto asking: 'Is there anything you can do, please, to help me?'[24] His letters continued in this vein until *Years of Command* was published two years later, and they make excruciatingly painful reading. In September, Peters waded in, agreeing to advance Bob £100 if Sholto would do the same, although Peters thought it was a derisory sum in view of Bob's problems. Peters wrote: 'His situation is due to circumstances over which you had no control namely your illness. But for that the book would have been finished months ago. But I think you must agree that you have a very strong moral obligation to help Bob through now.'[25] Sholto's response to both Bob and Peters was to say that he wished he could disabuse both of them of the idea that he was a rich man, and that he could not accept liability for half of Bob's expenses indefinitely, without an end date for the completion

of the manuscript. According to Sheila Brough, Hazel undoubtedly played a part in all this, because she was incredibly careful about
money (Sheila implied that she was mean), and she was having an
increasing influence in Sholto's affairs.

To add to Bob's difficulties, Sholto's memory was beginning to fail
him, and the tapes he was sending Bob were somewhat disjointed,
with lacunae in the telling of the story that required Bob to fill in the
gaps by consulting Sholto's former colleagues and friends. Strikingly,
the holes in Sholto's memory were those of the happier times. The
traumatic memories were indelibly etched in his psyche and returned
with unfailing regularity. Such a phenomenon has been described
movingly in an interview with a distinguished older veteran, conducted by the late Richard Holmes, a military historian:

> Often you can keep these things out of your mind when you are
> young and active, but they come back to haunt your nights in
> your old age. We thought we had managed all right, kept the awful
> things out of our minds, but now I'm an old man and they come
> out from where I hid them. Every night.[26]

Lord Moran also admitted to being haunted by traumatic memories
many years after events in WWI when, as a military doctor, he had
had to certify his unit as fit, saying that it was 'like signing the death
warrant of two hundred men. And I might be wrong.'[27] Writing in
1945, he admitted: 'Even now after twenty years my own conscience
is troubled.'[28] But, as in Sholto's case, it is the killing of civilians that
produces the most disturbing traumatic memories. Dave Grossman
has observed: 'Killing comes with a price, and societies must learn
that their soldiers will have to spend the rest of their lives living with
what they have done ... Although the mechanism of the firing squad
ensures killing, the psychological toll on the members of a firing
squad can be tremendous.'[29] Sholto may not have been an actual
member of a firing squad, but he had sent dozens of men out to be
part of them, and to face them.

Bob and Sholto now faced a race against Sholto's increasing infirmity, not helped by a bad fall in Barbados during a holiday in January

1965. He was angry and frustrated at his own incapacity, and as well as being bruised by what was happening with Bob, he himself could be incredibly hurtful. Bob wrote to Sholto in January 1966: 'The comments about the work that I have been doing that you have just made during our talk on the 'phone have hurt me more deeply than you will ever know. It is utterly incomprehensible to me that you can dismiss so lightly all that I have done.'[30] This was all the more painful because Sholto and Bob had been through so much together, in the heat of war at Fighter Command, and in the hell of post-war Germany. Sholto suffered further impairment following his car crash with Hazel at the wheel in June 1966, but somehow, he and Bob had managed to maintain some sort of relationship until the book was published in the same year.

All this drove Bob further into the arms of Dowding, on whom he was beginning to write a biography. Dowding's memory was also starting to fail him, which he admitted in a letter to Sholto in June 1966, in which he thanked him for sending him a copy of *Years of Command* and for 'the kindly things' that Sholto had said about him in the book.[31] Although friendly in this letter, expressing his concern for Sholto's health and hope for his recovery, Dowding's resentment against the treatment that he had received when he was dismissed from Fighter Command at the end of 1940 was as sharp as it had ever been. He expressed his anger to Bob, including over the part that he felt Sholto had played in the whole affair. The resulting biography contains a number of inaccuracies, which I have attempted to redress, but it was accepted for decades thereafter by historians who took their cue from it, and undoubtedly coloured their view of Sholto.

Sholto's death came in late October 1969. Due to his long period of infirmity and disintegration, his demise and the tributes to him that followed were more significant to me then than his life had been. These stellar accolades caused me to treat him as a distant hero, and I lost sight of the kind and loving man who had been my father for the last twelve years, to whom I had not been able to say a proper goodbye.

Nevertheless, Sholto would have been touched deeply by the tributes, many of which came from those for whom he had the greatest respect and fondness. Viscount Portal, former CAS and Sholto's boss for almost the whole of WWII, wrote to my mother:

> I was very sorry to hear on the news yesterday that we have lost Sholto. I did not know that he was in danger, though his absence from the B of B [Battle of Britain] film gala ought to have made me enquire about him. We are both very sad about it and offer you our sympathy in your loss.
>
> You can be very proud of him though. He did everything well, and his heart was as good as his head. During the whole of the war he was the most reasonable and the most unselfish of all the Commanders in Chief I had to deal with, and of course his post-war work with BEA was brilliant.
>
> I do hope that knowing how much he was liked and respected by all his friends is some comfort to you.[32]

The CAS at the time of Sholto's death, Sir John Grandy, one of Sholto's 'young men' whose career he had done so much to foster during WWII, wrote:

> Cécile and I send you and your daughter our heartfelt sympathy.
>
> I first met Sholto in the mid '30s – he became a great friend. He had that splendid ability of treating one – pretty junior in those days – absolutely as an equal, yet he retained your total respect.
>
> He was always a most wise counsellor and, above all, great fun.
>
> We are so sorry.[33]

Sholto's memorial service took place in a full Westminster Abbey on 5 December, at which the final tribute was paid by one of his oldest surviving friends, Harold Balfour, the brave and highly strung young man who had served in Sholto's squadron on the Western Front in WWI and who had worked with him as Under-Secretary of State in WWII. Balfour's eulogy captured Sholto perfectly, even if it paints a picture of Sholto and Hazel's marriage in his final years that was perhaps more rosy than the reality:

We gather to pay tribute to Lord Douglas of Kirtleside – known as 'Sholto' by so many – far and wide – great and humble.

We pay tribute to those qualities and characteristics which carried him to the highest positions of two distinct careers: first, service – in the Royal Flying Corps and Royal Air Force; secondly, civil – as chairman of British European Airways for fifteen years …

I know that nothing would have sickened him more than just words of fulsome adulation on such an occasion as today. He once described himself as a 'robust individual' – and I would go further – Sholto was a gloriously contentious character, and he would wish us to remember him as he was.

Looking back over the years, the qualities that I recall most vividly are his determination; judgement; his fairness and his loyalty to all those around him.

When our time comes, would that we could outweigh our faults, weaknesses and failures – of which every one of us is only too aware – with such qualities of heart and mind as possessed by Sholto.

Appreciations of the high manner he discharged his great responsibilities in the Royal Air Force – as Commander in Chief Fighter Command, and later as Commander in Chief Coastal Command, at the time of D-Day – and still later as Commander in Chief Germany – have been written about and there will be more in the future. Likewise, his achievements in the field of civil aviation.

But it is as the man we remember him today.

A moment ago I summarised some of his qualities as they struck me and I think others too. I would put in the van of all others his loyalty and sympathy towards all who worked with him. Now Sholto was not always an easy fellow, and particularly to those to whom he may have been answerable during his rise to high rank. If he differed, he was at no pains to hide this. In today's phraseology 'he made the message very clear'.

Yet to those on his staff from senior to junior clerk he extended limitless loyalty. All knew this.

He was a man trusted. This in itself is a lovely epitaph for any man.

If someone slipped up in his task, provided always, to use an expression of his, the man would 'come clean' on his failure, it was on to Sholto's broad shoulders that the responsibility of error was transferred.

Every individual who served under him – service or civil – knew that he could be relied on never to let them down.

Outside his official life – and this I know myself from 1917 onwards – Sholto allied himself to the left in politics, although I would never describe him as an 'ardent party man'.

It was his belief that by this particular allegiance he could best express his hopes for the less fortunate in life.

He felt deeply the human responsibilities of his position and once he told me that the most painful hour of his career was when justice demanded his signature on the death sentences for Goering and the other Nazi leaders after the Nuremberg trials.

In his own life he was gay and fun. He enjoyed the material good things of life. Good company, good food, good wine. How right he was – and he always ensured that those with him should share in such pleasures.

To travel with him on some service or civil mission was a tremendous experience. One saw welcome extended to all he met, yet work accomplished with orderly calm: there was fun and grand companionship.

Sholto's powerful personality had an inspiring effect on all those he met and to such extent that they in turn were able to pass on something of this to others who knew their Chief only by hearsay. Such is the effect of that indefinable human quality he possessed called 'Leadership'.

In this address it would be false to ignore the rough passages and sometimes stormy weather of his personal life. But then later in his life his ship sailed into calm waters. The sun shone and his marriage was blessed with a daughter, still young today.

He then enjoyed the happiness of being safely at anchor in harbour, though his last years were menaced by the gathering clouds of ill health.

To Lady Douglas and to Katharine we can express our deep sympathy. But also we can share with them the memory of a <u>big man</u> and a <u>true friend</u>.

Sholto may not have owed allegiance to ritual religion of the Church, but in his life and what he accomplished, I venture to say that he showed himself a better Christian than many of we who subscribe to orthodoxy.

Just a few days before he died, he was asked to inscribe a presentation volume of his memoirs for an Eton Library, and this is what he chose:-

> I have never been rich in the sense of money, but I have come to enjoy other riches that have been far greater than I ever thought would come my way.

Like it or not, and certainly not expecting any guard of honour, I do believe for Sholto 'So he passed over and all the trumpets sounded for him on the other side'.

CHAPTER TWENTY-SEVEN

A LIFETIME OF TRAUMA

Today, almost everyone has heard of post-traumatic stress disorder. Indeed, mention of this condition following a disaster like that of Grenfell Tower, in the context of overseas conflicts such as in Afghanistan, Iraq or Syria, more recently during the coronavirus pandemic, or subsequent to the Beirut explosion, produces a world-weary *ennui* in some quarters: 'Not *that* again,' as we see interviews with distressed, tearful people, obviously traumatised, on our TV screens. But can familiarity with the term actually preclude understanding? We *think* we know what it all means, but do we really? Perhaps we have a passing familiarity with some of the symptoms: nightmares, flashbacks, traumatic memories that won't go away, inability to feel positive emotions, angry outbursts, hypervigilance. These are just some of the many criteria for PTSD listed in the fifth edition of the Diagnostic and Statistical Manual of Mental Disorders, but do these symptoms, of which most people are aware, paint a whole picture?

Until I started researching this book, I had the common idea that PTSD stems usually from a single traumatic event, with images in my mind of shell-shocked soldiers in WWI, and that it is primarily a psychological disorder. Once I had grasped that it had been manifest to such a degree in my father, I realised how all-encompassing PTSD can be, its malign tendrils reaching into every part of the body and far back into the sufferer's childhood, exposing the tiniest vulnerabilities and wounds inflicted, whether psychic or physical, decades previously. Adverse life events, such as childhood poverty, prior to a traumatic episode are more common in those who go on to develop the chronic form of the illness.[1] With each reactivation of memories associated with the trauma(s), sometimes triggered by things that to the rest of us may seem inconsequential, sensitisation occurs.[2] It's like a wound that keeps being reopened, becoming increasingly sore with each insult. Eventually, the person's whole being is affected by the trauma, not just the brain and nervous system, with increasing physical as well as psychological morbidity.[3]

These things I witnessed in my father towards the end of his life, and in case you are tempted to think, as many have from WWI onwards, that it is only the 'weak', 'defective' or, in that most modern of concepts, those 'lacking in resilience'[4] (all of which have unpleasant eugenicist connotations) who break down, then it would be wise to consider Sholto. As you have seen, a more resolute, resilient person, at least outwardly, it would be hard to find, and it is an insult to every PTSD sufferer to think in those terms. The armed forces lexicon used to describe individuals exhibiting signs of distress following trauma may have changed over the course of a century, from 'cowardice under fire' to 'lack of moral fibre' to 'lacking in resilience', but the stigma and prejudice remain, only covered now by a veneer of so-called knowledge.

That is not to deny that pre-existing factors such as childhood adversity have a bearing on one's susceptibility to the condition, facilitating that process of sensitisation.[5] From the age of six, Sholto suffered his father's desertion, his mother's consequent distress, and poverty. Actually, from the age of two, following his father Langton's affair with the housemaid with whom he subsequently had twins, the bonds that might have held the family together disintegrated. All of Sholto's four siblings died, one before he was born, another when he was a young child, the third during WWI, and the last when he was in his thirties.

George Vaillant, in his book on the Grant study of adult development, observed: 'The reliable presence of people who love us facilitates our perception and toleration of painful reality.'[6] The Grant study is significant because one of the sample groups comprised Harvard graduates with educational backgrounds similar to Sholto's, one of whom was John F. Kennedy. The study showed that, unsurprisingly, childhood adversity exerts its effects throughout life. Men from bleak childhoods age more rapidly and experience more mental and physical illness than those from more positive ones. Vaillant commented: 'Mental illness in adult life was rarely the fault of any one person or event; for in human development, it is the sustained emotional trauma, not the sudden insult, that does the most lasting damage to the human spirit.'[7] In all of this, the mental health of parents is a crucial element, and Sholto's mother was chronically depressed. The study also showed that fathers' capacity to love was an important factor in determining how successful their sons were. An example that paralleled Sholto's experience almost exactly was of a boy of four whose father had left home, but who continued to pursue his father, whereas the boy's brother had excluded his father from his life. The brother who was the most successful in later life was the one who maintained contact with his father, which Sholto managed to do despite everything, almost wrenching his father's love out of him. Nevertheless, betrayal by an important attachment figure, such as Sholto experienced with his father, increases the risk of childhood traumatisation and PTSD as an adult.[8] Sholto himself complained of the 'inherent self-consciousness' that always bothered him, ascribing it to the break-up of his parents' marriage when he was very young. F. C. Bartlett, the first professor of experimental psychology at Cambridge, observed in his book *Psychology and the Soldier*, published in 1927, that 'an unusual degree of shyness, or lack of sociability, or secretiveness',[9] all of which Sholto displayed to some degree, were predisposing factors in 'mental breakdown under the conditions of modern warfare'. Bartlett ascribed such shyness and anti-social characteristics to the experience of being '"let down" by somebody for whom he had a great respect or a great love'.[10]

Since the Grant study, other investigations have shown that early life stress has a bearing not only on subsequent reactions to trauma but also on brain development in structures that are implicated in PTSD. Brain imaging in adults who have endured two or more adverse childhood events (ACEs) has demonstrated significant reductions in volume in two brain regions, the anterior cingulate cortex (ACC, part of the system concerned with managing responses to threat) and the caudate nuclei (involved in emotional regulation and inhibitory control of action, as well as habit learning), compared to people who have experienced none. And this was reported in a study population without clinically significant past or current psycho-pathology.[11] The ACEs included divorce and separation from other family members. In another imaging study looking at ACC volume in US military veterans with and without PTSD, and observing the contributions of both childhood and combat trauma, both PTSD and the interaction of early trauma and combat exposure were associated with smaller ACC volume. Such phenomena were not observed in those who had not experienced childhood trauma.[12]

In a New Zealand study in which the participants were followed from birth, childhood adversity, specifically maternal distress and loss of a parent due to death, divorce or separation prior to eleven years, was shown to be a predictor for PTSD at twenty-six years.[13] Other studies that involved military personnel have implicated childhood adversity, including economic deprivation, in the subsequent development of depression and PTSD,[14] as well as other mood and anxiety disorders,[15] above and beyond the role of combat exposure.[16] However, an alternative suggestion from another study involving combat veterans with PTSD is that the methods that a child uses in order to cope with the fear and anxiety associated with childhood trauma may actually assist an individual when later exposed to a combat situation. In this study, for those reporting high levels of combat exposure, increased levels of childhood adversity served to lower PTSD severity.[17] It is possible to see how this might work, particularly in Sholto's case, where he developed quite robust ways of coping as a child, but this did not hold true throughout his life and it is definitely a minority view. It is contradicted by findings from a more recent prospective study of Australian troops deployed to Afghanistan. This investigation demonstrated that the opposite happens: namely, greater pre-deployment trauma, including that occurring during childhood, has a cumulative negative effect, so that a higher number of traumatic events prior to deployment is associated with post-deployment PTSD and depressive symptoms.[18]

It's not simply the number of repeated exposures to traumatic events, including in combat situations, but also their duration, which increases the risk of PTSD, especially in those units that have had longer spells of deployment[19] with less time to recuperate in between,[20] as happened with Sholto and the squadrons in which he served in WWI. Another factor in the development of what were called war neuroses in WWI was the prolonged experience of danger without the ability to do anything about it, for example having to passively endure shelling if on the ground,[21] or being an observer in an aircraft as opposed to a pilot.[22] There was also the helplessness of experiencing the death of comrades and being unable to prevent it,[23] as when Sholto and so many others watched friends being shot down in flames. Sholto wrote repeatedly in *Years of Combat* of the deep distress that this engendered, usually compounded at the same time by the danger to his own life during aerial battles.

The Grant study also showed that after WWII, men with high combat exposure continued to report increased symptoms of PTSD up to forty years later. Perhaps more remarkably, they were also 'more likely to be in *Who's Who in America* and to enjoy a good psychosocial outcome, mature defences, and low neuroticism. However, exposure to repeated combat predicted poor future physical health.'[24] While this is another nail in the coffin of the 'weak', 'lacking in resilience' view of those with PTSD, the link with poor physical health in later life resonates not only with Sholto's situation but also with the concept of PTSD as a systemic illness involving multiple bodily systems.

There is also evidence of sensitisation with repeated deployments, but it reveals itself in more subtle ways. A study of the effects of prior combat experience on the expression of somatic (physical) and affective (emotional) symptoms in servicemen deployed to Iraq found that the more experienced soldiers reported limited affective complaints but greater somatic problems compared to those without combat experience. The authors attributed this to 'a greater reliance on repressive processes such as denial, distortion, or suppression of affect'.[25] They observed that their findings were consistent with other studies that have reported increased somatisation, that is, the manifestation of psychological distress by the presentation of physical symptoms, among soldiers with prior combat exposure, especially those with a history of PTSD. Increasing familiarity with the military culture brings greater awareness of the stigma and prejudice that still exist within that environment, meaning that soldiers do not want to be seen as 'weak' or 'less capable' in the eyes of their leaders and comrades, and sadly, those with the greatest need for mental health services are the least likely to seek help from them.[26] This is something with which Sholto and his comrades were even more familiar.

In the context of military service, combat exposure is not the only factor that increases the likelihood of PTSD. A study of 422 US veterans with PTSD found that other trauma exposures such as assaults (up to 39 per cent of their sample) rendered them more vulnerable to developing PTSD.[27] Sholto was subjected to just such an attack by the pilots in his squadron in 1918 that knocked him unconscious, leaving him concussed and lying on the ground.

There is a substantial overlap between what is termed 'post-concussive syndrome' (defined as a complex disorder in which various symptoms, including headaches and dizziness, last for weeks and sometimes months following the injury that caused the concussion) and PTSD.[28] Sholto had at least two such episodes in WWI, the first following that bad aircraft crash when he struck a horse on take-off and the second when he was assaulted. More recently, among US soldiers deployed to Iraq, mild traumatic brain injury caused by such events as blasts or explosions, shrapnel fragments, falls and vehicle accidents where the injury involved the head was strongly associated with PTSD and physical health problems three to four months after the soldiers returned home. This association was not seen to the same degree with injuries to other parts of the body.[29] Concussion is associated with such changes to brain tissue as stretching of nerve fibres, swelling and metabolic changes that may result in secondary loss of connections between nerve cells.[30] The authors of the Iraq study observed that 'PTSD and depression are important mediators of the relationship between mild traumatic brain injury and physical health problems'.[31] Not only is there a link between post-concussive syndrome and PTSD but there is also a link between both of these conditions and dementia in later life.[32]

An essential component in aiding recovery from traumatic events is the amount of social support that a person receives, lack thereof being a potent factor in determining whether a person goes on to develop PTSD.[33] Social support can take many forms, including acknowledgement in the community and the possibility of disclosing thoughts and feelings to a person with whom one is closely connected, whether a partner or friends. Those who develop PTSD initially but who are embedded in a supportive social network are at lower risk for developing the chronic form of the illness. The opposite is true for those who do not have the benefits of such help.[34] A frequent assertion by military personnel in WWI and in every conflict since then is that those at home understand nothing of what goes on in foreign combat situations, and servicemen and women returning from those wars meet with little real appreciation of what they have endured. That's possibly why many choose not to talk of their experiences even now. We saw how little there was of any kind of assistance, social, medical or familial, for Sholto and his fellows returning from WWI, and how isolated he felt when trying to make decisions about his future. His bonds with his parents were fragile, his mother still grieving for the loss of Archie, her favourite son, and his father preoccupied with financial worries, augmented by the growing number of children he had to support, although, reluctantly, he did point Sholto in the direction of an art historian who might be an avenue to future employment. Such 'anxious attachments', which must have been this way from Sholto's childhood, in which attachment figures are seen as inaccessible and/or unresponsive, predispose to the development of PTSD.[35] In the end, with the encouragement of Trenchard, who fulfilled a fatherly role to some extent, Sholto returned to what he knew best and where he felt most alive, the RAF, but in time this path would take him not only to positions of leadership but also right back to trauma.

Very little has been written about leaders having PTSD, although both the physician and psychologist William Rivers and a colleague of his, Charles Myers, offered what might now be considered class-ridden explanations of the different manifestations of war neurosis in officers as opposed to ordinary soldiers in WWI, and the reasons for them. But perhaps, as Rivers, well-known for treating Siegfried Sassoon in Craiglockhart War Hospital, suggested, it was all about the relationship of an officer to his men, resembling that of father to son,[36] meaning that the officer could not be seen to be vulnerable even though some officers undoubtedly did suffer. Myers reasoned that

> the forces of education, tradition and example made for greater self-control in the case of the Officer. He, moreover, is busy throughout a bombardment, issuing orders and subject to worry over his responsibilities, whereas his men can do nothing during the shelling, but watch and wait until the order is received for an advance.[37]

This explanation might have been appropriate for the Army at that time, but as the physician T. A. Ross, who treated many WWI combat survivors at the Cassel Hospital, observed, different conditions obtained in the Air Force. Subsequently, in WWII, Ross noted that although there was a high incidence of combat neurosis among those in Bomber and Flying Training Commands, as we have seen, ground staff could also be thus affected. These personnel, whom Ross termed 'the craftsmen', were 'in fact responsible for the safety of their officers', and many of them were overwhelmed by their responsibilities. Ross had treated some of them in peacetime prior to WWII. Often they had 'broken down' after an aircraft had crashed, when they wondered whether it was their carelessness that had caused the accident.[38]

As Ross and others have recognised, the element of control over one's own and others' circumstances is an important factor in the genesis of PTSD. A study of UK armed forces personnel at the time of the Iraq War in 2003 found that officers had a markedly lower risk of psychological symptoms than other ranks and that this was explained in part by higher job control, low job control being associated with adverse psychological symptoms even if the work was not particularly demanding.[39]

An account that examines long-term outcomes among veterans of the brutal Kokoda Trail campaign in the Far East in 1942, written by an esteemed Australian psychologist, the late John Raftery, examined soldiers' perceptions of their roles decades after the campaign. John and I shared a special interest because, like Sholto, his father, born just a year later, had fought in WWI. John wrote in his study of the Kokoda veterans that although the strain of combat was a common thread in the narratives of both officers and men, they had differing accounts of life after discharge. John observed: 'The officer believes that while a stressful experience does have a short-term effect, it dissipates without the need for expert intervention or particular adjustment. The militia soldier confesses to a lifetime of struggle.'[40]

Although Sholto did have periods of difficulty after both world wars, he managed to gather his forces and carry on. Perhaps, as the neurologist Henry Head, who had worked with Rivers, submitted to the 1922 inquiry into 'shell-shock', 'The officer ... is repressing all the time because, first of all, he must not show fear in any circumstances.'[41] This would have been Sholto's lifelong habit, and it was what enabled him and I suspect many like him who reached senior positions, for example Newall, the first CAS in WWII, to carry on until it was no longer possible.

Many times in Sholto's life, there are signs that he employed defence mechanisms to deal with the memories of distressing events. Such mechanisms include the unconscious repression of traumatic images, avoidance of people, places or situations that can act as reminders of trauma, and emotional 'numbing', in which the sufferer attempts to block out all feelings. Sholto remarked more than once that he did not experience either the highs or the lows of emotion, and was noted for his calmness and phlegmatic exterior, except in post-war Germany, when one of the US team of lawyers at the Nuremberg trials remarked that Sholto was 'explosive', and of course when he was older. The American psychiatrist Abram Kardiner described this blunting of emotions perfectly in his patients with what he called 'traumatic neuroses' but what would be termed PTSD today. He made many of his observations while studying survivors from WWI in the 1920s but published his book *The Traumatic Neuroses of War* in 1941 when it was clear to him that the lessons of the previous war had not been learned and there was an urgent need to revisit them.[42] He noted that 'the affective tone in traumatic neurosis is generally diminished, except for aggression and tenderness'.[43] Thus, in post-war Germany, Sholto's explosions were interspersed with open-mindedness and humanity when it came to considering those most unfortunate individuals whose lives he held in his hands. Much closer to home and years later, he alternated between angry outbursts to others and melting tenderness towards my mother and me.

Emotional numbing correlates with reduced activity in those networks in the brain associated with reward. This has been clearly demonstrated in an imaging study involving PTSD patients and trauma-exposed controls who had not developed PTSD. The participants were shown happy and neutral faces in random order and the responses within the networks of the brain that are activated by rewarding or reinforcing stimuli were monitored. Those with PTSD rated happy facial expressions as less intense than the control group, and at the same time showed reduced activation in reward processing networks, consistent with emotional numbing.[44] The reason this is so important is that the ability to interpret and respond to facial displays of emotion is essential to effective social functioning, something that is often lacking in those with PTSD.[45]

The conscious suppression of traumatic memories is a more mature defence mechanism, which PTSD sufferers use because they have a phobia of these memories that involves fear, disgust, shame or guilt, emotions that Sholto would have felt, but perhaps attempted to banish, many times during his life as a consequence of warfare, or of the actions he was compelled to perform in post-war Germany. Strikingly, feelings of shame are common among military personnel when discharged, the implication being that military training and discipline facilitate the suppression of debilitating emotional reactions such as shame but that this cannot be sustained on leaving the services.[46] The philosopher Peter Marin has suggested that on discharge, veterans have the opportunity to reflect on the meaning and moral significance of past events and that their remorse does not recede with the passage of time, making their view of life increasingly tragic.[47] Certainly, after Sholto's time in Germany, it was impossible to forget his profound moral anguish not only over the devastation caused by the war but also to a greater degree over the numerous death warrants he had had to sign. In fact, it was the major reason for him requesting leave of his post there. The primacy of such moral injury over other causative factors in the development of PTSD has been highlighted in a study which demonstrated that the best predictor of the prototypical re-experiencing symptoms of PTSD is not a threat to one's life, nor the traumatic loss of a comrade, but a morally injurious event of which one is the perpetrator.[48]

Rivers wrote a great deal about the repression and suppression of traumatic memories in war neuroses. Somewhat confusingly, he used the terms in the opposite way round to the sense in which they are employed today. For him, repression was 'the process by which we wittingly endeavour to banish experience from consciousness' and suppression the *unconscious* removal of unwanted material from awareness. He added that repression may be one way of producing suppression, but more often the latter occurs 'wholly without the intervention of volition, especially when it occurs as the result of some physical or mental shock'.[49] These defence mechanisms, whichever way round they are applied, are important because they are what enabled Sholto to continue right through his life until almost the end without an overt mental collapse. Rivers remarked that complete suppression of fear was possible even during the traumas of aerial combat in WWI, and in some cases it was 'so well established that this emotion remains completely absent even when the danger is so insistent and unavoidable that death or violent injury is inevitable. Thus, the emotion of fear may be completely absent during the fall and crash of an aeroplane in which death seems certain...' An alternative reaction to fear was something that Sholto recognised in himself, which was 'the assumption of an aggressive attitude towards the source of danger with the accompaniment of the affective state of anger'.[50] I suspect that Sholto employed this device, whether consciously or unconsciously, many times during his military career.

Rivers observed that suppression becomes 'less potent and effective with advancing years'.[51] A vital factor in Sholto's scenario was his retirement. While he had his absorbing job as chairman of BEA, he could keep the memories at bay, much like an Australian WWII veteran whose wife remarked: 'When his mind was full of [work] he was

OK, but once he retired the nightmares started ... It was terrible.'[52] Once again, Rivers described this process perfectly:

> If unpleasant thoughts are voluntarily repressed during the day, it is natural that they should rise into activity when the control of the waking state is removed by sleep or is weakened in the state which precedes and follows sleep and its intervals ... It is as if the process of repression keeps the painful memories or thoughts under a kind of pressure during the day, accumulating such energy by the time night comes that they race through the mind with abnormal speed and violence when the patient is wakeful, or take the most vivid and painful forms when expressed by the imagery of dreams.[53]

Rivers's patient Siegfried Sassoon wrote in one of his later poems, published in 1935, of 'that garret of uneasy gloom / Which is your brain'.[54] Similarly to Sassoon, whose memories of his traumatic WWI experiences were undiminished two decades later, Sholto's brain provided him with little respite in his old age.

This re-experiencing of traumatic memories is one of the fundamental symptoms of PTSD, in which not only is there psychological distress but also a reactivation of the stress response that occurred at the time of the trauma, sometimes called 'fight or flight'. Stress hormones such as cortisol and noradrenaline are activated, producing physiological symptoms such as sweating and increased heart rate. Repeated activation of the traumatic memory tends to cause a worsening of the associated stress response, meaning that there is a progressive increase in a person's reactivity with each recurrence.[55] An essential part in this cascade is played by the amygdala, a small, almond-shaped group of neurons, which has a key role in the processing of emotions, and forms part of the limbic system, which deals with emotion and memory. In PTSD, the amygdala mounts an exaggerated response that is the basis of the excessive acquisition of fear associations and the expression of fear responses.[56] Also central to this condition is a corresponding deficit of frontal cortical functioning, this being the part of the brain that has an important role in extinguishing the fear response. It is possible that declining function of parts of the frontal cortex with age would weaken further its modulating effect.[57] Another part of the brain involved in this whole story is the hippocampus, which has been shown to play a role in fear learning and appreciation of the context of safety. In PTSD, there is a deficit in hippocampal functioning, and recent imaging studies have shown that it decreases in size in this condition,[58] as well as undergoing microstructural changes that worsen its anatomical and functional integrity. Similar damage occurs in the caudate nuclei and, because of their role in habit learning, may underlie the flashbacks and reactivity to triggers seen in those with PTSD.[59] If these structures involved in fear and stress systems are overactivated repeatedly, as occurs in combat or other war-related situations, this results in increasing dysregulation over time.[60]

Chronic exposure to this cascade of events, termed 'allostatic load', has been shown to increase the risk for multiple physical disorders, which challenges the notion of PTSD as involving only the mind. In fact, it is unhelpful to think of it only in these terms, since this ignores the growing body of evidence that demonstrates the need to reframe it as a whole-body or 'systemic' condition.[61] Greater lifetime trauma exposure alone increases the possibility of developing a chronic medical condition, although the likelihood of poor physical health is greater in those with an actual diagnosis of PTSD.[62] Even back in 1941, Kardiner observed that 'the nucleus of the neurosis is a *physioneurosis*'.[63] Inclusion of the entire body in response to trauma, via excitation of stress systems including the hypothalamic-pituitary-adrenal (HPA) and sympathetic-adrenal-medullary (SAM) axes, increases a person's susceptibility to inflammatory conditions such as coronary artery disease,[64] and the factors associated with its development, including high blood pressure.[65] Those with combat-related PTSD have a higher risk of arterial disease in general, not just of the coronary arteries, increasing the probability of stroke,[66] and PTSD has been shown to predict cardiovascular mortality in a large population of combat veterans sixteen years after the traumatic events.[67] PTSD is also a risk factor for being overweight and obese,[68] and as we have seen in Sholto's story, repeated attention was drawn by others to his increasing girth. Although it can be a consequence of

PTSD, some individuals see it as a protective mechanism, a man in the Grant study observing that he actually wanted a fat abdomen 'in order to make myself more imposing'.[69] However, it can also indicate a condition known as metabolic syndrome, from which I am sure Sholto suffered. This is a cluster of symptoms that include increased blood pressure, high blood sugar, excess body fat around the waist, and abnormal cholesterol levels. This condition increases the risk of heart disease, heart attack and stroke, all of which were mentioned in Sholto's post-mortem report as causes of his death. An evaluation of many studies, called a meta-analysis, showed that the risk of meta-bolic syndrome among individuals in midlife with PTSD was almost double that of the general population.[70] Even more seriously, a brain imaging study of young military veterans has suggested that PTSD may be a catalyst for the association between metabolic syndrome and widespread reductions in the thickness of many areas of the cerebral cortex, predisposing individuals to premature ageing and substantial cognitive decline.[71]

Many clinicians treating those who have PTSD have recog-nised that their methods of dealing with trauma may lead to over-indulgence in tobacco, alcohol and also food,[72] tendencies that Sholto had displayed ever since WWI. Both AVM Salmond, later to become CAS, and Squadron Leader Craig, an RAF medical officer, reported in the 1922 inquiry into 'shell-shock' that excessive use of tobacco and alcohol was commonplace among pilots in WWI. Indeed, it was the way in which they 'sustained themselves'.[73] More recent investiga-tions have shown that even though rates in the general population are declining, smoking continues to be much more common in veterans with PTSD. But cause and effect are difficult to untangle, as pre-existing nicotine dependence has been shown to increase the likelihood of PTSD among military veterans.[74] This may be due to the effects of long-term smoking on the central nervous system. Nic-otine has been shown to promote the release of the stress hormone cortisol and to dysregulate the HPA axis, thereby sensitising neural stress systems,[75] and rendering individuals more vulnerable to PTSD after trauma exposure. It also modulates the activity of the hippocam-pus, amygdala and prefrontal cortex, those regions of the brain most implicated in PTSD, and may interfere with the extinction of the fear response, increasing fearful, defensive reactions.[76]

Regarding alcohol, there is a significant association between length of deployment and severe alcohol problems, which is due in part to combat exposure.[77] A study conducted in 2010 found that the prevalence of alcohol misuse in current members of the armed forces (10.9 per cent) was twice that in the general population (5.4 per cent). This rose to three times (15.7 per cent) in those service personnel deployed to either Iraq or Afghanistan or both.[78] However, the psychiatrist Bessel van der Kolk has observed that there is a circular relationship between PTSD and substance abuse, including drugs and alcohol, due to the temporary relief from trauma symptoms that they provide, but withdrawing from them causes additional problems as it increases hyperarousal, thereby intensifying nightmares, flashbacks and irritability,[79] making it very difficult to address substance dependence in those with PTSD.

The same brain structures and stress systems involved in other addictive behaviours relative to PTSD are implicated in the response to food. A deterioration in inhibitory learning and memory processes, functions mediated by the hippocampus, may interfere with the regulation of food intake that normally prevents excessive consumption. Moreover, activation of the HPA axis reduces the satisfaction and sense of reward that usually accompanies eating, which may cause sufferers to seek out sugary and fat-rich comfort foods, all of which adds to their weight gain.[80]

The long-term effects of combat, of which these kinds of addictions often form a part, were noted by Butler in his *Official History of the Australian Army Medical Services in WWI*. He wrote: 'Participation in the war had an inimical and far reaching influence on the "nervous system" which might lie dormant for many years, and determine a "breakdown" under adverse circumstances.'[81] This concept has been termed 'delayed-onset PTSD', and in the 1960s, there appeared in the scientific literature instances of chronic and even irreversible combat fatigue, as it was known then, among veterans twenty years after the end of WWII.[82] These findings have been augmented by studies since then,[83] but in common with many older people who display symptoms of PTSD, the difficulty with Sholto is determining whether its emergence was truly an example of delayed onset, or whether it had been festering away for almost his entire life only to manifest itself fully when his defences were down. What does delayed onset mean in this context? The research evidence suggests that 'true' delayed-onset PTSD, where there is no evidence of any previous symptoms, is uncommon.[84]

The psychologist Chris Brewin has noted that surveys documenting the natural course of PTSD over time have indicated that immediately following a traumatic event, such as a physical assault, many people display symptoms such as re-experiencing, avoidance and arousal that are sufficient to meet the diagnostic criteria for PTSD. Over the first three months after the event, the number of people suffering these symptoms drops off rapidly, after which it stabilises. However, as many as one third of victims go on to develop chronic symptoms lasting not just months but years thereafter. In some cases, the onset of full PTSD can be delayed by months or even years after the trauma and may follow a long period of someone being symptom-free.[85] Other investigators have postulated a similar U-shaped curve of PTSD in long-term survivors of trauma, in which symptoms are elevated shortly after a traumatic experience, decline thereafter and increase again in later life, in conjunction with other age-related problems.[86] Severe physical illness in old age, involving the loss of independence and inability to follow recreational activities, both of which indicate diminishing control, can lead to the emergence of PTSD symptoms.[87]

What I suspect happened to Sholto and occurs especially in former military personnel is that they have symptoms following a traumatic event or events that do not fulfil the criteria for PTSD at first but do so at a later stage.[88] This was demonstrated in a prospective military study in which data were collected over several time points. Many of those who were classed as having delayed-onset PTSD had had symptoms compatible with 'subthreshold' PTSD at an earlier phase of data collection.[89] The same study showed that psychiatric illness in the first phase, including subthreshold PTSD, increases the risk of so-called delayed-onset PTSD by the follow-up phase. Laboratory investigations also reveal a disruption in the underlying neurobiology of such individuals even though their symptom levels are well below the threshold for a full diagnosis of PTSD.[90] As might be expected, exposure to further stressful events following an initial trauma increases the likelihood of developing full-blown PTSD later.[91] This may be particularly true in military service, where personnel are subjected to multiple traumatic episodes.

One problem is the tendency by some clinicians and researchers to 'normalise' the early symptoms of distress following traumatic stress exposure, which means that early signs that are indicative of the future development of a chronic course of the disorder are downplayed.[92] This highlights the importance of longitudinal studies, i.e. those that follow a sample over a period of months and years, as against those that are cross-sectional, which only look at groups of subjects at a single point in time. All of this emphasises the need to take what the psychiatrist Sandy McFarlane and his co-authors call a 'staging approach' to PTSD, in which early symptoms of subclinical distress are not dismissed as 'normal reactions to abnormal events', as is often asserted by clinicians, but a longer-term approach is used, which monitors military personnel using models that reflect more accurately alterations in trauma symptoms over time and decreases the emphasis on studies involving single traumatic events.[93]

The Grant study also demonstrated the unchanging nature of traumatic memory as opposed to non-traumatic autobiographical recollections that tend to alter over time. The investigators interviewed their subjects in detail about their war experiences after WWII in 1945–46, and then again in 1989–90. At the second interview point, most of them gave very different accounts from those recorded forty-five years earlier. Over the years, the wartime events had been stripped of their horror. By contrast, those who had been traumatised and who had developed PTSD did not modify their accounts. Their memories were frozen intact four and a half decades after the war had ended.[94] In his study of the Kokoda veterans, John Raftery saw that in most cases, the traumatic memories not only did not fade but grew stronger with time.[95]

The psychiatrist Mardi Horowitz has observed that these types of memories 'may suddenly intrude only as sensory experiences and fragments of traumatic experience', and of course, what makes them all the more disturbing is that they have 'a sense of the trauma happening all over again in the present moment'.[96] Horowitz also noted that 'the unbidden images tend to occur most frequently when the person relaxes, lies down to sleep, or closes her [or his] eyes to rest'.[97] All of this happened to Sholto, the most intrusive symptoms being his bad dreams, followed by re-enactments that occurred in the space between wakefulness and sleep. Horowitz asserts that these types of 'highly important' memory, or flashbacks, are replayed over and over again in the brain until some sort of 'completion' occurs, involving their transfer from 'active memory storage', as though the events are still occurring, to inactive or long-term memory, where they are integrated into an organised memory structure.[98] Brewin has advanced a slightly different version of the theory of two different memory systems, which are subserved by different brain structures. He calls this 'the dual representation theory of PTSD'. The intense traumatic memories or flashbacks are processed by the perceptual memory system, which is present from birth and is based on visual images and other sensory information. These memories are egocentric, relying on the person's own viewpoint, are automatically activated by related cues or triggers and are relatively inflexible. Narrative memories of the trauma, meanwhile, are processed by the episodic memory system, which develops in early childhood and is dependent on language, with its contents expressed through verbal accounts of the traumatic events. These memories are selective, correspond to the focus of conscious attention, are allocentric in that they admit of alternative viewpoints, and they can be consciously as well as automatically retrieved.[99] The tragedy is that Sholto, like so many others, never had the treatment that would have enabled the flashbacks to be integrated into a more stable long-term memory structure. The disjunction between the two memory systems, perceptual and episodic, which lies at the heart of PTSD, continued until the end of his life.

The interaction between PTSD and dementia in older veterans is a complicated one, because although some of the long-term effects of military service, including combat exposure, can become bound up with the ageing process and accelerate it,[100] it is also the case that trauma symptoms in older adults can be mistaken for the onset of dementia, as was probably the case with Sholto. The authors of an interesting study that used focus groups to examine the emergence of trauma symptoms among military veterans in later life noted that the appearance in the elderly of stress reactions to earlier trauma, including signs of confusion, concentration problems, memory loss and functional impairment, all of which could be ascribed to dementia, can all clear once the trauma is addressed in treatment.[101] These investigators added: 'Moreover, older trauma survivors run the risk of being misdiagnosed with dementing processes, underscoring the potential for inappropriate medical and psychiatric treatment and the further loss of autonomy.'

Nevertheless, one cannot escape the fact that male military veterans diagnosed with PTSD are at a nearly two-fold higher risk of developing dementia compared to those without the condition,[102] and rates of what is called 'incident dementia', i.e. dementia following an event such as a stroke, are higher for those with PTSD than for patients without.[103] It is also the case that the degeneration of higher brain structures seen in older veterans with dementia may also cause the resurgence of trauma memories, which can result in re-enactments. These episodes, involving flashbacks that are quite dramatic and disruptive, mostly occur at night and, as with Sholto, are often accompanied by vocalisations of war-related references.[104]

Another factor in the interaction between PTSD and dementia is sleep disturbance. It is a common symptom of PTSD that is manifest in recurrent nightmares, restless sleep and difficulty falling and staying asleep.[105] For much of his adult life, Sholto had suffered sleep deprivation, especially in the intense activity of the two world wars, but as he entered old age, his sleep became even more disrupted. Sleep disturbance has been shown to cause oxidative stress in the brain, which contributes to cognitive decline and neurodegeneration. The longer someone lives with PTSD, the worse are the effects on the integrity of brain structures and connections,[106] which would in turn predispose to dementia. I did not see those in charge of Sholto's care bearing his trauma in mind, but in view of the long-term duration of PTSD symptoms, which investigators had begun to discern even then,[107] a more trauma-centred approach than I observed would have been so helpful in alleviating his distress.

As well as the occurrence of flashbacks, another deeper structural dislocation can arise in those with PTSD. In Chapter One, I described how Sholto seemed to have left a piece of himself in the situation that caused him the most distress, post-war Germany with all of those death warrants, and that when he was old and at his most vulnerable following strokes, that missing part came back to haunt him, taking us back there with him. This phenomenon has been called 'dissociation', and van der Kolk has described precisely what I witnessed: 'The overwhelming experience is split off and fragmented, so that the emotions, sounds, images, thoughts, and physical sensations related to the trauma take on a life of their own. The sensory fragments of memory intrude into the present, where they are literally relived.'[108] Whether this involves a separate though incomplete personality, or whether it is simply a nexus of the features outlined above, brought to the forefront of a person's mind by some sort of vulnerability or perhaps a triggering event, has been the subject of considerable debate within the trauma specialist community ever since the concept was first articulated by the French physician and psychologist Pierre Janet in 1886.[109] He expounded this theory of 'dissociation' in a paper about unconscious acts and double personality during induced somnambulism, although he actually used the word 'dissociation' in a paper the following year.[110]

Rivers asserted that it was important not to confuse 'dissociation' with 'suppression', something of which he said he had been guilty himself, even though the two phenomena are linked. In the case of dissociation, 'the suppressed experience does not remain passive, but acquires an independent activity of its own'. The emergence of this separate consciousness has continued to be referred to as a 'fugue', in which, Rivers continued, 'a person shows behaviour, often of the most complicated kind, and lasting it may be for considerable periods of time, of which he is wholly unaware in the normal state'.[111] Dissociative fugues may occur during waking, but what I witnessed with my father happened during the night and is more usually described as 'somnambulism'. Rivers wrote that this was 'of especial interest as an example of dissociation on account of its very close resemblance to a fugue'. The person walking in his sleep may perform quite complicated actions 'which are wholly independent of the activities of his normal life'. He may be aware of these actions in the form of a dream that he remembers when he wakes, but 'more often any consciousness which may have accompanied the somnambulistic acts becomes inaccessible as soon as the sleeper awakes'. Nevertheless, somnambulism fulfilled Rivers's definition of dissociation as it displays both independent activity and independent consciousness, so he concluded that 'there is, in fact, no difference between a fugue and a somnambulistic attack except that one occurs in sleep and the other in the waking state'.[112]

Certainly, when I first heard of and read about dissociation, it resembled most closely what I observed of my father's behaviour: the emergence of what seemed to be someone else at night, the person who was stuck in post-war Germany, although he was not completely unrecognisable. The key piece of evidence that clinches this for me was that during the day in his normal, conscious state, Sholto was wheelchair bound and required lifting, whereas at night during his somnambulistic episodes, he could get himself out of bed and walk, albeit holding on to something. Similar phenomena have been observed in others for whom dissociation is part of their condition, including by Myers, who witnessed them in those acutely traumatised following combat in WWI. When these soldiers were operating in their 'apparently normal' personality as Myers termed it, they suffered mutism, paralysis or contractures of the limbs, but during dissociative episodes, often occurring during sleep, a different 'emotional' personality emerged and the disorders that were there during waking were no longer present. Myers wrote: 'On waking, however, the "apparently normal" personality may have no recollection of the dream state and will at once resume his mutism, paralysis, etc.'[113] This is similar to what I witnessed in Sholto and is generally referred to as 'somatoform dissociation' as it involves a lack of normal integration of those components of experience involving sensation and motor functions.[114]

How is dissociation different from flashbacks? It has been

suggested that there are two different subtypes of PTSD, dissociative and non-dissociative, which involve different patterns of activity in the regions of the brain implicated in the condition. However, these processes are not completely distinct, and individuals with PTSD may show both response patterns either simultaneously or at different times.[115] In the non-dissociative subtype, also called re-experiencing/hyperarousal PTSD, in which reliving experiences such as flashbacks predominate, there is a failure of inhibition (termed 'emotional undermodulation') of limbic system activity, including in the amygdala, by those areas involved in arousal modulation and emotional regulation, including the prefrontal cortex. This leads to intense, intrusive feelings and compulsive action. In contrast, in the dissociative form of PTSD, there is abnormally high activation of the brain regions involved in emotional regulation, causing decreased limbic system activity, which constitutes emotional overmodulation and produces a state of denial and emotional numbing, at least during 'normal' daytime activity. PTSD sufferers with prolonged traumatic experiences such as childhood adversity and/or combat trauma often display chronic symptoms of dissociation, as opposed to those victims of more acute or single-episode forms of trauma who suffer more from flashbacks.[116] The dissociative subtype is also associated with more severe PTSD.

However one looks at this conundrum, Ross wrote of his patients' fear of 'vivid dreams of a loathsome kind which were almost worse than any experience they had gone through at the Front'.[117] Much more recently, van der Kolk has reported from experience with his patients that this process of reliving can be worse than the trauma itself. Although Sholto's account in *Years of Command* of his feelings about the sentences at the time is distressing enough, his consternation at the resurgence of these events was arguably more upsetting. As van der Kolk has commented: 'Reenactments are frozen in time, unchanging, and they are always lonely, humiliating, and alienating experiences.'[118]

I appreciate that I may not have left you with much hope, but I am not a clinician and so cannot inspire you with first-hand accounts of the successful treatment of PTSD, although undoubtedly they exist.

However, I have always believed that the more one understands a condition, the better one is able to find solutions to treat it. This was the guiding principle in my scientific study of pain mechanisms in infants, and it has been the same in my examination of my father Sholto's life. Tragically, it's too late for him, but my hope is that those involved in the field of trauma will continue, in the most compassionate and rigorous ways, to investigate and find creative means to alleviate the suffering of those with PTSD. It is also up to all of us to encourage those afflicted, which may include ourselves, to come forward and ask for help, without fear of stigma or discrimination, phenomena that are nevertheless remarkably difficult to eradicate. This is particularly relevant to military personnel of senior rank who, because of their often isolated position, are reluctant to reveal hidden traumas and unconsciously repress or actively suppress them, which is part of their armoury of self-protection. The way forward lies in enabling these staff to understand and acknowledge that they may have a problem and to engage with the consultation and treatment process, which should be confidential and easily accessible in every unit.

I leave you with the words of Sholto's favourite war poet, Siegfried Sassoon:

> Break silence. You have listened overlong
> To muttering mind-wrought voices. Call for lights.
> Prove these persistent haunting presences wrong
> Who mock and stultify your days and nights.
>
> Dawn comes, and recreates the sleepless room;
> And eyesight asks what arguing plagues exist.
> But in that garret of uneasy gloom
> Which is your brain, the presences persist.[119]

ENDNOTES

FOREWORD

1 Sholto Douglas, *Years of Combat* (London, Collins, 1963), p. 340.
2 B. S. McEwen, 'The neurobiology of stress: from serendipity to clinical relevance', *Brain Research*, 15 December 2000; 886 (1–2): 172–89.
3 A. G. Butler (ed.), *The Australian army medical services in the war of 1914–1918*, Volume 3 (Australian War Memorial, 1943).
4 K. A. Lee et al., 'A 50-year Prospective Study of the Psychological Sequelae of World War II Combat', *American Journal of Psychiatry*, 1995; 152 (4): 516–22.
5 Douglas, *Years of Combat*, op. cit., pp. 358–9.
6 Imperial War Museum, transcript of a tape recorded by Lord Douglas for the purposes of his autobiography, Box P32.
7 Erich Maria Remarque, *All Quiet on the Western Front* (London, Pan Books, 1987), p. 101.

CHAPTER ONE: MY MEMORIES OF THE DARK GRAY MAN

1 Imperial War Museum (IWM), Duxford, Archives of the Guinea Pig Club, *The Guinea Pig*, August 1948.
2 William Simpson, *I Burned My Fingers* (London, Putnam, 1956 [1955]), p. 10.
3 E. R. Mayhew, *The Reconstruction of Warriors: Archibald McIndoe, the Royal Air Force and the Guinea Pig Club* (London, Greenhill Books, 2004), pp. 58–9.
4 Simpson, op. cit., p. 9.
5 Ibid., p. 228.
6 Garry May, *The Challenge of BEA: the story of a great airline's first 25 years* (London, Wolfe Publishing Ltd, 1971), p. 152.
7 Lord Moran, *Winston Churchill: The struggle for survival, 1940–1965* (London, Constable, 1966), pp. 432, 444.
8 Ibid., p. xv.
9 A. Lähdepuro et al., 'The Impact of Early Life Stress on Anxiety Symptoms in Late Adulthood', *Nature Scientific Reports*, 2019, 9 (1): 4395, published online 13 March 2019.
10 Ben Shephard, *A War of Nerves: Soldiers and Psychiatrists, 1914–1994* (London, Pimlico, 2002 [2000]), p. 207.
11 Roy Richard Grinker and John Paul Spiegel, *War Neuroses in North Africa: The Tunisian Campaign, January to May, 1943* (New York, NY, Josiah Macy Jr Foundation, 1943), p. 157.
12 Shephard, op. cit., p. 215; RxList, Internet Drug Index, information on Nembutal, https://www.rxlist.com/nembutal-side-effects-drug-center.htm, accessed 13 June 2019.
13 Grinker and Spiegel, op. cit., pp. 164–6.
14 Eric J. Ettema, Louise D. Derksen and Evert van Leeuwen, 'Existential loneliness and end-of-life care: A systematic review', *Theoretical Medicine and Bioethics*, April 2010, 31 (2): 141–69.

15 Steven Mee et al., 'Psychological pain: A review of evidence', *Journal of Psychiatric Research*, 2006, 40: 680–90.

16 The term 'shell-shock' was used first in the medical literature by the physician Charles Myers, in a paper entitled 'A contribution to the study of shell shock', published in 1915 (*The Lancet*, i, pp. 316–20). Before WWI, Myers had worked with W. H. R. Rivers in the psychology laboratory at Cambridge, and subsequently became chief specialist in nervous shock to the British Army in France during WWI. Later, although Myers had not invented the term, he regretted using it as it in no way described the condition to which it applied, and the term 'war neurosis' came to be used more frequently by the medical profession.

17 Herbert C. Archibald and Read D. Tuddenham, 'Persistent Stress Reaction After Combat', *Archives of General Psychiatry*, Vol. 12, May 1965, pp. 475–81.

18 John Raftery, *Marks of War: War Neurosis and the Legacy of Kokoda* (Adelaide, Lythrum Press, 2003), p. 118.

CHAPTER TWO: THE BEGINNINGS OF THE DARK GRAY MAN

1 This attractive but probably fictitious suggestion for the origins of the name 'Sholto Douglas' was made by David Hume of Godscroft (1558–1629), a historian, political theorist and controversialist who was private secretary to his relative Archibald Douglas, 8th Earl of Angus. He wrote in *History of the House and Race of Douglas and Angus* (published in 1644) that when King Solvathius, a Celtic king, enquired about the knight who had done such valuable service in helping him to win a battle (mythical or otherwise) in 767AD, somebody exclaimed 'Sholto du glasse!' … 'Behold the black gray man!' This has been the explanation that has been handed down in our family for generations, whether apocryphal or not!

2 Douglas, *Years of Combat*, op. cit., p. 18.

3 Ibid., p. 27.

4 TNA, J77/713/1682, Divorce Court File: Appellant: Margaret Jane Douglas, Respondent: Robert Langton Douglas, Wife's petition.

5 K. C. Koenen et al., 'Early childhood factors associated with the development of post-traumatic stress disorder: results from a longitudinal birth cohort', *Psychological Medicine*, 2007, 37: 181–92.

6 O. A. Cabrera et al., 'Childhood Adversity and Combat as Predictors of Depression and Post-Traumatic Stress in Deployed Troops', *American Journal of Preventive Medicine*, 2007, 33 (2), pp. 77–81.

7 TNA, J77/733/2301, Divorce Court File: Appellant: Margaret Jane Douglas, Respondent: Robert Langton Douglas, Wife's petition.

8 Ibid.

9 Douglas, *Years of Combat*, op. cit., p. 25.

10 Ibid., p. 28.

11 Letter from Sholto to his father Langton dated 5 March 1908, personal collection, Katharine Campbell.

12 Douglas, *Years of Combat*, op. cit., p. 29.

13 Ibid., p. 23.

14 Ibid., p. 24.

15 *The Tonbridgian*, 1911.

16 BE stands for Blériot Experimental, a British single-engine 'tractor' two-seat biplane designed and developed at the Royal Aircraft Factory. Early versions of the BE2 entered squadron service with the Royal Flying Corps in 1912. A 'tractor' configuration means that the propeller is in front of the engine.

17 Douglas, *Years of Combat*, op. cit., p. 34.

18 Ibid., p. 17.

19 *The Tonbridgian*, November 1912.

20 Imperial War Museum (IWM), Documents, 22964, Personal papers of Lord Douglas of Kirtleside. William Sholto Douglas' final report from Tonbridge School, in Robert Wright, Synopsis for *Years of Combat*, Box P32.

21 Douglas, *Years of Combat*, op. cit., p. 36.

22 Anthony Storr, *Churchill's Black Dog and Other Phenomena of the Human Mind* (London, HarperCollins, 1997 [1989]), p. 35.

23 Douglas, *Years of Combat*, op. cit., p. 37.

24 Ibid., p. 39.

CHAPTER THREE: THE SIREN CALL TO WAR

1 Walter Raleigh, *The War in the Air: Being the Story of the part played in the Great War by the Royal Air Force*, Volume I (Oxford, The Clarendon Press, 1922), p. 423.

2 Douglas, *Years of Combat*, op. cit., p. 41.

3 Ibid.

4 That is, pits lined with masonry and/or sandbags.

5 Douglas, *Years of Combat*, op. cit., p. 51.

6 Cyril Falls, *The First World War* (Longmans, London, 1960), p. 17.

7 Douglas, *Years of Combat*, op. cit., p. 55.

8 Ibid., pp. 57–8.

9 Ibid., p. 65.

10 Raleigh, op. cit., p. 420.

11 TNA, AIR 1/2386/228/11/13, An account by course students of war experiences, 1914–1918, Squadron Leader W. S. Douglas, First Course, RAF Staff College, Andover, October 1922, p. 1.

12 John H. Morrow Jr, *The Great War in the Air: Military Aviation from 1909 to 1921* (Washington DC, Smithsonian Institution Press, 1993), p. 116.

13 Raleigh, op. cit., p. 444.

14 H. A. Jones, *The War in the Air: Being the Story of the part played in the Great War by the Royal Air Force*, Volume II (Oxford, The Clarendon Press, 1928), p. 89.

15 TNA, AIR 1/2393/240/1, Record of air photography – 1915. January–March.

16 Jones, Vol. II, op. cit., p. 91.

17 Maryam Philpott, *Air and Sea Power in World War I: Combat and Experience in the Royal Flying Corps and the Royal Navy* (London and New York, I. B. Tauris, 2013), p. 106.

18 Douglas, *Years of Combat*, op. cit., p. 75.

19 Basil Collier, *Heavenly Adventurer: Sefton Brancker and the Dawn of British Aviation* (London, Secker & Warburg, 1959), p. 47, in Morrow, op. cit., p. 114.

20 Jones, Vol. II, op. cit., p. 137.

21 Cecil Lewis, *Sagittarius Rising* (London, Frontline Books, 2009 [1936]), p. 64.

22 TNA, AIR 1/2386/228/11/13, op. cit., p. 4.

23 RAF Museum, DC73/23/2, Letter from 2nd. Lieut. W S Douglas to Mrs Rhodes-Moorhouse, 28 April 1915.

24 RAF Museum, DC71/46/1&2, Pilot's Flying Log Book of 2nd Lieut. W. S. Douglas, 26 May 1915–31 August 1916.

25 Ibid.

26 Denis Winter, *The First of the Few: Fighter Pilots of the First World War* (London, Allen Lane, 1982), p. 36.

27 Douglas, *Years of Combat*, op. cit., p. 94; Lewis, op. cit., p. 40.

28 Raleigh, op. cit., p. 446.

29 Douglas, *Years of Combat*, op. cit., p. 98.

30 Ibid., p. 102.

31 Ibid., p. 104.

32 TNA, AIR 1/688/21/20/8, History of 8 (Bomber) Squadron RAF.

33 Arthur Gould Lee, *Open Cockpit: A Pilot of the Royal Flying Corps*, second edition (London, Grub Street, 2016 [1969]), p. 70.

34 RAF Museum, DC71/46/1&2, op. cit.

35 Professor Johannes Werner, *Boelcke: Der Mensch, der Flieger, der Führer der deutschen Jagdfliegerei* (Leipzig, K. F. Köhler, 1932), p. 107.

36 W. H. R. Rivers, *Instinct and the Unconscious: A Contribution to a Biological Theory of the Psycho-neuroses* (Cambridge University Press, 1920), p. 57.
37 Hannah Arendt, *On Violence* (Orlando, Harcourt Inc., 1969), p. 62.
38 Werner, op. cit., pp. 160–61. Reproduced by kind permission of Casemate UK.

CHAPTER FOUR: FIRST TASTE OF COMMAND
1 Douglas, *Years of Combat*, op. cit., p. 135.
2 R. R. Money, *Flying and Soldiering* (London, Ivor Nicholson & Watson, 1936), p. 73.
3 Ibid.
4 Letter from Campbell Chesterman to Provost Colin O'Brien, 2005, private collection of Katharine Campbell.
5 *Tonbridge School and the Great War of 1914 to 1919* (Tonbridge, The Whitefriars Press, 1923), p. 107.
6 Ibid.
7 IWM, Personal papers of Lord Douglas of Kirtleside, Box P31.
8 Douglas, *Years of Combat*, op. cit., p. 145.
9 RAF Museum, Trenchard Papers, MFC 76/1/4, *Short Notes on the Battle of the Somme*, 1 July–11 November 1916. In: Morrow, op. cit., p. 173.
10 Douglas, *Years of Combat*, op. cit., p. 146.
11 IWM, Personal Papers of Lord Douglas of Kirtleside, Box P31. Letter copyright Siegfried Sassoon, reproduced by kind permission of the estate of George Sassoon.
12 Harold Balfour, *Wings over Westminster* (London, Hutchinson, 1973), p. 36.
13 Douglas, *Years of Combat*, op. cit., p. 161.

CHAPTER FIVE: THE FIGHTING COCKS AND THE WHITE HORSE
1 Douglas, *Years of Combat*, op. cit., p. 165.
2 Harold Balfour, *An Airman Marches: Early Flying Adventures, 1914–1923* (London, Greenhill Books, 1985 [1935]), p. 69.
3 Ibid., p. 85.
4 Ibid., p. 88.
5 Douglas, *Years of Combat*, op. cit., p. 168.
6 Ibid., p. 170.
7 Morrow, op. cit., p. 175.
8 Balfour, *An Airman Marches*, op. cit., p. 80.
9 Douglas, *Years of Combat*, op. cit., p. 171.
10 Morrow, op. cit., p. 276.
11 Jones, Vol. III, op. cit., p. 370.
12 Balfour, *Wings over Westminster*, op. cit., pp. 39–40.
13 Balfour, *An Airman Marches*, op. cit., p. 93.
14 Douglas, *Years of Combat*, op. cit., p. 178.
15 Ibid., p. 193.
16 Ibid., p. 194.
17 Lee, *Open Cockpit*, op. cit., p. 168.
18 Douglas, *Years of Combat*, op. cit., p. 203.
19 Letter from Wilfrid Freeman to Sholto Douglas, 2 July 1917, private collection of Katharine Campbell.
20 Denys Sutton, *Robert Langton Douglas, Connoisseur of Art and Life*, *Apollo Magazine* special supplement, 1979, p. 157.
21 Arthur Gould Lee, *No Parachute: A Classic Account of War in the Air in WWI* (London, Grub Street, 2013 [1968]), p. 97.

CHAPTER SIX: TACTICS AND RETREAT
1 Douglas, *Years of Combat*, op. cit., p. 53.
2 TNA, AIR 1/1138/204/5/2286, 8 Brigade Reserve Aerodromes, May 1918.

3   Douglas, *Years of Combat*, op. cit., p. 240.
4   Falls, op. cit., p. 284.
5   Douglas, *Years of Combat*, op. cit., p. 240.
6   Lee, *Open Cockpit*, p. 169.
7   Douglas, *Years of Combat*, op. cit., p. 242.
8   Lee, *No Parachute*, p. 205.
9   Douglas, *Years of Combat*, op. cit., p. 248.
10 Balfour, *An Airman Marches*, p. 47.
11 Philpott, op. cit., p. 77.
12 William Bishop, *Winged Warfare* (New York, George H. Doran Co., 1918), p. 145.
13 Douglas, *Years of Combat*, op. cit., p. 253.
14 Ibid.
15 Lewis, op. cit., pp. 66–7.
16 Grafton Elliot Smith and T. H. Pear, *Shell Shock and Its Lessons*, second edition (Manchester University Press, 1918), p. 19.
17 Douglas, *Years of Combat*, op. cit., p. 253.
18 Encyclopaedia Britannica Online, https://www.britannica.com/event/Battle-of-Cambrai-1917, accessed 8 January 2021.
19 Douglas, *Years of Combat*, op. cit., p. 261.
20 Boscombe Down Aviation Collection, Old Sarum, RFC 23–0078, Letter from W. Sholto Douglas to Mrs McCudden, March 1918.
21 Jones, Vol. IV, p. 292.
22 Douglas, *Years of Combat*, op. cit., p. 262.
23 Jones, Vol. IV, p. 273.
24 Falls, op. cit., p. 315.
25 Jones, Vol. IV, p. 340.
26 Douglas, *Years of Combat*, op. cit., p. 278.
27 Gary Sheffield and John Bourne, *Douglas Haig: Diaries and Letters 1914–1918* (London, Weidenfeld & Nicolson, 2015), entry for 3 April 1918.

CHAPTER SEVEN: BIRTH AND TRIUMPH

1   Mark Wilkins, 'The Dark Side of Glory: An early glimpse of PTSD in the letters of World War I aces', *Air & Space Magazine*, February 2018, https://www.airspacemag.com/military-aviation/world-war-i-pilot-ptsd-180967710/, accessed 23 October 2019.
2   Wilkins, op. cit.
3   Douglas, *Years of Combat*, op. cit., p. 305.
4   Jones, Vol. VI, pp. 443–4.
5   Douglas, *Years of Combat*, op. cit., p. 326.
6   Stewart K. Taylor, '"Mum's the Word": An Evening Major W. Sholto Douglas MC DFC would Prefer to Forget', *Cross & Cockade International Journal*, Vol. 37, No. 2, 2006, pp. 116–19.
7   Douglas, *Years of Combat*, op. cit., p. 321.
8   Supplement to *Edinburgh Gazette* of 7 February 1919, 11 February 1919, Issue 13400, p. 796.
9   Douglas, *Years of Combat*, op. cit., p. 337.
10 Ibid., p. 340.
11 Falls, op. cit., p. 21.

CHAPTER EIGHT: A TROUBLED AFTERMATH

1   Douglas, *Years of Combat*, op. cit., p. 342.
2   Ibid., p. 343.
3   Huan Song et al., 'Stress related disorders and subsequent risk of life threatening infections: population based sibling controlled cohort study', *British Medical Journal*, 2019, 367: l5784.
4   Douglas, *Years of Combat*, op. cit., p. 345.

5   Ibid., p. 347.
6   Ibid., p. 348.
7   Ibid., pp. 358–9.
8   Smith and Pear, op. cit., p. xiv.
9   Ibid., p. xv.
10 Ibid., p. 24.
11 Ibid., p. 47.
12 A. C. Iversen et al., 'Help-seeking and receipt of treatment among UK Service personnel', *British Journal of Psychiatry*, 2010, 197 (2): 149–55. In: Rafferty et al. 2017, op. cit., p. 9.
13 Smith and Pear, op. cit., p. 80.
14 Abram Kardiner, *The Traumatic Neuroses of War* (New York, Paul B. Hoeber Inc., 1941), p. 236.
15 Robert Graves and Alan Hodge, *The Long Week-end: A Social History of Great Britain 1918–1939*, second edition (London, Faber & Faber, 1950 [1940]), p. 27.
16 Douglas, *Years of Combat*, op. cit., p. 364.

CHAPTER NINE: RETURN TO THE FOLD AND CLIMBING THE LADDER

1   Sholto Douglas with Robert Wright, *Combat & Command: The Story of an Airman in Two World Wars* (New York, Simon & Schuster, 1966), p. 303.
2   Robert Wright, *Dowding and the Battle of Britain* (London, Macdonald, 1969), p. 45.
3   TNA, AIR 1/2386/228/11/13, op. cit.
4   Giulio Douhet, *The Command of the Air*, translated by Dino Ferrari (Washington DC, Air Force History and Museums Program, 1998 [1921]), p. 90.
5   Sutton, op. cit., p. 166.
6   Paul Kelly, *Biplane to Monoplane: Twenty Years of Technological Development in British Fighter Aircraft, 1919–1939*, thesis for PhD in Science and Technology Studies, University of Edinburgh, 2013, p. 126.
7   Denis Richards, *Portal of Hungerford* (London, Heinemann, 1977), p. 85.
8   Douglas, *Combat & Command*, op. cit., p. 325.
9   Ibid., p. 326.
10 RAF Museum, AIR 69/85, *The Air Aspect of the Military Problems of the Sudan*, by Group Captain W. S. Douglas, précis of a lecture given at RAF Staff College, Andover, 10th Course, 5 October 1932. Notes on the discussion after the lecture are included also: Notes, p. 5.
11 IWM, op. cit., Box P32.
12 Douglas, *Combat & Command*, op. cit., p. 329.
13 RAF Museum, AIR 69/85, op. cit.: Notes, p. 4.
14 Pat Malone, 'Don't forget Ernst Udet', *Pilot* magazine, Spring 2018, p. 32.
15 Douglas, *Combat & Command*, op. cit., p. 331.

CHAPTER TEN: THE STUNT PILOT, THE RED ALFA AND A CHAIN OF PROTECTION

1   Douglas, *Combat & Command*, op. cit., p. 332.
2   IWM, op. cit., transcript of a tape recorded by Sholto for the purposes of his autobiography, Box P32.
3   TNA, J77/3038/3653, Divorce Court File, Appellant: William Sholto Douglas, Respondent: Beatrice May Douglas, Co-respondent: Charles K Turner-Hughes, Type: Husband's petition for divorce.
4   Arthur Bryant, *The Turn of the Tide: A History of the War Years based on the diaries of Field Marshal Lord Alanbrooke, Chief of the Imperial General Staff* (London, Collins, 1957), p. 17.
5   Douglas, *Combat & Command*, op. cit., p. 333.
6   G. T. Garratt, *Mussolini's Roman Empire*, third edition (London, Penguin Books, 1938), pp. 81, 109.
7   Douglas, *Combat & Command*, op. cit., p. 343.
8   Ibid.
9   GCI was a ground-based 360-degree radar that plotted the position of attacking and defending aircraft on a map-like display, allowing ground control of intercepting fighters fitted with AI.

10 TNA, AIR 2/2625 – Flying arrangements for Biggin Hill experiments, 1936–1938, letter from Douglas to Joubert de la Ferté, 14 July 1936.

11 Royal Air Force Signals, 1939–1945, *Official History by the Air Historical Branch of the Ministry of Defence*, Volume V: Fighter Control & Interception, Chapter 1: Biggin Hill Experiments, pp. 12, 19–20.

12 Sir Robert Watson-Watt, *Three Steps to Victory: A Personal Account by Radar's Greatest Pioneer* (London, Odhams Press, 1957), p. 163.

13 Basil Liddell Hart, 'The Military Strategist', in *Churchill: Four Faces and the Man* (Harmondsworth, Penguin Books, 1973 [1969]), p. 181.

14 TNA, HW 22/2 – Air Staff Intelligence Reports on the Spanish Civil War, May 1937–March 1938, Report no. 35, 3 May–9 May 1937.

15 TNA, HW 22/2, op. cit., Notes of an interview on 26 June 1937, with Mr Steer, a *Times* correspondent in Spain.

16 Winston S. Churchill, *The Gathering Storm: The Second World War*, Volume 1 (London, Cassell, 1949), p. 253.

17 Ibid., Letter Mr Churchill to Mr Eden, 18 May 1938, p. 254.

18 Orange, *Dowding*, op. cit., p. 93.

CHAPTER ELEVEN: FLYING TOWARDS THE CRASH

1 TNA, AIR 2/2615 – RADAR and Radio Countermeasures (Code B, 61), Method of deciding whether bombers located by RDF are friendly or hostile, 1936–1938.

2 Douglas, *Combat & Command*, op. cit., p. 352.

3 Ibid., p. 353.

4 Hansard, HC Deb, 5 October 1938, Vol. 339, col. 373.

5 Douglas, *Combat & Command*, op. cit., p. 355.

6 TNA, AIR 2/3103, Inter-service committee on RDF: final report of CHL Planning sub-committee, 1938–1941.

7 Denis Richards and Hilary St George Saunders, *Royal Air Force 1939–1945, Volume I: The Fight at Odds* (London, HMSO, 1974 [1953]), p. 31.

8 TNA, AVIA 46/111, Boulton and Paul Defiant, 1935–1943.

9 Douglas, *Combat & Command*, op. cit., p. 361.

10 TNA, AVIA 12/41, Inter-service committee on RDF: meetings 1–5, 1938–1939.

11 Air Marshal Sir Victor Goddard KCB CBE MA, *Skies to Dunkirk: A Personal Memoir* (London, William Kimber, 1982), p. 36.

12 C. Galletly et al., 'Working memory in posttraumatic stress disorder – an event-related potential study', *Journal of Traumatic Stress*, 2001, 14: 295–309.

13 Sholto Douglas with Robert Wright, *Years of Command: The second volume of the autobiography of Sholto Douglas, Marshal of the Royal Air Force Lord Douglas of Kirtleside* (London, Collins, 1966), p. 47.

CHAPTER TWELVE: AN EVIL DREAM WORLD

1 Marshal of the Royal Air Force Sir John Slessor, *The Central Blue: Recollections and Reflections* (London, Cassell and Co., 1956), p. 236.

2 Douglas, *Years of Command*, op. cit., p. 49.

3 Service file for Robert Langton Douglas, Army Personnel Centre, Support Division, Historical Disclosures.

4 Douglas, *Years of Command*, op. cit., p. 51.

5 Ibid., p. 57.

6 Ibid., p. 59.

7 Richards and Saunders, op. cit., Vol. I, p. 89.

8 John Terraine, *The Right of the Line* (London, Hodder & Stoughton, 1985), p. 118; Richards and Saunders, op. cit., Vol. I, p. 104.

9 Major-General Sir Kenneth Strong, *Men of Intelligence: A study of the roles and decisions of Chiefs of Intelligence from World War I to the present day* (London, Cassell, 1970), p. 115.

10 Douglas, *Years of Command*, op. cit., p. 62.

11 Ibid.

12 Terraine, op. cit., p. 118.

13 IWM, Personal papers of Lord Douglas of Kirtleside, Box P31.

14 Douglas, *Years of Command*, op. cit., p. 64.

15 IWM, Personal Papers of Lord Douglas of Kirtleside, Box P31.

CHAPTER THIRTEEN: MORE CATASTROPHE

1 Douglas, *Years of Command*, op. cit., p. 76.

2 TNA, AIR 2/3034, Fighter Command, Strength: policy, 1938–1939.

3 Ibid.

4 Terraine, op. cit., p. 145.

5 Max Hastings, *Bomber Command* (London, Pan Books, 2010 [1979]), p. 197.

6 TNA, AIR 27/485/18-28, Squadron Number 50. Record of Events. Y (Operations Record Books).

7 TNA, AIR 14/194, Air Bombardment: Air Ministry Policy regarding various plans. 1939 Sept.–1940 Sept., Letter from Douglas to Portal, 4 June 1940.

8 Ibid., Review of Bombing Policy, October 1940, Note by Air Officer Commanding-in-Chief, Bomber Command.

9 TNA, AIR 20/4341, Air Defence of Great Britain: Fighter Deployment, 1938 Oct.–1940 Oct.

10 TNA, CAB 106/1193, Despatch on the Battle of Britain, 1940–1941, by Air Chief Marshal Sir Hugh C. T. Dowding, Air Officer Commanding-in-Chief, Fighter Command, Royal Air Force (Supplement to London Gazette 37719) (HM Stationery Office, 1946).

11 Peter Flint, *Dowding and Headquarters Fighter Command* (England, Airlife Publishing Ltd, 1996), pp. 79–80.

12 TNA, CAB 106/1193, Dowding's despatch, op. cit.

13 TNA, AIR 2/7281, ROYAL AIR FORCE: Fighter Command (Code B, 67/12) Tactics against German mass formations, Operations by No. 11 Group Units over France, May–June 1940.

14 Hansard, HC Deb, 4 June 1940, Vol. 361, cols 787–98.

15 Terraine, op. cit., p. 162. Richards and Saunders, op. cit., Vol. I, p. 150.

16 TNA, AIR 20/2759, Miscellaneous papers, DCAS, 1 May 1940–28 February 1942, Memo from DCAS to VCAS, 9 June 1940.

17 Douglas, *Years of Command*, op. cit., p. 70.

CHAPTER FOURTEEN: INFIGHTING CHAOS IN THE BATTLE OF BRITAIN

1 Alan C. Deere, *Nine Lives* (Manchester, Crécy Publishing Ltd, 2012 [1959]), p. 167.

2 IWM, Personal papers of Lord Douglas of Kirtleside, Notes for Years of Command, Box P31.

3 TNA, AIR 16/330, Reinforcement of No. 11 Group. 1 August 1940–31 December 1940, Minutes of a Conference held at Headquarters Fighter Command, on 7 September 1940.

4 TNA, AIR 6/70, Meetings 1–11. Air Council Minutes & Memoranda, 1 July 1940–31 December 1940.

5 TNA, AIR 20/10727, Flying Stress, DGMS (RAF)'s correspondence, 1940–46, memo by AMP, 23 August 1941.

6 TNA, AIR 16/330, op. cit.

7 Ibid.

8 Ibid.

9 TNA, AIR 2/5246, Enemy air offensive against Great Britain: Attacks on England from 11 September 1940–31 October 1940, No. 11 Group Report.

10 Douglas, *Years of Command*, op. cit., p. 88.

11 TNA, AIR 2/3080, ROYAL AIR FORCE: Fighter Command (Code B, 67/12): Early introduction of Very High Frequency Radio Telegraphy equipment, 1939–1940.

12 Flint, op. cit., p. 90.

13 Air Chief Marshal Sir Kenneth 'Bing' Cross with Professor Vincent Orange, *Straight and Level* (London, Grub Street, 1993), pp. 118–19.

14 TNA, AIR 41/16, The Air Defence of Great Britain, Appendices and Maps, 1945 [but refers to 1940], Appendix 37, German views on the Battle of Britain.

15 TNA, AIR 2/7281, op. cit., Letter from Park to Stevenson, 15 October 1940.

16 TNA, AIR 2/7281, op. cit., Report from Leigh-Mallory to Dowding, 17 September 1940.

17 John Ray, *The Battle of Britain: New Perspectives – Behind the Scenes of the Great Air War* (London, Brockhampton Press, 2000 [1994]), p. 145.

18 Cross and Orange, op. cit., p. 119.

19 Peter Townsend, *Duel of Eagles* (Ealing, Corgi Books, 1974), pp. 470–71.

20 TNA, AIR 2/7281, op. cit., Employment of Duxford Wing during Operations – 29 October 1940.

21 Wright, *Dowding and the Battle of Britain*, op. cit., p. 89.

22 Sebastian Ritchie, 'A Political Intrigue Against the Chief of the Air Staff: The Downfall of Air Chief Marshal Sir Cyril Newall', *War & Society*, May 1998: 16 (1): 83–104.

23 Churchill Archive, CHAR 20/8/14–15, Sinclair to Churchill, 15 November 1940.

24 Ibid.

25 IWM, Personal papers of Lord Douglas of Kirtleside, Notes for Years of Command, Box P31.

26 Air Commodore Henry Probert and Mr Sebastian Cox (eds), *The Battle Re-Thought: A Symposium on the Battle of Britain*, 25 June 1990, 9. Digest of the Group Discussions, Comment by Denis Richards.

27 Leo McKinstry, 'We won the Battle of Britain — just', *The Spectator*, 2 July 2020.

28 IWM, Personal papers of Lord Douglas of Kirtleside, Notes for Years of Command, Box P31.

CHAPTER FIFTEEN: NIGHT TERRORS

1   Douglas, *Years of Command*, op. cit., p. 91.

2   King's College London, Liddell Hart Military Archives, MA 15/4/141. Newspaper cuttings relating to RAF organisation and appointments of senior officers, 1940–1945.

3   RAF Museum, DC76/74/1424, Biographical file on Marshal of the Royal Air Force, Lord Douglas of Kirtleside, Biographical note, 15 November 1942.

4   Douglas, *Years of Command*, op. cit., p. 96.

5   TNA, AIR 40/307, Observations by Sir Sholto Douglas on Fighter Command when he was C-in-C.

6   Douglas, *Years of Command*, op. cit., p. 103.

7   TNA, AIR 16/622, Sir W Sholto Douglas, C-in-C Fighter Command: correspondence with Sir C. F. A. Portal, Chief of Air Staff, December 1940–November 1942, Letter from Douglas to Portal, 9 December 1940.

8   TNA, AIR 41/17 in John Ray, *The Night Blitz: 1940–1941* (Edison NJ, Castle Books, 2004 [1996]), p. 191.

9   TNA, AIR 16/524, Night Defence, Note by Sir Henry Tizard, 31 December 1940.

10 Douglas, *Years of Command*, op. cit., p. 109.

11 RAF Museum, A944, Brief account of the London Blitz as witnessed by Mrs Helen Margaret Nimmo and RAF Officers billeted at Sparrows Herne Hall. Reproduced by kind permission of Mrs Nimmo's grandchildren.

12 Douglas, *Years of Command*, op. cit., p. 129.

13 Ibid., p. 132.

14 Adolf Galland, *The First and the Last* (USA, Popular Classics Publishing, 2014 [1952]), p. 37.

15 Metallised leaflets were a radio countermeasure, originally named WINDOW by the British and *Düppel* by the Germans (from the Berlin suburb where they were first developed), in which incoming aircraft spread a cloud of small, thin pieces of black paper backed with aluminium foil cut to half of the target radar's wavelength, which either appears as a cluster of primary targets on radar screens or swamps the screen with multiple returns.

16 Jones, op. cit., p. 293.

17 Ray, *Night Blitz*, op. cit., p. 238.

18   TNA, AIR 40/307, op. cit.
19   Ray, *Night Blitz*, op. cit., p. 242.

CHAPTER SIXTEEN: 'FIT TO FLY'
1   Douglas, *Years of Command*, op. cit., p. 151.
2   Ibid., p. 155.
3   Ibid., p. 156.
4   IWM, Personal papers of Lord Douglas of Kirtleside, notes for *Years of Command*.
5   TNA, AIR 2/8591, RAF Personnel (Code B, 68), Aircrew who refuse or are unfit to fly, disposal policy.
6   TNA, AIR 20/10727, Flying Stress, DGMS (RAF)'s correspondence, 1940–46.
7   TNA, AIR 57/12, Air Ministry and Ministry of Defence: Flying Personnel Research Committee: REPORTS. Nos 601–625. 1 October 1944–31 July 1945. FPRC 601, Dr Bradford Hill and Wing Commander Denis Williams, 'Investigation into psychological disorders in flying personnel: the reliability of psychiatric opinion in the Royal Air Force', October 1944.
8   J. L. Birley, Goulstonian Lectures on the Principles of Medical Science as applied to Military Aviation, Lecture I, *The Lancet*, Vol. 195, Issue 5048, 29 May 1920, pp. 1147–51.
9   T. A. Ross, *Lectures on War Neurosis* (London, Edward Arnold & Co., 1941), p. 66, Ross had been director of the Cassel Hospital, founded in 1919, which treated cases of 'shell-shock' from WWI. His series of lectures, published in 1941, were intended to equip 'battalion medical officers and general practitioners to deal with patients under war strain'.
10   TNA, AIR 2/6345, Proposal for selection of candidates for aircrew by combined psychiatric and psychological methods, 1941–1943, Gp Capt. C. P. Symonds, 'Predictability of Breakdown under War Conditions'.
11   TNA, AIR 20/10727, op. cit., C. P. Symonds, 'The Human Response to Flying Stress, Lecture 1: Neurosis in Flying Personnel', *British Medical Journal*, 4 December 1943, pp. 703–6.
12   TNA, AIR 2/4935, Disposal procedure of members of aircrews who forfeit confidence of their commanding officers, 1941–1944, letter from Symonds to U.S. of S., 10 December 1942.
13   Ibid., memo from Whittingham to AMP, 21 February 1944.
14   TNA, AIR 2/6252, MEDICAL (Code B, 48): Psychological disorders in flying personnel: occurrence reports, 1942–1945, memo from Whittingham to AMP, 25 April 1945.
15   TNA, AIR 2/6252, op. cit., Flying Personnel Research Committee, Symonds and Williams, Investigation into psychological disorders in flying personnel, Section 1. A critical review of the published literature, January 1942.
16   TNA, AIR 2/8038, Aircrew – length of operational tour, Part I, 1940–1942, minute from ACAS to AMP, 27 February 1940.
17   Ibid., minute from AMP to DGMS, 28 February 1940.
18   Ibid., minute from DGMS to AMP, 4 March 1940.
19   John McCarthy, 'Aircrew and "Lack of Moral Fibre" in the Second World War', *War & Society*, 1984, 2 (2): 87–101.
20   TNA, AIR 2/8038, Part I, op. cit., Letter from Douglas to U.S. of S., 8 January 1941.
21   Christ Church College Oxford, Lord Portal Papers, RAF Archive, Folder 7, Correspondence with C-in-C Fighter Command, 1941, Letter from Portal to Douglas, 3 October 1941.
22   TNA, AIR 2/8038, Part I, op. cit., Letter from Bottomley to Douglas, 9 October 1941.
23   Ibid., Letter from Douglas to Bottomley, 12 October 1941.
24   Christ Church College Oxford, Lord Portal Papers, RAF Archive, Folder 7, Correspondence with C-in-C Fighter Command, 1941, Letter from Douglas to Portal, 10 December 1941.
25   TNA, AIR 20/2859, op. cit., memo from AMP to VCAS, 21 November 1942.
26   Ibid.
27   'Johnnie' Johnson (Group Captain J. E. Johnson), *Wing Leader* (London, The Reprint Society, 1958 [1956]), pp. 120–21.
28   Jimmy Rawnsley and Robert Wright, *Night Fighter* (London, Collins, 1957), p. 201.
29   Ibid., p. 265.

30 AIR 20/2859, op. cit., memo from SO to VCAS, 14 November 1942.

31 Rawnsley and Wright, op. cit., p. 265.

32 RAF Air Historical Branch (AHB), Wing Commander Lawson Memorandum on Executive Action (LMF), 23 November 1945.

33 A. C. McFarlane, 'The Vexed Construct of Medical Resilience: Friend or Foe?', Introduction on 'Medical Resilience' in: Leo van Bergen and Eric Vermetten (eds), *The First World War and Health: Rethinking Resilience* (Leiden, Brill Publishers, 2020).

CHAPTER SEVENTEEN: DAY SWEEPS

1   TNA, AIR 16/367, Organisation of Fighter Wing, December 1940–March 1943, Letter from Leigh-Mallory to Douglas, 7 December 1940.

2   Douglas, *Years of Command*, op. cit., p. 99.

3   Squadron Leader W. S. Douglas, MC, DFC, 'A Lecture on Fighting in the Air', Lecture II, Essays based on lectures given by officers to the third course of the RAF Staff College, 1924–25. In: *Air Power Review*, Vol. 21, No. 1, Spring 2018.

4   Johnson, *Wing Leader*, op. cit., p. 80.

5   Ibid., pp. 86–8.

6   Deere, *Nine Lives*, op. cit., p. 205.

7   Vincent Orange, *Sir Keith Park: A biography of Air Chief Marshal Sir Keith Park* (London, Methuen, 1985 [1984]), p. 138.

8   TNA, AIR 16/663, Fighter Operational Records, September 1939–February 1942, Letter Douglas to all Groups, 25 April 1941.

9   Johnson, *Wing Leader*, op. cit., p. 87.

10 Galland, op. cit., p. 44.

11 Ibid., p. 45.

12 Douglas, *Years of Command*, op. cit., pp. 145–6.

13 Ibid., pp. 148–9.

14 TNA, AIR 19/313, Memoranda by Sir Hugh Dowding on economics in personnel and equipment, 1941–1942, Memo from Air Staff to Sinclair, 15 November 1941.

15 Ibid., Memo from DGD to VCAS, 15 November 1941.

16 Collier, op. cit., p. 294.

17 Christ Church College Oxford, Lord Portal Papers, RAF Archive, Folder 7, Correspondence with C-in-C Fighter Command, 1941, Letter from Douglas to Portal, 10 December 1941.

18 TNA, ADM 116/4528, Escape of German battle cruisers *Gneisenau* and *Scharnhorst* and heavy cruiser *Prinz Eugen* up the Channel: Operation 'Fuller' and Board of Enquiry, Evidence of Air Marshal Sir Sholto Douglas, KCB, MC, DFC, C-in-C Fighter Command.

19 Douglas, *Years of Command*, op. cit., p. 165. Swordfish were biplane torpedo bombers that were already obsolete at the start of WWII.

20 'Report of the Board of Enquiry appointed to enquire into the circumstances in which the German Battle Cruisers SCHARNHORST and GNEISENAU and Cruiser PRINZ EUGEN proceeded from Brest to Germany on February 12 1942, and on the operations undertaken to prevent this movement, March 2 1942, published March 1946' (Bucknill Report), p. 8.

21 Douglas, *Years of Command*, op. cit., p. 165.

22 Galland, op. cit., p. 66.

23 Lord Tedder, *With Prejudice* (London, Cassell, 1966), p. 256.

24 Douglas, *Years of Command*, op. cit., p. 173.

25 Ibid., p. 162.

26 TNA, AIR 16/760, Operation 'Rutter', 1 June 1942–31 December 1942, Douglas to Leigh-Mallory, 30 June 1942.

27 David Stubbs, 'An Analysis of Factors Affecting the Royal Air Force Contribution to the Raid on Dieppe, 1942', *Canadian Military History*, 2016; 25 (1): Article 12.

28 Douglas, *Years of Command*, op. cit., p. 175.

29 Eric Maguire, *Dieppe, August 19* (London, Jonathan Cape, 1963), p. 11.
30 Johnson, *Wing Leader*, op. cit., p. 145.
31 Richards, *Royal Air Force 1939–1945*, Vol. I, op. cit., p. 384.
32 Douglas, *Years of Command*, op. cit., p. 115.
33 TNA, PREM 3/15, Commands, Prime Minister's Office: Operational correspondence and papers. AIR, Commands, 1941 May–1945 July, Letter from Churchill to Sinclair, 14 November 1942.
34 Ibid., Letter from Churchill to Portal, 14 November 1942.
35 Ibid., Letter from Portal to Churchill, 15 November 1942.
36 Ibid., Letter from Sinclair to Churchill, 15 November 1942.
37 Ibid., Minute from Churchill to Sinclair and Portal, 19 November 1942.
38 Ibid., Telegram for Prime Minister from Lord Moyne (Deputy Resident Minister of State in Cairo), 29 November 1942.
39 Liddell Hart, op. cit., p. 196.
40 Douglas, *Years of Command*, op. cit., p. 176.

CHAPTER EIGHTEEN: CAIRO: DISAPPOINTMENTS AND SNARES

1   Douglas, *Years of Command*, op. cit., p. 176.
2   Tedder, op. cit., p. 399.
3   Christ Church College Oxford, Lord Portal Papers, Denis Richards Archive, V – World War II, PREM 3/15, Minute, Churchill to Sinclair and Portal, 8 February 1943.
4   Ibid., Archive 2, Box C, Folder 5, Letter Freeman to Portal, January 1943.
5   Anthony Furze, *Wilfrid Freeman: The Genius behind Allied Survival and Air Supremacy, 1939–1945* (Staplehurst, Spellmount, 2000), pp. 183–4.
6   Christ Church College Oxford, Lord Portal Papers, Archive 2, Box C, Folder 5, Letter Douglas to Portal, 8 February 1943.
7   Douglas, *Years of Command*, op. cit., p. 179.
8   TNA, AIR 23/1361, Demi-official correspondence, Air C-in-C, MAC, 1943, Letter Douglas to Tedder, 5 June 1943.
9   IWM, Personal papers of Lord Douglas of Kirtleside, notes for *Years of Command*, section on Middle East Command.
10 Christ Church College Oxford, Lord Portal Papers, RAF Archive, Folder 12, Correspondence with C-in-C Middle East Command, 1940–1945, Letter Douglas to Portal, 20 March 1943.
11 Ibid.
12 Ibid., Archive 2, Boxes D & E, Folder 5, Handwritten letter Douglas to Portal, 27 May 1943.
13 Ibid., Letter Portal to Sinclair, 17 June 1943.
14 Noël Coward, *Middle East Diary* (London, William Heinemann, 1944), p. 49.
15 Ibid., pp. 81–2.
16 Ibid., p. 101.
17 Lord Killearn (Sir Miles Lampson), *The Killearn Diaries, 1934–1946*, edited by Trefor E. Evans (London, Sidgwick & Jackson, 1972), pp. 213–14, 4 February 1942.
18 Douglas, *Years of Command*, op. cit., p. 197.
19 Ibid., p. 198.
20 Killearn, op. cit., p. 259, 18 August 1943.
21 Douglas, *Years of Command*, op. cit., p. 201.
22 Ibid., p. 205.

CHAPTER NINETEEN: AN ILL-FATED OPERATION AND SHOLTO'S NADIR

1   Field Marshal Lord Alanbrooke, *War Diaries 1939–1945*, Alex Danchev and Daniel Todman (eds) (London, Phoenix Press, 2002), p. 458, 7 October 1943.
2   Christ Church College Oxford, Lord Portal Papers, RAF Archive, Folder 12, Correspondence with C-in-C Middle East Command, 1940–1945, Letter Douglas to Portal, 4 May 1943.
3   Tedder, op. cit., p. 486.

4   Richards and Saunders, Vol. II, *The Fight Avails*, op. cit., p. 345.

5   Winston Churchill, *Closing the Ring, The Second World War*, Vol. 5 (Boston, Houghton Mifflin, 1951), p. 193.

6   Douglas, *Years of Command*, op. cit., p. 225.

7   Ibid.

8   Alanbrooke, op. cit., p. 421, 17 June 1943.

9   BOLERO was the code name of the United States military troop build-up in the United Kingdom during World War II.

10 Churchill Archive, CHAR 20/114/79, Former Naval Person to President Roosevelt, 7 July 1943.

11 Ibid., CHAR 20/114/117–18, President Roosevelt to Prime Minister, 9 July 1943.

12 Ibid., CHAR 20/115/76, Personal for Prime Minister from Field Marshal Dill, 18 July 1943.

13 Ibid., CHAR 20/115/81–82, Personal for Prime Minister from Field Marshal Dill, 19 July 1943.

14 Ibid., CHAR 20/117/119, Prime Minister from Minister of State [in Egypt, Richard Casey], 4 September 1943.

15 TNA, PREM 3/15, Commands, Prime Minister's Office: Operational correspondence and papers. AIR, Commands, 1941 May–1945 July, Minute Churchill to Sinclair, 7 September 1943.

16 Ibid., Minutes Churchill to Sinclair, 13 and 22 October 1943.

17 Ibid., Minute Sinclair to Churchill, 24 October 1943.

18 Ibid., Minute Churchill to Sinclair, 27 October 1943.

19 Ibid., Letter Sinclair to Churchill, 28 October 1943.

20 Ibid., Letter Churchill to Sinclair, 30 October 1943.

21 Moran, op. cit., p. 728.

22 Christ Church College Oxford, Lord Portal Papers, Archive 2, Boxes D & E, Folder 3, Letter Freeman to Portal, 29 September 1943.

23 Douglas, *Years of Command*, op. cit., p. 229.

24 Alanbrooke, op. cit., p. 481, 26 November 1943.

25 Ibid., p. 493, 9 December 1943.

26 TNA, AIR 23/6041, Middle East and Mediterranean Air Command: re-organisation, 1943–44, Letter Douglas to Mediterranean Allied Air Forces, 26 December 1943.

27 Victor Thompson, 'Monty's Successor', *Illustrated*, 1 June 1946, p. 25.

28 Douglas, *Years of Command*, op. cit., p. 239.

29 Ibid., p. 240.

30 Ibid., p. 242.

31 Ibid.

32 TNA, PREM 3/15, op. cit., Letter Douglas to Churchill, 1 January 1944.

33 Ibid., Letter Brereton to Douglas, 4 September 1943.

34 Churchill Archive, CHAR 20/130/111, Prime Minister to Secretary of State for Air and CAS, 29 December 1943.

35 TNA, PREM 3/15, op. cit., Telegram Secretary of State for Air to Prime Minister, 29 December 1943.

36 Churchill Archive, CHAR 20/130/128, Prime Minister to Secretary of State for Air and CAS, 31 December 1943.

CHAPTER TWENTY: VICTORY AT LAST

1   Douglas, *Years of Command*, op. cit., p. 248.

2   RAF Museum, X001–3540/012/006, Speech by AOC Fighter Command on occasion of WAAF Anniversary.

3   Douglas, *Years of Command*, op. cit., p. 251.

4   Alanbrooke, War Diaries, op. cit., p. 547.

5   Andrew Browne Cunningham, *A Sailor's Odyssey: The Autobiography of Admiral of the Fleet Viscount Cunningham of Hyndhope* (London, Hutchinson & Co., 1951), p. 604.

6   TNA, AIR 2/5721, Coastal Command's participation in Operation *Overlord*, 1944–1946. The work of Coastal Command in the Invasion of Europe, 25 August 1944.

7   TNA, CAB 106/1042, Despatch on operations of Coastal Command, Royal Air Force in operation 'Overlord' – the invasion of Europe 1944 May–August, by Air Chief Marshal Sir Sholto Douglas, Air Officer Commanding-in-Chief, Coastal Command (Supplement to London Gazette 38111) (HM Stationery Office, 1947), p. 5128.

8   TNA, AIR 2/5721, op. cit., Minute from H. A. Jones, Minute Director of Public Relations, to Private Secretary to Secretary of State for Air, 26 July 1944.

9   Christ Church College Oxford, Lord Portal Papers, RAF Archive, Folder 8, Correspondence with C-in-C Coastal Command, 1944, Letter Douglas to Portal, 12 August 1944.

10 TNA, AIR 15/311, Aircraft wastage: records of statistics, 1 August 1943–30 April 1946, Figures for July 1944–April 1945.

11 IWM, Personal Papers of Lord Douglas of Kirtleside, Captain D. V. Peyton-Ward, A brief account of events in the period Jan. 1944 to May 1945, 21 November 1963.

12 TNA, CAB 106/351, Despatches on the operations of Coastal Command, Royal Air Force, 1939 September–1945 May, IV. – Despatch by Air Chief Marshal Sir Sholto Douglas, KCB, MC, DFC, AOC-in-C from January 1944 to May 1945, p. 204.

13 Douglas, *Years of Command*, op. cit., p. 277.

14 Ibid., p. 278. and Saunders, *Royal Air Force 1939–1945*, Vol. III, *The Fight is Won*, op. cit., p. 276.

15 Christina J. M. Goulter, *A Forgotten Offensive: Royal Air Force Coastal Command's Anti-Shipping Campaign, 1940–1945* (London, Frank Cass, 1995).

16 Christ Church College Oxford, Lord Portal Papers, Denis Richards Archive, VII – WWII, Folder VIIa. Handwritten letter from Douglas to Portal, marked 'Sholto Douglas – tribute', 11 May 1945.

17 Ibid., Archive 2, Boxes D & E, Folder 3, Letter Freeman to Portal, 9 August 1944.

18 Ibid., Folder 4, Letter Freeman to Portal, 25 May 1944.

19 Ibid., Draft Letter Portal to Sinclair, 9 July 1944.

CHAPTER TWENTY-ONE: 'MISERY AND STARVATION'

1   Douglas, *Years of Command*, op. cit., p. 285.

2   Ibid., p. 287.

3   Douglas, *Years of Command*, op. cit., p. 299.

4   Ibid., p. 300.

5   TNA, AIR 55/18, Commander-in-Chief's visit to Warsaw to open the RAF Exhibition on 29 October 1945, Report by Douglas on his Interview with Marshal Rola-Zymierski, Minister of Defence in the Polish Government at Warsaw, 1 November 1945.

6   TNA, FO 371/47815, Royal Air Force Exhibition in Warsaw. Code 55, File 11839, 1945. Letter from R. M. A. Hankey, 1st Secretary British Embassy Warsaw to The Right Honourable Ernest Bevin MP, Secretary of State for Foreign Affairs, 6 November 1945, Appendix B.

7   TNA, FO 371/47815, op. cit., Letter from Air Attaché Warsaw, Gp Capt. C. B. E. Burt-Andrews, to H. E. Mr V. F. W. Cavendish-Bentinck, British Ambassador in Poland, 6 November 1945.

8   Douglas, *Years of Command*, op. cit., p. 300.

9   TNA, FO 371/47815, op. cit., Letter from Hankey to Bevin, op. cit., 6 November 1945.

10 TNA, AIR 55/18, op. cit., Letter, Grieg to Douglas, 31 October 1945.

11 Ibid., Letter Douglas to Portal, 3 December 1945.

12 Institut Pamięci Narodowej (Institute for National Remembrance) Warsaw, IPN BU 00170/74/2, Teczka robocza 'KALINA' [Marian Duriasz] [Work file of Secret Informer ‹KALINA'], pp. 119–20.

13 Ben Shephard, *The Long Road Home: The Aftermath of the Second World War* (London, Vintage Books, 2011), p. 75.

14 TNA, AIR 55/21, Disposal of enemy war materiel, policy. 1945 August–1946, October, Letter Douglas to Montgomery, 14 August 1945.

15 Ibid., Cipher Message Montgomery to Admiralty, cc. BAFO, among others, 3 November 1945.

16 Captain Eric 'Winkle' Brown, *Wings on my Sleeve* (London, Phoenix, 2007 [2006]), pp. 97–8.

17 Bernadette M. Cortese PhD, Kimberly Leslie RN and Thomas W. Uhde MD, 'Differential

Odor Sensitivity in PTSD: Implications for Treatment and Future Research', *Journal of Affective Disorders*, 1 July 2015; 179: 23–30.

18 Eric Vermetten MD, and J. Douglas Bremner MD, 'Olfaction as a Traumatic Reminder in Post-traumatic Stress Disorder: Case Reports and Review', *Journal of Clinical Psychiatry*, February 2003; 64 (2): 202–7.

19 TNA, AIR 55/22, Organisation of a post-war Royal Air Force Headquarters: policy, 1 October 1945–30 November 1946. Letter Douglas to Air Marshal Hollinghurst, Air Member for Supply & Organisation, 26 October 1945.

20 Douglas, *Years of Command*, op. cit., p. 305.

21 Ibid.

22 Ian Buruma, *Year Zero: A History of 1945* (London, Atlantic Books, 2013), p. 63.

23 RAF Museum, B2497, Diary of Flying Officer R.M. Williams, 1945.

24 Shephard, op. cit., p. 133.

25 Douglas, *Years of Command*, op. cit., p. 306.

26 Ibid., p. 308.

27 Ibid., p. 309.

28 TNA, AIR 8/1126, Post-war control in Germany: higher appointments. 1 March 1946–30 September 1949, p. 301. Minute Stansgate to Prime Minister, 16 January 1946.

29 TNA, FO 1030/323, DO correspondence with Commander-in-Chief, handwritten letter from Montgomery to Robertson, 27 January 1946.

30 Douglas, *Years of Command*, op. cit., p. 310.

31 TNA, AIR 55/17, Lectures by Air Commanders-in-Chief, August 1945–June 1947, RAF Staff College, Sixteenth War Course, British Air Forces of Occupation (Germany) by Air Chief Marshal Sir Sholto Douglas, Air Commander-in-Chief, BAFO.

32 TNA, AIR 55/23, Revision of contraction programme, BAFO 1946, 1 February 1946–31 March 1947. Letter AOC-in-C BAFO to Under Secretary of State, Air Ministry, 23 February 1946.

CHAPTER TWENTY-TWO: IN THE MIDST OF CHAOS

1 Douglas, *Years of Command*, op. cit., p. 318.

2 Michael Balfour and John Mair, *Four-Power Control in Germany and Austria 1945–1946* (London, Oxford University Press, 1956), p. v.

3 TNA, FO 1030/148, Directives and memoranda issued by Military Governor, 1945–1946. Field Marshal Montgomery: Notes on the German Situation, 1 May 1946.

4 TNA, DEFE 5/5 (136), MOD Chiefs of Staff Committee. Memoranda. Internal security situation in the British Zone of Germany: memorandum by Sir Sholto Douglas. 28 June 1947.

5 TNA, FO 1030/170, C-in-C's Lectures, Lecture to the Imperial Defence College on Germany, 12 June 1947.

6 Douglas, *Years of Command*, op. cit., p. 321.

7 Ibid., p. 322.

8 RAF Museum, X002–5661, Gp Capt. John Alexander Kent papers, 1935–1945.

9 RAF Museum, Records of Afro-Caribbean pilots, used in online exhibition 'Pilots of the Caribbean', entry for Flying Officer Errol Walton Barrow.

10 RAF Museum, A2084, Reminiscences of the RAF, 1939–1945, Speech by Air Chief Marshal Sir Sholto Douglas to the People of the British West Indies.

11 TNA, FO 1049/1092, Entry Permit, D. G. H. Douglas, 1947. Letter from Director SIO, Advanced Headquarters, Intelligence Division, HQ CCG for Germany (British Element), to I. T. M. Pink, Political Division, 24 November 1947.

12 Reuters Archive, Letter from Alfred Geiringer to Walton Cole, 17 July 1946.

13 TNA, FO 1049/1092, op. cit., Dossier written by I. T. M. Pink, Mr D. G. H. Douglas, 1 December 1947.

14 TNA, FO 371/55578, CCG organisation and functions: status of Control Council, 1946, article in *Manchester Guardian* on CCG in Germany by G. L. Watson, 21 September 1946.

15 Ibid., Telegram Strang to Foreign Office, 20 October 1946.

16 TNA, FO 371/55529, op. cit., *British Zone Review*, 17 August 1946. C-in-C on staff problems.

17 Douglas, *Years of Command*, op. cit., p. 325.

18 This was an advisory body set up by the CCG, formed of representatives of the states, central offices, political parties, trade unions and consumer organisations within the British Zone.

19 TNA, FO 371/55529, op. cit., *British Zone Review*, 8 June 1946, 'C-in-C meets Zonal Advisory Council'.

20 Ibid., *British Zone Review*, 3 August 1946. Macfee Kerr (Reuters), 'What's wrong with British administration? Some reasons for the decline of our popularity in the Zone'.

21 Melita Maschmann, *Fazit: Kein Rechtfertigungsversuch* (Stuttgart, dva, 1963), in Mary Fulbrook, *Reckonings: Legacies of Nazi Persecution and the Quest for Justice* (Oxford, Oxford University Press, 2018), p. 210.

22 David Phillips, *Educating the Germans: People and Policy in the British Zone of Germany, 1945–1949* (London, Bloomsbury Academic, 2018), pp. 114–16.

23 Robert Birley, Introduction to Annedore Leber, *Conscience in Revolt* (English version, London, Vallentine, Mitchell, 1957), p. xxii.

24 Douglas, *Years of Command*, op. cit., p. 328.

25 IWM, Personal papers of Lord Douglas of Kirtleside, Notes for *Years of Command*.

26 TNA, FO 1030/170, op. cit.

27 TNA, FO 371/55529, op. cit., *British Zone Review*, 11 May 1946, 'Ave Atque Vale'.

28 TNA CAB 79/50, Chiefs of Staff Committee, Minutes of Meeting held on 3 July 1946.

29 TNA, FO 371/55578, op. cit., Telegram Strang to Foreign Office, 20 October 1946.

30 Ibid., Memo by Patrick Dean, 23 October 1946.

31 https://www.youtube.com/watch?v=ee87x7TWNMc

32 TNA, FO 371/55578, op. cit., Telegram Strang to Foreign Office, 20 October 1946.

33 TNA, FO 800/466, Foreign Office, Private Offices: Various Ministers' and Officials' Papers, Bevin, Ernest. Germany. 1945–1947. Questions relating to Germany. Economic Principles and Reparations. Statement by the Head of the UK Delegation, 17 March 1947.

34 Ibid., Cipher Bevin to Attlee, 29 March 1947.

35 Ibid., Cipher Douglas to Bevin, 10 May 1947.

36 Douglas, *Years of Command*, op. cit., p. 352.

37 TNA, FO 800/466, op. cit., memo Pakenham to Bevin, 23 June 1947.

38 TNA, FO 1030/170, op. cit.

39 Dieter Tasch, 'Britische Idee wurde zum Deutschen Erfolg' ['A British Idea became a German Success'], *Hannoversche Allgemeine Zeitung*, 11 August 1977.

40 TNA, FO 1030/188, Housing in British Zone, 1946–1947, Letter Douglas to Robertson, 3 July 1946.

41 Ibid., Letter Douglas to three Service Cs-in-C and Deputy Military Governor, 5 November 1946.

42 Ibid., Letter Douglas to Sir Richard McCreery, C-in-C BAOR, 17 November 1946.

43 Ibid., Second letter Douglas to Sir Richard McCreery, C-in-C BAOR, 17 November 1946.

44 Ibid., Letter McCreery to Douglas, 21 November 1946.

45 Ibid., Letter Douglas to Berry, 3 December 1947.

46 TNA, FO 1030/171, Letter Douglas to Major-General E. P. Nares, General Officer Commanding British Troops, Berlin, 1 May 1947.

47 TNA, FO 800/466, op. cit., Cipher Bevin to Prime Minister (Attlee), Minister of Defence (Alexander) and Chancellor of the Exchequer (Dalton), 12 March 1947.

48 Ibid., Telegram Sir Orme Sargent [Permanent Under-Secretary at the Foreign Office] to Bevin, March 1947, Civilianisation of *Dienstgruppen*.

49 R. M. Douglas, *Orderly and Humane: The Expulsion of the Germans after the Second World War* (New Haven, Yale University Press, 2012), p. 1.

CHAPTER TWENTY-THREE: PLEAS FROM NUREMBERG

1 Hartley Shawcross, *Life Sentence: The Memoirs of Lord Shawcross* (London, Constable, 1995), pp. 86–7.

2   The London Charter, 8 August 1945, https://www.un.org/en/genocideprevention/documents/atrocity-crimes/Doc.2_Charter%20of%20IMT%201945.pdf, accessed 14 May 2020.
3   Shawcross, op. cit., p. 97.
4   Rebecca West, *A Train of Powder* (London, Macmillan & Co., 1955), p. 30.
5   Douglas, *Years of Command*, op. cit., p. 329.
6   IWM, Personal papers of Lord Douglas of Kirtleside, Notes for *Years of Command*, op. cit.
7   TNA, FO 1060/1383, Pleas for clemency (Goering and others): Vol. III, 1946. Article by H. A. Smith (Professor of International law in the University of London), *Free Europe*, Vol. 13, No. 162, July 1946.
8   Shawcross, op. cit., p. 96.
9   https://www.trumanlibrary.gov/library/research-files/letter-robert-jackson-harry-s-truman?documentid=3&pagenumber=7, accessed 15 May 2020.
10 David Maxwell Fyfe, *Political Adventure: The Memoirs of the Earl of Kilmuir* (London, Weidenfeld & Nicolson, 1964), p. 111.
11 TNA, FO 1060/1378, Judgments and Sentences; Vol. I, 1946.
12 Shawcross, op. cit., p. 110.
13 West, op. cit., pp. 15–16.
14 Robert H. Jackson, *The Case Against the Nazi War Criminals* (New York, Alfred A. Knopt Inc., 1946), p. 85. In: Brian Imiola, 'The Duty of Diligence: Knowledge, Responsibility, and Selective Conscientious Objection', in Andrea Ellner, Paul Robinson, David Whetham (eds), *When Soldiers Say No: Selective Conscientious Objection in the Modern Military* (London, Routledge, 2016 [2014]), p. 24.
15 David Fisher, 'Who Guards the Guards? The Importance of Civilian Control of the Military', in Ellner et al., op. cit., p. 68.
16 Douglas, *Years of Command*, op. cit., p. 335.
17 TNA, FO 1060/1385, op. cit., Allied Control Authority, Control Council Minutes of the Fortieth Meeting, 20 September 1946.
18 Douglas, *Years of Command*, op. cit., p. 336.
19 Telford Taylor, *The Anatomy of the Nuremberg Trials: A Personal Memoir* (New York, Alfred A. Knopf, 1992), p. 604.
20 TNA, FO 800/466, op. cit., Cipher from Foreign Office to Paris, 5 October 1946, Text of personal message CCG 45949 from Douglas to Sir Gilmour Jenkins (Permanent Secretary to Foreign Office), 5 October 1946.
21 Taylor, op. cit., note on p. 605.
22 Ibid., Cipher from Paris to Foreign Office, Bevin to Attlee, 5 October 1946.
23 Douglas, *Years of Command*, op. cit., p. 338.
24 TNA, FO 945/332, Appeals against judgments at Nuremberg Trials, 1946. Meeting of Ministers, 7 October 1946, Brief: Appeals against Nuremberg Sentences.
25 Ibid., Telegram Hynd to Douglas, 7 October 1946.
26 Douglas, *Years of Command*, op. cit., p. 338.
27 Ibid., p. 340.
28 Ibid., p. 341.
29 TNA, WO 311/707, War crimes: personal history of accused; includes Albert Speer, Hermann Goering, Joachim von Ribbentrop, Julius Streicher, Franz von Papen and Rudolf Hess, 1945 September 01–1945 September 30.
30 TNA, FO1060/1386, Top secret folder containing twenty-two short histories of major war criminals and judgment, 1945–1946. Goering.
31 TNA, FO 1060/1381, Pleas for clemency (Goering and others): Vol. I, 1946. Letter from Allied Control Authority, Allied Secretariat, to Chairman of the Quadripartite Commission for the Execution of Sentence Pronounced against the Major War Criminals, Hermann Goering, 11 October 1946.
32 TNA, FO 1060/1386, op. cit., Hess.
33 TNA, FO 1060/1382, Pleas for clemency (Goering and others): Vol. II, 1946. Dr Alfred Seidl,

Attorney-at-Law. To the Secretary General of the IMT. Regarding Rudolf Hess concerning crimes against the peace, execution of Art. 29 of the Charter of the IMT of 8 August 1945. 4 October 1946.

34 TNA, FO 1060/1382, op. cit., Joachim von Ribbentrop, Attorney-at-law, Dr Martin Horn, 4 October 1946.

35 Ibid., Joachim von Ribbentrop, Anneliese von Ribbentrop, 4 October 1946.

36 TNA, FO 1060/1386, op. cit., Handwritten notes by Sholto on Keitel.

37 TNA, FO 1060/1383, op. cit., Application under Paragraph 29 of the Charter for the Defendant Alfred Rosenberg.

38 TNA, WO 311/707, op. cit.

39 TNA, FO 1060/1386, op. cit.

40 TNA, FO 1060/1383, op. cit., Re. Dr Hans Frank, for War Crimes and Crimes against Humanity, in accordance with Article 29 of the Charter for the IMT.

41 TNA, FO 1060/1382, op. cit., Dr Fritz Sauter, Counsel for the Defendant W. Funk, To the Secretary-General of the IMT, Nuremberg, 4 October 1946.

42 Ibid., Handwritten note by Sholto on Doenitz.

43 Ibid., Captain Otto Kranzbühler, Defense Counsel for Grand Admiral Karl Doenitz, To the Control Council for Germany through the Secretary-General of the IMT, Nuremberg, 4 October 1946.

44 TNA, FO 1060/1386, op. cit.

45 TNA, FO 1060/1383, op. cit., Grand Admiral Dr H. C. Erich Raeder, To the Allied Control Council for Germany in Berlin through the General Secretary of the IMT, Nuernberg.

46 TNA, FO 1060/1386, op. cit.

47 TNA, FO 1060/1382, op. cit., Plea for Mercy on behalf of the defendant Fritz Sauckel by the Attorney-at-Law, Dr Robert Servatius. To the Control Council for Germany through the General Secretary of the IMT, Nuremberg, 5 October 1946.

48 TNA, FO 1060/1386, op. cit.

49 TNA, FO 1060/1381, op. cit., Luise Jodl to the Allied Control Council for Germany, 5 October 1946.

50 TNA, FO 1060/1382, op. cit., Dr Gustav Steinbauer, Defense Counsel for Dr Seyss-Inquart, Control Council for Germany, Nuremberg, 3 October 1946.

51 TNA, FO 1060/1386, op. cit.

52 Douglas, *Years of Command*, op. cit., p. 342.

53 TNA, FO 1060/1386, op. cit.

54 Trial of The Major War Criminals before the IMT. Nuremberg 14 November 1945–1 October 1946. Vol. I. Official Text in the English Language, Indictment, p. 34.

55 TNA, FO 1060/1381, op. cit., Dr Hanns Marx, Attorney-at-law, Defense Counsel for the defendant Streicher, To the Control Council for Germany Berlin. Nuernberg, 5 October 1946.

56 TNA, FO 1060/1386, op. cit.

57 TNA, FO 1060/1381, op. cit., Dr Otto Freiherr von Luedinghausen, Attorney-at-law and notary. Defense counsel for Constantin Freiherr von Neurath. To the Supreme Control Council Berlin, through the General Secretary of the IMT Nuernberg, Berlin 5 October 1946.

58 TNA, FO 1060/1388, op. cit. Letter from Richard Georgi (Major-General, Retired), Otto Sichtschlag (Colonel, Retired) and Arno Einke (Colonel, Retired) to Air Marshal Douglas, CCG; HQ, Mil. Gov.

59 IWM, op. cit.

60 Douglas, *Years of Command*, op. cit., p. 343.

61 Ibid., p. 344.

62 Ibid., p. 346.

63 West, op. cit., pp. 44–6.

64 Douglas, *Years of Command*, op. cit., p. 346.

65 Jürgen Rose, 'Conscience in Lieu of Obedience: Cases of Selective Conscientious Objection in the German *Bundeswehr*', in Ellner et al., op. cit., p. 183. Rose is a former Lieutenant Colonel

of the Bundeswehr who came to public notice in 2007, when he successfully requested to be relieved from military duties relating to the conflict in Afghanistan on grounds of conscience.

66 Shawcross, op. cit., p. 136.

67 Douglas, *Years of Command*, op. cit., p. 347.

68 Joseph I, Greene (ed.), *The Essential Clausewitz: Selections from On War* (New York, Dover Publications Inc., 2003), p. 112. In: Lt. Col. Dave Grossman, *On Killing: The Psychological Cost of Learning to Kill in War and Society* (New York, Back Bay Books, 2009 [1995]), p. xxxv.

CHAPTER TWENTY-FOUR: 'A DIFFERENT KETTLE OF FISH ALTOGETHER'

1 Douglas, *Years of Command*, op. cit., p. 359.

2 Shawcross, op. cit., p. 132.

3 TNA, FO 1060/1389, Trials of members of organisations declared criminal by IMT Nuremberg. 1946–1947.

4 TNA, FO 371/55529, *British Zone Review*, 6 July 1946, 'Crimes against Humanity: World conscience demands Nazi oppressors be brought to justice'.

5 TNA, FO 1060/1389, op. cit., Letter Douglas to Regional Commissioners, 13 February 1947.

6 Douglas, *Years of Command*, op. cit., p. 359.

7 Ibid., p. 361.

8 F. S. V. Donnison, *Civil Affairs and Military Government North-West Europe 1944–1946* (London, HMSO, 1961), p. 388.

9 TNA, FO 1060/938, Review of Mil Gov Courts proceedings and death sentences: Vol. VI, 1946 May–August.

10 Ralf-Markus Lehmann, Jürgen Balke, *Aus Besatzern wurden Freunde: Erinnerungen aus dem Hauptquartier [Occupiers became Friends: Memories of the Headquarters] British Air Forces of Occupation, Second Tactical Air Force, 1945–1955* (Heimat Kultur Verein Eilsen E.V., 2012), p. 74.

11 TNA, FO 1060/937, Review of Mil Gov Courts proceedings and death sentences: Vol. V, 1946 February–May.

12 Ibid.

13 TNA, FO 1060/938, op. cit.

14 Ibid.

15 TNA, FO 1049/557, Military Government Courts. 1946. Extract from article in *Manchester Guardian*, 8 August 1946.

16 TNA, FO 1060/938, op. cit.

17 TNA, FO 1060/939, Review of Mil Gov Courts proceedings and death sentences: Vol. VII, 1946 August–December.

18 Ibid.

19 Ibid.

20 TNA, FO 371/55529, op. cit.

21 TNA, FO 1060/939, op. cit.

22 TNA, FO 1030/153. Review of sentences by Military Government Courts, 1946–1947.

23 TNA, FO 1060/939, op. cit.

24 Ibid.

25 A. T. Williams, *A Passing Fury: Searching for Justice at the End of World War II* (London, Jonathan Cape, 2016), pp. 146, 159, 173.

CHAPTER TWENTY-FIVE: THEFT AND CORRUPTION

1 TNA, FO 936/653, Loss of valuables from Schloss Bückeburg, 1946–1948, Statement of Dr Wolrad Schwertfeger, Curator of Schloss Bückeburg, July 1947.

2 TNA, FO 936/738, Bückeburg: reports and statements, 1947–1948. Report on Bückeburg Schloss, 20 September 1945.

3 TNA, FO 936/738, op. cit., Statement of Helmut Riepe.

4 Ibid., Notes of statement made by Mr Ellis Waterhouse, Magdalen College, Oxford, 31 July 1947.

5   TNA, FO 936/653, Letter from Personal Staff Officer to Commander-in-Chief to Property Control Branch, HQ Military Government, Hannover, 18 September 1946.

6   TNA, FO 1032/1371, Schaumburg-Lippe case (claims by Princess Feodora): Vol. III, July–September 1947. Notes on the meeting held in the Commander-in-Chief's office at 11.00 hours on 17 July 1947 concerning *Daily Mail* article and investigation into the Property of Schaumburg-Lippe.

7   TNA, FO 1032/1461, Schloss Bückeburg: enquiry into missing property of Prince Wolrad of Schaumburg-Lippe, Vol. II, Hayward Report, 30 December 1947.

8   Ibid.

9   TNA, FO 936/653, op. cit., Report on Property of Prince Wolrad of Schaumburg-Lippe missing from Schloss Bückeburg by T Hayward (final), 30 June 1948.

10 Christopher Knowles, *Winning the Peace: The British in Occupied Germany, 1945–1948* (London, Bloomsbury Academic, 2017), p. 57.

11 TNA, FO 1030/151, C-in-C's Residence in Berlin, 1946–1947, Letter Douglas to S. P. Chambers, 3 October 1946.

12 Ibid., Letter Chambers to Douglas, 7 October 1946.

13 Jane Macaskie's Berlin Letters 1946–1948, Letter from Jane to her eldest daughter Florence, 27 November 1946, http://www.sophialambert.com/JaneMacaskiesBerlinletters1946-48.htm, accessed 27 April 2020.

14 FO 936/743, Allegations and investigations of cases of corruption in CCG, British Zone, 1946–1948. Statement by Ralph C. Tarlton, 318 L/R Detachment, Military Government, BAOR, 15 June 1946.

15 Ibid., Letter Robertson to Street, 30 May 1946.

16 Ibid., Statement by Ralph C. Tarlton.

17 Ibid., Letter Robertson to Jenkins, 31 October 1946.

18 Ibid., Minute Dean to Street, 29 November 1946.

19 TNA, FO 936/741, Operation 'Sparkler' and large-scale black market activities, 1946–1947. Report by the Economic Information Section, CCG, Berlin: Illegal Trading in Germany, 17 July 1946.

20 *The Advertiser* (Adelaide), 13 May 1947, p. 3.

21 TNA, FO 936/425, Appointment of successor to Sir Sholto Douglas, 1947. Handwritten letter, Douglas to Bevin, 15 May 1947.

22 TNA, FO 800/466, op. cit., Memo, Bevin to Attlee, 21 June 1947.

23 TNA, FO 936/425, op. cit., Memo, Attlee to Bevin, 16 September 1947.

24 TNA FO 800/466, op. cit., Memo, Bevin to Attlee, 7 October 1947.

25 RAF Museum, MF 10111/11. Pilot's Flying Log Book of Wing Commander Neville Blake Freeman, 1 December 1943–28 January 1948.

26 Douglas, *Years of Command*, op. cit., p. 362.

27 Lord Pakenham, *Born to Believe: An Autobiography* (London, Jonathan Cape, 1953), pp. 177–8.

CHAPTER TWENTY-SIX: 'AND ALL THE TRUMPETS SOUNDED'

1   Douglas, *Years of Command*, op. cit., p. 362.

2   Ibid., p. 363.

3   Pakenham, op. cit., p. 206.

4   Brian Woosey, 'Exit the Fighting Pilot', *Daily Herald*, 31 March 1964.

5   Stevenson Pugh, 'He's still in command, and still a fighter.' *Daily Mail*, Saturday 21 March 1959.

6   May, op. cit., p. 20.

7   Ibid., pp. 148–9.

8   Letter, Jean Douglas to Gloria Muirhead, 21 August 1951, private collection of Katharine Campbell.

9   May, op. cit., p. 149.

10 Hansard, HL Deb, 26 May 1954, Vol. 187, col. 950.

11 May, op. cit., p. 40.

12 TNA, AIR 19/602, Civil Aviation Policy, 1949 December–1957 June, Civil Aviation Policy (Memorandum by the Minister of Transport and Civil Aviation, [John Boyd-Carpenter]) 19 July 1955.

13 Ibid., Cipher from Foreign Office to British Embassy, Moscow, 8 July 1955.

14 Hansard, HL Deb, 26 May 1954, Vol. 187, cols 944–5.

15 Hansard, HL Deb, 16 May 1956, Vol. 197, cols 456, 461.

16 May, op. cit., p. 153.

17 Letter, Steve Wheatcroft to Sholto, 19 December 1958, private collection of Katharine Campbell.

18 May, op. cit., p. 149.

19 Phil Lo Bao, *An Illustrated History of British European Airways* (Feltham, Middlesex, Browcom Group PLC, 1989), p. 86.

20 May, op. cit., p. 152.

21 IWM, Personal papers of Lord Douglas of Kirtleside, Letter Vaughan Berry to Sholto, 4 April 1964.

22 BEA says goodbye to its greatest captain, *The Observer* (Pendennis), 29 March 1964.

23 IWM, op. cit., Letter Peters to Douglas, 24 January 1964.

24 Ibid., Letter Wright to Douglas, 1 July 1964.

25 Ibid., Letter Peters to Douglas, 14 September 1964.

26 Grossman, op. cit., p. 74.

27 Lord Moran, *The Anatomy of Courage* (London, Robinson, 2007 [1945]), p. 140.

28 Ibid., p. 187.

29 Grossman, op. cit., p. 194.

30 IWM, op. cit., Letter Wright to Douglas, 28 January 1966.

31 RAF Museum, AC95/124/7, Letter Dowding to Douglas, 1 June 1966.

32 Letter, Viscount Portal to Lady Douglas of Kirtleside, 31 October 1969, private collection of Katharine Campbell.

33 Letter, Air Chief Marshal Sir John Grandy to Lady Douglas of Kirtleside, 31 October 1969, private collection of Katharine Campbell. Reproduced by kind permission of Sir John Grandy's son, John Grandy.

CHAPTER TWENTY-SEVEN: A LIFETIME OF TRAUMA

1   A. C. McFarlane, 'The Longitudinal Course of Posttraumatic Morbidity', *The Journal of Nervous and Mental Disease*, 1988, 176; 1: 30–39.

2   A. C. McFarlane, 'The long-term costs of traumatic stress: intertwined physical and psychological consequences', *World Psychiatry*, February 2010; 9 (1): 3–10.

3   Ibid.

4   A. C. McFarlane, 'The Vexed Construct of Medical Resilience: Friend or Foe?', Introduction on 'Medical Resilience' in L. van Bergen and E. Vermetten (eds), *The First World War and Health: Rethinking Resilience* (Leiden, Brill Publishers, 2020).

5   C. Heim and C. B. Nemeroff, 'The role of childhood trauma in the neurobiology of mood and anxiety disorders: preclinical and clinical studies', *Biological Psychiatry*, 2001; 49: 1023–39.

6   George E. Vaillant, *Adaptation to Life* (Cambridge, Massachusetts, Harvard University Press, 1995 [1977]), p. 28.

7   Ibid., p. 297.

8   R. E. Bernstein and J. J. Freyd, 'Trauma at Home: How Betrayal Trauma and Attachment Theories Understand the Human Response to Abuse by an Attachment Figure', *New Directions in Psychotherapy and Relational Psychoanalysis*, 2014; 8 (March): 18–41.

9   F. C. Bartlett, *Psychology and the Soldier* (Cambridge, Cambridge University Press, 1927), p. 199.

10 Ibid., p. 213.

11 R. A. Cohen et al., 'Early Life Stress and Morphometry of the Adult Anterior Cingulate Cortex and Caudate Nuclei', *Biological Psychiatry*, 2006; 59: 975–82.

12 S. H. Woodward et al., 'Early adversity and combat exposure interact to influence anterior cingulate cortex volume in combat veterans', *Neuroimage: Clinical* 2, 2013: 670–74.

13 K. C. Koenen et al., 'Early childhood factors associated with the development of post-traumatic stress disorder: results from a longitudinal birth cohort', *Psychological Medicine*, 2007; 37: 181–92.

14 O. A. Cabrera et al., 'Childhood Adversity and Combat as Predictors of Depression and

Post-Traumatic Stress in Deployed Troops', *American Journal of Preventive Medicine*, 2007; 33 (2): 77–82. A. C. Iversen et al., 'Influence of childhood adversity on health among male UK military personnel', *British Journal of Psychiatry*, 2007; 191: 506–11. A. C. Iversen et al., 'Risk factors for post-traumatic stress disorder among UK Armed Forces personnel', *Psychological Medicine*, 2008; 38: 511–22.

15 J. Sareen et al., 'Adverse childhood experiences in relation to mood and anxiety disorders in a population-based sample of active military personnel', *Psychological Medicine*, 2013; 43: 73–84.

16 Cabrera et al., op. cit. Sareen et al., op. cit.

17 G. P. Owens et al., 'The Relationship Between Childhood Trauma, Combat Exposure, and Post-traumatic Stress Disorder in Male Veterans', *Military Psychology*, 2009; 21: 114–25.

18 A. K. Searle et al., 'The impact of antecedent trauma exposure and mental health symptoms on the post-deployment mental health of Afghanistan-deployed Australian troops', *Journal of Affective Disorders*, 1 October 2017; 220: 62–71.

19 A. B. Adler et al., 'The Impact of Deployment Length and Experience on the Well-Being of Male and Female Soldiers', *Journal of Occupational Health Psychology*, 2005; 10 (2): 121–37. R. J. Rona, N. T. Fear and S. Wessely, 'Mental health consequences of overstretch in the UK armed forces: first phase of a cohort study', *BMJ*, 2007; 335 (7620): 603.

20 McFarlane (2010), op. cit.

21 Michael Roper, *The Secret Battle: Emotional survival in the Great War* (Manchester, Manchester University Press, 2009), p. 248.

22 Raleigh, op. cit., p. 444.

23 Roper, op. cit., pp. 263–4.

24 K. A. Lee et al., 'A 50-year Prospective Study of the Psychological Sequelae of World War II Combat', *American Journal of Psychiatry*, 1995; 152 (4): 516–22.

25 W. D. S. Killgore et al., 'The effects of prior combat experience on the expression of somatic and affective symptoms in deploying soldiers', *Journal of Psychosomatic Research*, 2006; 60: 379–85.

26 Ibid.

27 C. P. Clancy et al., 'Lifetime Trauma Exposure in Veterans With Military-Related Posttraumatic Stress Disorder: Association with Current Symptomatology', *Journal of Clinical Psychiatry*, 2006; 67 (9): 1346–53.

28 J. V. Rosenfeld et al., 'Blast-related traumatic brain injury', *Lancet Neurology*, 2013; 12: 882–93.

29 C. W. Hoge et al., 'Mild Traumatic Brain Injury in U.S. Soldiers Returning from Iraq', *New England Journal of Medicine*, 2008; 358: 453–63.

30 M. A. McCrea, *Mild traumatic brain injury and postconcussion syndrome: the new evidence base for diagnosis and treatment* (New York, Oxford University Press, 2008).

31 Hoge, op. cit.

32 Rosenfeld et al., op. cit.

33 Chris R. Brewin, *Post-traumatic Stress Disorder: Malady or Myth?* (New Haven, Yale University Press, 2003), pp. 56–7. Grossman, op. cit., p. 288.

34 C. Steinert et al., 'The course of PTSD in naturalistic long-term studies: High variability of outcomes. A systematic review', *Nordic Journal of Psychiatry*, 2015; 69 (7): 483–96. K. C. Koenen et al. (2003), op. cit.

35 J. Bowlby, *Attachment and Loss: Separation, Anxiety and Anger* (Harmondsworth, Pelican Books, 1973), pp. 213, 197.

36 Rivers, op. cit., p. 217.

37 Charles Myers, *Shell Shock in France, 1914–1918* (Cambridge, Cambridge University Press, 1940), p. 40.

38 Ross, op. cit., pp. 60–61.

39 N. T. Fear et al., 'Job Strain, Rank, and Mental Health in the UK Armed Forces', *International Journal of Occupational and Environmental Health*, 2009; 15 (3): 291–8.

40 Raftery, op. cit., p. 79.

41 *Report of the War Office Committee of Enquiry into 'Shell-Shock'* (London, The Naval & Military

Press Ltd in association with The Imperial War Museum Department of Printed Books [HMSO, 1922]), p. 70.

42 Kardiner, op. cit., p. v.

43 Ibid., p. 100.

44 K. L. Felmington et al., 'Reduced Amygdala and Ventral Striatal Activity to Happy Faces in PTSD Is Associated with Emotional Numbing', *PLoS ONE*, 2014; 9 (9): e103653.

45 Ibid.

46 M. J. Horowitz and G. F. Solomon, 'A prediction of delayed stress response syndromes in Vietnam veterans', *Journal of Social Issues*, 1975; 31: 67–80.

47 P. Marin, 'Living in Moral Pain', *Psychology Today*, 1981 (November): 66–80.

48 N. R. Stein et al., 'A Scheme for Categorising Traumatic Military Events', *Behavior Modification*, 2012; 36 (6): 787–807.

49 Rivers, op. cit., p. 17.

50 Ibid., p. 242.

51 Ibid., p. 126.

52 Raftery, op. cit., p. 109.

53 Rivers, op. cit., p. 199.

54 Siegfried Sassoon, Poem 17, in *Vigils* (London, William Heinemann Ltd, 1935), p. 17. Copyright Siegfried Sassoon, reproduced by kind permission of the estate of George Sassoon.

55 A. C. McFarlane et al. (2002), op. cit.

56 M. Wicking et al., 'Deficient fear extinction memory in posttraumatic stress disorder', *Neurobiology of Learning and Memory*, 2016; 136: 116–26.

57 J. O. Goh et al., 'Frontal Function and Executive Processing in Older Adults: Process and Region Specific Age-Related Longitudinal Functional Changes', *Neuroimage*, 1 April 2013; 69: 43–50.

58 M. W. Logue et al., 'Smaller Hippocampal Volume in Posttraumatic Stress Disorder: A Multisite ENIGMA-PGC Study: Subcortical Volumetry Results From Posttraumatic Stress Disorder Consortia', *Biological Psychiatry*, 1 February 2018; 83 (3): 244–53.

59 D. Waltzman et al., 'Altered Microstructural Caudate Integrity in Posttraumatic Stress Disorder but Not Traumatic Brain Injury', *PLoS ONE*, 12 (1): e0170564. doi: 10.1371/journal.pone.0170564.

60 McFarlane (2010), op. cit.

61 A. C. McFarlane, 'Post-traumatic stress disorder is a systemic illness, not a mental disorder: is Cartesian dualism dead?', *Medical Journal of Australia*, 3 April 2017; 206 (6): 248–9.

62 E. M. Sledjeski, B. Speisman and L. C. Dierker, 'Does number of lifetime traumas explain the relationship between PTSD and chronic medical conditions? Answers from the National Comorbidity Survey-Replication (NCS-R)', *Journal of Behavioral Medicine*, 2008; 31 (4): 341–9.

63 Kardiner, op. cit., p. 195.

64 N. Ahmadi et al., 'Post-traumatic Stress Disorder, Coronary Atherosclerosis, and Mortality', *American Journal of Cardiology*, 2011; 108: 29–33. M.-L. Gander and R. von Känel, 'Myocardial infarction and post-traumatic stress disorder: frequency, outcome, and atherosclerotic mechanisms', *European Journal of Cardiovascular Prevention and Rehabilitation*, 2006; 13: 165–72.

65 M. M. Burg et al., 'Risk for Incident Hypertension Associated with PTSD in Military Veterans, and The Effect of PTSD Treatment', *Psychosomatic Medicine*, 2017; 79 (2): 181–8.

66 S. S. Coughlin, 'Post-traumatic Stress Disorder and Cardiovascular Disease', *The Open Cardiovascular Medicine Journal*, 2011; 5: 164–70.

67 J. A. Boscarino, 'Posttraumatic Stress Disorder and Physical Illness: Results from Clinical and Epidemiologic Studies', *Annals of the New York Academy Sciences*, 2004; 1032: 141–53.

68 W. V. R. Vieweg et al., 'Posttraumatic stress disorder as a risk factor for obesity among male military veterans', *Acta Psychiatrica Scandinavica*, 2007; 116: 483–7.

69 Vaillant, op. cit., p. 211.

70 S. Rosenbaum et al., 'The prevalence and risk of metabolic syndrome and its components among people with posttraumatic stress disorder: a systematic review and meta-analysis', *Metabolism*, 2015; 64 (8): 926–33.

71 E. J. Wolf et al., 'Posttraumatic Stress Disorder as a Catalyst for the Association Between Metabolic Syndrome and Reduced Cortical Thickness', *Biological Psychiatry*, 2016; 80 (9): 363–71.

72 Mardi J. Horowitz, *Stress Response Syndromes: PTSD, Grief, Adjustment, and Dissociative Disorders*, fifth edition (Lanham, Maryland, Jason Aronson, 2014), p. 35. Van der Kolk, op. cit., p. 208.

73 *Enquiry into 'Shell-Shock'*, op. cit., pp. 84, 86.

74 K. C. Koenen et al., 'A Twin Registry Study of the Relationship Between Posttraumatic Stress Disorder and Nicotine Dependence in Men', *Archives of General Psychiatry*, 2005; 62: 1258–65.

75 J. D. Kassel, L. R. Stroud and C. A. Paronis, 'Smoking, stress, and negative affect: correlation, causation, and context across stages of smoking', *Psychological Bulletin*, 2003; 129 (2): 270–304.

76 A. M. Rasmusson, M. R. Picciotto and S. Krishnan-Sarin, 'Smoking as a complex but critical covariate in neurobiological studies of posttraumatic stress disorders: a review', *Journal of Psychopharmacology*, 2006; 20 (5): 693–707.

77 K. C. Koenen et al. (2003), op. cit. R. Kulka et al., op. cit.

78 N. T. Fear et al., 'What are the consequences of deployment to Iraq and Afghanistan on the mental health of the UK armed forces? A cohort study', *The Lancet*, 2010; 375 (May): 1783–97.

79 Van der Kolk, op. cit., p. 327.

80 A. B. Levine, L. M. Levine and T. B. Levine, 'Posttraumatic Stress Disorder and Cardiometabolic Disease', *Cardiology*, 2014; 127: 1–19.

81 Arthur Graham Butler, *Official History of the Australian Army Medical Services, 1914–1918*, Vol. III: Special Problems and Services. Section IV: The Aftermath of War. First edition: 1943, p. 817.

82 H. C. Archibald and R. D. Tuddenham, 'Persistent Stress Reaction After Combat', *Archives of General Psychiatry*, Vol. 12, May 1965, pp. 475–81.

83 Z. Solomon, M. Mikulincer, 'Trajectories of PTSD: a 20-year longitudinal study', *American Journal of Psychiatry*, 2006; 163: 659–66.

84 B. Andrews B et al., 'Delayed-onset posttraumatic stress disorder: A systematic review of the evidence', *American Journal of Psychiatry*, 2007; 164 (9): 1319–26.

85 Brewin, op. cit., pp. 31–3.

86 Steinert et al., op. cit.

87 S. Hiskey et al., 'The Emergence of Posttraumatic Distress in Later Life: A Review', *Journal of Geriatric Psychiatry and Neurology*, 2008; 21: 232–41.

88 L. Goodwin and R. J. Rona, 'PTSD in the armed forces: What have we learned from the recent cohort studies of Iraq/Afghanistan?', *Journal of Mental Health*, 2013; 22 (5): 397–401.

89 L. Goodwin et al., 'Prevalence of delayed-onset post-traumatic stress disorder in military personnel: Is there evidence for this disorder? Results of a prospective UK cohort study', *Journal of Nervous and Mental Disease*, 2012; 200 (5): 429–37.

90 A. C. McFarlane et al., 'The Need to Take a Staging Approach to the Biological Mechanisms of PTSD and its Treatment', *Current Psychiatry Reports*, 2017; 19 (2): 10. See references 28–32.

91 R. H. Pietrzak et al., 'Trajectories of posttraumatic stress symptomatology in older persons affected by a large-magnitude disaster', *Journal of Psychiatric Research*, 2013; 47 (4): 520–26.

92 A. C. McFarlane et al. (2017), op. cit.

93 Ibid.

94 K. A. Lee et al., op. cit.

95 Raftery, op. cit., p. 89.

96 Horowitz, *Stress Response Syndromes*, op. cit., p. 81.

97 Ibid., p. 12.

98 Ibid., pp. 83, 85.

99 C. R. Brewin, 'Episodic Memory, Perceptual Memory, and Their Interaction: Foundations for a Theory of Posttraumatic Stress Disorder', *Psychological Bulletin*, 2014; 140 (1): 69–97.

100 A. Spiro and R. A. Settersten, 'Long-Term Implications of Military Service for Later-Life Health and Well-Being', *Research in Human Development*, 2012; 9 (3): 183–90.

101 E. H. Davison et al., 'Late-Life Emergence of Early-Life Trauma: The Phenomenon of Late-Onset Stress Symptomatology Among Aging Combat Veterans', *Research on Aging*, 2006; 28 (1): 84–114.

102 S. U. Qureshi et al., 'Greater prevalence and incidence of dementia in older veterans with posttraumatic stress disorder', *Journal of the American Geriatrics Society*, 2010; 58 (9): 1627–33.

103 K. Yaffe et al., 'Posttraumatic Stress Disorder and Risk of Dementia Among US Veterans', *Archives of General Psychiatry*, 2010; 67 (6): 608–13.

104 D. L. Dallam et al., 'Trauma Reenactments in Aging Veterans with Dementia', *Journal of the American Geriatrics Society*, 2011; 59 (4): 766–8.

105 M. W. Miller and N. Sadeh, 'Traumatic stress, oxidative stress and post-traumatic stress disorder: neurodegeneration and the accelerated-aging hypothesis', *Molecular Psychiatry*, 2014; 19 (11): 1156–62.

106 E. R. Lindemer et al., 'Reduced cortical thickness with increased lifetime burden of PTSD in OEF-OIF veterans and the impact of comorbid TBI', *Neuroimage: Clinical*, 2013; 2: 601–11.

107 Archibald and Tuddenham, op. cit.

108 Van der Kolk, op. cit., p. 66.

109 Pierre Janet, 'Les actes inconscients et le rédoublement de la personnalité pendant le somnambulisme provoqué', *Revue philosophique*, 1886; xxii: 577–92.

110 Pierre Janet, 'L'anesthésie systematisée et la dissociation des phénomènes psychologiques', *Revue philosophique*, 1887; xxiii: 449–72.

111 Rivers, op. cit., p. 73.

112 Ibid., p. 114.

113 Myers, op. cit., p. 67.

114 O. van der Hart et al., 'Somatoform Dissociation in Traumatized World War I Combat Soldiers: A Neglected Clinical Heritage', *Journal of Trauma and Dissociation*, 2000; 1 (4): 33–66.

115 R. A. Lanius et al., 'Emotion Modulation in PTSD: Clinical and Neurobiological Evidence for a Dissociative Subtype', *American Journal of Psychiatry*, 2010; 167 (6): 640–47.

116 B. A. van der Kolk et al., 'Dissociation, somatization, and affect dysregulation: the complexity of adaptation to trauma', *American Journal of Psychiatry*, 1996; 153 (July Festschrift suppl.): 83–93.

117 Ross, op. cit., p. 74.

118 Van der Kolk, op. cit., p. 180.

119 Sassoon, op. cit.

SELECT BIBLIOGRAPHY

Complete references for all the items that I have consulted are contained in the endnotes for the chapters, but here is a list of books and documents that I found particularly interesting. Some of the books have been published a long time ago, but their insights are relevant still.

BOOKS

WORLD WAR I MEMOIRS

Sholto Douglas, *Years of Combat* (London, Collins, 1963).
Arthur Gould Lee, *No Parachute: A Classic Account of War in the Air in WWI* (London, Grub Street, 2013 [1968]).
Arthur Gould Lee, *Open Cockpit: A Pilot of the Royal Flying Corps*, second edition (London, Grub Street, 2016 [1969]).
Cecil Lewis, *Sagittarius Rising* (London, Frontline Books, 2009 [1936]).
L. A. Strange, *Recollections of an Airman* (London, John Hamilton, 1935 [1933]).
Professor Johannes Werner, *Knight of Germany: Oswald Boelcke, German Ace* (Philadelphia and Newbury, Casemate, 2009 [1932]).

WORLD WAR II MEMOIRS

Captain Eric 'Winkle' Brown, *Wings on my Sleeve* (London, Phoenix, 2007 [2006]).

Air Chief Marshal Sir Kenneth 'Bing' Cross with Professor Vincent Orange, *Straight and Level* (London, Grub Street, 1993).

Alan C. Deere, *Nine Lives* (Manchester, Crécy Publishing, 2012 [1959]).

Sholto Douglas, *Years of Command* (London, Collins, 1966).

Adolf Galland, *The First and the Last* (USA, Popular Classics Publishing, 2014 [1952]).

Richard Hillary, *The Last Enemy* (London, Vintage, 2010 [1942]).

'Johnnie' Johnson (Group Captain J. E. Johnson), *Wing Leader* (London, The Reprint Society, 1958 [1956]).

Jimmy Rawnsley and Robert Wright, *Night Fighter* (London, Collins, 1957).

William Simpson, *I Burned My Fingers* (London, Putnam, 1956 [1955]).

POETRY OF THE WORLD WARS

Siegfried Sassoon, *Vigils* (London, William Heinemann, 1935).

MEMOIRS AND BIOGRAPHIES OF PUBLIC FIGURES

Field Marshal Lord Alanbrooke, *War Diaries 1939–1945*, Alex Danchev and Daniel Todman (eds) (London, Phoenix Press, 2002).

Clement Attlee, *As It Happened: His Autobiography* (London, William Heinemann, 1954).

Andrew Boyle, *Trenchard, Man of Vision* (London, Collins, 1962).

Noël Coward, *Middle East Diary* (London, William Heinemann, 1944).

Peter Flint, *Dowding and Headquarters Fighter Command* (England, Airlife Publishing, 1996).

Professor R. V. Jones, *Most Secret War* (London, Hamish Hamilton, 1978).

Lord Moran, *Winston Churchill: The struggle for survival, 1940–1965* (London, Constable, 1966).

Vincent Orange, *Sir Keith Park: A biography of Air Chief Marshal Sir Keith Park* (London, Methuen, 1985 [1984]).

Lord Pakenham, *Born to Believe: An Autobiography* (London, Jonathan Cape, 1953).

Denis Richards, *Portal of Hungerford* (London, Heinemann, 1977).

OFFICIAL HISTORIES

J. B. Collier, *Official History of World War II, The Defence of the United Kingdom* (London, HMSO, 1957).

H. A. Jones, *The War in the Air: Being the Story of the part played in the Great War by the Royal Air Force*, Volume II (Oxford, Clarendon Press, 1928).

H. A. Jones, *The War in the Air: Being the Story of the part played in the Great War by the Royal Air Force*, Volumes III–VI and Appendices (Uckfield, The Naval & Military Press, and London, Imperial War Museum, 2002 [1931]).

Walter Raleigh, *The War in the Air: Being the Story of the part played in the Great War by the Royal Air Force*, Volume I (Oxford, Clarendon Press, 1922).

Denis Richards and Hilary St George Saunders, *Royal Air Force 1939– 1945*, Volumes I–III (London, HMSO, 1974 [1953]).

OTHER HISTORIES OF THE WORLD WARS

Artemis Cooper, *Cairo in the War, 1939–1945* (London, Penguin, 1995 [1989]).

Cyril Falls, *The First World War* (London, Longmans, 1960).

WARFARE, ON THE GROUND AND IN THE AIR

Carl von Clausewitz, *On War*, Michael Howard and Peter Paret (eds) (Princeton, Princeton University Press, 1989 [1832]).

Giulio Douhet, *The Command of the Air*, translated by Dino Ferrari (Washington DC, Air Force History and Museums Program, 1998 [1921]).

MILITARY AVIATION

John H. Morrow Jr, *The Great War in the Air: Military Aviation from 1909 to 1921* (Washington DC, Smithsonian Institution Press, 1993).

Maryam Philpott, *Air and Sea Power in World War I: Combat and Experience in the Royal Flying Corps and the Royal Navy* (London and New York, I. B. Tauris, 2013).

THE RAF AND ITS COMMANDS

Stephen Bungay, *The Most Dangerous Enemy: A History of the Battle of Britain* (London, Aurum Press, 2000).

Christina J. M. Goulter, *A Forgotten Offensive: Royal Air Force Coastal Command's Anti-Shipping Campaign, 1940–1945* (London, Frank Cass, 1995).

John Ray, *The Battle of Britain: New Perspectives – Behind the Scenes of the Great Air War* (London, Brockhampton Press, 2000 [1994]).

John Terraine, *The Right of the Line* (London, Hodder & Stoughton, 1985).

THE ABYSSINIAN CRISIS AND THE SPANISH CIVIL WAR

G. T. Garratt, *Mussolini's Roman Empire*, third edition (London, Penguin Books, 1938).

Nicholas Rankin, *Telegram from Guernica* (London, Faber & Faber, 2003).

Hugh Thomas, *The Spanish Civil War*, fourth edition (London, Penguin Books, 2012 [1961]).

GERMANY, UNDER THE NAZIS AND POST-WAR

Ian Buruma, *Year Zero: A History of 1945* (London, Atlantic Books, 2013).

R. M. Douglas, *Orderly and Humane: The Expulsion of the Germans after the Second World War* (New Haven, Yale University Press, 2012).

Annedore Leber, *Conscience in Revolt*, English edition (London, Vallentine, Mitchell, 1957).

Keith Lowe, *Savage Continent: Europe in the Aftermath of World War II* (London, Penguin Books, 2013 [2012]).

David Phillips, *Educating the Germans: People and Policy in the British Zone of Germany, 1945–1949* (London, Bloomsbury Academic, 2018).

Ben Shephard, *The Long Road Home: The Aftermath of the Second World War* (London, Vintage, 2011).

Chester Wilmot, *The Struggle for Europe* (London, Collins, 1952).

THE NUREMBERG TRIALS

G. M. Gilbert, *Nuremberg Diary* (Boston, Da Capo Press, 1995 [1947]).

Philippe Sands, *East West Street: On the Origins of Genocide and Crimes Against Humanity* (London, Weidenfeld & Nicolson, 2016).

Telford Taylor, *The Anatomy of the Nuremberg Trials: A Personal Memoir* (New York, Alfred A. Knopf, 1992).

Rebecca West, *A Train of Powder* (London, Macmillan & Co., 1955).

A. T. Williams, *A Passing Fury: Searching for Justice at the End of World War II* (London, Jonathan Cape, 2016).

POST-TRAUMATIC STRESS DISORDER

Leo van Bergen and Eric Vermetten (eds), *The First World War and Health: Rethinking Resilience* (Leiden, Brill Publishers, 2020). Introduction on 'Medical Resilience': Alexander McFarlane, 'The Vexed Construct of Medical Resilience: Friend or Foe?'

Chris R. Brewin, *Post-traumatic Stress Disorder: Malady or Myth?* (New Haven and London, Yale University Press, 2003).

Grafton Elliot Smith and T. H. Pear, *Shell Shock and Its Lessons*, second edition (Manchester, Manchester University Press, 1918).

Mardi J. Horowitz, *Stress Response Syndromes: PTSD, Grief, Adjustment, and Dissociative Disorders*, fifth edition (Lanham, Jason Aronson, 2014).

Abram Kardiner, *The Traumatic Neuroses of War* (New York, Paul B. Hoeber Inc., 1941).

Bessel van der Kolk, *The Body Keeps the Score: Brain, Mind, and Body in the Healing of Trauma* (New York, Viking, 2014).

Charles Myers, *Shell Shock in France, 1914–1918* (Cambridge, Cambridge University Press, 1940).

John Raftery, *Marks of War: War Neurosis and the Legacy of Kokoda* (Adelaide, Lythrum Press, 2003).

W. H. R. Rivers, *Instinct and the Unconscious: A Contribution to a Biological Theory of the Psycho-neuroses* (Cambridge, Cambridge University Press, 1920).

Michael Roper, *The Secret Battle: Emotional Survival in the Great War* (Manchester, Manchester University Press, 2009).

T. A. Ross, *Lectures on War Neurosis* (London, Edward Arnold & Co., 1941).

Ben Shephard, *A War of Nerves: Soldiers and Psychiatrists, 1914–1994* (London, Pimlico, 2002 [2000]).

George E. Vaillant, *Adaptation to Life* (Cambridge, Massachusetts, Harvard University Press, 1995 [1977]).

PSYCHOLOGY OF VIOLENCE AND KILLING

Hannah Arendt, *On Violence* (Orlando, Harcourt Inc., 1969).

Lt. Col. Dave Grossman, *On Killing: The Psychological Cost of Learning to Kill in War and Society* (New York, Back Bay Books, 2009 [1995]).

Robert Jay Lifton, *The Nazi Doctors: Medical Killing and the Psychology of Genocide* (New York, Basic Books, 2000 [1986]).

MEDICAL MILITARY HISTORY

E. R. Mayhew, *The Reconstruction of Warriors: Archibald McIndoe, the Royal Air Force and the Guinea Pig Club* (London, Greenhill Books, 2004).

ARCHIVES

Imperial War Museum:
Duxford, Archives of the Guinea Pig Club.
London, Personal papers of Marshal of the Royal Air Force Lord Douglas of Kirtleside.
Henry Tizard Archive, HTT38, Correspondence between Henry Tizard and Sholto Douglas.

Churchill College, Cambridge University: Churchill Archive.

Christ Church, Oxford University: Papers of Marshal of the Royal Air Force Viscount Portal of Hungerford.

The National Archives, Kew: documents that I have consulted there are cited in full in the endnotes.

RAF Museum, Hendon, London.

SCIENTIFIC PAPERS ON COMBAT STRESS/ POST-TRAUMATIC STRESS DISORDER

J. L. Birley, 'Goulstonian Lectures on the Principles of Medical Science as applied to Military Aviation, Lectures I–III', *The Lancet*, 1920.

O. A. Cabrera et al., 'Childhood Adversity and Combat as Predictors of Depression and Post-Traumatic Stress in Deployed Troops', *American Journal of Preventive Medicine*, 2007; 33 (2): 77–82.

E. H. Davison et al., 'Late-Life Emergence of Early-Life Trauma: The Phenomenon of Late-Onset Stress Symptomatology Among Aging Combat Veterans', *Research on Aging*, 2006; 28 (1): 84–114.

K. L. Felmington et al., 'Reduced Amygdala and Ventral Striatal Activity to Happy Faces in PTSD Is Associated with Emotional Numbing', *PLoS ONE*, 2014; 9 (9): e103653.

K. C. Koenen et al., 'Early childhood factors associated with the development of post-traumatic stress disorder: results from a longitudinal birth cohort', *Psychological Medicine*, 2007; 37: 181–192.

R. A. Lanius et al., 'Emotion Modulation in PTSD: Clinical and Neurobiological Evidence for a Dissociative Subtype', *American Journal of Psychiatry*, 2010; 167 (6): 640–647.

K. A. Lee et al., 'A 50-year Prospective Study of the Psychological Sequelae of World War II Combat', *American Journal of Psychiatry*, 1995; 152 (4): 516–522.

A. C. McFarlane, 'The long-term costs of traumatic stress: intertwined physical and psychological consequences', *World Psychiatry*, February 2010; 9 (1): 3–10.

A. C. McFarlane, 'Post-traumatic stress disorder is a systemic illness, not a mental disorder: is Cartesian dualism dead?', *Medical Journal of Australia*, 3 April 2017; 206 (6): 248–249.

A. C. McFarlane et al., 'The Need to Take a Staging Approach to the Biological Mechanisms of PTSD and its Treatment', *Current Psychiatry Reports*, 2017; 19 (2): 10.

S. Rosenbaum et al., 'The prevalence and risk of metabolic syndrome and its components among people with posttraumatic stress disorder: a systemic review and meta-analysis', *Metabolism*, 2015; 64 (8): 926–33.

J. V. Rosenfeld et al., 'Blast-related traumatic brain injury', *Lancet Neurology*, 2013; 12: 882–93.

E. M. Sledjeski, B. Speisman and L. C. Dierker, 'Does number of lifetime traumas explain the relationship between PTSD and chronic medical conditions? Answers from the National Comorbidity Survey-Replication (NCS-R)', *Journal of Behavioral Medicine*, 2008; 31 (4): 341–349.

Z. Solomon and M. Mikulincer, 'Trajectories of PTSD: a 20-year longitudinal study', *American Journal of Psychiatry*, 2006; 163: 659–666.

N. R. Stein et al., 'A Scheme for Categorising Traumatic Military Events', *Behavior Modification*, 2012; 36 (6): 787–807.

D. Waltzman et al., 'Altered Microstructural Caudate Integrity in Posttraumatic Stress Disorder but Not Traumatic Brain Injury', *PLoS ONE*, 12 (1): e0170564. doi: 10.1371/journal.pone.0170564.

M. Wicking et al., 'Deficient fear extinction memory in posttraumatic stress disorder', *Neurobiology of Learning and Memory*, 2016; 136: 116–126.

ARTICLES IN PRINTED MEDIA

Ben East, 'Inside a compelling conspiracy on the eve of war', Review of Robert Harris, *Munich*, *Guardian Review*, 17 September 2017.

Leo McKinstry, 'Did Neville Chamberlain create the conditions for the RAF to win the Battle of Britain?', *New Statesman*, 24 April 2018.

Leo McKinstry, 'We won the Battle of Britain – just', *The Spectator*, 2 July 2020 online.

Susan Pedersen, 'Narrow-minded inflexible prime ministers get the big questions of history wrong, as appeasement shows', Review of Tim Bouverie, *Appeasing Hitler: Chamberlain, Churchill and the Road to War*, *Guardian Review*, 6 April 2019.

SYMPOSIA

Air Commodore Henry Probert and Mr Sebastian Cox (eds), 'The Battle Re-Thought: A Symposium on the Battle of Britain', 25 June 1990.

MILITARY ARTICLES

Squadron Leader W. S. Douglas, MC, DFC, 'A Lecture on Fighting in the Air, Lecture II, Essays based on lectures given by officers to the third course of the RAF Staff College, 1924–25', in *Air Power Review*, Volume 21, Number 1, Spring 2018.

Allan D. English, 'A Predisposition to Cowardice? Aviation Psychology and the Genesis of "Lack of Moral Fibre"', *War & Society*, 1995; 13 (1): 15–34.

Edgar Jones, '"LMF": The Use of Psychiatric Stigma in the Royal Air Force during the Second World War', *Journal of Military History*, 2006; 70: 439–458.

John McCarthy, 'Aircrew and "Lack of Moral Fibre" in the Second World War', *War & Society*, 1984; 2 (2): 87–101.

Sebastian Ritchie, 'A Political Intrigue Against the Chief of the Air Staff: The Downfall of Air Chief Marshal Sir Cyril Newall', *War & Society*, May 1998; 16 (1): 83–104.

David Stubbs, 'An Analysis of Factors Affecting the Royal Air Force Contribution to the Raid on Dieppe, 1942', *Canadian Military History*, 2016; 25 (1): Article 12.

INTERNET SOURCES

The London Charter, 8 August 1945, https://www.un.org/en/genocideprevention/documents/atrocity-crimes/Doc.2_Charter%20of%20IMT%201945.pdf

International Military Tribunal Nuremberg, Volume I, 14 November 1945–1 October 1946, https://www.loc.gov/rr/frd/Military_Law/pdf/NT_Vol-I.pdf

ACKNOWLEDGEMENTS

I am so grateful to all those who have helped me on my journey of eight years to complete this book. Special thanks go to my husband Peter for his support in so many ways and his advice on diverse matters, particularly those involving aviation, the military and grammar! Jane McIntosh, the wife of my cousin Jake Douglas, has been my most staunch editor and friend, always encouraging me. Our neighbour and friend Peter Davidson, a former judge, has given me much-needed advice on legal matters and has been a most valuable reader of my chapters on post-war Germany.

I am deeply indebted to Professor Alexander (Sandy) McFarlane, director of the University of Adelaide's Centre for Traumatic Stress Studies and internationally renowned expert on post-traumatic stress disorder, who has provided constant scientific support, information and advice as well as friendship. He also introduced me to Dr Walter Busuttil, director of research and training at Combat Stress, who has become a friend as well as an adviser. Other scientists who have provided invaluable help are my friend and former colleague Professor Andrew Rice (Imperial College London) and his associate at Imperial, Dr Emily Mayhew; Dr Amanda Williams (University College London); the late and much-missed Professor Stephen Morley (University of Leeds); and the late and also much-lamented Dr John Raftery (University of Adelaide). Dr Smadar Bustan (Université Paris Diderot) of the Pain and Suffering Project put me in touch with someone who, in a way similar to Sandy McFarlane, has been a faithful guide on all things PTSD and a dear friend, Professor Emeritus Onno van der Hart (University of Utrecht).

Two of my closest first half-cousins, Robert Hutchison, very sadly now deceased, and his sister Erica Filby have provided me with documents from their particular part of our Douglas family and have been wonderful supporters. My father Sholto's only surviving sibling out of seventeen, my half-aunt, Dr Claire Douglas Salinger, has been a great source of information and wise comment, and an example to follow. Sadly, two wonderful women who were immensely supportive are no longer with us: my mother's cousin Hilary Rees-Roberts and Mary Douglas, the wife of my late first cousin Duncan. My kinsman William Douglas has been a tremendous source of information on Douglas clan history. Close family friends who have refreshed my memory and been sources of wonderful nuggets of information have been one of my dear former nannies, Jutta Füller, and Sholto's late PA, Sheila Traynor, née Brough.

Special friends from the Royal Air Force, both retired and serving, have provided valuable contacts and information. These include Air Chief Marshal Sir Joe French; Air Chief Marshal Sir Simon Bryant; Air Vice-Marshal Dr Peter Dye; Air Commodores Richard Mason and Rob Cunningham (also a wonderful reader!); Wing Commanders Andy Moir and Bill Preece (all retired); and Group Captain Jim Beldon. Two extraordinary veterans from World War II have provided me with incredible insights concerning Sholto: Phyllis Felton (née Davies), who worked on his staff at Coastal Command and who celebrated her 100th birthday in 2020, and Britain's greatest pilot, the late Eric 'Winkle' Brown, who combined wisdom and humour in his observations on air tactics, and whose vivid first-hand account of the conditions in 1945 of Belsen concentration camp I will never forget.

Many historians have advised me in my endeavours, notably Sebastian Cox and Mary Hudson (Air Historical Branch); Drs Christina Goulter and David Jordan (Defence Academy, Shrivenham); Professor David Phillips (St Edmund Hall, Oxford University); Dr Garry Campion (University of Northampton); Drs Christopher Knowles and Marcus Faulkner (King's College London); and Ross Mahoney (formerly of the RAF Museum). Stephen Bungay and David Stubbs have provided valuable thoughts on the Battle of Britain and the Dieppe raid respectively, and Andrew Bird on Middle East Command.

I had a most enjoyable time working with French and English historians on Sholto's World War I airfields, the French contingent providing Peter and me with generous hospitality. Je suis très reconnaissante à Serge et Dominique Comini et Hugues Chevalier, and very grateful to Air Vice-Marshal Sir Roger Austin (retired), who provided me with excellent maps, and Wing Commander 'Jeff' Jefford (retired), whose book on RAF squadrons is a wonder. Campbell Chesterman, a resident of Stirling, furnished me with amazing details on Sholto's time with No. 43 Squadron there in 1916, learned from his mother.

I am especially thankful to two experts who helped me with understanding radar and Sholto's role in its development: Squadron Leader Mike Dean (retired), who is keeper of the Historical Radar Archive, and Ian Brown, assistant curator for aviation at the National Museums of Scotland.

My visits to places in Germany with which Sholto was associated were exceptionally moving, and I was greatly helped by Hugh Pierson (British Forces Germany Legacy Project coordinator); Dr Bettina Blum (University of Paderborn); Friedrich Winkelhake (historian, Bad Eilsen); Alexander Perl (administrator) and Oliver Glißmann (historian), Schloss Bückeburg. Similarly, I have received great help from those in Poland whom I met during my visits there and who have been sources of rare information, namely: Anna Żalińska (née Wrońska, formerly with the Institute for National Remembrance (Instytut Pamięci Narodowej), Warsaw); Anna Dziegiel (my translator); Franciszek Grabowski, an endless mine of unusual data; and Bolesław Ludwiczak, who helped with arrangements and communication.

Huge thanks must go to Phil Tomaselli, writer and researcher, who has assisted me by photographing documents from the National Archives at Kew when I could not get there, especially during the coronavirus pandemic, and been a great source of encouragement and friendship. Other staff at Kew have been very helpful, including Clive Hawkins and Michael McGrady.

This brings me to all the other staff in archives who have given me assistance, especially at the Imperial War Museum, where most of Sholto's papers and photographs are housed, including Robert

Rumble and Anthony Richards. At the RAF Museum, which contains Sholto's logbooks and some of his effects, I have appreciated the help of Peter Devitt, Belinda Day, Guy Revell and Ewan Burnet. Researching family history, those who have aided me for this particular project are: John Chignoli (British Library, Asia, Pacific and Africa Collections) and Hugh Cahill (Lambeth Palace Library). Stuart Bridges, paleographer at Hampshire Record Office, deciphered old family documents for me. Concerning Sholto's education, David Walsh (Tonbridge School) and Andrew Mussell and Lindsay McCormack (Lincoln College, Oxford) provided essential facts. Information about the Fabian Society in Oxford, which interested Sholto, was provided by Bodleian Library Special Collections and the London School of Economics Archive. I obtained copies of service records for Sholto, his brothers and his father Langton from Derrick Fawcett at RAF Disclosures, Cranwell, and the Army Personnel Centre, Historical Disclosures. My account of Sholto's time in Stirling in WWI was enhanced by information from Pam McNicol at Stirling Council Archives.

I could not have done without the generous help and encouragement of Dr Cristina Neagu, keeper of Special Collections, and Alina Nachescu, Photographic and Special Collections assistant, both at Christ Church Upper Library, where the Portal Archive is housed and where I spent some happy days, and also Alena Ptak-Danchak, formerly keeper of the Scientific Books and Head of Science and Medical Libraries at University of Oxford, based at the Radcliffe Science Library. Sophie Bridges at the Churchill Archives Centre, Cambridge, in particular, and also Diana Manipud at Liddell Hart Military Archives, King's College London, provided copies of valuable documents. Images of some beautiful photographs of Sholto's time in Khartoum between the world wars were sent to me by Francis Gotto and Mike Harkness of Durham University Archives and Special Collections. Important information on Sholto's half-brother Donald was provided by John Entwisle of the Reuters Archive and Gzegorz Sztoler of the Polskapresse Archive in Sosnowiec, Poland.

I learned a lot about Sholto's time as chairman of BEA from

material searched out by Jim Davies and Keith Hayward at British Airways Speedbird Centre, for which I am very thankful.

I am grateful to Philippa Fitzgerald at the coroner's office, Northampton, for acceding to my requests for Sholto's post-mortem report. It did not make easy reading, but it provided some closure.

Finally, heartfelt thanks to my agent Caroline Dawnay and her assistant Kat Aitken for believing in this project, and to my wise and diligent editor Olivia Beattie and everyone at Biteback Publishing for making it a reality.

INDEX